John Le Patourel

With the author's thanks and
best wishes

Kenneth Rose

25.9.69

# The King's Lieutenant

*Henry of Grosmont, First Duke of Lancaster*
*1310–1361*

Kenneth Fowler

# The King's Lieutenant

*Henry of Grosmont, First Duke of Lancaster*
*1310–1361*

Elek   London

© Kenneth Fowler 1969

Published by
ELEK BOOKS LIMITED
2 All Saints Street London N 1
and simultaneously in Canada by
The Ryerson Press
299 Queen Street West Toronto 2B

SBN 236 30812 2

 PRINTED BY Unwin Brothers Limited
THE GRESHAM PRESS OLD WOKING SURREY ENGLAND

*Produced by Letterpress*

A member of the Staples Printing Group          (HL3834)

# Contents

5

6

# List of plates

# List of maps

# Acknowledgements

The publishers wish to thank the following from whom the illustrations were obtained:

The British Museum, the Archives Photographiques, Paris, Stonyhurst College, Lancashire, the Public Record Office, Mr. Edwin Smith

To John Le Patourel
*With Affection and Gratitude*

# Preface

This book owes more than can be adequately expressed to Professor John Le Patourel, who first suggested the subject to me and has seen it through all its various stages. His insight into medieval Anglo-French affairs has everywhere informed my own approach to them and he has both guided and stimulated the researches upon which this work is based.

These were made possible by generous grants from the University of Leeds, the Institute of Historical Research and the French Government. With their assistance I was able to carry out extensive work in both English and French archives and libraries; but I should have found little there without the help of Dr E. B. Fryde and Dr Pierre Chaplais, who suggested to me many of the sources utilized in the following pages, and the staffs of the libraries and archive collections in which they are deposited, who were both efficient and patient in meeting my many requests.

To Dr Fryde I also owe the information on Lancaster's imprisonment in the Low Countries in 1340–1, which is largely based upon notes which he most generously placed at my disposal. Professor M. Dominica Legge offered a number of valuable suggestions concerning his *Livre de Seyntz Medicines*, and Dr R. G. Nicholson helped me on a number of points connected with the Scottish campaigns in which the duke took part and the earldom of Moray which was so mysteriously bestowed upon him.

I should also like to thank Professor May McKisack and Sir Goronwy Edwards for the constant kindness and encouragement which they showed to me during the course of my researches and for offering many helpful criticisms and suggestions.

Finally, I should like to record my indebtedness to my wife, who has listened to the book with patience and forbearance. Without her constant encouragement it would never have been completed.

K.F.  *Edinburgh, December 1968*

# Abbreviations

Except where otherwise stated, references to manuscript sources are to documents in the Public Record Office. Chronicles have been cited either by the name of the author (e.g. *Knighton* represents *Chronicon Henrici Knighton vel Cnitthon monachi Leycestrensis*) or by the most distinctive word in the title (e.g. *Chronographia* for *Chronographia Regum Francorum*). Other abbreviations used in the notes are as follows:

| | |
|---|---|
| Arch. dép. | Archives départementales |
| Arch. nat. | Archives nationales |
| Bibl. nat. | Bibliothèque nationale |
| BM | British Museum |
| *CCR* | *Calendar of Close Rolls* |
| *CChR* | *Calendar of Charter Rolls* |
| *CDRS* | *Calendar of Documents Relating to Scotland* |
| *CFR* | *Calendar of Fine Rolls* |
| *CIPM* | *Calendar of Inquisitions Post Mortem* |
| *CPL* | *Calendar of Entries in the Papal Registers: Letters* |
| *CPMR* | *Calendar of Plea and Memoranda Rolls of the City of London* |
| *CPP* | *Calendar of Entries in the Papal Registers: Petitions* |
| *CPR* | *Calendar of Patent Rolls* |
| *Foedera* | *Foedera, Conventiones, Litterae, etc.*, or *Rymer's Foedera* |
| *GEC* | *The Complete Peerage*, ed. G. E. Cokayne |
| *JGR* | *John of Gaunt's Register* |
| PRO | Public Record Office |
| *Rot. Parl.* | *Rotuli Parliamentorum* |
| *Rot. Scot.* | *Rotuli Scotiae* |
| *VCH* | *Victoria History of the Counties of England* |

Chancery:

| | |
|---|---|
| C 47 | Miscellanea |
| C 49 | Parliament and Council Proceedings |
| C 61 | Gascon Rolls |
| C 71 | Scottish Rolls |
| C 76 | Treaty Rolls |
| C 81 | Warrants for the Great Seal |

Duchy of Lancaster:

| | |
|---|---|
| DL 10 | Royal Charters |
| DL 25 | Ancient Deeds, series L |
| DL 27 | Ancient Deeds, series LS |
| DL 28 | Accounts Various |
| DL 29 | Ministers' Accounts |
| DL 37 | Chancery Rolls |
| DL 40 | Returns of Knights' Fees |
| DL 41 | Miscellanea |
| DL 42 | Miscellaneous Books |

Exchequer:

| | |
|---|---|
| E 36 | Treasury of Receipt, Miscellaneous Books |
| E 40 | Treasury of Receipt, Ancient Deeds, series A |
| E 43 | Treasury of Receipt, Ancient Deeds, series WS |
| E 101 | King's Remembrancer, Accounts Various |
| E 159 | King's Remembrancer, Memoranda Rolls |
| E 163 | King's Remembrancer, Miscellanea |
| E 326 | Augmentation Office, Ancient Deeds, series B |
| E 364 | Lord Treasurer's Remembrancer, Enrolled Foreign Accounts |
| E 372 | King's Remembrancer, Enrolled Foreign Accounts |
| E 401 | Receipt Rolls |
| E 403 | Issue Rolls |
| E 404 | Treasury of Receipt, Writs and Warrants for Issue |
| LR 14 | Office of the Auditors of Land Revenue, Ancient Deeds, series E |

Transcripts:

| | |
|---|---|
| PRO 31/8 | Transcripts from Foreign Archives |

Special Collections:

| | |
|---|---|
| SC 1 | Ancient Correspondence |
| SC 8 | Ancient Petitions |

Trésor des Chartes:

| | |
|---|---|
| J | Layettes |
| JJ | Registres |

Monuments Historiques:

| | |
|---|---|
| K | Cartons des rois |
| KK | Comptes |

Parlement de Paris:

| | |
|---|---|
| X1a | Parlement Civil, Registres |
| X1b | Parlement Civil, Minutes |
| X1c | Parlement Civil, Accords |
| X2a | Parlement Criminel, Registres |

# Note on money

Except where otherwise stated, references to money are given in £ s d sterling. Other monies of account which are referred to are: the English mark and the *livre bordelais*, which were worth 13s 4d and 4s od sterling respectively throughout the period covered in this book, the *livre tournois*, which was worth 4s od sterling, and the *livre parisis*, which was worth 5s od sterling.

The sterling value of the coinage referred to was subject to some fluctuation. The gold crown or *écu à la couronne* was generally worth 3s 9d sterling and the gold franc or *mouton*, first minted in 1360, was worth 4s od sterling; but the florin of Florence, which was worth 3s od sterling in 1340, had fallen to 2s 10½d by 1356.

# Introduction

By far the greater part of Henry of Grosmont's public career was taken up with the first phase of the Hundred Years War, in which he played a major role as a soldier, administrator and diplomat in shaping England's foreign policy.

Historians seem now to be agreed that the deeper causes of that conflict lay in the possession by the king of England of the duchy of Aquitaine, which included Gascony, and other territories in France which had been secured for the Crown by the accession of Henry Plantagenet in 1154.[1] Although the extent of these dominions was greatly reduced by the French monarchy during the course of the thirteenth century, nevertheless a community of political, economic and cultural interests still bound close to England the maritime provinces of western France which formed or had once been part of the Plantagenet empire.[2]

Political unity was still a tender plant in fourteenth-century France which, by contrast with England, had developed more as a federation of duchies and counties tied together by a feudal bond, but each possessing a considerable measure of independence from the king.[3] Into these semi-autonomous areas the royal authority had made dramatic but by no means complete inroads. Nevertheless, the growing implications of French claims to sovereignty and the persistent attempts of the kings of France to centralize and institutionalize their authority by expanding the competence of the judicial and other organs of royal government threatened to undermine the authority of the great feudatories, and even of lesser nobles, and it provoked resistance from many of those who felt that their interests were at stake.[4] Not least among them was the duke of Aquitaine who, because he was also the king of England, possessed considerably larger resources with which to resist his overlord.

Many of the sources of conflict over Aquitaine can be traced back to the treaty of Paris of 1259, which for the first time sought to define the limits of the Plantagenet dominions in France and the form of homage by which they were in future to be held.[5] But, in the absence of maps and the more modern concept of frontiers consistent with the developing notions of sovereignty, it was not possible to be precise about the feudal geography of the territories involved and the treaty consequently created more problems than it solved. Most important of all, the stipulation that the duchy was in future to be held by liege homage obliged the duke to assist his French overlord with troops in his foreign and domestic wars and not to support his enemies. In addition it enabled the king of France to receive judicial appeals from the duke's courts and to hear cases in dispute between their respective subjects, even when they occurred within the marches of the realm or at sea. It was consequently impossible for the king of England to govern his duchy without interference from Paris or to conduct an independent foreign policy without the threat of reprisals and the confiscation of the territories which he held in France. And yet to keep the wine trade open with Gascony and the salt trade with the bay of Bourgneuf in the marches of Poitou, the king of England relied upon the friendship or at least the neutrality of the duke of Brittany. For the sea route to the south was necessarily a coastal one, and if the Gironde estuary was the Suez of the fourteenth century, the rocky coast of Finistère was the Gibraltar. Moreover, consideration of the wool trade made it essential to keep on friendly terms with Flanders; it was through alliances with Castile that some protection was afforded to Gascony; the defence of northern England involved keeping a vigilant eye on Scotland; and in all of these places the French pursued policies which were often opposed to English interests.

For more than half a century before the outbreak of war in 1337 Anglo-French relations had been marked by conflict over Gascony. Reprisals and confiscations had been followed by unfulfilled treaties, which in turn became the occasion of further conflict. War flared up in 1294 when Edward I refused to appear in Paris to answer to a dispute that had arisen between a number of Gascon and Norman sailors, and again in 1324 when one of Edward II's vassals raided and burnt down the place of Saint-Sardos, where the king of France had authorized the building of a *bastide*. On each of these occasions the duchy was confiscated and only partially restored after a number of years had elapsed. Attempts were made to settle the outstanding disputes by judicial process, at Montreuil in 1306, Périgueux in 1311 and at Agen in 1322–3; but all of these failed, as much because the

Plate 1.   Henry of Grosmont, first duke of Lancaster, from the Bruges Garter Book
(*BM MS Stowe 594 fo. 8*)

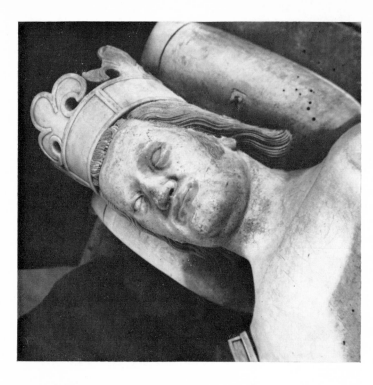

Plate 3. Effigy of Philip VI, from his tomb in the Abbey of St Denis

Plate 2. Effigy of Edward III, from his tomb in Westminster Abbey

French commissioners insisted on acting as judges, by virtue of their king's claims to sovereignty, as because the immediate issues were in themselves beyond solution. The inability to reconcile the development of a more centralized form of monarchy with an older and looser feudal relationship with its roots in the past was a constant source of friction in Anglo-French relations and seemed bound, sooner or later, to lead to a show-down.

But in 1328 a new dimension was added to the old disputes when the last Capetian king, Charles IV, died without a son to succeed him and his third wife gave birth to a posthumous daughter.[6] The situation was not without recent precedents, for all three sons of Philip IV (1285–1314) had failed to secure a male heir. The eldest of them, Louis X (1314–16), left a seven year old daughter, Joan (though she was of doubtful legitimacy), by his first wife and his second wife was pregnant. When the son to whom the queen gave birth died within a few days, Louis' brother Philip V (1316–22), who had already assumed the regency, seized the throne at the expense of his niece Joan and his elder sister Isabella. On Philip's death Charles IV (1322–8) likewise thrust aside Philip's daughters; but when Charles died there remained only one child of Philip IV: Isabella, the mother of Edward III of England.

Historians have argued, as princes, councillors and lawyers argued in 1328 and on many occasions thereafter, as to the merits of Edward III's claim to the French throne and the part which it subsequently played in his war policy. In default of a male heir, could a woman succeed to the French throne or, if she could not, could she transmit her right to her eldest son or even to her husband? And if a woman could succeed, did Isabella have a better claim than her nieces? Or should the crown go to one of the surviving cousins of Charles IV: to Philip of Valois, who was the grandson of Philip III (1270–85) by his second wife, or to Philip of Evreux, who was the grandson by his third wife, but was married to Louis X's daughter?

There were no rules to which the great assembly which met to discuss these crucial questions on the death of Charles IV could refer, since for more than three centuries before 1316 the crown of France had passed in continuous and uninterrupted succession from father to son. To counter the claims of Isabella's nieces, both Edward III and Philip of Valois must have agreed that a woman could not herself succeed or transmit her rights to her husband, although Edward II had at least considered claiming a share in the French kingdom on the death of Louis' posthumous son in 1317.[7] Edward's claim was therefore advanced by his proctors on the grounds that his mother could transmit her rights to him and that by virtue of those rights he was the nearest male heir to Charles IV—a fact that is incontestable, since he was the only nephew of the late king, whereas Philip of Valois was only the cousin. If his general argument was to be accepted he thus had a watertight case; but there were sound reasons why the assembly should reject it. For if one of Edward's cousins were subsequently to give birth to a son, the latter would be a grandson to one of the last three Capetian kings, whereas Edward was only the nephew. The dangers in accepting his argument were thus very real and in part confirmed by subsequent events. For in 1332 Louis X's daughter gave birth to Charles of Navarre, who was later able to maintain that he was more closely related to one of Philip IV's sons than either Philip of Valois or Edward III. But the main objections to Edward's candidature were probably political. For although his ancestry was as 'French' as Philip's, though he spoke French, was duke of Aquitaine, count of Ponthieu and a peer of France, he was at the time only fifteen and clearly not his own master, whereas Philip of Valois was thirty-five and Philip of Evreux twenty-three. Moreover, the prospect of Isabella and her lover Roger Mortimer ruling in France was hardly likely to appeal to the assembly any more than the power of a king who would add the domain of the English Crown and the Plantagenet fiefs in France to that of the Capetians. Edward's claim was therefore rejected by the assembly, which appointed Philip of Valois as regent (a position he appears to have already been occupying before Charles IV's death) and decided that if the queen gave birth to a son, Philip was to remain regent until the child's majority; but if the child was a daughter, he was then to ascend the throne. Thus between 1316 and 1328 the French succession was decided, not by any predetermined or Salic law, but by a series of *faits accomplis*, and for the time being there was nothing that the young king of England could do about it.

The importance that Edward attached to his claim in pursuing the war is a different matter. It has frequently been suggested that the homage which he did to Philip VI in Amiens Cathedral on 6 June 1329, and which he subsequently declared (30 March 1331) was to be recognized as liege homage, implies his acceptance of Philip's right to the throne; but Edward was at that time still a minor and the political situation in England and Gascony hardly favoured an active policy in pursuit of his rights. Not until October 1337 was he again in a position to lay serious claim to the throne of France, and it was not until two years later, after a revolution in Flanders in his favour, that he assumed the French royal title. More specifically, it is argued that this striking act of megalomania, which was celebrated with great pomp in Ghent on 26 January 1340, was no more than a tactical device, that it was never really taken seriously and that it was easily thrown over for territorial concessions.[8] According to this view, Edward's real aim was no more than an enlarged and sovereign Aquitaine and the main purpose of his assumption of the French royal title was to rid himself of the obligation to render homage for the lands which he held in France. But it has also been argued that his claim was put forward in all sincerity, that it deserves to be taken seriously, both as to its merits and in his war aims, and that this is demonstrated by the whole manner in which he fought the war, by his military strategy, his diplomacy and the way in which he fostered and used the unrest which revealed itself in the French provinces.[9]

In all of these activities, Henry of Grosmont played a vital and often the leading role; so much so that it is difficult to give an adequate account of his public career without virtually writing a history of English foreign affairs during the period of his lifetime. For while in the early campaigns of the war, in Scotland, the Low Countries and Brittany, Edward III consistently directed military operations himself, his assumption of the title 'king of France' in 1340 and his intervention in Brittany following a succession dispute which arose there in the following year, led to a completely different way of directing the war.

While Edward was simply a foreign claimant, direct invasion, such as he attempted in 1339 and 1340, was the natural method of prosecuting his claim. But once he had taken the French royal title, a policy of winning over his new subjects piecemeal and of supporting every local rising against King Philip might well be more profitable, for the Valois throne was far from secure in the 1340s. Some of the families of the maritime provinces of western France resented the predominance of Burgundians and other men from the eastern regions of the kingdom in Philip's court and council, and when things went badly wrong some of them began to wonder if he was the rightful king after all, for he had not succeeded to the throne in a manner that could be regarded as either normal or customary.[10] In the 1350s disenchantment with the policies of his son even spread to the eastern regions of the kingdom.[11] Rightly handled, these divisions in France could provide splendid opportunities for Edward III. The assumption of the French royal title gave a name and a cause to which all those discontented with Valois rule could rally and it associated them, in terms of the contemporary law of arms, in a 'just' war prosecuted in Edward's name.[12] To take advantage of these local conditions it might be necessary to have two or even three armies operating at once, either independently or in concert, and however important each might be it would be necessary to delegate the command of some of them at least. If a commander of one of these armies were to operate in a province recognizing Edward as king of France or, basing himself on that province, to operate in France at large, it would be necessary to make him the king's captain-general and lieutenant there, with virtually viceregal powers. Herein lay the chance to win fame that was offered to Lancaster and the earl of Northampton, as it was later offered to the Black Prince and John of Gaunt.

To lead a single army into France implies the hope of a decisive engagement; to send several armies into France, each with a more or less local assignment, implies a war of opportunity. When the opportunity passes, or the initial impetus is exhausted, it is to everyone's advantage to make a truce. And so the war, from the conclusion of the first Breton campaign until the peace of Brétigny in 1360, took the form of short bursts of activity, usually in several theatres at once, followed by rather long periods of quiescence, of ill-kept truce. And since the papacy was constantly endeavouring to convert each truce into a 'firm peace', each period of truce was also a period of intense diplomatic activity. In the fourteenth century governments did not employ permanent, resident ambassadors.[13] Diplomacy was consequently a matter of *ad hoc* embassies and every embassy included a quorum of high-ranking nobles. Much of the real work was done by the legal experts, while the presence of nobles gave the occasion such importance and urgency as might be desired; but sometimes the noble took an active and leading part in negotiations, as Lancaster did on more than one occasion. Here was another field in which to win distinction.

In the years down to 1361, Henry of Grosmont had greater opportunities in all of these fields than any other of Edward III's subjects. He served on no less than fifteen separate military expeditions, had supreme command of six of them and held the office of king's lieutenant on seven separate occasions. He headed six major diplomatic missions abroad and was involved in twelve truce conferences. Yet amid a crowded public life he still found time to supervise the administration of his vast estates, to indulge in crusades to Algeciras and

North Africa against the Moors and to Prussia against the Slavs, to fight a duel in Paris, found a collegiate church at Leicester and write a unique devotional treatise. In the following pages an attempt has been made to investigate the part he played in the affairs of Edward III's reign, to reconstruct his varied and active life, and so to see what use he made of his manifold opportunities.

# I Father and son (1310-1332)

When Edmund Crouchback, the youngest son of King Henry III, died at Bayonne on 5 June 1296, he left his second wife Blanche, the widowed queen of King Henry of Navarre and count of Champagne, with three sons—Thomas, Henry and John—all under age. As earl of Lancaster and Leicester his estates were widely scattered, in a manner typical of baronial holdings, from the North Sea in Yorkshire to the coasts of Lancashire, from Dunstanburgh in the northern marches to the south of Wales, with the more concentrated holdings in the Midlands, in the counties of Derby, Stafford, Leicester and Northampton and the Trent valley where he was the greatest lord.[1]

The bulk of these estates were inherited by his eldest son Thomas, who greatly added to them by marriage to Alice de Lacy, heiress to the lands of the earldoms of Lincoln and Salisbury. The youngest brother, John, secured the lordships of Beaufort and Nogent-sur-Marne in France, acquired by Edmund through his second marriage. But when John died in 1317 these interests in Champagne and Brie passed to Edmund's second son, Henry, who went to France in 1318 to render his homage and take over the lordships, from one of which he assumed the title of lord of Beaufort.

As his part of the inheritance Henry had already acquired estates in South Wales and the Welsh marches, notably Monmouth honor and castle, the castles of Grosmont, Skenfrith and Whitecastle which were situated in that county, all his father's lands beyond the river Severn and Rodley and Minsterworth in Gloucestershire. Through his marriage to Maude, the daughter and heiress of Patrick Chaworth, he acquired further Welsh lands in the counties of Glamorgan and Carmarthen which lay round the castles of Kidwelly and Ogmore and a number of manors in Hampshire and Wiltshire. Maude bore him six daughters—Blanche, Mary, Isabella, Maude, Eleanor and Joan[2]—and an only son, also called Henry, who was born around 1310, probably at Grosmont castle.[3]

Of the early life of this Henry, the subject of this book, relatively little is known, but his young manhood must have been quite eventful. The family could not but be involved in his uncle Thomas' manoeuvres and ultimate rebellion in 1322, while his father took so large a part in the revolution of 1327 and the removal of the queen's lover, Roger Mortimer, in 1330 that Edward III might well have felt that he almost owed his throne to him.

Born into a reign of civil war and upheaval, young Henry's opportunities and fortunes were inextricably bound up with the tragic events of these years. By birth and wealth and as the greatest subject of the realm, his uncle Thomas had been cast for great achievement but, lacking the necessary qualities and purpose, he had failed in that part. His ambition was satisfied by the exercise of a predominantly negative influence in the affairs of state. He had made a sorry mess of his public career and succeeded only in ruining himself and, more than anyone else, was responsible for ruining King Edward II's reign. The rebellion which he led against the king resulted in his execution outside Pontefract in 1322 and was followed by the forfeiture of his estates.

Henry's father, the elder Henry, might well have suffered a similar fate.[4] He was among those barons who forced Edward II to agree to the appointment of a baronial reform committee in 1310 and, along with other adherents of Thomas, he had a hand in the execution of the king's favourite, Piers Gaveston. As a marcher lord he was no friend of the Despensers and joined a confederacy against them in 1320 when civil war raged for a time in South Wales. But as chance had it he was on the king's service in France in 1322[5] and so took no part in his brother's rebellion in that year.

Three months after Thomas' execution he began the process of recovering for himself and his heirs the family fortune which his brother had so recklessly thrown away. In 1324 he secured the return of the county and honor of Leicester and won back the title of earl of Leicester. When Isabella and Mortimer returned from the continent with an army of invasion two years later he joined them and headed the baronial opposition which led to a general desertion of the king's cause. He captured Edward II and the Despensers at Neath and took the king to Kenilworth where he was responsible for his custody. Through this association with Isabella and Mortimer he was given the honors of Lancaster, Tutbury and Pickering, together with their castles and other parts of the family estates, and the same year he assumed the title of earl of Lancaster and Leicester.

Edward III's reign thus began with Lancastrian influence once again in the ascendant. Earl Henry was present at the young king's coronation, he knighted him, was appointed his guardian and chief of the regency council, where he had the support of friends and relatives like John Stratford, his chief clerical friend, his son-in-law Thomas Wake of Liddell and the northern barons Henry Percy (who also married one of his daughters) and John Ros. It was therefore hardly unexpected that when, in the first parliament of the new reign, he petitioned for a reversal of the judgement on his brother, he was reinstated in the inheritance.

However, when the queen and Mortimer strove to deprive him of the authority with which he had been invested by general assent of the magnates, when they replaced Lancastrian officials with their own men, when the earl found himself unable to control or advise his young charge, he was again forced into opposition, and decided on rebellion. Together with Wake and others he declined to attend the parliament which met at Salisbury in October 1328, when Mortimer was created earl of March; he assembled troops at Winchester and prepared for war. Some attempts were made to patch up a peace by negotiation, but these failed. Mortimer's troops entered the Lancastrian lands in January 1329, occupied Leicester and forced Henry to make terms near Bedford. According to the Leicester chronicler, Henry Knighton, who says much of the ravages committed by Mortimer's troops, the desertion of the earls of Kent and Norfolk was the cause of the Lancastrian defeat.[6] Among the rebels who made large recognizances in accordance with a rather humiliating oath which they were compelled to swear were Henry himself, Hugh d'Audley, Wake, the earl of Atholl, Henry de Ferrers and many other lords.[7] Henry de Beaumont, Sir Thomas Rosselin, Sir William Trussell and Thomas Wyther, who had been specifically excluded from the pardon offered by the king on 29 December, were obliged to leave the country.[8]

But that was not the last Mortimer was to hear of Lancaster. In the spring of the following year, when the earl of Kent was executed for treason, it must have been evident to Henry that his life and those of his supporters were in danger. To guard against this threat he enlisted the support of two members of the royal household—Richard Bury, keeper of the privy seal, and a yeoman of the household called William Montagu—in the hope that they would be able to inform the king of his plight. Mortimer was captured in Nottingham castle in October, speedily removed to London, and a few weeks later sentenced to be drawn and hanged as a traitor. The young king had joined the conspirators and although the *coup* was largely carried out by Montagu it could not have been accomplished without Lancastrian support.

In 1322 Henry of Grosmont was heir to no more than the lordships of Beaufort and Monmouth. By 1327 he could hope for the greater part of the Lancastrian inheritance. But even after the removal of Mortimer in 1330 he could not have felt sure of it. There was no reason to believe that the troubles of the last two decades had been brought to an end, but in the years that lay ahead the family's relations with the king promised to be harmonious. Not only had the elder Henry taken a leading part in the revolutions and scuffles that had finally secured Edward III upon the throne, but his son and the king shared the same interests and were of much the same age.[9]

Of young Henry's upbringing we know very little, but his education, though doubtless orthodox, was to produce a knight true to his period, endowed with both ability and charm, conventional, yet in some ways in advance of his time. In a devotional treatise entitled *Le Livre de Seyntʒ Medicines*, which he wrote himself when he was in his early forties—in itself an illuminating commentary upon the man—he tells us that he was a good-looking youth. Tall, fair and slim, he was fond of hunting and jousting and proud of his dancing and his armour. But he also says that he was a poor writer, having learnt late and by himself, and that being English he had little acquaintance with French—though on the latter point he was modest about his own accomplishment.[10]

He is said to have spent much of his youth abroad, fighting the paynim wherever he was to be found,[11] but it is probable that he spent the greater part of it in England. Henry could not have been much more than twelve when his mother died and was buried at Mottisfont Priory, which lay close to the old Chaworth lands in Hampshire.[12] He first appears on record, as 'Sir Henry de Grosemound', at Leicester in 1324.[13] Six years later he was married to Isabella, the daughter of Henry Lord Beaumont, a foreigner who had been rewarded for his services to Edward II with considerable grants of land, chiefly in Lincolnshire; he was a friend of the elder Henry and had been forced to flee the country for his part in the earl's rebellion in 1328–9.[14] It was in 1330 that Henry's sister Eleanor was married to Beaumont's son and heir, John.[15] By that time all but two of his sisters had been married off to his father's friends and supporters—Blanche to Lord Wake of Liddell, Maude to William de Burgh, earl of Ulster, and Joan to John Lord Mowbray. Shortly afterwards Mary was married to Henry Lord Percy. The sixth sister, Isabella, became a nun.[16]

Nevertheless, all the children long remained dependent on their father for money. The earl's accounts show that Henry received numerous advances from his father, who also met many of his daily expenses.[17] It is possible that Earl Henry took him on Edward III's first campaign against the Scots, and he may have been present at the young king's marriage to Philippa of Hainault in York Minster in January 1328. In the following month he went to see a tournament at Blyth with his brother-in-law William de Burgh who was of much the same age and who appears to have been brought up in the Lancastrian household.[18] They paid a short visit to Hereford from Kenilworth at the end of May and spent some time at Grosmont with Henry's father in June. Nothing is known of his movements during the earl's rebellion of October 1328 to January 1329, but he may have accompanied him to France on the occasion of Edward's homage to Philip of Valois.[19]

He next appears on the scene at the beginning of June 1330, when he was at Leicester with his sister Blanche. The same month he joined his wife at Tutbury and they together paid a short visit to Bolton. He was constantly on the move about his father's estates during the course of that year, travelling from Witney near Oxford to Kempsford in Gloucestershire, then awaiting his father at Leicester. He was still at Leicester in September, but paid a short visit to Melbourne in Derbyshire during the course of that month. Also in September his wife Isabella and his sister Eleanor travelled down to Leicester from York. His sisters Maude, Joan and Blanche, although married, still spent most of their time at one or other of their father's favourite castles—at Tutbury, Kenilworth, Higham Ferrers or Leicester. The Blounts (who were among the family's most trusted servants) stayed with them and Simon Simeon—Simkyn as he was known to his friends—Henry's future chamberlain and most trusted confidant hunted with the earl's hounds at Duffield and Needwood together with John Blount.[20]

Nothing is known of Henry's movements during the *coup* of October 1330, other than that he was involved in journeys up and down the country while his wife and sister Eleanor were staying at Kenilworth.[21] But about this time his father became blind and he was consequently given added responsibilities.[22] He now took an active part in the earl's council and represented him in parliament;[23] it was also during the course of that year that he was knighted.[24]

His journeys also took him further afield than the family estates, to Peterborough, Cottingham, Lichfield, Northampton, Cambridge,

Savernake, Bedford, Stafford, Dartford, Newmarket, and to a council meeting in London. In April 1331 he accompanied the king to France when Edward, disguised as a merchant, had a secret meeting with Philip of Valois at Pont-Sainte-Maxence. Together with his sisters and some of his father's retainers and councillors, he attended the jousts at Cheapside in September, when the grandstand collapsed and the queen narrowly escaped injury. He was present at the parliament which commenced at the close of that month, travelled to Hampshire in December, attended parliament in London in January 1332, went to Deeping with his sister Eleanor in February, attended parliament again in March, but during the course of the same month spent some time at Grosmont with his wife, who had travelled down from Leicester to join him there. During the course of that year he went abroad—to Brabant and elsewhere—but was back in September 1332 for the parliament held at the beginning of that month. Around the same time he visited Abingdon, Deeping, Uppingham, and was at Woodstock when the queen gave birth to her first daughter, Isabella.[25]

During the course of the year to Michaelmas 1332 his father had paid all his expenses, which amounted to over £666, of which £158 was spent on his household. There is no mention of this in his father's accounts for the previous year, but the bills were up some £200, mainly due to his journeys abroad.[26] Yet even this had not been enough to meet his needs and in March he was granted 500 marks at the Exchequer 'for the special affection which the king bore him, because his father had not yet made such provision for him as became his estate and also for his better maintenance in the king's service'.[27]

However, in the following year Earl Henry gave him a large part of the family lands in South Wales, which made him lord of Kidwelly, two Yorkshire manors and the profits from Pickering forest eyre. At the great distribution of honours to the younger baronage in March 1337 he was created earl of Derby and was granted a further annuity of 1,000 marks a year during his father's lifetime. In the following August, Earl Henry settled several of the Chaworth manors on him and his wife, and from February 1342 he was in possession by lease of Pontefract honor. While he was at Roxburgh with the king in 1334 he secured the custody of the lands of Isabella of Hastings during the minority of Laurence de Hastings—notably of Abergavenny castle—and in 1342 the custody of the castle, town and county of Carmarthen and the lordship of Cantref Mawr was granted to him for ten years.[28] By that time his active public career was already assured.

# II  Early campaigns (1333-1343)

In the ten years following his return from Brabant in 1332, much of Henry's time was taken up with campaigns in Scotland, where the initiative of his father-in-law, Henry Beaumont, led to a renewal of the Anglo-Scottish wars. When these in turn resulted in a further deterioration in Anglo-French relations he was involved in the campaigns in the Low Countries and in Brittany which marked the beginning of major hostilities on the continent and during the course of which he was imprisoned in Brabant as a surety for the king's debts. While in all of these military enterprises Henry seldom played a leading role, they formed an invaluable apprenticeship for the years which lay ahead.

On 7 June 1329 King Robert the Bruce died at Cardross in Dunbartonshire leaving a five year old son, David, to succeed him on the Scottish throne. While these circumstances augured badly for the future, during the next three years the government of Scotland was carried on by the young king's cousin Thomas Randolph, earl of Moray—an able man—and David's throne seemed secure. By the treaty of Northampton (17 March 1328), which followed a Scottish offensive begun on Edward III's accession to the English throne in the previous year, the English government, under the control of Roger Mortimer, had recognized the independence of Scotland and arranged for the marriage of Edward's sister, Joan of the Tower, to the infant David. But in October 1330 Mortimer was overthrown, Randolph died two years later and there were powerful opponents to the 'shameful peace' of 1328. In effect, the treaty of Northampton had made only partial restoration to the 'disinherited' lords—among whom Henry's close relatives Thomas Wake and Henry Beaumont were the most prominent—of the Scottish lands which they had forfeited for adherence to the English side. Led by Beaumont, they resolved to put forward Edward Balliol as claimant to the Scottish throne, of which Edward I had deprived his father. At the end of July 1332, a few days after the death of Moray, they sailed for Fife with a small but eager force. Edward III, while officially prohibiting their expedition, secretly connived at it. He authorized Beaumont to conduct Balliol from his ancestral estates in Picardy to England and evidently received his homage and fealty as king of Scotland before their military adventure began. On 11 August they won a resounding victory over the Scottish forces under the command of the new regent, the earl of Mar, at Dupplin Moor and, after hastening to Perth, they contrived to have Balliol crowned king of Scotland by the bishop of Dunkeld. On 23 November following he formally recognized the overlordship of Edward III and promised, in return for Edward's assistance, to cede him lands in Scotland to the value of £2,000 a year, including the castle, town and county of Berwick.[1]

For a time Edward kept up the pretence of neutrality. At York in February 1333 he received messengers from both Balliol and David, whose pleas were reinforced by Philip VI of France. But heartened by Balliol's astounding good fortune, anxious to reverse the defeat inflicted on his father's forces at Bannockburn in 1314 and the 'shameful peace' concluded by his mother's lover in 1328, he soon gave open support to Balliol and prepared an army for the siege of Berwick. In May 1333 the great border port and fortress, whose fortifications had been built by his own grandfather, was invested by the English forces and, after a siege of two months, on 19 July a Scottish force which attempted to relieve it was decisively defeated at Halidon Hill. Endeavouring to cross a marsh and attack uphill, they were overwhelmed by showers of English arrows and suffered enormous casualties. The tactics which Balliol and Beaumont had first used at Dupplin Moor—of dismounting their men-at-arms and combining them with archers—were once more used to good effect. Henry may or may not have been with the king on this memorable occasion, since part of the English forces had to be left before Berwick; but his seal was affixed to the articles of surrender of the town and he was one of a smaller number of magnates who consented to Edward's charter to its inhabitants.[2]

However, Halidon Hill did not give Edward III or Balliol control of Scotland, and the Franco-Scottish alliance, first concluded by Balliol's father in 1295 and renewed by Bruce in 1326, was now given practical effect. Philip VI did his best to foster resistance in Scotland and invited David Bruce and his queen to seek refuge in France. Around the middle of May 1334 they disembarked in Normandy, where Richard the Lionheart's great fortified castle of Château Gaillard was placed at their disposal. This was a serious setback for both Edward III and Balliol and when, on 12 June, the English king obliged his Scottish vassal to assign him territories in the Lowlands and on the Border which amounted to most of English-speaking Scotland, both parties made a serious mistake. Resentful of the dismemberment of their kingdom, but boosted by the prospect of French aid and the return of the new earl of Moray, John Randolph, from France, the Scots resisted the threat to their independence and Balliol found himself with a serious rising on his hands with which some of his former supporters threw in their lot. Edward III was again called upon to give his assistance to Balliol and a futile expedition, in which Henry took part,[3] was organized for the winter of 1334–5. Edward advanced to Roxburgh with a force of 4,000 men and spent the whole of December and January there demanding further support. At the beginning of February, when this had failed him, he abandoned his plans and returned to England.

The ensuing months saw considerable diplomatic activity. Philip VI, encouraged by the new pope Benedict XII, was determined to intervene in the Anglo-Scottish issue with diplomacy if not with arms. When Edward returned to Newcastle he was met by Philip's envoys, who persuaded him to negotiate with the Scots at Nottingham, where a truce was concluded to last from Easter until Midsummer. Henry took part in the discussions on each of these occasions;[4] but nothing enduring emerged from them. In granting the truce Edward was merely serving his own ends, since the north of England was devoid of troops and the larger English army which he had determined to raise could not be assembled before Midsummer. By the time the truce expired he had gathered together at Newcastle an army totalling over 13,000 troops—perhaps the largest he ever raised. The Lowlands of Scotland were to be caught in a pincer movement: Edward advanced from Carlisle through Annandale with one force, to which Henry belonged,[5] while Balliol (who, according to a pre-arranged plan of campaign, left Berwick on the same day that Edward left Carlisle) proceeded up the east coast with another. After holding a council of war at Glasgow the combined forces advanced on Perth, where they arrived early in August with the help of a supporting fleet in the Forth, which had by then reached the Tay. Assistance was also secured from Ireland for an attack on Rothesay in Bute and, two days after news arrived of the landing of the Irish expeditionary force, Lancaster joined Balliol in a raid 'beyond the mountains of Scotland' from Perth,[6] which was possibly intended to establish contact with the Irishmen or to supplement their attack on Rothesay with a simultaneous attack on Dumbarton. Whatever the case, he arrived in Berwick from the ultramontane foray on 15 October. Meanwhile, Edward had begun to disband his army and, at the beginning of September, he had left Perth for the south, making arrangements for the rebuilding of Edinburgh castle which, together with Stirling, was intended to defend the nothern border of the annexed lands. The garrisons of Berwick and Roxburgh were accordingly reduced on the grounds that the frontier had supposedly moved north to the Forth, and for the first time an attempt was made to establish an effective English administration in the newly acquired territories based on Roxburgh, Caerlaverock, Berwick and Edinburgh.

Three-cornered negotiations between the English, the French and the Scots occupied the spring of 1336, and among the Scottish negotiators were now included some from David Bruce's *émigré* court at Château Gaillard. Short truces were made until Edward was ready to promote another campaign, when they were allowed to lapse. On this occasion, Lancaster was appointed captain and leader of the army by the king and council and was sent to take command of Perth until Edward came north with the main body of his army and took over.[7] He was given full disciplinary power over its members and all royal ministers in the annexed territories and in Northumberland (as well as over the troops to be raised in Scotland and the Border counties of England) and was empowered to receive enemies into the king's peace and grant them pardons. Henry proceeded north with a force of 500 men-at-arms and 1,000 mounted archers and, after encountering some resistance at Monkland and Dunfermline, he reached Perth during the first half of June.[8] Meanwhile, the king made his way north from Newcastle on 14 June and joined Lancaster at Perth on 1 July. Twelve days later he started out on his most daring and romantic Scottish expedition—his destructive dash into the Highlands. Having heard that the earl of Atholl's widow was besieged in Lochindorb castle in Moray, he went to her rescue with a small escort. Leaving Perth on 12 July, he succeeded in relieving Lochindorb by the 16th. Then he proceeded to burn Forres and Elgin, thence on by Cullen to Aberdeen, both of which were burnt, and returned by way of Dunnottar, Brechin and Forfar to Perth for 28 July.

On his return to Perth, Edward ordered new defences to be constructed, and arranged for the castles of St Andrews and Leuchars to be rebuilt. Then, moving on to Stirling, he saw to the building of a peel, but left Lancaster in command there when, at the beginning of September, he returned south to hold parliament at Nottingham. Once

Plate 4.   Obverse and reverse of the Great Seal of Henry of Grosmont as duke of Lancaster
(*PRO DL 27/324*)

Plate 5.   Privy Seal of Henry of Grosmont
as earl of Lancaster
(*PRO DL 27/127*)

The seals are reproduced by permission of the Chancellor and
Council of the Duchy of Lancaster

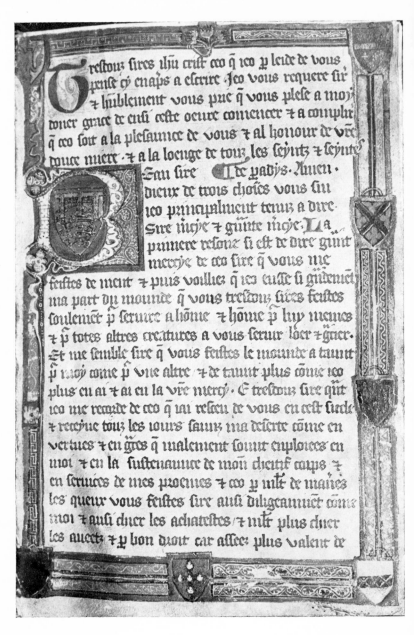

Plate 6. Page from *Le Livre de Seyntz Medicines* showing the duke's arms in the decorated initial (*Stonyhurst College Library*, *MS CCCC no. 128*)

again Henry had supreme authority over the English forces in Scotland for about six weeks until Edward returned to Stirling at the beginning of November and sent him back to England to organize measures for the defence of the south coast.[9]

To the king and his councillors this matter now seemed of the utmost importance. The French, through their intransigence, were making it impossible for him to deal a decisive blow to the Scots and in the spring of 1336, when Benedict XII cancelled the Crusade, Philip VI transferred the fleet (which was ostensibly to have taken him to the East) from the Mediterranean to the Norman ports. Edward was convinced that he intended a large-scale intervention on behalf of the Scots. He had now come to regard war with France as inevitable. In the parliament at Nottingham, discussions took place on the measures necessary to meet a possible invasion and all other contingencies. Lancaster was instructed to hold a conference in London with the archbishop of Canterbury, John de Warenne, earl of Surrey and Sussex, William de Clinton, constable of Dover castle and warden of the Cinque Ports, and John de Hampton, to formulate defence arrangements.[10] The city of London and some forty-four ports west of the Thames also sent representatives and a similar conference was held at Norwich to arrange defence for ports and other towns to the north.[11] Meanwhile, during the first fortnight in December, Edward withdrew the greater part of his forces from Scotland, instructed the seneschal of Aquitaine to put the duchy into a state of defence and began to seek allies in the Low Countries and Germany.

In May 1337 an elaborately-equipped embassy, with considerable financial resources, was sent to Valenciennes in Hainault. Within a short time the counts of Hainault, Gelderland, Berg, Cleves and Marck, the count palatine of the Rhine, the margrave of Juliers and the elector of Brandenburg promised to give their support to Edward in return for huge pensions and other payments. Lancaster appears to have taken no part in these diplomatic preparations. While the English ambassadors were setting out on their mission he was again sent to Scotland—on this occasion with the earls of Warwick and Arundel[12]— and when he returned south in June the breach with France had already occurred and the first hostilities that marked the beginning of open war had commenced. On 24 May Philip VI had declared Gascony confiscate and in July an army under the command of the constable of France was sent into the Garonne valley where it captured the key fortresses of Saint-Macaire and La Réole. By way of reply Edward III seized all French property in England, issued a manifesto to his subjects and on 7 October once again laid claim to the throne of France. But although Lancaster had an early taste of military action on the continent in August 1337 when, as one of the captains of the naval escort which conducted the wool convoy to Dordrecht, he made a raid on Cadzand,[13] it was not until the following summer that the king was able to make the decisive move.

That he was able to do so then was in no small measure due to a revolt in Flanders organized by a wealthy artisan of the patriciate of Bruges, James van Artevelde, and it was brought about by the prohibition on the export of wool to Flanders by the English government in August 1336, with the intention of bringing the count into alliance with Edward III. In future all English wool was to be shipped to Dordrecht in Brabant and from the following September a complete blockade of the Flemish ports was enforced. As a result, an alternative government was organized under the hegemony of the councils of Ghent, Ypres and Bruges, which in July 1338 agreed to be neutral in the war with France in return for the ending of the blockade, and which subsequently (3 December 1339) recognized Edward as the rightful king of France.

On 16 July 1338 the English forces set sail for the Low Countries, where they endured a long and frustrating winter during which Edward was unable either to pay or induce his Netherlandish allies to engage the enemy. Lancaster appears to have been with the king throughout these agonizing months—at Antwerp, Ghent and Brussels, and at Coblenz where, on 5 September 1338, Edward held an ostentatious meeting with the Emperor Lewis to seal the imperial vicariate which had recently been bestowed upon him. In the following year, when military hostilities eventually broke out, he led a detachment in the Thiérache campaign and was drawn up with the king at Buironfosse for the battle with Philip VI that never took place.[14] In January 1340 he was among the English ambassadors appointed to meet cardinals Peter and Bertrand, who were sent by the pope to Valenciennes to discuss the mediation of a peace or truce, which was intended to prevent the Anglo-Flemish alliance, concluded in the previous month, from achieving permanency.[15] Having been offered, together with the earl of Salisbury, as a hostage to Duke John of Brabant, he returned to England in late February.[16] His presence there was of short duration. On 22 June he once again set sail with Edward from Orwell; he was present at the decisive naval engagement at Sluys and subsequently led a section of the army in the Tournai campaign that followed.[17] Together with the duke of Brabant, the earl of Northampton and the bishop of London, he was among the English commissioners who negotiated the truce of Espléchin (25 September 1340) between France and the allies which ended ingloriously the campaign of 1340.[18]

Almost immediately he was obliged to enter prison in Malines as one of the sureties for the king's debts to the Malines and Louvain creditors who had met Edward's obligations to his Netherlandish allies when insufficient money was forthcoming from England for this purpose.[19] The Malines debt totalled £9,450 and should have been repaid at Easter 1340. Since Henry was personally bound to John Rikier, William Kerman and Walter le Chaungeair, the Malines creditors, for its repayment, he was arrested at Brussels and obliged to give them a fresh bond for the sum on 24 July 1340, promising repayment on 24 September. The earls of Northampton and Warwick appear to have been detained with him.[20] For damages because of non-payment at Easter and for having respite for payment till 24 September, he paid them £1,500. To procure the necessary money he had to raise a loan of 800 *livres gros tournois* 'in pannis' at Brussels: 336 *livres* apparently through the intermediary of the Malines creditors and the remaining 464 *livres* from the sale of velvet given to him for the purpose by the queen. He undertook that if the debt was not repaid wholly or in part on 24 September 1340 he would return in person to Malines on 25 September and remain there until it was. On this condition he was allowed by the merchants to proceed to the siege of Tournai, which started at the beginning of August 1340.

He was also bound, together with Northampton, to Edward's Louvain creditors and, together with Warwick, to his Brussels creditors.[21] For the former debt four knights of either earl were held as hostages at Louvain; imprisonment at Malines covered the latter. Both the Malines and Louvain creditors had insisted on having the earls as sureties and had refused to have anyone else instead.[22] They knew that in this way the repayment not only of the main debt but of all the interest and damages was assured them. The repayment of these debts was entrusted in the first instance to the Italian banking houses of Bardi and Peruzzi and secondly to that of the Leopardi of Asti. The sums necessary for the release of the earls were to have been raised by assignments on the ninth and on the wool levy. That the firms were unable to meet their obligations was due to the king's inability to raise the cash and wool necessary to meet his.

Edward did everything he could. On 18 August 1340 he instructed the council to secure 2,000 sacks of wool and to have them delivered to the attorneys of Henry and Northampton 'as quickly as you can . . .

to avoid disgrace and damage to us and our said cousins'.[23] Since 1 August the four knights of either earl had been detained at Louvain and on 25 September Henry was obliged to re-enter Malines as a hostage. Northampton appears to have been detained with him, as in a letter of 9 October, which was sent from Ghent, Edward wrote that they both 'lay in prison'.[24] The king's concern was mounting. Sufficient wool was not forthcoming and it had to be made clear that it had been ordered and assigned 'for the deliverance of our said cousins and for nothing else'. To this end two envoys from either earl, well known as their officers and retainers—Sir Hugh de Hastings and Sir Peter de la Mare for Henry, Oliver de Bohun and Peter Favelore for Northampton—were sent to act as their special attorneys.[25] Edward was clearly disturbed by the 'very great damages and perils which, God forbid, might come about if our said cousins remain any longer in prison'. November passed without any change in the situation and when Edward returned to England on 30 November Northampton returned with him but Henry remained in prison at Malines. The king probably magnified the perils which he thought might befall his cousin, since the earl was in no real danger of being treated harshly. He was paid five marks a day expenses and apart from the initial licence which he secured to be present at the siege of Tournai, on 9 December he obtained another to go to the jousts at *Le Bure*, providing that he was back for 15 December.[26]

The Bardi and Peruzzi having failed to procure his release, in January 1341 a new arrangement was made with the Leopardi. Since they were unable to advance the necessary sums, contraction of loans on the spot became the only way in which the earl could speedily end his imprisonment. He managed to raise £7,650 from various financiers, for the payment of which he was able to secure a provisional release for himself and the earl of Warwick on 23 May 1341, on condition that they would return to Malines if the remaining £1,800 still due out of the £9,450 was not repaid on 8 July following. He also had to pay damages of £1,200 for non-repayment of the debt of 24 September 1340, and for licence to leave Malines he had to pay an additional £900.

The £7,650 necessary for his release was raised from three loans, one of £450 from the Buonacorsi and two others of £3,600 each received from unknown financiers. He lost £653 13s 6d on these three loans and his account also mentions £320 in cloths at Brussels on which he is said to have lost more than £500. The £1,200 still due to the Malines merchants does not appear to have been repaid until September

1341. A letter which they sent to the earl on 15 August reveals how, after returning to England, Henry sent Sir Thomas Cok and William de Duvenvaerde to ask a further postponement of the term of repayment of the remaining debt. The merchants complained that the terms of the agreement were not being adhered to, that the full sum had not been paid, and asked for satisfaction. It was not until 20 September that they restored the earl's letters patent and acquitted him, the king and the earl of Warwick of all further liability for the debt. The repayment of the loans contracted by the earl to procure his release may have dragged on even longer.

Besides being bound personally for the repayment of these debts, he paid £969 in wool and cash to retrieve the royal crown, pawned by Edward to pay his debts, and pledged all the jewels he then had with him—some £1,500 worth all told—to a number of Ghent merchants in order that Edward could get back to England.[27]

On returning to England, Henry spent some time on the family estates—at Pickering and elsewhere; but it was not for long that he was free from public duties. About the same time that he secured his release from prison, David II of Scotland returned to his native country after seven years' exile in France, and in early autumn he raided Northumberland as far as the Tyne. On 7 October, to deal with this emergency, Henry was appointed the king's lieutenant in the north of England and in Scotland and captain and leader of the army destined for those parts.[28] By the time he reached Newcastle on 2 December, however, the king had assumed the command of the English forces,[29] and meanwhile Henry Percy had been sent ahead to recapture Stirling and supervise the defence of the March until he arrived.[30] Hostilities seem to have been half-hearted and a truce for the period until May was concluded. Christmas was spent jousting at Roxburgh and at Melrose, and when the English forces returned to Berwick they continued the tournaments there.[31] But Lancaster spent the entire winter on the Border and at the beginning of April he was at the head of a commission appointed to negotiate an extension of the truce or a peace; these negotiations appear to have been held at Berwick during the course of that month.[32] When he returned to London towards the middle of May, English expeditionary forces were embarking for Brittany.

On the death of Duke John III of Brittany in 1341 a dispute had arisen over the succession to the duchy. The candidate favoured by the king of France was Charles of Blois, who claimed the succession by right of his wife, while Edward III supported John de Montfort.

When war broke out between the partisans of these two claimants, Edward offered Montfort his support, and sent no less than three consecutive expeditions—Sir Walter Mauny in May 1342, the earl of Northampton with Robert of Artois in August, and finally he followed himself, with Lancaster, in October.[33] It seems likely that it had been necessary to send over an expeditionary force quickly, more quickly than the main army under the king's command could be assembled, and that the expeditions led by Mauny and Northampton were in the nature of advance guards to secure ports for disembarking the main force. But it is also possible that Edward's original plan was for a three-pronged attack on France and that he had himself intended to cross to Flanders—for his fleet was assembled at Sandwich—while Sir Oliver de Ingham, at the time seneschal of Aquitaine, was sent back to the duchy with sufficient funds to promote the war in the south. Whatever the case, it is clear that as soon as the king landed in Brittany he took over the direction of all operations.

Preparations for Lancaster's passage in the king's ship *La Robynet* were already under way on 22 June but, owing to the delay in the assembly of the main army, he did not leave England until towards the end of October.[34] Of his subsequent movements there is little to be said, but it seems probable that he was with the king for the greater part of the time. Together with the earl of Northampton, he was among the English envoys who in January 1343 negotiated a truce in the priory of St Mary Magdalen at Malestroit and was among its guarantors.[35] Edward returned to England with part of his army at the end of February. By that time Lancaster was on his way south to Spain.[36]

# III The first expedition to Aquitaine: Preparations (1343-1345)

During the next four years much of Lancaster's time was taken up with affairs in the south, where he was employed in diplomatic negotiations with Castile and the papacy and in the reorganization of the government of Gascony. All of these activities were to pave the way for an expedition, to recover the king's possessions in Aquitaine in 1345-6, which was placed under his command. Up to 1343 the English military effort had been largely concentrated in northern France, while the situation in Gascony steadily deteriorated. The French had made alarming progress there by the beginning of 1343. When the English expeditionary forces crossed to Brittany in 1342, the bishop of Beauvais, then Philip VI's lieutenant in Languedoc, besieged strategically vital places along the Garonne valley between La Réole and Port-Sainte-Marie: Saint-Bazeille, Coussan, Damazan and Lavardac.[1] But no less important was his activity in distributing pardons and rewards to tempt men into French obedience. The situation was a grave one.

Ultimately, English interests in Gascony depended upon the loyalty of the lords and the towns. Ever since the French invasion of the duchy in 1324, following the incident at Saint-Sardos, the area under English rule (that is the number of lords and towns acknowledging allegiance to the king-duke) had been contracting, until there were few places that could be relied upon outside the immediate surroundings of Bordeaux, Bayonne and Saint-Sever. The fall of La Réole in 1324 had brought about the submission of almost all the duchy, the Anglo-Gascons maintaining themselves only in these three strongholds, Bourg and Blaye on the Gironde, and a few castles of less importance. Although in the following year Charles IV had agreed to restore the duchy and actually began its evacuation, the turn of events had led him to order its reoccupation shortly afterwards. While the treaty of Paris of 1327 provided for the restoration of lands occupied by either side

39

since the treaty of 1325, in fact the Capetians (who had long since reinstated themselves in Limousin, Périgord and Quercy) kept certain territories to the west of the Garonne in the Bazadais, in addition to the Agenais, which they secured by the treaty.[2] French penetration had been accompanied by an extension of administrative and judicial as well as military control, even in those areas—the Agenais and parts of Gascony proper—most recently occupied by French arms. The latter two areas had been formed into a single *sénéchaussée* administered on similar lines as was to be found elsewhere in France and, on and off after 1324, the king of France appointed a lieutenant in Languedoc and, although this was not expressly stated in each commission, Gascony.[3]

It was the confiscation of the duchy by the French king (for the third time in forty years) in May 1337 which gave the signal for the recommencement of hostilities.[4] Philip VI appointed lieutenants in Languedoc and Gascony and between 1337 and 1340 fighting was fairly constant. War flared up in the Agenais and then enveloped the Bordelais. French armies penetrated the Garonne valley, seized La Réole and laid siege to Saint-Macaire, advanced down the Dordogne valley as far as Libourne and Saint-Emilion and ravaged the rich vine-growing district of Entre-Deux-Mers.[5] Bourg, which is situated sixteen miles to the immediate north of Bordeaux in the southern confines of Saintonge and commanded the entrance to the Dordogne, was taken by the French. So also was Blaye, situated a little further to the north-west and commanding the northern bank of the Gironde estuary. These were serious strategic losses which threatened the lifeline of the duchy with England, and they almost resulted in the occupation of Bordeaux.[6]

Between 1340 and 1344, French successes in the field were followed up by judicious grants of land, money and privileges to those entering French obedience. In March 1344 Philip VI invested his eldest son John with such parts of Aquitaine as were then in French control.[7] During the summer and autumn of that year the duke made a tour of his new possessions, took the homage of his subjects and promised to respect their customs, franchises and liberties. Until his accession to the throne in 1350 he styled himself 'duke of Normandy and Guyenne, count of Poitou, Anjou and Maine'.[8]

English interests had reached their lowest ebb. The accounts of the constable of Bordeaux (who was the king's chief financial officer in the duchy) for the year commencing September 1342 amply demonstrate the desperate state of affairs.[9] The collection of revenues was largely

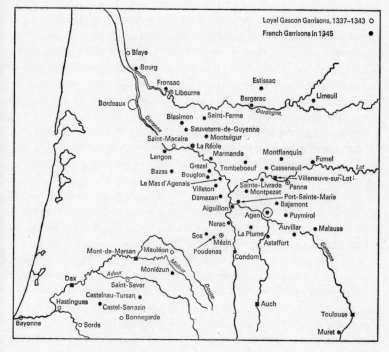

Map I.   Garrisons in Gascony, 1337–1345

limited to the narrow coastal strip between the mouth of the Gironde and the Pyrenees. Much that had not already been taken by the French or made valueless by the ravages of war had been granted by the king and the seneschal of Aquitaine (his chief officer in the duchy) to those supporting the Anglo-Gascon cause, either in recognition of their services or in compensation for the losses sustained by them in those parts of the duchy occupied by the enemy. There was little else accounted for other than the returns from the *prévôtés* of Bordeaux, Bayonne, Saint-Sever, Salles and Aulas, the *bailliage* of Blanquefort and a few isolated castellanies like that of Saint-Macaire. Meetings with the French seneschals of Saintonge and the Agenais to discuss the observation of the truce were held in the frontier districts which ran between Blaye and Bourg to the north of Bordeaux and between Saint-Macaire and Caudrot to the east. There were no returns for the *bailliage* of Bonnegarde because it was under constant attack from the French.

The defence of the duchy had been left very much to the Gascons themselves. The responsibility for organizing and directing that effort rested with the king's ducal administration acting under the seneschal of the duchy and the captains-general and lieutenants appointed by the king. On a smaller scale there was a remarkable parallel in the opening years of the war between Edward's policy of distributing money fiefs to the princes of the Low Countries and his provisions for enlisting support in Gascony. Both were marked by an attempt to secure military support in return for pensions and other payments. In the month following the confiscation of the duchy by Philip VI in May 1337, Edward empowered Sir Oliver de Ingham, then seneschal of Aquitaine, and John Diens to retain in the king's service whatever persons they could, either for life or for a year, and to treat with them of the wages they were to receive for themselves and their men-at-arms. On 1 July 1338 Bernard Ezi, lord of Albret, and Ingham were appointed joint lieutenants in the duchy. They were instructed to retain in the king's service all those who would be valuable to the king and they were to arrange pensions and other payments with them. Eighteen months later, when Bernard Ezi was once more appointed to the office, together with another Gascon called Hugues de Genève, they received substantially the same powers.[10] Indentures were drawn up between the seneschal and a number of Gascon lords which laid down the fees to be received by the latter for their services. There is ample evidence that the practice of enlisting support in return for pensions was common in the early years of the war. Gascon lords, knights, esquires and even some of the more influential burgesses and citizens of the towns figure among the names of those receiving royal pay.

Surviving records of payments made and outstanding to the troops in the years 1337–43 show that those Gascon lords, knights and esquires supporting Edward III maintained retinues of men-at-arms and foot sergeants and garrisoned castles and other places situated on their lands upon enlistment by the seneschal of Aquitaine and on the pay of the constable of Bordeaux. They were also responsible for garrisoning the more important towns and castles of the duchy remaining in English control, contributing men to the forces and the more important of them serving as captains and castellans.[11]

These troops were of two kinds: cavalry, made up of men-at-arms and mounted armed men (*hominibus ad arma* and *hominibus armatis equitibus*) and infantry, made up of foot sergeants (*servientibus peditibus*). In the years 1337–43 the infantry formed the overwhelming majority ($86\frac{1}{2}\%$) of the total number of troops in the king's pay and over half of them ($59\%$) were employed in the garrisons of towns and castles. These figures reflect an essentially defensive policy. As long as the infantry were in such preponderance there could be little manoeuvrability of the forces with which to facilitate effective military strategy. War had necessarily to be prosecuted by way of sieges and defensive tactics in established positions.

Both the seneschals of Aquitaine and the captains-general and lieutenants appointed by the king could retain, co-ordinate, direct and command the Gascon forces; but the troops were invariably enlisted by the seneschal. Sometimes he delegated his powers of enlistment to his subordinates, but their action was then subject to his confirmation. When a captain-general and lieutenant was appointed in the duchy the seneschal was expected to have assembled the Gascon army and to be ready for him to take over command of it. The troops were enlisted for service either in the garrison (*in municione et custodia*) of a specified town or castle or to serve in a Gascon field army (*in servicio domini regis et ducis*). There are numerous references to the ducal army, which was sometimes commanded by the captain-general and lieutenant, sometimes by the seneschal. The troops were enlisted to serve in it on prescribed rates of pay—the same as those operative in the English army—and it was staffed by marshals, marshals of the horse, royal standard-bearers and surgeons appointed to attend the wounded. The final direction and deployment of the troops was within the powers of either office, but it was usually exercised by one or both occupants acting in consultation with the king's council in the duchy—those important barons still in allegiance to Edward and the functionaries who sat alongside them, clerks retained to serve as the king's councillors and who drew his pay.

If Gascony could not defend itself against the French advance it was primarily due to financial causes rather than to lack of support for the Anglo-Gascon cause. Armies could be and were raised by the Gascons themselves. But the loyalty of the troops depended upon regular pay and their successful deployment could only be realized if they were placed under the authority of an experienced commander with adequate backing.

Theoretically, the cost of the war in Gascony was to have been met out of the ducal revenues; in practice, it became increasingly apparent as it proceeded that it must be financed from England. In the years 1337–43 the maintenance of military forces reached such proportions that the Bordeaux administration could not meet its commitments, the more so as its revenues decreased with the progressive reduction of the area under its control as a result of increasing French encroachment. The situation was further aggravated by the alienation of what lands and revenues remained, in order to secure the support of the leading towns and barons.[12] By 1341 the constable was in debt to the Gascon lords in respect of enormous sums for troops maintained by them since the beginning of the war.[13] During the summer of that year the king's council in England was bombarded with petitions for these arrears to be paid; its instructions to the constable that the sums in question should be met out of the ducal revenues showed a complete failure to grasp how limited his resources were and the extent of his commitments. Already towards the close of 1340 Bernard Ezi had requested further financial assistance from England; and Edward, who had overtaxed the country's resources and blamed his ministers for failing to procure the necessary sums, had promised to see that it was sent.[14] When this was not forthcoming, Bernard left Gascony for England and, in a report of the situation in the duchy which he made to the council at Westminster on 2 December 1341, he related how very little remained in the king's obedience save the cities of Bordeaux and Bayonne, how the troops were deserting because they were not paid; and he again requested—as he had done a year earlier—that he might be relieved of his lieutenancy.[15] Fearing that Albret might defect from the English cause, the council agreed that he should have his money, but the overall situation hardly improved during the next few years. In the following July, when the earl of Northampton was appointed king's lieutenant in Brittany, Sir Oliver de Ingham (who had been recalled from Gascony to give a full report on the situation there) was sent back to the duchy with special funds to be administered by Walter Weston, who was appointed treasurer of the Gascon army.[16] Many of the troops who had been enlisted in the king's pay were suspected of having inadequate arms and horses. To prevent this from happening in the future the troops were to be mustered monthly, their horses were to be branded and valued, and in future only those forces serving in the garrisons of royal towns and castles were to be paid during periods of truce. Weston was not to pay any old debts out of the money allocated to him for the war and, together with Ingham, he was to inform the king of excessive grants which had been extorted from him. Weston's funds were, however, clearly inadequate, even for current expenses.[17] The attempt to get the Gascons to run the war in the south themselves had proved a failure.

Immediately after the conclusion of the campaign in Brittany in 1343, Lancaster was sent to Spain, where he was officially described as 'fighting against the enemies of God and Christianity'.[18] The Castilian chroniclers tell how he arrived in Alfonso XI's camp outside the walls of Algeciras (at the time still controlled by the Moors), of how the king was heartened by their arrival, and of how Henry and the earl of Salisbury who accompanied him gained general respect for their bravery. Alfonso is said to have been so pleased by their presence that in order to intimidate the Moors he conducted one of their diplomatic missions over the English camp. But as well as taking part in the siege, the two earls also accompanied the admiral of the Castilian fleet, Egidio Boccanegra, when he descended on the African coast with a fleet of galleys to attack the Moorish fleet off Ceuta.[19]

Lancaster and Salisbury had not, however, primarily gone to Spain in pursuit of a chivalrous reputation; they went as professional diplomats. Although they had been in Castile for several months when, on 2 September, they were empowered to treat with Alfonso concerning maritime disputes between the two countries,[20] as early as 14 March Edward had informed the chancellor of England that 'our dear and faithful cousin the earl of Derby has gone to Spain on great necessities and charges and, among other things, we have instructed him to speak of certain matters to our cousin the king of Spain'.[21] The principal of these matters was a marriage alliance between Alfonso's eldest son and one of Edward's daughters and its purpose was to secure the support, or at least the neutrality, of the Castilian fleet in the war with France.

Castile was at the time a major naval power for, unlike England and France, who had to rely on impressed merchant ships for their defence, she had a permanent fleet of galleys. These ships were commanded by professional naval officers and they were renowned for their speed and their manoeuvrability. In addition, the Castilians also had at their disposal a large merchant fleet which was maintained by the numerous sea ports along her Atlantic coast. If the French were to secure the support of the Castilians in the war with England they might be able to cut off communications with Gascony and once again secure a strong position in the English Channel.[22]

The English government had, however, started with a remarkable ignorance of domestic politics in the Iberian Peninsula, and this constituted a serious handicap in its quest for allies there. In 1336 the French had concluded an alliance with Castile and it was one of the main purposes of the English mission to break their monopoly of influence there. By the beginning of November Lancaster had returned to England,[23] but in the following January the council gave the prior of Rochester and Sir William Trussell—significantly a Lancastrian official of some standing—charge of an embassy sent to Spain 'to treat with our dear cousin the king of Castile of a marriage alliance and other alliances to be made between him and us' and gave them £1,000 to pay 'to certain men of the council of the said king, wherever it seems to them that the money can be best employed to expedite the necessities touching the aforesaid treaty according to the charge given to them'.[24]

Meanwhile, on 24 March 1344, Lancaster and the earl of Arundel were appointed lieutenants in Aquitaine and (though this is not expressly stated in their commissions) Languedoc.[25] Among other things they were empowered to negotiate alliances with three of the Iberian kingdoms (Castile, Portugal and Aragon) and to treat with them on outstanding maritime disputes. Leaving England towards the close of that month with other pilgrims bound for Santiago[26]— including Lancaster's sister Eleanor who was having an affair with Arundel—their mission was veiled in secrecy,[27] but of its main purpose there can be no doubt. In subsequent correspondence between Edward and Alfonso, Edward claimed to have 'opened his heart' to Lancaster on the subject of an alliance. But although the earl made his way southwards to join Alfonso at the siege of Algeciras, when he arrived at Logroño on the frontier between Navarre and Castile he was informed that Algeciras had surrendered to the king and, abandoning his journey, he returned to Bayonne and appointed John de Brocas and Guillaume Sanche, lord of Pommiers, to treat in his name.[28] At some point, however, he joined Egidio Boccanegra on board one of his galleys and managed to secure a tentative offer of the support of the Castilian fleet.[29]

Now that the ground had been laid, the way was open for less important embassies to settle the details of a closer understanding between the two countries. Sir William Trussell and and Sir William Stury were sent out in the late autumn of 1344, the prior of Rochester and Trussell in March 1345 and the bishop of Bayonne and Gérard du Puy, two of Edward's Gascon councillors, in the summer of 1345.[30] The two earls had impressed Alfonso sufficiently for him to continue the negotiations for a marriage alliance. It is clear from Edward's subsequent correspondence with the Castilian court that Lancaster had acquired a very shrewd idea of the political situation there, for he now knew who to approach in order to bring the alliance to fruition.[31] He wrote to Alfonso's mistress, Leonor de Guzmán, as well as to the queen and to their respective supporters. He declared that, although he regretted having been unable to attend the siege of Algeciras in person, he now intended to come on a pilgrimage to Santiago. By 1346 Alfonso had been persuaded to agree to the marriage of his son and heir Don Pedro to Edward's daughter Joan. Although the young princess died before the marriage could be celebrated, Lancaster's work had not been in vain.[32] Alfonso did not give active support to the French when the war was renewed with England in 1345 and, as a result of Lancaster's efforts, the government had secured an invaluable insight into Spanish domestic affairs.

By the spring of 1344 the situation in Aquitaine had become critical. The finances of the duchy were in a chaotic state and the granting of lands and revenues to secure and maintain the support of the Gascons had reached such staggering proportions and had been so badly administered that it was defeating the purpose it was intended to serve.[33] Although there was something to be said for placing the responsibility for the distribution of such large grants in the hands of the government in Westminster, since the seneschal might be open to local persuasion, the king and council could not always have a clear picture of the situation in Gascony. In the spring of 1344, shortly before Lancaster and Arundel arrived in the duchy, the seneschal, Nicholas de la Beche, reported to the council that the king should secure information about certain grants which he had made to several not particularly deserving people, explaining that Edward had granted so much away that there was very little left with which to reward the deserving and pointing out that he had overburdened the customs at Bordeaux. He advised that the king should secure information about what he was

47

granting, about how much it was worth and about the loyalty of the proposed beneficiaries.[34] The evils inherent in parcelling out Gascon lands and revenues in Westminster were thus abundantly clear and in March 1344, when the duke of Normandy was invested with those parts of the duchy then in French control and shortly afterwards began his homage tour, the need to send one or more high-ranking official representatives to Bordeaux became a top priority.

On 24 March Lancaster and Arundel were given their commissions for the reform of the government of the duchy.[35] They were appointed the king's lieutenants in Aquitaine and Languedoc and were given extensive powers to recover what they could there. They could treat with both individuals and communities and receive them into the king's allegiance; they could take their homage, reward them with grants of land or, conversely, they could confiscate the lands of those who had deserted the king's allegiance and employ such properties as they saw best. In case the truce lapsed and the war was renewed, they were given full military authority, with full powers to assemble and command the Gascon army. They were also given overriding judicial and administrative authority and were to make a thorough overhaul of the ducal administration: they were to investigate the work of the king's ministers there and appoint or dismiss them at their discretion. In an attempt to improve the financial situation, they were to see that all customary dues were performed and that rents were paid. Since the king had been given to understand that he had been deceived and had made excessive grants in the duchy, they were to recover all the castles, lands and liberties which he had granted away—without exception of persons—and enquire into the merits of the gifts. They were to annul all those which had been fraudulently engineered and restore the others to their holders. They were to do everything they could to see that the truce of Malestroit was observed.

The two earls doubtless gave some attention to the government of the duchy, but much of Lancaster's time was taken up at Avignon in connection with peace discussions first agreed to at Malestroit in January 1343. At some point between Edward's final acceptance of papal arbitration on 12 May and the announcement of the departure of the English embassy on 3 August he was involved in secret negotiations with the pope at Villeneuve-les-Avignon.[36] This may have been an unofficial visit to secure the necessary dispensations for Arundel's marriage to his sister Eleanor, but if so it was one which Clement used for his own purposes.[37] According to the chronicler Adam Murimuth, Lancaster arrived back in England on 7 July, and on the 11th a council was called to hear his report, which was kept secret but said to be unpleasant. Edward therefore sent the dean of Lincoln, John de Ufford, together with Nicholas de Luca and Hugh Neville to Avignon, where they stayed until after the conference began.[38] It would thus appear that the final decision to accept papal arbitration and the final briefing of the English ambassadors were made on the basis of Lancaster's report. Before the conference opened at the beginning of October the earl was in correspondence with Ufford (who was one of the English envoys) by way of his confessor John de Rippis.[39] From their letters it is clear that Lancaster had proposed a secret meeting with the pope to discuss Edward's terms for a settlement. Clement, however, would only agree on the condition that Edward should state what lands and money he would require to make peace. He seems to have been attempting to make the king accept conditions quite different from those which Edward had in mind.

The discussions which took place during the autumn peace conference are known in some detail from a number of letters sent back by the English envoys and a journal written by one of them.[40] These show that they began by stating Edward's claim to the French throne without qualification; and that although they discussed other proposals that might have resulted in a peace, they insisted on Edward's demand for the French throne as his right. The French delegates, on the other hand, maintained that the origins of the war lay in Aquitaine and that a settlement must solve the problem of the duchy. Given these two opposed positions, no agreement could be reached.

Lancaster was not present at the conference, and plans to send him on a secret mission to the curia upon its conclusion—whatever its purpose—were abandoned.[41] On 10 January he was present at a council meeting summoned to hear the report of Hugh Neville, who had returned from Avignon at Christmas.[42] According to subsequent correspondence with the pope, it was agreed in council on 17 January that Lancaster and Bartholomew de Burghersh should be sent to the curia to prevent the breakdown in the negotiations from drifting into war.[43] The government seems to have considered this suggestion, but in the final analysis they never went. Edward had decided to secure his duchy by a reversion to arms.

During the spring and summer of 1345 three fleets totalling no less than 443 ships were assembled in the harbours of Portsmouth, Sandwich and Southampton. The Portsmouth flotilla was destined for Brittany with an army under the command of William de Bohun, earl of Northampton; that assembled at Sandwich was to cross to Flanders with an army under the command of the king; the Southampton flotilla—some 152 ships manned by a crew of nearly 3,000—was bound for Gascony with an army under Lancaster's command.[44] They were the product of long and careful preparations.

On Sunday 13 March 1345 Lancaster was party to an indenture with the king by the terms of which he undertook to go to Gascony (for six months in the first instance) as the king's lieutenant in command of an expeditionary force of 2,000 men who were to be assembled at Southampton on the evening of 14 May, ready to set out for Gascony.[45]

Among other things, the indenture specified the powers he was to have as the king's lieutenant in the duchy. Four commissions were proposed. The first empowered him to take into the king's hands such lands, tenements, towns, castles, franchises, customs, profits of money and anything else in the duchy as he saw fit. The second charged him to conclude a truce, should he consider it necessary to do so in order to safeguard the king's interests and those of himself and his men. The third authorized him to supervise the work of the king's ministers, to dismiss those who were incompetent (with the exception of the seneschal and the constable) and replace them by others. The fourth empowered him to banish the king's enemies or, conversely, to receive them into the king's peace and grant them pardons. If any of these powers were meanwhile issued to any other person they were to be revoked before Lancaster took up his command. The truce of Malestroit was to be allowed to run out and the earl was to be informed to that effect before he began military operations.[46]

Meanwhile, Ralph Stafford, whose son Ralph had married Lancaster's eldest daughter Maude on 1 November 1344, was appointed seneschal of Aquitaine on 25 February and sent out to the duchy to prepare the way for Henry's arrival.[47] On 16 March he was given a series of instructions relating to his duties.[48] In the military sphere he was to see that the troops enlisted in Gascony were well supplied with horses and arms. He could treat with nobles and others for their return into the king's allegiance, to grant them pardons and, wherever necessary, to reward them with goods taken from the king's enemies. He was also given extensive administrative powers: several of the king's councillors and other ministers and officers in the duchy were not fulfilling their duties and were spending too much; he was to inspect and supervise their work and, wherever necessary, to remove and replace them, with the exception of the constable and the mayor of Bordeaux. The king and his officers were once again said to have made excessive grants in the duchy; he was to investigate the merits of these. To secure the neutrality of Castile he was authorized to treat with Alfonso XI for a settlement of maritime disputes.

A series of commissions issued to Lancaster on 10 May, four days before his scheduled embarkation, embodied most of the powers granted to him and Arundel in the previous year and those outlined in his indenture, some of which had meanwhile been granted to Stafford.[49] He was appointed the king's captain-general and lieutenant in Aquitaine and Languedoc. The two posts combined not only gave him full military authority, with powers to assemble and lead an army, but overriding judicial and administrative authority, with powers to dismiss and appoint local officials at his discretion. To some extent he was the king's viceroy; he could receive individuals and communities into the king's allegiance, take their homage, grant them letters of pardon and reward them with grants of land; conversely, he could confiscate the lands of those who had deserted the king's allegiance and employ such properties as he thought best.

During late May and early June, the forces placed under Lancaster's command were assembled at Southampton and arrangements were made for their provisioning and pay.[50] Meanwhile, on 17 April, a month after Lancaster had concluded his indenture, the earl of Northampton had contracted with the king to go to Brittany as captain and guardian of the duchy and on 24 April, just over a fortnight before Lancaster received his commission as captain-general and lieutenant in Aquitaine and Languedoc, he was given a similar commission as Edward's captain-general and lieutenant in 'the kingdom of France and the duchy of Brittany', significantly in co-operation with John de Montfort, the English candidate in the Breton succession dispute.[51] Both earls were thus designated captains-general and lieutenants and they divided France between them. Lancaster was to operate in the south and Northampton in the north, based on Gascony and Brittany respectively.

By 11 June, Northampton had left for Brittany and Lancaster had embarked the greater part of his men and horses and was ready to leave for Gascony. The sheriffs of London were instructed to have it proclaimed that all those going to the duchy with him were to join him at Southampton as quickly as possible.[52] Ten days later the mayors and bailiffs of the southern ports were instructed not to allow any seaworthy vessel which could be used to transport the forces to France to leave England unless it was to carry the troops under the command of the king or Lancaster.[53] A huge fleet had been raised and equipped—

almost entirely in English ports—to transport the earl's expeditionary force to Bordeaux. The feat of organization had been staggering but, held up by contrary winds and storms at sea, it was not until some two months after its intended departure that, on Saturday 23 July, it was able to put out from Falmouth. Seventeen days later, having passed down the Gironde estuary, it arrived in the harbour of Bordeaux.[54]

# IV  The first expedition to Aquitaine:
# The campaigns (1345-1347)

It was a sadly diminished duchy of Aquitaine into which Lancaster set foot when he disembarked at Bordeaux on Tuesday 9 August 1345. French armies had advanced down the Garonne valley as far as Langon, which they had taken, and along the Dordogne to the gates of Libourne. To the north much of Saintonge, to the east Périgord and the Agenais, together with Bazas and a good many places in the Bazadais, were firmly in French control, while on the southernmost boundaries of the duchy the vicomté of Béarn and the county of Armagnac were rallied to French obedience by their respective lords. The area effectively in English control had been reduced to the immediate neighbourhood of Bordeaux, Bayonne and Saint-Sever and the eastern seaboard country which separated them. A maritime strip without any deep hinterland, with hostile neighbours on every side save the open sea which lay to the west, was all that remained of King Edward's heritage in the south of France.

Once he arrived in the duchy, Lancaster was joined by those Gascon lords remaining in English allegiance and whose principal possessions lay in the Bordelais. Among the most prominent was Bernard Ezi, lord of Albret, whose lands were concentrated in the region between the river Adour and the north of Landes, but which included a string of important lordships in the Bordelais. Twice the king's lieutenant in the opening years of the war, he had over a thousand troops in his pay.[1] His brother Bérard was a baron of almost equal importance. Lord of Vayres, Vertheuil and Gironde since 1326, he had bought the lordship of Rions in the following year and, after persuading Bernard Ezi to return into English obedience in 1339, had been rewarded for his services to the Crown by a grant of the lordships of Puynormand, Cubzac and a part of Blasimon, together with the custody of several fortresses for his sons.[2] Like his brother, he also was able to muster a large number of troops.

Several important Gascon barons served in Lancaster's retinue: Guillaume-Sanche, lord of Pommiers, and his brothers Élie and Guillaume de Pommiers, Pierre de Grailly, *vicomte* of Benauges and Castillon-sur-Dordogne, Jean de Grailly, *captal* of Buch, Bertrand, lord of Montferrand and Arnaud de Durfort, lord of Castelnoubel.[3] Guillaume-Sanche controlled a strong castle at Saint-Félix-de-Pommiers, situated in an admirable position on a rock promontory above the river Vignagne, a tributary of the Drot, near to La Réole. His family had remained loyal to the Crown for over a century.[4] The Graillys, whose family had settled in the Bordelais in the thirteenth century, possessed the lordships of Puy-Paulin and Castillon-de-Médoc which lay to the south of the Gironde estuary.[5] The barony of Montferrand and a grant of the castellany of Blaye in 1341 made Bertrand de Montferrand's loyalty both certain and vital: these possessions commanded the entry to the Dordogne valley and the northern bank of the river Gironde.[6] Arnaud de Durfort held two of the strongest castles in the Agenais: Castelnoubel and Bajamont, only ten kilometres from Agen. A long-standing quarrel with that town over the jurisdiction of the former castle made him unique as a lord of the Agenais still in English allegiance.[7] Besides these Gascon barons Lancaster was also joined by Bérard d'Albret's sons Bérard and Amanieu, by Guillaume-Sanche's brother Bertrand de Pommiers, by Bertrand de Montferrand's brother Amalvin, by the *vicomtes* of Fronsac and Tartas, Élie de Saint-Symphorien, lord of Landiras, Bernard d'Escoussans, lord of Langoiran, the lords of Lesparre, Lescun, Audenge and Thouars, Alexander de Caumont and several others.[8]

## The first campaign

Lancaster stayed in the Gascon capital for no more than a few days. Almost immediately his army had disembarked he made his way down the Garonne valley to Saint-Macaire (a loyal town which had remained in English control) and joined up forces with the seneschal of Aquitaine, Ralph Stafford, who was then besieging Langon with a Gascon army. From there he did not proceed further down the Garonne valley to La Réole (then in French hands) as might have been expected, but cut across country to Bergerac, over forty miles to the north-west, surprised a French force commanded by Henri de Montigny, seneschal of Périgord and Quercy, which was besieging Montcuq, and routed it beneath the walls of Bergerac.[9]

Bergerac was then the headquarters of an army commanded by Bertrand, count of l'Isle-Jourdain, the largest French force then con-

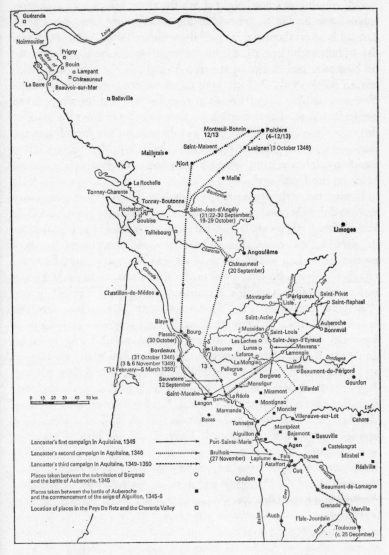

Map II.   Lancaster's Campaigns in Aquitaine, 1345–1350

centrated in Gascony. Situated on the northern bank of the Dordogne, the town was (and still is) connected to the south bank by a long bridge running at some height above the river. Montigny's retreating forces were unable to get within the walls before Lancaster's army pressed in upon them and trapped them on the bridge. The attack was driven home with heavy fire from the archers on the flanks and followed up by a mounted charge by the men-at-arms. In the confusion which ensued many of the French were taken prisoner or killed. Both the *Chronique de Bazas* and Froissart describe how the archers worked particular havoc. The defending force was unable to close the gates or drop the portcullis and Lancaster's army pursued the French into the faubourgs, routed some, whilst others, including Montigny, tried to escape by another gate; some of the troops and inhabitants fled by boats on the Dordogne.

Having taken the faubourgs by a dash in which he had completely surprised the French, it could only be a matter of time before the main French force, still secure behind the ramparts, would have to surrender or abandon the town. Meanwhile, Lancaster maintained a heavy assault. According to Froissart he combined his operations with those of a fleet of boats brought up from Bordeaux and the defending force under the command of l'Isle-Jourdain retreated to La Réole.[10]

Bergerac surrendered on 24 August, only fifteen days after the expeditionary force had disembarked. It was a magnificent opening to Lancaster's military operations and the chroniclers leave us in no doubt that it greatly impressed contemporaries. The whole expeditionary force was present—the earl of Pembroke, Sir Walter Mauny, Ralph Stafford and their retinues—and several Gascon contingents, including that of Bernard Ezi. Pierre de Grailly, Bernard d'Escoussans, Bertrand de Montferrand and his brother Amalvin, Guillaume-Sanche and his brother Élie, Bertrand de Durfort, and the lord of Audenge were knighted. Adam Murimuth gives the names of ten lords taken at Bergerac; Robert of Avesbury states that there were eleven. They included Henri de Montigny and Jean de Galard, lord of Limeuil. According to the *Chronique de Guyenne* many other barons, knights and burgesses of the town were also taken.[11] Galard, who was detained in the Bordelais for a considerable period of time, was later accused of having sworn obedience to Lancaster and undertaken to support Edward III against the French; but he was certainly put to ransom. He was obliged to sell property to the value of 600 *livres tournois* and received a grant of 10,000 gold *écus* in order to pay the sum demanded.[12] Henry Knighton tells us of the loot Lancaster is reputed to have collected at Bergerac, 52,000 marks of which he is said to have expended on his manor of the Savoy in London.[13]

Bergerac was a considerable town situated in a strong position, an important road centre then as it is today. It gave command of the Dordogne valley to whatever party held it and effectively blocked progress to either east or west to whichever side did not. The enforced expulsion of the French army under the command of the count of l'Isle, and the capture of Henri de Montigny, seneschal of Périgord and captain of Bergerac, Jean de Galard, lord of Limeuil, and some nine lords did the Valois cause no good. In taking Bergerac Lancaster acquired a strong town in a strategically important position and a base from which operations could be carried into the surrounding country. Whoever held Bergerac would soon be able to control the smaller neighbouring places. The town fell on 24 August and Lancaster remained there until 10 September.[14] During this period and for some time after he used it as a base for expeditions which resulted in the capture of a number of not inconsiderable places: La Mongie, Lalinde, Laforce, Lunas, Beaumont, Montagrier, Pellegrue and Montségur.[15]

Before leaving Bergerac he made an indenture with Bernard Ezi and Bérard d'Albret, appointing them captains of the town, in the first instance until 9 October.[16] They were to maintain a garrison of 298 cavalry and 1,200 infantry during the first fortnight and 250 cavalry and the same infantry during the second fortnight at customary wages. In case they did not wish to hold the custody of the town after 9 October, Lancaster was to be free to appoint another captain or captains in their place. Once every eight days they were to muster the troops for review by a deputy to be appointed by the earl. Upon the command and advice of this deputy they were to have carried out all works and repairs necessary in the town and they were to have the faubourgs and barriers reinforced, repaired or destroyed, whichever was most in the interests of the king and of the safety of the town. Lancaster undertook to provide artillery (bows, crossbows, siege engines), also by way of his deputy, on condition that it would be available to him there or to take elsewhere at his convenience and that it was to be returned to the deputy on 9 October. The two brothers could surrender the captaincy on that day provided that they made their intentions known to the earl in the meantime. If, however, Lancaster preferred that they should continue to hold office, they were to be paid wages in advance at the same rates as in the initial period for as long as they continued to do so. If the wages were not forthcoming they could surrender the captaincy without loss of favour, provided they notified him in advance. Their horses were to be appraised and compensation given for those lost. Together with the constable of Bordeaux, John Wawyn, they were authorized to invite the inhabitants of Bergerac to return into the town, to grant them pardons, make agreements with the previous garrison forces, bring them into the king's pay for service in Bergerac or elsewhere in the neighbourhood and, in general, to treat with all those who wished to enter the king's obedience. Lancaster undertook to confirm whatever the two captains did in conjunction with his deputy. These provisions indicate the importance which the earl attached to Bergerac, the strength of the allied assault and his distrust of the faubourgs by which his forces had entered. It was with a siege engine transported from Bordeaux to Bergerac and thence to Montségur, that he took the latter town.[17] Both Froissart and the *Chronique de Bazas* comment on the flight of some of the inhabitants and the latter chronicle makes it clear that some of these were part of the French defending force.

Lancaster left Bergerac for Périgueux, which he approached by an indirect route. Passing north-north-west to Mucidan, he took Maurens, Saint-Jean-d'Eyraud and Les Lèches on his way. He then changed his direction, swung to the north-east and advanced on Périgueux by way of Saint-Louis, Saint-Astier, Isle and Montagrier, thus securing control of the lower course of the river Isle between Mucidan and Périgueux. He did not attempt to take the city, which was too well fortified to be taken by assault. Turning east-south-east he passed up the valley of the Manoir (a tributary of the Isle) and took Bonneval and Auberoche. His movements between the submission of Auberoche and the famous and much more important battle which took place there some weeks later are uncertain. In one edition of his chronicles Froissart places him at Bordeaux, in another at Libourne, from where he is said to have received the news that took him to relieve the siege of Auberoche by the count of l'Isle. But it is possible that he passed northwards and, taking Saint-Privat and Saint-Raphael, continued his operations in the north of the *département* of the Dordogne, in the confines of Limousin and Quercy.[18]

On the morning of Tuesday 21 October 1345, just over a month after he had taken Bergerac, his forces defeated a French army commanded by the count of l'Isle which was encamped before Auberoche in Périgord.[19] It was the most disastrous setback to French arms in Aquitaine during the reign of Edward III until the capture of King John of France at the battle of Poitiers more than ten years later and it was certainly the greatest single achievement of Lancaster's entire military career. Together with the capture of Bergerac and subsequently of La Réole it was the essential key to the re-establishment of English control in much of the duchy, since it paralysed all effective French resistance in Aquitaine until the arrival of a large army commanded by the duke of Normandy in the spring of the following year. In the meantime the whole of the Agenais, much of Périgord and parts of Quercy were brought into English control.[20] The Florentine chronicler Giovanni Villani, who was extremely well-informed on affairs in Aquitaine during the course of Lancaster's campaigns, remarks that on the day of the battle a large French army commanded by the king's son John was no more than ten leagues away. John was in Aquitaine both as his father's lieutenant and in his own right as duke.[21] A week before Lancaster disembarked at Bordeaux he was at Carcassonne. Passing northwards through Limousin, Poitou and Touraine, preparing the defence of these provinces, he crossed Périgord shortly before Lancaster took Bergerac and by the end of August had reached Sablé-sur-Sarthe and Le Mans. On 2 September he was at Marmoutiers near Tours, where he ordered the seneschal of Carcassonne to be at Angoulême on 11 September with all the forces which could be raised in his *sénéchaussée*. He had returned south to Poitiers by 19 September and left there for Limoges around the time that Lancaster was moving north-eastwards towards Périgueux. On 4 and 5 October he authorized the inhabitants of Limoges to fortify the town and instructed the royal officers of the *sénéchaussée* of Carcassonne to send him all the money which they could get together for the prosecution of the war. The treasury of the army was at Pons during the greater part of August and September, but had moved to Limoges by 10 October. On 19 October, two days before the battle, Duke John was in Angoulême. Thus during September and October, at the very time that Lancaster, having taken Bergerac, was moving north-eastwards through Périgord, John was concentrating in Limousin and the Angoumois the greater part of the French troops then in Aquitaine and was moving into the theatre of Lancaster's operations.

Meanwhile on 8 August, the day before Lancaster had disembarked at Bordeaux, Philip VI appointed the duke of Bourbon his lieutenant in Languedoc and Gascony; the commission was issued at Sablé, doubtless after consultation with Duke John.[22] By 22 September Bourbon had made his way to Cahors, where he appointed deputies for the prosecution of the war. Between 27 September and 8 October he was at Gourdon, where he assembled his troops. He had, therefore, concentrated his forces on the frontiers of Quercy and Périgord, just to the south of Lancaster's army. Duke John had moved south from Le Mans to Marmoutiers, Poitiers, Limoges and Angoulême, where we know him to have been on 19 October; he was still there three days after the battle. Bourbon had moved north from Cahors to Gourdon. On 21 October the count of l'Isle, who had made his way to Auberoche from La Réole, was encamped before the castle with his troops. If the three armies were to join forces they would be able to surround Lancaster's expeditionary force and cut off his one line of retreat, to the south-west in the direction of Bergerac and Bordeaux. Had he acted quickly, Lancaster might have retreated by way of the places which he had taken along the valleys of the Dronne and the Isle, but at the expense of sacrificing Auberoche. The alternative was to attack the considerable forces of the count of l'Isle before Duke John arrived. There was no time to await help from Pembroke. The French army was still encamped before Auberoche when Lancaster's forces moved in upon it, and the engagement, disastrous to French control in Aquitaine, took place before the walls of that town.

There can be no doubt about the importance of Lancaster's victory. It momentarily paralysed any effective action on the part of the dukes of Normandy and Bourbon and it left La Réole without sufficient garrison forces. It gave the Anglo-Gascon forces a free hand to extend the area in English control, for there was no longer any effective opposition. Duke John retreated to the north. Although he remained in Angoulême until the end of the first week in November, shortly afterwards he made his way by Caunay and Lusignan in Poitou to Châtillon-sur-Indre, situated just below the Loire valley to the south-east of Tours. He had arrived there by 23 November and set up headquarters for the winter. It was not until spring of the following year that he once more came south to begin a long siege of Aiguillon. The duke of Bourbon retreated to Agen, where he set up winter quarters.

The earl made a considerable profit out of his victory. 'There were taken', Froissart comments, 'nine counts and *vicomtes* and so many barons and knights that there was not a man-at-arms among the English that did not have for his share two or three, from which they later had great profit.' Several lists were compiled of the prisoners; both Murimuth and Avesbury state that they included three counts, seven *vicomtes*, three barons and fourteen bannerets, although Murimuth, who gives the fullest list, names two counts (of l'Isle and of Valentinois), eight *vicomtes* and twenty-four other lords and knights. Lancaster's indenture with the king had provided that if the earl or his troops took prisoners, Lancaster could 'do what he wished with them' and he was to have 'all other advantages of war'. If Pembroke or his men took prisoners, Edward would 'give him satisfaction'. Froissart puts the ransom figure for the captives at 300,000 gold *écus* (£56,562 10s 0d)—a sum remarkably close to Villani's estimate of £50,000. Some of the prisoners were temporarily liberated upon their promise to surrender themselves at Bordeaux or Bergerac by a certain day, but the greater part were taken to Bordeaux, where the bargaining over individual ransoms took place. Many of them were still captives in the following summer and the payment of some ransoms dragged on throughout 1348.[23]

In spite of his overwhelming victory Lancaster did not, as Froissart asserts, return to Bordeaux for the winter, but made the most of the advantage which he had clearly acquired. By 2 November, less than a fortnight after his victory at Auberoche, he had taken the town of La Réole, some sixty-five miles to the south-west, thereby acquiring the keys to the Garonne valley, as the capture of Bergerac had given him those of the Dordogne. It was here that he set up winter quarters.[24]

The succeeding months were far from inactive. During this period the Agenais succumbed to English control: Aiguillon, Castelsagrat, Monclar, Villeréal, Bajamont, Beauville, Montagnac, Réalville, Mirabel, Montpézat and Miramont were among the places brought into allegiance to the king. Many of these places were taken by separately-operating armies. The submission of Aiguillon some time before 10 December is almost certainly to be attributed to Ralph Stafford, for at the time Lancaster was at La Réole. Just as Bergerac had acted as a base from which the upper Dordogne valley had been secured and a good many strongholds in Périgord taken, La Réole and Aiguillon were the two centres from which the Garonne valley which separated them was secured, the lower reaches of the Lot controlled and numerous important fortresses and towns in the Agenais and Quercy were acquired. By the spring of 1346 the Agenais was overwhelmingly in English control.[25]

The capture of Bergerac and the victory of Auberoche, which were achieved in a remarkably short space of time, had an immediate impact among the Gascon lords and towns. The two English successes compelled men whose fortunes depended upon choosing rightly between an English and a French suzerain to come to a decision. La Réole was in English control so soon after the battle of Auberoche that there can be no question, therefore, of the long siege related by Froissart. The authors of the *Chronique normande* and the *Grandes Chroniques* are much more accurate in recording that the town was taken with the consent of the inhabitants; there is ample documentary evidence with which to substantiate this voluntary submission.[26] Lancaster was quick to reward the burgesses and inhabitants. He granted them complete exemption from the custom which they had hitherto been required to pay at Bordeaux for all their wines made from vines grown within the honor and district of the town, as well as the right to sell them there at any time of the year. He also granted them the right to levy an *impôt* of 1s 8d *bordelais* on every barrel of wine and other goods transported along the Garonne before the town; half of the proceeds were to be used for the repair of the castle. Anxious to avoid any resentment which the entry of his troops might have caused, he granted them 2,000 gold florins for wine, corn and other provisions which they had commandeered. Upon the request of the jurats and community he ratified all the customs, privileges and liberties of the town. When the castle surrendered to him he entrusted it to the lord of Pommiers—an appointment which greatly pleased the jurats and community. It was upon Lancaster's advice that on 3 June 1347 Edward agreed to a series of petitions from the town. He confirmed a charter of King John to the burgesses, granted that they might sell their wines at Bordeaux as freely as their ancestors had done, undertook never to alienate the town from the English Crown and promised the municipal cornmills to the jurats and community after the death of Raymond Seguin, to whom Lancaster gave them to fulfil Edward's pledge that he should have them as soon as La Réole came into English control. All of these grants were made to the burgesses and inhabitants for having freely and of their own accord returned into the king's obedience.[27]

In their petitions to the king the jurats and community stated the names of five members of the family of Pins who had 'more than anyone else treated and brought to a conclusion that the said town came into your obedience'. Lancaster rewarded them and other burgesses with annuities, pensions and offices. Nearly all of these grants were made either in recognition of past services, in particular in connection with the submission of La Réole, or as incentives for some impending service; the rewards they offered were invariably located in territories at the time in French control—places in the Agenais which were for the most part secured in the winter and spring following the surrender of La Réole.[28]

Military success for the Anglo-Gascons also forced the lords to think of their fortunes. It was vital to families like the Durforts, one of the oldest and most powerful in the Agenais, to know which way the wind was blowing. Gaillard de Durfort, by rights lord of Duras in the Agenais and of Blanquefort near Bordeaux, possessed two of the strongest fortified castles in Gascony, but seemed condemned to lose one or the other. The side to which he rallied depended upon what seemed least disadvantageous to him in a choice between his distant lordships, or upon the conditions which might allow him to hold both.[29] In November 1345, when Lancaster had accomplished the victory of Auberoche and the capture of La Réole, he came over to the English side. The earl made it worth his while. He restored possession of the castle and castellany of Blanquefort to him and granted him a life annuity of 2,000 gold *écus*, to be had from rents in the duchy—a grant which encouraged him to capture the *bastides* of Miramont and Castelsagrat in the Agenais and Molières and Beaumont in the Sarladais, in order to secure his rent there. When he made his submission to Lancaster, 'many towns, places, castles and nobles came and returned into our (i.e. the king's) obedience', for he is said to have brought 'towns, places, several castles and many nobles into the obedience of our said lord the king'.[30] Gaillard de Durfort's submission, which was accompanied by that of other branches of his family,[31] goes a long way to explain how the Agenais, much of Périgord and parts of Quercy were brought back into English control in the winter of 1345–6. Lancaster had wisely rewarded him and in the following summer, when the earl conducted a raid north into Poitou, he placed him in command of that part of his forces which was left to operate in the Agenais.[32]

'When the inhabitants of Aiguillon saw the English coming,' the author of the *Chronique normande* commented, 'during the night they killed and imprisoned the soldiers who were there for the king of France and surrendered to the English.'[33] Situated in a strong position at the confluence of the rivers Garonne and Lot, the town was well fortified and commanded the Gascon plain. It was composed of two bourgs: Guillaume III and Gualard de Lunas, sons and heirs of Astorg II de Lunas, were co-lords of Lunas d'Aiguillon together with Arnaud IV de Montpézat and Rainfroid II, lord of Montpézat; Amanieu III du Fossat, lord of Madaillan, and Gautier VI du Fossat were lords of Fossat d'Aiguillon.[34] The town appears to have been surrendered by all or some of these lords. The seneschal Ralph Stafford probably received the submission of the town early in December, when he granted Guillaume de Lunas and Arnaud Garsie du Fossat the right to levy a toll each on every barrel of wine transported down the rivers

Lot and Garonne before Aiguillon. Arnaud Garsie proved a faithful adherent. Rainfroid, lord of Montpézat, was particularly well rewarded by Lancaster. He granted him the places of Saint-Sardos and Saint-Amans near Agen together with their appurtenances, a life annuity of £60 to be had from the properties of the king's enemies or in lands already acquired or which would in future be acquired by him (and which in the meantime was to be recovered from the constable of Bordeaux or the treasurer of Agenais), a single sum of £400 to be had from the properties of the king's enemies, full jurisdiction at Pech Bardar and in the parishes of Sainte-Foy and Lacépède (also near Agen) in the manner in which his ancestors had exercised it, similar jurisdiction in the parishes of Saint-Michel and Rides, restitution of the possessions which his ancestors had held in the place of the lands of the abbey of Pérignac and exemption (for himself, his household and his immediate subjects) from the summons and cognizance of the *bailli* and other officials of the *sénéchaussée* of Agen and, in matters touching them, from the jurisdiction of the court of the seneschal and *bailli* of the Agenais.[35]

Those rewarded could be given responsibilities. By the late spring and early summer of 1348 Gautier du Fossat was captain of the bourg of Fossat d'Aiguillon, and Guillaume de Lunas of that of Lunas d'Aiguillon.[36] Amanieu du Fossat appears to have lost by what his co-lords gained. He entered French obedience, did homage and fealty to Philip VI and secured letters of remission, the restitution of certain castles which had been confiscated from him for serving the Anglo-Gascons and a new grant. It was not until December 1349, when Lancaster was once again sent to Aquitaine with an expeditionary force, that he was persuaded to enter English obedience by a number of very advantageous grants.[37]

The submission of Bazas admirably illustrates the means by which much of Aquitaine was brought back into English allegiance. In a letter written at La Réole on 13 November 1345 Lancaster commanded the inhabitants of the town to return into English obedience—a request rejected by the French captain, Thibaut de Barbazan, on the following day.[38] Shortly afterwards Bernard Ezi and John Wawayn, constable of Bordeaux, opened negotiations with the jurats, consuls and community, promising them that if they would return into obedience to the king, Edward would grant them complete exemption from the custom due on their wines at Bordeaux for all wines made from vines grown within a league of Bazas.[39] On 17 November Lancaster granted the *prévôté* of the town to Arnaud Micol de Bazas, a citizen of Bordeaux, as soon as it was brought back into English control.[40] This was straightforward bribery.

The city surrendered on 3 January 1347.[41] There can be little doubt that it was as a result of the machinations of at least some of the inhabitants. Jean de la Tour, a burgess of the town, 'treated and procured that the said city, previously in the hands of the French, returned into the obedience of our said lord the king'. By way of reward he was granted all the goods and other possessions in the town confiscated from Gaillard de Cabositz, the lands of another French collaborator, called Rossignol de Cozin, a life annuity of 100 *livres tournois* and compensation for other losses which he had sustained because of his fidelity. Two other citizens, Bernard and Geraud Cestor, were similarly rewarded for 'coming freely into the obedience of our lord the king and treating and procuring that the city of Bazas, together with its inhabitants, came into the said obedience'.[42]

Allegiance was made attractive to the community as a whole. Upon the request of the jurats and consuls the city was never to be alienated from the English Crown, the seneschal of Aquitaine and the constable of Bordeaux were to inspect all its charters of privileges, liberties and customs and confirm them, the inhabitants were to be allowed to sell wines made from vines grown within a league of the city without paying the wine custom at Bordeaux, and they were to be allowed to levy certain *impôts* to subsidize the defence of the city.[43]

There were numerous administrative matters which Lancaster was expected to supervise whilst he wintered in La Réole. The extension of English control in the duchy created many new offices to which appointments needed to be made: sub-seneschals, baillis, councillors, proctors, notaries, keepers of the royal seals, masters of the mint, collectors and receivers. These offices were remunerative enough to be distributed as rewards to the deserving, and they were frequently supplemented by annuities and other grants.[44]

It is evident that Lancaster could not be expected to have a detailed knowledge of the often essentially local matters with which he had to deal; in making these grants and appointments to offices he was assisted by the king's council in the duchy. This was composed of the most important Gascon barons in English obedience and a number of professional councillors, it was normally presided over by the seneschal and it was held wherever he convened it. When a lieutenant took up office in the duchy it was customary for the council to continue its functions 'as an advisory body to the lieutenant himself' and it is clear from the notes of warranty on the original copies of the earl's letters that the grants and appointments which he made in Aquitaine were carefully scrutinized by it; some were only made after close consultation with it and clearly required its assent. The council thus exercised a measure of control over the earl, but at the same time provided him with invaluable information and assistance without which he would have been unable to carry out his administrative responsibilities.[45] But Lancaster also kept in close contact with the king,[46] and during the spring of 1346 reinforcements, money, victuals and other supplies were sent out to him from England.[47]

## The second campaign

In late February or early March the duke of Normandy left his winter quarters at Châtillon-sur-Indre and, passing south through Cahors, appeared on the Garonne with a large army during the course of the latter month. Between 10 and 15 April he pitched his tents before Aiguillon.[48] Lancaster, who entrusted the defence of the town to Pembroke and Mauny,[49] was probably then in Bordeaux; but by 1 May he had returned to La Réole where he remained during the greater part of the siege, directing the defence, running men, reinforcements and supplies to the garrison and thus making it necessary for the duke of Normandy, who conducted his siege from the right bank of the Garonne on the south side of the town during April and May, to move his camp to the north of the town on the side of La Réole between Aiguillon and Tonneins in mid-June.[50]

Lancaster's forces and the successes which they had achieved were threatened by the strength of the French forces. The initial plan for three more or less simultaneous landings in France in the previous year, which would have prevented the French from concentrating their forces to meet any single one of them without leaving the other two a free hand, had foundered in Flanders with the murder of James van Artevelde. Edward had been obliged to return to England.[51] But now that a large French army had been drawn into the south of France his intervention could be opportune and his assistance was imperative, perhaps obligatory. In the indenture which Lancaster had made with him it was expressly stated that 'the king has agreed that if it shall happen that the said earl is besieged or beset by so great a force that he cannot help himself unless he be rescued by the king's power, then the king is bound to rescue him in one way or another, provided that he can be rescued easily'. Similar provision had been made for Northampton. On 12 July Edward landed at Saint-Vaast-La-Hougue in the Cotentin with an army generally believed to have been assembled to relieve Aiguillon and, under the guidance of a Norman renegade called Godfrey d'Harcourt, he began the campaign which culminated in the battle of Crécy and the capture of Calais. He did more. When the duke of Normandy heard of his landing, on 20 August he raised the siege and hurried north to help his father, once again leaving the Anglo-Gascons with a free hand in Aquitaine. Edward had rescued Lancaster in the north of France. The duke of Normandy was too late. On 26 August his father's army suffered a disastrous defeat at Crécy and shortly afterwards Lancaster conducted a raid north into Poitou.

The earl's dispatch of his second campaign, which is thoroughly substantiated by documentary evidence,[52] enables us to trace his movements from the eve of Normandy's departure from Aiguillon. On 12 August he left La Réole for Bergerac, where he assembled an army and held a council of war. Overtures from Normandy for a truce were firmly rejected since Lancaster had foreknowledge of Edward's landing. On 20 August John raised the siege, made his way down the Garonne valley to Agen and Moissac, then left for the north of France. Lancaster immediately moved into the Agenais, received the submission of Villeréal and other towns and castles in the district, garrisoned them and then made his way to Tonneins and Aiguillon, where he repeated the process. He then returned to La Réole, where he stayed for eight days and held another council of war. There were still places in the Agenais and the Bazadais that were not securely in English control, notably Bazas, Marmande, Port-Sainte-Marie and a number of places along the Lot and Garonne valleys below Aiguillon in the direction of Agen. To secure these places he divided his forces into three contingents, two of which he wisely entrusted to local lords: Bernard Ezi and Bérard d'Albret, Alexander de Caumont and other Gascon lords were given command of a contingent which was to operate in the Bazadais, while Gaillard de Durfort and other lords of Agenais were given command of another that was to operate around La Réole.

Lancaster moved into Saintonge with a comparatively small force of 1,000 men-at-arms. The raid began on 12 September with his departure from La Réole. The town of Sauveterre was surrendered to him on the same day and his troops spent the night there. The following morning, having taken the homage of the inhabitants, he began an eight-day march, uninterrupted by any attempt to take town or castle, until he arrived at Châteauneuf-sur-Charente on the 20th. The river, which lies to the north of the town, was too deep to ford and it was necessary to repair the bridge, which had been destroyed by the French, before his troops were able to continue on the following day. News of the imprisonment of Sir Walter Mauny (who had previously proceeded northwards with a safe conduct from the duke of Normandy to join Edward in northern France) in Saint-Jean-d'Angély, and of his difficult escape, determined Lancaster to take the town by force, release the remaining prisoners, oblige the inhabitants to do homage and punish the opposition. He stayed there eight days in all. On the 30th he left for Poitiers, took Lusignan by assault on 3 October, received the surrender of the castle and garrisoned it. On 4 October, after the inhabitants had refused to surrender, he took Poitiers by force.

The city was the northernmost point reached on the raid. He stayed there for eight days, but appears to have made no attempt to hold it. On the 12th or 13th he began his return south by way of Montreuil-Bonnin, Saint-Maixent and Niort.[53] By the 19th he was once more in Saint-Jean-d'Angély, where the dispatch was written. Several towns and castles in Saintonge were surrendered to him; they included Rochefort, Soubise, Taillebourg and Tonnay-Charente. He was then proposing to return to Bordeaux, but expected to encounter enemy resistance. He was still there on the 29th, but had reached Plassac (situated to the north of the Gironde estuary, between Blaye and Bourg) by the 30th. The following day he was in Bordeaux. The raid had been accomplished in seven weeks.

Both the nature and the consequences of the second campaign were fundamentally different, but no less significant, than those of the first. A raid deep into hostile territory called for more stringent military methods. Burning and bloodshed replaced negotiations and reward. In October 1346 Clement VI wrote to the earl exhorting him to restrain his men from destroying and robbing churches and ecclesiastics.[54] Some of the prisoners taken at Saint-Jean-d'Angély were put to ransom, the Benedictine monastery there was systematically looted by the troops and the incumbents forcibly expelled and ransomed.[55] The castle of Montreuil-Bonnin and the town of Saint-Maixent were burned.[56] The speed of Lancaster's successes was in part due to lack of preparations by the French. The towns and castles of Poitou were insufficiently garrisoned and in a bad state of defence and the inhabitants of many of them preferred to surrender than suffer plunder.[57] At Poitiers the earl's army is said to have 'carried away gold, silver and countless precious things' and 'destroyed and carried off many things, including religious ornaments'.[58] The clergy had to be compensated for 'all the possessions—books, chalices, vestments, silver vases, relics and other ornaments—taken from the churches'.[59]

According to Froissart the soldiers on their departure were 'so laden' with the riches they found there 'that they made no account of cloths unless they were of gold or silver or trimmed with furs'. When they returned to Bordeaux the troops were 'altogether rich and burdened with good things'.[60]

At other places captured or surrendered to him during the raid Lancaster extracted retribution and distributed rewards. At Saint-Jean-d'Angély he imposed the occupation costs of 200 men-at-arms and 600 infantry upon the inhabitants during wartime and increased their rents by 4,000 écus over and above the sum they had previously paid to the French monarchy.[61] Those who had supported the French were disinherited and only the most ardent loyalists were rewarded. As at Poitiers the property held in the town by the Lombards was confiscated and several French merchants were imprisoned and forced to swear fealty to the king of England.[62] Before he left, he appointed Gaillard, lord of Guassac, captain and marshal of the town and empowered him to continue the redistribution of properties.[63]

The castle of Rochefort, which guarded the entry to the river Charente, he granted to Sir Frank de Hale, a soldier of some reputation and possibly one of his retainers.[64] Soubise and Taillebourg surrendered to him. By way of reward the inhabitants of Soubise received certain new liberties from him and to support the costs of fortifying the town he granted them the right to levy an increased pedage on wine and other merchandise transported down the river Charente by the king's enemies.[65] The castle and castellany he granted to Pierre Beguer de la Russelle of Bordeaux, who was to have an annuity of 500 gold écus from the property of the king's enemies within the marches of the castellany for its defence.[66] At Tonnay-Charente he granted the inhabitants certain liberties and undertook that Edward would never separate the town, nor anything within its jurisdiction from the Crown, except should it be to the heir presumptive.[67] He committed the custody of both town and castle to a loyal Gascon baron, Élie de Saint-Symphorien, lord of Landiras. In return for undertaking the inhabitants' custody for life Lancaster granted him 500 *livres petits tournois* in the property of the king's enemies in the town and castellany—a grant which the king increased to all the revenues arising from the properties of his enemies.[68]

Other towns which may have been taken by Lancaster at the same time included Cannac, which was in English obedience by 4 January 1347, Tonnay-Bouton, in English obedience by September 1348, and the priory of the monastery of Saint-Agnant, situated to the south of

Tonnay-Charente on the road to Saint-Jean-d'Angle, which was granted by him, together with all its revenues and profits, to Guillaume de Montségur.[69] Lusignan he garrisoned with 100 men-at-arms and a body of infantry, appointed Bertrand de Montferrand captain and Arnaud de Miramont as castellan with right to all the revenues and profits of the castellany.[70]

There can be no doubt of the importance of the acquisition of these towns and castles. Although Poitiers was once more in French control by July 1347 and Saint-Maixent before the end of the year, Lusignan was a base from which the enemy were harried until 1351.[71] Their control allowed the Anglo-Gascons to conduct raids into Saintonge and Poitou and afforded a line of well-garrisoned and well-supplied advance bases to assist English and Gascon troops operating in what was otherwise hostile territory. The river Charente subsequently became a lifeline along which victuals, troops and money were constantly poured into Rochefort, Tonnay-Charente and Taillebourg and, from the confluence of the Charente and the Bouton, along the latter river to Tonnay-Bouton and Saint-Jean-d'Angély, and thence over land to Lusignan.

Lancaster was once more in Bordeaux on 31 October and he appears to have remained there throughout November.[72] There were friends to be rewarded, administrative affairs to be seen to. During the course of December he left the city for England, where he arrived with his retinue on 1 January. Pembroke had also returned with his on 20 December and Mauny on 3 January.[73] On 1 February, in order that he might aid the king, who was besieging Calais, he was officially released from the office of captain and lieutenant in Aquitaine.[74] If there had been any plan for him to join Edward direct from the duchy, it had been abandoned; but almost as soon as he arrived back in England preparations were started for his crossing to Calais.[75] Nevertheless, it was not until the middle of May that Edward (who had learned that Philip was preparing to relieve Calais and who was finding it necessary to concentrate almost the whole of England's military might before the town) summoned him to bring reinforcements over from England. On 19 May the admiral to the west was instructed to find shipping in Sandwich and Dover for him and his 'huge force' and by 1 June the earl had joined Edward in the siege.[76]

Lancaster stayed with the besieging force at Calais until the fall of the town on 4 August. When Philip made his last attempt to relieve it on 27 July, the only approach to the English positions was by a bridge over the river Hem, to the south-west of the town near to Fort

Nieulay and known as the Nieulay Bridge. Lancaster was put in command of the troops holding this position;[77] but no serious action developed. On the same day Cardinals Annibal Ceccano and Étienne Aubert approached the earl and a number of other army leaders about peace negotiations, which were agreed to.[78] A conference was arranged in two tents erected between the opposing forces on Lancaster's orders and the earl was clearly at the head of the English delegation which spent a fruitless four days parleying there. No agreement was reached, since the French delegates insisted that the siege should be terminated and would offer no more in compensation for the abandonment of Edward's claims to the French throne than the duchy of Guyenne (as Edward I had held it) and the county of Ponthieu, which the English delegates considered too little. Philip then offered battle, to which Edward agreed; but before dawn on 2 August—the day before the battle was to take place—Philip's army retreated, pursued by Lancaster's forces, who succeeded in cutting off its rear.[79]

After the capitulation of the town, Lancaster was a member of the English delegation which negotiated the truce of 28 September and he was appointed one of the judges of infringements of its terms.[80] Knighton tells us of the great state which the earl maintained in Calais and of considerable daily expenses which could only have been met out of the profits of his campaigns in the south.[81] He was at the height of his fame. No one but the king had won such military glory, for the Black Prince had still to prove himself. His work in Aquitaine was undoubtedly his most brilliant achievement as military commander and administrator. It won the king's gratitude, established his reputation and added greatly to his wealth.

By letters dated by Calais on 1 June, 'in gratitude for his victorious deeds in Aquitaine' Edward granted him the castle, town and castellany of Bergerac.[82] He thus became lord of Bergerac and no time was wasted on seeing to its defence. On 7 June the chancellor was instructed to order the constable of Bordeaux to pay the wages of John Diens, then captain of the town, and three days later he was instructed to provide a ship for William de Arenton, one of the earl's valets, to sail to Gascony with victuals and other things necessary for the defence of Bergerac.[83] The earl was not, however, to be put to any expense in its defence. Since the town was a strategically vital outpost of English influence in Aquitaine, on 17 June provision was made for its garrison with 100 men-at-arms and 200 foot sergeants who were to be paid by the constable of Bordeaux.[84] In England his services were rewarded with some of the remaining lands forfeited by Earl Thomas. Since the annuity of 1,000 marks granted to him at the time of his creation as earl of Derby was surrendered on the death of his father (23 September 1345), the king 'having regard for the good service and great honour which our said cousin has done us in Gascony and elsewhere by the said name of earl of Derby and greatly wishing that the aforesaid name and title should not be lost but should be maintained to perpetual memory', upon Lancaster's request, restored him and his heirs in the castle and honor of Pontefract.[85] These had been granted to the queen in 1330 and in order to effect their transfer to the earl, Edward instructed the chancellor to inquire where he could assign Philippa lands and rents of the same value. The letters were dated before Calais on 10 July, although the formal resumption and release took place in November 1348.[86] It was for the same reasons that he granted Lancaster the castle of Horston in Derbyshire and £40 yearly from the farm of the county,[87] and it may also have been whilst he was with the king before Calais that he was promised Clitheroe (given to Queen Isabella in 1327), which was granted to him in November 1348.[88] On 3 and 8 October, after the town had capitulated, he secured grants of lands, vineyards and other goods of those prisoners in Saint-Jean-d'Angély who had not paid their ransoms as well as the property (houses, inns, wine-presses, young vines, lands, meadows, pastures, woods and rents) of Bernard Barraut, a burgess of the town who had refused to enter English obedience.[89] He also acquired a considerable number of houses in Calais itself, and this grant was confirmed in 1360.[90]

There can be no doubt about the importance of Lancaster's work in Aquitaine; it had brought about a considerable extension in the frontiers of the duchy and resulted in significant changes in military and financial organization there. The extension of the area under English control called for radical changes in the structure of the Gascon army. The effort required to defend a large number of towns and castles scattered over extensive territory was much greater than that required to defend a relatively small number of places situated within narrow territorial limits. Prior to the arrival of his expeditionary forces the majority of the troops were employed in a few strategically vital garrisons and they were made up almost entirely of infantry. After Lancaster's campaigns it was not possible to raise either the men or the money to do this in the much greater area in English control. Already in the years 1337–43 it had proved impossible to finance them over an extended period. What was now needed was an effective, manoeuvrable, fighting force which could be called into service during periods of military threat, either to engage the enemy in the field or to strengthen the defence of any place, town or castle. This was done by replacing the infantry by cavalry, by employing English archers and organizing the troops into compact retinues under the command of the Gascon lords.[91]

These changes had already taken place by the close of 1347 and by 1350, when the accounts of the constable of Bordeaux speak of a *novus exercitus* operating in the duchy, the reforms were complete. The troops were organized into smaller and more compact retinues on the English model and the majority of them were retained by Gascon lords, many of whom had entered English service during the earl's lieutenancy. From then until the Black Prince's expedition of 1355–7 five different corps were in service in the duchy, largely Gascon, but including a small percentage of English troops. The men-at-arms formed the greater part of the cavalry, but they were accompanied by mounted sergeants and mounted archers. The infantry was made up of foot sergeants and foot archers, but the cavalry were now in the majority.[92] The foot sergeant had been replaced by the mounted sergeant and the number of sergeants now maintained, along with the size of retinues, had been considerably reduced. The troops (including the garrison forces) were no longer maintained on a more or less permanent basis, but were enlisted for relatively short periods of time to accomplish specific tasks. Many of them were in the king's pay for no more than a few months, some for no more than a few weeks at a time; but since they had therefore to be employed more effectively, the part played by the seneschal and the king's council in directing military operations greatly increased.[93] The forces were frequently divided into separate companies and were sent to the main trouble spots, or to promote an offensive. Each company was placed under the command of a captain of proved ability who received a commission and instructions from the seneschal and council.

In this way an efficient and more economic use was made of the military resources of the duchy. Nevertheless, the financial position, far from improving, steadily deteriorated and was aggravated by the practice—of which Lancaster had made such extensive use—of encouraging loyalists and winning new adherents to the English cause by grants of lands, castles, annuities, pensions and other sources of revenue. Thus, although the earl's campaigns resulted in an extension of English control in Gascony, no new revenues were made available to the Bordeaux treasury and existing returns decreased. Not only had he alienated lands and revenues to supporters as rewards for their services, but he had also assigned ducal revenues to the upkeep and repair of the castles and fortresses which he granted to them. The account of the constable of Bordeaux for 1348 shows that there were no returns from the *bailliages*, *prévôtés* and castellanies then in English control because all the revenues which should have been collected from them had been assigned by Lancaster and the king to the construction and repair of fortresses, or else they had been granted to loyalists in return for their support. In August 1349, when the earl was given another commission as lieutenant in Aquitaine and Languedoc, he was once again empowered to inquire into excessive grants of land which had been made in the king's name in the duchy and to resume all those which had been secured by fraud so that on his advice Edward and the council could redistribute them. But although some attempt was then made to cut them down, no solution was found. In the thirteen years from September 1348 to September 1361 new assignments on the Bordeaux treasury still averaged £1,992 annually, to which must be added the alienation of revenues elsewhere in the duchy which were not recorded in the constable's accounts—save as an absence of revenues—and these were very considerable. In 1359 the constable was excused returns for all the *bailliages* and *prévôtés* in the duchy because they had been alienated by the king, his lieutenants (Lancaster, Stafford and the Black Prince) and other royal officers in the duchy. The problem was not solved until there was a return to more peaceful conditions after the treaty of Brétigny, when the duchy was elevated into a principality for the Black Prince and the government was no longer obliged to honour its concessions to the Gascons.

After Lancaster's campaigns it was therefore no longer possible to pretend that the war in Gascony could be financed out of the ducal revenues—they had already proved totally inadequate. The dispatch of the expeditionary forces under his command was in itself an admission of that impossibility and of the need to finance the Gascon forces from England if the war was to be prosecuted effectively in the duchy. This position was recognized after 1348 and thereafter the income of the Bordeaux treasury was greatly augmented by subsidies from the English Exchequer. In the period from September 1348 to September 1361 they amounted to more than half of the revenues received by the constable[94] and they were almost entirely spent on the wages of the troops.[95] During these thirteen years the English government had to subsidize the war in Gascony to the extent of £85,470 out of total revenues of £161,503. The inheritance which Edward III had been called upon to defend was henceforth a financial liability to the English Crown.

# V  Louis de Male and the two treaties of Dunkirk (1348)

There can be little doubt that the campaigns of 1345–7 had brought Edward substantial territorial gains. Quite apart from his victory at Crécy, which made him a hero, Lancaster's campaigns in Aquitaine had completely restored the English position and prestige there, the earl of Northampton and Sir Thomas Dagworth had strengthened and extended his hold on Brittany and in the town of Calais he had acquired a much needed port of disembarkation and a base for operations in north-eastern France. Much of this was due to the change in military strategy, but it had been accompanied by the loss of nearly all his allies in the Low Countries.

This decline in Edward's diplomatic prestige had set in with his military and financial failure as early as 1340, and by the time of the fall of Calais little remained of the structure of alliances which he had laboriously erected at so great a cost.[1] The French had disengaged the Emperor Lewis IV, thereby depriving Edward of the imperial vicariate —his sole source of authority over the princes. Hainault, Holland and Zeeland had withdrawn their support, John of Hainault had deserted him and was ready to join Philip VI, and the duke of Brabant had concluded marriage alliances with the duke of Guelders and the count of Flanders and had allied himself with Philip. Only the margrave of Juliers and the Flemings remained faithful to him; but the margrave could effect nothing in his isolation and the Flemings might sooner or later be forced to modify their policy because of their dissensions and because of the policy of the duke of Brabant. It was up to Edward to see that they did not. To this end Lancaster was appointed the king's lieutenant in Flanders and the Calais region and empowered to conduct truce negotiations with the French which were to act as a cover for more important discussions intended to secure the alliance of the count of Flanders for a further military venture into France.

Since 1340 Edward's foothold in Flanders—recognition of him as king of France—had been determined by two factors: his alliance with the burghers of the county led by James van Artevelde, and the unswerving allegiance which Count Louis de Nevers had given to Philip of Valois ever since the king had assisted the count to defeat his rebellious subjects at the battle of Cassel in 1328. Although Artevelde had been assassinated in the summer of 1345 and the hegemony of the great Flemish cities had passed to a wealthy urban faction—the weavers—the alliance with England nevertheless still held good. But a year later Louis de Nevers was killed fighting for the Valois cause at Crécy.[2]

The way was thus cleared for a new settlement of the complex relationship between England and Flanders and in 1347 it appeared as if Edward would profit greatly by the deaths of both his friend and his enemy. English influence in Flanders was no longer bound up with the dominant personality of Artevelde and Edward still had the enthusiastic support of the strongest faction in Ghent, Bruges and Ypres. Louis de Nevers' son and successor Louis de Male was young. All parties in Flanders were eager for the return of their count and were apparently prepared for a reconciliation which would find expression in united support of the English cause. With Louis de Nevers and Artevelde removed from the scene it appeared at the time as if Edward would obtain both the alliance of the Flemish burghers and the friendship of their count. Under pressure from his subjects, in March 1347 young Louis de Male was constrained to promise marriage with Edward's daughter Isabella. But almost immediately afterwards he fled to France, where he repudiated the whole project and by July he was married to the duke of Brabant's daughter Margaret, whose family were now firmly allied to Valois France.

Edward was once more back where he had started; but in the following summer the situation became really critical and his alliances with the Flemish towns were also threatened. Revolts broke out against the domination of the weavers in the Flemish cities and against the hegemony of Ghent.[3] There was a rising in Bruges in favour of Louis de Male. Oudenarde, Grammont and Termonde opened their gates and were garrisoned by his forces. In Bruges and Ypres the weavers were massacred in great numbers. Only Ghent, which had opened its gates to refugees from the other towns, still held out. Unless Edward acted quickly he would lose what support he still had there. Upon urgent appeals from the Flemings for assistance,[4] he appointed Lancaster lieutenant in the county on 25 September and the earl immediately left Westminster for Calais.[5]

Less than a year had elapsed since Henry had returned to England.[6] He had spent much of it jousting, at Eltham, Lichfield, Lincoln, Windsor and Canterbury; but some of his time had also been taken up on his estates and with affairs of state.[7] Although the truce concluded at Calais on 28 September 1347 was not due to expire until 8 July 1348, it had been agreed that before that date embassies for either monarch would be sent to the papal curia to treat of a peace.[8] At the end of November Edward accordingly sent his envoys to Avignon to make the necessary arrangements with the pope and a report was expected to arrive from them in time for parliament which assembled in January when the whole matter was to have been discussed. In the event no news was forthcoming before its conclusion and another parliament was therefore convoked for the end of March and the dispatch of an embassy to treat for peace was suspended.[9]

Meanwhile the pope, who was determined to secure at least an extension of the truce, wrote to Edward requesting him to empower John de Carlton, who was then at the curia, to renew it. A procuration for an extension of one year was issued to Carlton and others on 15 May, and on 30 May Clement requested Philip to send envoys with similar powers. A meeting was held between the two embassies before the pope and cardinals and the truce of Calais was extended for one year as it stood. The arrangement was to be confirmed by more solemn envoys who were expected to arrive at Avignon to treat of a final peace around Michaelmas. On 28 July Edward requested letters of safe-conduct for the bishop of Norwich, Lancaster, Arundel and Bartholomew de Burghersh, who were to be given a procuration for his part. But the embassy was never sent owing to the turn of events in Flanders.[10]

Among its many clauses the truce of Calais had stipulated that Count Louis de Male was not to return to Flanders or make war on the Flemings and that neither Philip nor Edward was to seek alliances or foment trouble in the county. But with the outbreak of the revolts in the summer, Louis returned to Flanders with Philip's backing and French troops proceeded to conduct military operations there.[11] There could not have been a more flagrant violation of the truce and it had been clear from its inception that the extension would be short-lived. Edward had only given instructions for its proclamation on the proviso that Philip did likewise and that he did not infringe its terms.[12] There were now only two courses open to him—to recommence the war or to insist upon the truce or some new arrangement. Since it was impossible to assemble an expeditionary force in time to save the situation, negotiation was the only practicable alternative, presuming that Philip and Louis were willing to talk.

To this end Lancaster was empowered to conduct negotiations with Raoul de Brienne, count of Eu and Guines, who had been detained in England since his capture at Caen in 1346. Together they drew up a short truce which was published in London on 5 September. On the English side this was entirely Lancaster's work and the final terms set out bore his seal. The main purpose of the arrangement was to secure negotiations with Philip and Louis. A truce to last for six weeks was concluded. During this period embassies for either monarch were to be appointed to conclude a permanent peace. The queens of France and England were to go to Boulogne and Calais respectively for 30 September, ready to treat on the frontier. They were to be accompanied by envoys of their choice and certain others specified in the terms of the agreement.[13]

The French accepted the proposal and in accordance with the articles two embassies were drawn up to treat. As had been envisaged the English embassy included the bishop of Norwich, Lancaster, the earl of Suffolk, Sir Walter Mauny and John de Carlton. But on the French side Philip's choice fell on none of those who, like Gautier de Brienne, duke of Athens, Louis de Savoie, lord of Vaud, and Galois de la Baume, were either relatives or close friends of Raoul de Brienne. Instead, it was made up of some of Philip's most ardent councillors: the bishop of Laon, the lord of Offémont, Geoffrey de Charny and Robert de Houdetot.[14]

Had Edward hoped to secure a pliant embassy? Certainly Brienne's actions were already suspect. He held the counties of Eu and Guines in the Pas-de-Calais, which, together with his lands in Poitou and Saintonge and the fief of Belleville-Clisson (which was occupied by the English) formed a string of territories stretching down the Atlantic seaboard between Brittany and Gascony. Until the commencement of the war he also held considerable fiefs in England and Ireland and, by marriage to the daughter of Louis de Savoie, he held lands in Savoy for which he was not obliged to do homage to Philip VI. He had much to gain from an independent arrangement with Edward. Already in August 1347—a month before the truce of Calais—he had negotiated a private truce for his possessions and, in view of the fact that he was executed for treason on his return to France in 1350, it is not impossible that he had reached some measure of agreement with Edward.[15]

Meanwhile, Louis de Male sent to Edward an embassy which was headed by one of his councillors, Henry, brother to Henry of Flanders, and which included other envoys who were already known in England.[16] Having heard what they had to say, on 25 September—the same day as the procuration was issued to the English envoys to treat with the French—Edward appointed Lancaster his lieutenant in Flanders, Calais and 'elsewhere in the kingdom of France'.[17] The commission empowered him to treat on his own, take homages, fealties and oaths of any persons wishing to enter the king's allegiance, confirm agreements made in the king's name, take securities, issue letters of safe-conduct and do anything else which he saw fit. Whilst Louis was looking for a settlement with his subjects which would enable him to exercise his authority throughout the county,[18] Lancaster was empowered to look after the king's interests there and to treat with whomever he saw fit. Both commissions were issued in council, where the envoys were briefed and the programme was mapped out before they left the city for Dover on 26 September. Two days later they crossed to Calais with retinues amounting to nearly 450 men on board 28 ships.[19]

Negotiations appear to have been conducted with the French envoys and Louis' council at Boulogne-sur-Mer. All of them had ostensibly assembled to discuss the truce; but it was clear that some arrangement for Flanders would also have to be worked out. Whilst Louis' envoys had to ensure the count's authority, the French had to endeavour to steer him clear of Edward's envoys whose primary concern was the maintenance of English influence in the county; but there was a good deal more going on behind the scenes.[20] On 11 October the English envoys were given an additional procuration to treat with the count and the king's supporters in the county[21] and during the course of the month they drafted a secret treaty of alliance with Louis.[22]

This provided for a truce to be concluded with the French which was to last until 1 September 1349. Before it expired Louis was to send an embassy to Philip to demand the restoration of the 'western provinces' of Flanders, notably of the county of Artois and the towns and castellanies of Lille, Douai, Béthune and Orchies, which had been annexed by the king of France in 1305 under the terms of the treaty of Athis-sur-Orge—the humiliating settlement which followed the battle of Courtrai. If Philip agreed, the count would be satisfied; but the inhabitants of the county, towns and castellanies were not to be hostile to Edward and the alliances which he had made with the great Flemish cities were to remain in force. On the other hand, if Philip refused and Louis' demands were not met, the count was to defy him and revoke all homages which he owed to him. In this case an offensive alliance was to be concluded between Edward and Louis for the duration of the war, by the terms of which they would assist one another to secure their respective 'rights' in France.

The proposed alliance was to stipulate that they were not to make peace or conclude a truce or other agreement without mutual consent. They would agree to assist one another to conquer their 'rights' from Philip and his allies. If in the process Edward acquired the county of Artois or part of it (save Calais, Marck and Oye, which he already held), the city of Tournai, or any of the four towns and castellanies (Lille, Douai, Béthune and Orchies), he was to hand them over to the count immediately. Conversely, if Louis conquered anything in France or elsewhere touching Edward's quarrel with Philip, he was to hand it over to Edward. If this alliance were concluded, Louis was to undertake to observe its terms in a letter under his seal obliging himself to pay Edward 200,000 *livres gros tournois* if he defaulted. For his part Edward was to designate someone of his lineage to swear on his behalf to respect the treaty. The final details were to be settled at Dunkirk in November, when the agreement embodying all these clauses was to be drawn up and Louis was to issue the letter of obligation.

The negotiations which resulted in this draft treaty took place at Boulogne during the six weeks in which truce negotiations were being conducted there with the French, and it appears to have been concluded around 11 November.[23] Two days later a truce to last until 1 September 1349 was published on the frontier between Calais and Guines. There had clearly been some very insincere bargaining over this, for it provided that the French were not to treat with the Flemings, either secretly or openly, with intent to secure an alliance, but the English only undertook not to treat with anyone on Philip's side. Both sides undertook not to make any offensive alliances during its duration— but the English already had. Upon its conclusion the English envoys proceeded to Dunkirk,[24] where negotiations took place with a markedly pro-English embassy led by Henry of Flanders, lord of Ninove, Sohier, lord of Enghien and Jaqueme Metteneye, a burgess of Bruges, who were together empowered to treat for Louis; the towns of Ghent and Ypres were also represented.[25]

Nothing is known of the actual parleyings at Dunkirk, but the agreements reached during the course of the negotiations were embodied in two very different treaties, one of them the projected alliance. The formal document embodying its provisions was drawn up in the form of a chirograph, each half being sealed by either party.[26]

It fixed the date of Louis' defiance and his revocation of homage to Philip to within three weeks of 1 September—the day of expiry of the truce—when the offensive alliance was to come into force. Louis was to assist the English to install Edward as 'the rightful king of France' (the change of wording here is noteworthy) and as long as the counties of Nevers and Rethel were withheld from him, Edward was to pay an annual pension of 40,000 gold *écus*. Three articles were specified for inclusion in the offensive alliance, namely: that Louis was to abide by its terms by reason of being *conjoint* and obliged in the sum of 200,000 *livres gros tournois*; that both Louis and Edward were to secure a promise from the towns of Ghent, Ypres and Bruges to the effect that they would not accept Louis' heirs and successors as count until he had sworn to abide by its terms; and that the count's alliances with Brabant were not to be abrogated. In accordance with these terms Louis issued the letter obliging himself in the 200,000 *livres gros tournois*.[27]

For obvious reasons this agreement was not entered on the English chancery rolls; but another agreement drawn up by the envoys at Dunkirk and ratified by both Edward and Louis early in December was.[28] This was very different from the treaty of alliance. It merely declared peace between the two countries, guaranteed the cities of Flanders their old freedoms, arranged a settlement between Louis and the towns and guaranteed Edward's alliances in the county. Around 30 November Edward himself crossed to Calais to complete the negotiations[29] and it was probably there that he attached his seal to the treaty of alliance.[30]

As far as the English were concerned the treaty of alliance was the instrument which bore weight, for it was clearly very much in English interests. Edward was to lose none of the support and recognition which he had hitherto enjoyed in Flanders and, on the surface of things, was almost certain to secure recognition from Louis; for it was doubtless clear to the envoys that Philip would never agree to surrender the lost provinces. Taken on its own the other agreement was far from advantageous. For whilst it declared peace between the two countries, Edward appeared to be leaving his staunchest supporters in the county at the mercy of the count. Even the French could find little to grumble at in this agreement, which was doubtless put out for their benefit.

Louis had nothing to lose. His ambitions were altogether different from those of his father Louis de Nevers. He was more concerned with his own dynastic interests and the commercial interests of the county than with his obligations as a loyal vassal of the king of France.[31] Having secured French support to intervene in the civil war which had broken out in the county in order to secure recognition there, the treaty of alliance with Edward held out the promise of the western provinces whose return he so greatly coveted and both agreements made certain his authority in the county. In these negotiations, as in those of the previous year, he revealed something of the mettle which was to distinguish him in the future as a most skilful diplomat. From the beginning he showed himself to be a practical person, utterly self-interested and quite unscrupulous.[32] Although he was only eighteen in 1348[33] and was doubtless advised by able councillors,[34] the sly expression on his face, the sharp look, the thin lips, correspond well with the character which he had already revealed in the negotiations of the previous year.[35] He was not very brave and preferred the ruses of diplomacy to the brutal solutions of war. It was no part of his intention to sacrifice his position as count to the duties which he owed as a vassal of Philip VI; he wished to govern himself and to make his will felt among his subjects. He had a very clear idea of the conditions upon which he could exercise his authority in Flanders, for he understood that as ruler of a county of great industrial towns he must allow its powerful economic activity to go on unimpeded. The policy which he pursued in subsequent years was not lost on the future dukes of Burgundy.

He had played his cards well. Edward's support had helped him to reach a settlement with his subjects. He had a weapon with which to bargain with Philip over the lost provinces and should the king of France refuse to comply with the request he had been promised English military assistance. If he did not wish to take advantage of it he need not feel obliged to put the treaty of alliance into effect. For before the negotiations were completed at Dunkirk and before they were terminated at Boulogne, he annulled the letters which he was later to issue, obliging himself to pay Edward 200,000 *livres gros tournois* if he failed to stand by its terms.[36] In accordance with the second agreement with Edward he pardoned the citizens of Ghent and Ypres their rebellion and made arrangements for the settling of disputes which might subsequently arise.[37] By September 1349 he stood the chance of securing the obedience of the entire county—and then matters could take their course.

Lancaster and his colleagues arrived back in England on 16 December[38] in the firm belief that they had secured that alliance with the count of Flanders which Edward had so persistently but unsuccessfully pursued since the beginning of the war. For it seemed certain that Philip would refuse Louis' demands, that when the count revoked his homage to Philip he would recognize Edward as king of France and that his recognition would be sealed with active military support. For they had no reason to doubt that Louis had bound himself as *conjoint*, on pain of being perjured and in the enormous sum of 200,000 *livres gros tournois*.

# VI   The second expedition to Aquitaine (1349-1350)

When Henry returned from Flanders for the Christmas of 1348 England was in the grip of the Black Death. The parliament which he was to have attended at Westminster in the following April had to be prorogued because of the mounting toll of deaths in London and the Home Counties, and he appears to have spent most of his time until late August well away from the capital, at Kenilworth, Rothwell and Leicester. But during the course of the following year he was to lead another expedition to Aquitaine and was involved in a major naval engagement with the Castilian fleet, which not only endangered his voyage to and return from the duchy and possibly prevented him from taking action in a dispute between two of the king's lieges in the marches of Brittany and Poitou, but through its presence in the Channel also threatened communications with Calais and Flanders.

On the basis of the secret treaty concluded at Dunkirk, a series of campaigns was scheduled for the autumn of 1349. Louis de Male was to operate in north-eastern France with English assistance and Lancaster was once again to be sent with an expeditionary force to Gascony. On 28 August the earl was given a new commission as the king's captain-general and lieutenant in Aquitaine and Languedoc and preparations for his departure were put under way at the beginning of September.[1] In accordance with the agreements concluded at Dunkirk, envoys were sent to Flanders to secure oaths of fealty from the captains and other prominent citizens of the Flemish cities, and the lieutenant of the captain of Calais, Sir Robert de Herle, and Sir Richard Totesham were appointed to treat with Louis about the execution of the terms of the alliance.[2]

In the intervening period another conference was held between Calais and Guines in accordance with the terms of the truce of 13 November 1348, which had stipulated that envoys for either monarch were to assemble there on 22 March to treat of peace. If no agreement could be reached within a period of six weeks (extendible for 15 days) they were to conclude the negotiations, but the truce was to stand firm.[3] Accordingly, on 8 and 10 March envoys for either side were appointed.[4] Two papal nuncios, Pastor, archbishop of Embrun, and Bertrand, bishop of Sénez were sent to join the embassies and on 19 March the English envoys crossed to Calais.[5]

Of the deliberations we know very little, but a treaty may have been drafted. Sir Reginald de Cobham, who was one of the English envoys, was sent back to England to report on the proceedings and he returned with a statement of the king's wishes on the same to be given to the bishop of Norwich.[6] According to the chronicler Geoffrey Baker, the French would not hear of peace until Calais was returned to them.[7] But on 13 April another commission was issued to the envoys which only empowered them to treat of an extension of the truce. By 2 May the negotiations were completed. The truce was extended to 16 May 1350 and this provided for envoys to be sent to Avignon for 1 November 1349 to negotiate in the presence of the pope.[8]

Edward never had any serious intention of sending an embassy and the negotiations in the spring were no more than a cover to his military plans for the year. He rejected the pope's request for envoys to be sent to the curia as arranged on the grounds that Philip had broken the truce. It was in vain that Clement sent the archdeacon of Perpignan, Bernard de Caulesone, to try and induce him to send his envoys to Avignon not later than 2 February 'to confirm the treaty of peace' and not to send Lancaster to Gascony.[9]

For their part, the French appear to have been making considerable progress in Aquitaine.[10] The territories Lancaster had secured there were threatened by the acquisition of strategically important places in the Garonne valley (notably Aiguillon and Port-Sainte-Marie) and the investment of a number of vital places in the Charente valley (in particular Tonnay-Charente).[11] Moreover, whilst preparations for the embarkation of the earl's forces were in progress a quarrel broke out between two of the king's officers in France, Sir Walter Bentley and Raoul de Caours, soldiers with conflicting interests in the marches of Brittany and Poitou. The dispute, in threatening the defection of Caours to the French, menaced English control in the *pays de Retz* and south-eastern Brittany. In order to meet this emergency, on 18 October Lancaster was given a further commission as the king's captain-general and lieutenant in Poitou.[12]

Considerably less is known about the earl's second expedition to Aquitaine than about his first. Froissart, who wrote at considerable length on the campaigns of 1345–6, does not even mention it and no dispatch is available like that for his raid into Poitou in 1346. The expedition of 1349–50, as events turned out, was of less importance than that begun four years earlier. The plan for two simultaneous campaigns starting in the autumn broke down owing to the failure of Louis de Male to keep his part of the bargain struck at Dunkirk.[13] It was further frustrated by the diversion in the *pays de Retz* and it took place in the winter and in violation of the truce. It was only a small retinue of which Lancaster had command[14] and his military operations, which occupied little more than a month, ended early in 1350 in the conclusion of a truce with the French.

Lancaster left England towards the end of October and disembarked at Bordeaux at the beginning of the following month.[15] During the first week of October the French, who had expected him to land in Normandy, alerted the coastal defences there.[16] Rather more serious, the Castilians, who were now firmly allied with Philip, had sent a number of ships to the mouth of the river Gironde and still more to that of the river Charente, where they were operating under the command of Guy de Nesle, recently appointed Philip's captain-general in Saintonge.[17] When Lancaster arrived in the duchy, Nesle was besieging the town of Tonnay-Charente with the help of a number of Aragonese miners and the flotilla.[18] In order to prevent the delivery of a shipment of money and victuals which were being sent out to the garrison of Saint-Jean-d'Angély, he ordered ships to be sunk in the river before Tonnay.[19] Allied garrisons in Saintonge and Poitou were thereby threatened. One of Lancaster's first administrative actions in the duchy was to have the assignment diverted to Bordeaux.[20]

When he arrived in Gascony, Henry was joined by those Gascon lords loyal to the English connection, and the bulk of his army was recruited from the forces under their command.[21] As early as 20 June Sir Frank de Hale had been appointed seneschal of the duchy and was responsible for enlisting troops in preparation for the earl's arrival.[22] Among the retinues assembled were those of the Albrets, the Graillys, the Durforts, Bertrand de Montferrand, the lords of Lesparre and of Pommiers and that of Bernard of Béarn, alias *Aspes*.[23]

As in 1345, Lancaster stayed in Bordeaux for no more than a few days. By 27 November the *jurats* of Agen reported that his forces were moving down the south bank of the Garonne in the *Brulhois*.[24] The country was easy prey. Many of the towns were not walled and were unprepared for the attack; their garrisons were small and insufficiently victualled. There was a panic in Agen where the *jurats* and notables, hearing that he was in the neighbourhood, made hurried arrangements for its defence and sent messengers to King Philip to report upon the critical situation and to seek royal assistance. By Christmas the earl's army was before Toulouse.[25] Laplume, Astaffort, Cuq, Fals, Dunes and Beaumont-de-Lomagne were taken.[26] Grenade, where the bridge was destroyed by order of the *capitouls* of Toulouse, and Merville, some twenty kilometres to the north-west of the city, were pillaged.[27]

The pope, determined at all costs to preserve the truce and still vainly hoping for the conclusion of a peace settlement, did everything he could to repair the breach. On 22 November he wrote to Lancaster and the archbishop of Auch, then Philip's lieutenant in Gascony and Languedoc, requesting the earl to remove hindrances to the peace treaty by respecting the truce and requiring the archbishop to use his influence to that effect. He informed them that he proposed to send nuncios to treat with them on the matter and requested appropriate safe-conducts.[28]

Lancaster received the pope's letters by way of one Giovanni Maingheti and sent his reply with Guillaume de Savignac, a canon of Bayonne. The earl's attitude was further expounded to the pope by Simon de Brisley, the dean of Lincoln, and Richard de Wymondwold, an English advocate then at the curia. Clement promised to convey a reply to what they had to say by way of the nuncios whom he was sending out to the earl and the archbishop of Auch. On 8 December the archbishops of Braga and Brindisi were given a procuration empowering them to treat with Lancaster and the archbishop of Auch concerning the peace treaty and the observance of the truce. The two lieutenants and other parties involved were requested to give credence and favourable attention to them in order 'to end the discord'.[29]

It is not known where Lancaster received the papal nuncios. He had returned to La Réole by 30 December[30] and negotiations appear to have begun during the course of January. On 6 February Clement wrote to the earl thanking him for receiving the nuncios favourably and to Jacques de Bourbon, count of La Marche (who had been sent into Languedoc with a special commission as lieutenant of Philip), requesting him to co-operate with the archbishop and Lancaster. Some time before 3 March, after 'much discussion' between the papal nuncios and the three lieutenants, a truce was concluded to last until 12 April, by which time embassies for either monarch were to meet the nuncios between Calais and Guines to treat of peace or prolongation of the truce.[31]

It is quite clear that an arrangement of this kind had been envisaged. Lancaster's commission, issued to him in five separate letters, not only gave him full military, judicial and administrative authority similar to that with which he had been invested in 1345, but it also empowered him to prolong the truce and if necessary to conclude a new one.[32] On the same day Michael de Northburgh and Andrew de Ufford, archdeacons of Suffolk and Middlesex, Richard de Wymondwold, doctor of laws, and master Robert de Askeby, canon of Salisbury, were given similar powers to treat of the truce and they appear to have left for Gascony with Lancaster.[33]

By 14 February the earl was back in Bordeaux, where he remained until at least 5 March.[34] There can be no doubt about the success of his *chevauchée*. It was spectacular. None of Edward's armies had hitherto penetrated so deeply into French territory, for the Black Prince's raid to Narbonne lay in the future. The French were unprepared and had been taken by surprise. The archbishop of Auch had at the time left Toulouse for Carcassonne and Jacques de Bourbon was given his commission as lieutenant too late to assemble an army capable of resisting the lightning attack.[35] Lancaster had chosen to conclude a truce before an effective opposition could be brought up and had thus momentarily secured his conquests. But in the long run the territorial consequences of the raid were negligible. During the summer, after the earl had returned to England, most of the places taken by his forces were recaptured by the French in the course of a short campaign conducted by the count of Armagnac and Robert de Houdetot, master of the French crossbowmen and newly appointed captain-general in Languedoc. Beaumont-de-Lomagne, Cuq, Fals, Astaffort, Dunes and Laplume were rapidly reoccupied, although Port-Sainte-Marie (which had been surrendered to the Anglo-Gascons by the inhabitants) was not taken until some time later, after Houdetot had acquired the tower of Saint-Laurent-du-Port, situated on the left bank of the Garonne before the town.[36]

Before Lancaster left the duchy there were old friends to see and supporters to be rewarded.[37] On 5 March, after some of the horses belonging to his troops had been sold to the constable of Bordeaux for use in the duchy, he left the city for England; but there was evidently some trouble about the return voyage. Whether held up by the Castilian fleet, to turn his attention to the *pays de Retz*, by contrary winds, storms at sea, or some other cause, he had not yet left the mouth of the Gironde by 20 March and only arrived in London on 10 May, almost ten weeks after he had set out from Bordeaux.[38]

Edward had not heard from him for a long time and had been making preparations to land in northern France in late spring.[39] The two-pronged attack was to be carried out without Louis de Male. Arrangements were therefore made for the provisioning of Lancaster's forces in the duchy and for substantial reinforcements to be sent to join him there. On 15 January general and special mandates were issued to sheriffs, mayors, bailiffs and other royal officers ordering them to send food to Lancaster and those with him in the king's service in Gascony,[40] and by 7 March 220 men-at-arms and 222 mounted archers were assembled at Plymouth to join him in the duchy; but they were held up there until his return on 10 May.[41] The king's army was scheduled to assemble at Sandwich for 23 May and during March and April mobilization was in full swing.[42] According to Baker these preparations were suspended on the arrival of messengers from Gascony with news of the truce concluded by Lancaster,[43] but they were not finally abandoned until after the earl's return to England. Before that happened Lancaster was engaged in the settlement of the dispute between Sir Walter Bentley and Raoul de Caours.

The year 1346, the year of the Crécy-Calais campaign and of Lancaster's raid into Poitou, had been a particularly successful period for England, and those captains and men who made a practice of fighting on the winning side were quickly transferring allegiance from Philip VI to Edward III. One such person was Raoul de Caours, who had already changed sides twice in the course of the Breton war and once again found that his interests lay with Edward. Initially a supporter of Montfort in the Breton succession dispute, he held lands in Guérande.[44] During the course of 1345 he deserted Edward's allegiance for that of the French,[45] but returned into the Montfort party during the course of the following year.

With a record of recent service to his name, in January 1347 he sought out the king before Calais and secured a commission as his captain and lieutenant in Poitou and the *pays de Retz*, excepting those lands, castles and towns taken by Lancaster in 1346.[46] Arrangements were made for him to cross to the duchy in the company of Sir Thomas Dagworth, newly appointed as the king's captain and lieutenant in Brittany, and four ships were to be supplied for his passage.[47]

Raoul evidently served himself and the king well. In the summer of the following year, in recognition of his good service, Edward granted him £1,000 rent in lands which he had already acquired and would acquire in the *pays de Retz*, Brittany, Poitou and the surrounding parts. A business-like indenture was drawn up between them whereby, in return for the grant, Raoul undertook to support Edward in his wars in Brittany and Poitou at his own cost.[48]

His territorial aggrandizement in the *pays de Retz* brought him into conflict with Sir Walter Bentley, a soldier of considerable abilities who was later to serve as the king's captain and lieutenant in Brittany.[49] Bentley had secured a personal interest in the duchy through an opportune marriage to Jeanne de Belleville, the widow of Olivier III de Clisson (who had been executed by the French for supporting John de Montfort in the early years of the succession dispute) and who had herself been banished from France and her possessions declared confiscate by judgement of the *parlement de Paris*.[50]

The dispute arose, amongst other things, over certain lands in the *pays de Retz* which Bentley claimed as part of the inheritance of his wife. On 20 June 1349 Edward, having forbidden Raoul and Walter to start a private war on the matter and ordered them to accept his mediation, arranged for his valet Richard de Cardoil to secure information on the dispute, to do summary justice and execute a judgement.[51] Walter's claims were accepted. On 20 October Edward granted him, Jeanne and Jeanne's heirs in perpetuity possessions in the bay of Bourgneuf which were judged to be in his wife's inheritance. They included all the domains, castles, fortresses, towns, manors, lands and places of Beauvoir-sur-Mer, Lampant, La Barre-de-Monts and Châteauneuf, together with the islands and domains of Noirmoutier and Chauvet, a moiety of the islands of Bouin and all the saltings and appurtenances of these places.[52]

News was not slow in getting to the French. Quite apart from the economic importance of the saltings, the bay of Bourgneuf was a link in the chain of halting-places for English coasting vessels on their way between England and Gascony and its strategic importance was almost as great as that of the west Breton ports and the Charente towns. French control of the area would therefore be of a value out of all proportion to its size and the cost of maintaining it in a state of defence. To this end Philip instructed three knights—Jean de Beaumanoir, Foulques de Laval and Maurice Mauvinet—to treat with Raoul. Together they drew up an agreement by the terms of which Raoul was once more to enter French obedience and service. He entrusted the knights with the custody of Beauvoir-sur-Mer, Lampant and the islands of Chauvet and Bouin pending the accomplishment by the king of France of certain clauses drawn up between them.[53] These provided that the king was to pay him 10,000 gold *écus* wages for his troops and, as a security, he would surrender the island of Chauvet to the knights. If the king did not wish to accept the agreement the knights were to retain the custody of the castle of Chauvet until Raoul had restored the 10,000 *écus*, but the other three fortresses (Beauvoir-sur-Mer, Lampant and Bouin) were to be returned to him immediately. If, on the other hand, the king did wish to accept the arrangement, all the fortresses were to remain in Raoul's possession, unless the king wanted them, in which case he was to pay Raoul 60,000 *écus* in place of the £1,000 in lands and rent granted to him by Edward. Raoul was to be responsible for the defence of the fortresses and all the saltings were to remain his personal property, unless the king wished to buy salt, in which case it was to be valued by officials acting on behalf of them both, and the king was to have a quarter of the profits. If Philip agreed to all these clauses Raoul undertook to change allegiance and to do as much damage to the English as he could. He was not, however, to be bound to bear arms for either king if he did not wish to; but if he did wish to, then Philip was to grant him lands to a value to be agreed between them.

It was one thing to render judgement in favour of Bentley, quite another to execute it. The possibility of a change of allegiance on Raoul's part had not been overlooked and arrangements were made for Lancaster to have a special commission empowering him to assume the entire inheritance of Jeanne and her children together with all the saltings in Poitou.[54] Raoul was to be obedient and carry out all that the earl or his deputies should command him regarding the matter. The custodians of the castles of Noirmoutier and La Barre-de-Monts and of the fortresses of Chauvet and Bouin were also to be under his command. William d'Aubigny, captain of Guérande, and his subjects were to do nothing contrary to the custodianship.

On 18 October, two days before the grant in favour of Bentley, Lancaster was given his patent of appointment as the king's captain and lieutenant in Poitou.[55] Already on 1 September he had been empowered to grant £1,000 in land and rent 'to certain persons according to his ordinance', and the constable of Bordeaux was instructed to meet out of the ducal revenues his expenses 'for expediting our negotiations'.[56] On 6 November the sheriffs of London were instructed to proclaim that no merchants were to buy salt from the bay or elsewhere in Poitou, except from Lancaster.[57]

It is probable that the earl did not personally take any action. A Castilian naval squadron under the command of Alfonso XI's eldest son Don Carlos arrived off Guérande about the same time that he set out from England and it may have obliged him to make straight for

Bordeaux. Although his return from the duchy took almost ten weeks, there is no evidence that the delay was occasioned by a visit to the *pays de Retz*. On the other hand, it is obvious that he was expected to take some kind of action. On 15 December he was instructed to take Jeanne de Belleville and her children into his protection together with their lands and possessions.[58] He was to maintain them in their inheritance, defend them against any injury or violence which might befall them and take the children into his safe custody. However, since he was preoccupied in Gascony, one of the king's sergeants-at-arms, Roger de Baildon, was appointed the earl's deputy in this matter and he was directed to execute the grant of 20 October giving seisin to Walter and Joan.[59]

Raoul had no alternative but to embrace more fully the Valois cause. The agreement with the three knights was confirmed. Beauvoir-sur-Mer, Lampant and the islands of Chauvet and Bouin were to be restored to him, to be held of the king of France by homage and service, together with their saltings. A grant of 2,000 *livres tournois* was made to him at the treasury in Paris and a rent for himself and his heirs in perpetuity. But Edward had not yet heard the last of Raoul de Caours.[60]

Lancaster's experiences in the winter and spring of 1349–50 had revealed the threat of Castilian ships in the Channel and on the sea route to Bordeaux. This was a relatively new development. Ever since the great naval victory at Sluys in 1340 Edward had been free to send troops almost anywhere he cared in western France. For although Philip, with the pope's backing, had concluded a marriage alliance with Alfonso XI of Castile in July 1345 and had thereby secured a promise of naval assistance, for his part Alfonso was in no immediate hurry to implement the treaty. In the following year he had agreed to the marriage of his eldest son Don Pedro to an English princess. But although Edward's daughter Joan of Woodstock left for Gascony on her way to marry the Castilian heir in 1348, she died of plague at Bordeaux and English plans for a marriage alliance were brought to an abrupt conclusion. French ascendancy in Castile was promptly re-established and the Franco-Castilian alliance was given concrete form in the winter of 1349.[61]

Lancaster presumably gave a very full report on the situation when he arrived back in London on 10 May. During the course of that month preparations were put under way for the assembly of a fleet to meet the Castilians. Orders were given for the manning of ships. Rigging and stores, carpenters and other workmen, were provided for ships, pinnaces and barges.[62] On 22 July Sir Robert de Morley was reappointed admiral of the northern fleet[63] and on the following day instructions were given for ships and sailors to be arrested and sent to Sandwich.[64] Before the vessels put to sea they were furnished with standards and streamers.[65]

The Castilian fleet, under the command of Charles de la Cerda, was then in the roads of Sluys, about to return to Spain. La Cerda, who had been informed of Edward's intention to attack him, recruited soldiers, crossbowmen, and archers, mainly in Flanders, and armed his ships with every kind of artillery and missile, including large iron bars.[66] On 10 August Edward wrote to the archbishops of Canterbury and York from Rotherhithe to the effect that the Castilians had robbed his ships and slain his subjects at sea and that they had collected an immense fleet in Flanders with which they not only boasted that they would utterly destroy English shipping and dominate the Channel but also threatened to invade the realm and exterminate the people. He was then about to proceed against them and he requested the prelates to cause divine service to be celebrated, processions made, and alms given in order that he might secure victory.[67]

Edward proceeded to Winchelsea about the middle of August and embarked in his favourite ship the *Cog Thomas* on the 28th.[68] The Black Prince, John of Gaunt and other nobles including Lancaster, were placed in command of the other vessels with their respective retinues of men-at-arms and archers. The ensuing battle,[69] which took place a few miles off Winchelsea on 29 August, was waged from vespers until nightfall. In his inimitable way Froissart tells us how Edward explained to all his knights the order of battle he would have them follow and posted himself in the prow of his ship. He was dressed in a black velvet jacket, and wore on his head a small beaver hat, which was said to have become him much. Some of the knights who were with him told Froissart that they had never seen the king in better spirits. He ordered his minstrels to play a dance which had recently been introduced from Germany by Sir John Chandos and for his amusement he made Chandos sing with them, which greatly delighted him.

The Castilian fleet had the wind in its favour and since it had a greater tonnage and sail power than did the English fleet, it might have swept down the Channel. But instead, La Cerda chose to engage the English ships. There was no manoeuvring in naval warfare in the fourteenth century. Since the fleets were virtually floating armies, naval tactics were not essentially different from those which prevailed on the battlefield. They were for the most part limited to grappling the enemy ships with chains and hooks, boarding them and fighting it out. Such engagements took place between individual ships, so that to an observer 'the battle was not in one place, but in ten or twelve at a time'. Froissart inevitably singled out for attention those actions in which some of the leading personages were involved: the king, the prince, Lancaster and Robert de Namur. Having been grappled to a Castilian vessel, Edward III's ship was sinking and the king and crew were only able to save themselves by boarding the enemy. Seeing that the prince's ship was grappled, sinking and had the worst of the fight, Lancaster is said to have laid his ship along the other side of the Castilian vessel, grappled and boarded it.[70] Not only was the prince's life saved, but also that of young John of Gaunt.

Apart from these picturesque details we have very little idea of the combat, and no overall view of the battle. The Castilian fleet is said to have been made up of 40 great ships, of which a number (variously estimated at between 14 and 30) are said to have been captured. The strength of the English fleet was not stated, but if it was superior in numbers to that of La Cerda, the Castilians had the advantage of the size and height of their ships, which towered above the English cogs and smaller vessels known as *pinnaces* and *barges*.

In the course of the fighting the Castilians were therefore able to throw large stones and bars of iron on to the English vessels from the 'castles' on their masts and they had the advantage of height in showering arrows from their crossbows on to the English decks. On the other hand, the fell aim and longer range of the English archers, which compelled the Spanish artillery-men as well as the crossbowmen to shelter themselves behind the bulwarks and castles and thus checked the discharge of missiles, once more stood Edward in good stead; the desperate fury with which his sailors and men-at-arms attacked their assailants in hand-to-hand combat ultimately proved irresistible. The losses on either side, both killed and wounded, were considerable.

Soon after nightfall, when the English ships returned to Rye and Winchelsea, they had certainly won the battle; but their victory was not complete. Although the title of 'King of the Sea' was later bestowed on Edward in parliament,[71] a large part of the Castilian fleet remained at sea. On 8 September the king warned the inhabitants of Bayonne of the danger and requested them to disregard the truce and to equip their ships against the enemy.[72] In October measures were taken to provide warships to convoy the wine ships to Gascony in order to defend them against attacks by the Castilians. On 11 November, by which time the Castilian ships had returned to Sluys, Sir Robert de Herle, captain of Calais, and others were appointed to treat with the masters and mariners of Castile in that port and elsewhere in Flanders, for the purpose of bringing hostilities to an end. But Edward had a good deal of trouble with enemy ships in the Channel during the course of the following year, and only the conclusion of a twenty-year truce with the maritime towns of Castile on 1 August 1351 removed the threat to English shipping until the 1370's.

# VII  Louis de Male and Margaret of Flanders (1350-1351)

After he returned from Gascony in the spring of 1350, much of Lancaster's time was again taken up with diplomatic work. Edward, who was determined to regain a foothold in the Low Countries, continued to press for an arrangement with Louis de Male and he intervened in a succession dispute which broke out in Hainault, Holland and Zeeland. The pope made even more determined efforts to convert the truce into a 'firm peace' and entrusted the work of mediation to one of his most ardent cardinals and self-seeking courtiers, Guy de Boulogne, bishop of Porto. Up to the spring of 1354 neither Edward, Clement nor Innocent met with much success, since French influence remained predominant in the Low Countries and Edward was determined not to come to terms with his adversary. But in the protracted negotiations of these years Lancaster played a leading part.

The truce which the earl had concluded in Gascony was to last until 12 April 1350, by which time envoys for each monarch were to assemble before the papal nuncios on the frontier between Calais and Guines to treat of peace or the extension of the truce. On 20 March the archbishops of Braga and Brindisi, who had gained the pope's confidence through their successful mediation in the south, were given a procuration to treat with the French and English envoys as arranged. Philip VI, Edward, and their respective ambassadors were requested to give credence to the nuncios and a number of other persons including Lancaster were asked to assist them in their work.[1]

Edward, however, chose to hold up the appointment of the English envoys until after Lancaster returned from Bordeaux, and Clement, who suspected that he was refusing to treat, made arrangements for the nuncios to cross over to England. But on 15 May, when the pope wrote to Edward requesting him to receive the two archbishops and to provide them with safe-conducts,[2] a procuration was issued to the bishop of Norwich, the earl of Suffolk, Sir Thomas Cok and Sir Robert de Herle, empowering them to negotiate a peace or truce with the French;[3] this embassy crossed to Calais from Sandwich during the course of the following week.[4]

Meanwhile, Edward wrote to the pope proclaiming his readiness to treat with the French and on 6 June Clement exhorted the two embassies to do everything in their power to conclude a peace treaty.[5] But it was of no avail. On 13 June the truce was once again renewed for one year as from 1 August,[6] and although it stipulated that envoys should assemble in Avignon before 1 November to continue the negotiations for peace, Edward's actions during the previous year made it unlikely that an English embassy would be sent to the curia. A week later the English envoys arrived back in London, where the bishop of Norwich reported to the council.[7]

Lancaster was appointed one of the English judges of infringements of this truce, which envisaged the possibility that he and the earl of Northampton would be among the envoys who were to be sent to Avignon. On 18 June Edward intimated to the pope that he would send the bishop of Norwich, Lancaster, the earl of Arundel and Bartholomew de Burghersh.[8] On 28 July they were given a procuration to negotiate at the curia, although they were not scheduled to leave England until around Christmas.[9] Letters of protection were requested for them and were issued on 30 August.[10]

Edward was in no mood for peace negotiations. Contrary to the tenor of the truce, he made preparations for the engagement with the Castilian fleet and when one of his sergeants, Robert Tanny, was killed at Tours on his way to Gascony to announce the truce, he made a great deal of fuss about it and used it as a demonstration of how he could not trust his adversary's safe-conducts.[11] It was not safe, he claimed, to send his envoys to Avignon. It was irrelevant that Tanny was assassinated before the death of Philip VI on 22 August. From Edward's point of view John II was as untrustworthy as his father. It was in vain that the pope implored him to confirm the truce and to send his embassy to the curia as had been planned.[12]

Fearing a renewal of hostilities, Clement did what he could to save something from the wreckage. He sent a canon of St Paul's called Raymond Pelegrini as his nuncio to Edward and requested Lancaster and a good many others to give him credence.[13] André de la Roche, abbot of Saint-Seine and Cluny, was sent to Paris with instructions to get another safe-conduct for the English envoys from King John, to have it sent to Pelegrini and to make arrangements for a meeting between Boulogne and Calais so that, in the meantime, the truce could be prorogued.[14] The nuncios were partially successful, for at the beginning of November Sir Robert de Herle, captain of Calais, and Andrew de Ufford, archdeacon of Middlesex, were empowered to confirm the truce.[15] But it is quite clear that there was a good deal of discussion before agreement was reached. Ufford, who had already left London for Calais on 21 October, only arrived back in the city on 28 January.[16] Edward could not ignore the assistance which the Flemings had afforded to the Castilian fleet during the summer and, since by the beginning of November Spanish ships had again put into the Flemish ports, he also commissioned Herle and Ufford to treat with their masters and mariners.[17]

By the end of November it had finally become clear to the pope that the English would not send the proposed embassy to Avignon. Clement therefore wrote to Edward proposing that a new time and place should be arranged for a conference with the French, that it might be held before one or two cardinals and the archbishops of Braga and Brindisi, and that he would get John to arrange a safe-conduct for his envoys.[18] At the beginning of December he wrote to the two embassies meeting between Boulogne and Calais informing them of his proposals.[19] The discussions were becoming too important for Herle and Ufford to deal with alone and on 12 January Lancaster was sent to Calais with a retinue of 340 riders 'to treat with the councils of France and Flanders'.[20]

Edward was still hankering after an arrangement with Louis de Male. In April the young countess of Flanders had given birth to a daughter, also christened Margaret after her mother.[21] Philip had wasted no time in attempting to turn this to his own advantage. During the course of that month he sent an embassy to treat with the count and the Flemish towns of differences between them and to arrange a marriage alliance between the infant Margaret and one of his sons.[22] The competition for the Flemish heirloom had thus already begun, for Margaret was Louis' only child and was the heiress to the counties of Nevers and Rethel in addition to that of Flanders. Louis was determined to make the most of it. When the Castilian fleet put in at Sluys in the summer he gave it shelter and permitted La Cerda to recruit troops and to take ammunition aboard his ships.[23] But when Philip died in August he resurrected the secret treaty of Dunkirk, and refused to do homage to John until Lille, Douai, Béthune and Orchies were restored to him. When John declined he immediately got into touch with Edward.[24]

Very little is known of the negotiations which followed; but at the beginning of October the lord of Enghien (who was one of the chief Flemish negotiators of the secret treaty) arrived in England ostensibly having fled from Flanders fearing for his life. A tale was being circulated that he had planned to poison Louis, the countess and Louis de Namur. Having requested Edward to clear him of suspicion, arrangements were made for representatives from the councils of the count and the duke of Brabant to assemble at Gravelines before 2 February 1351 and for representatives from the king's council to assemble at Calais by the same date. Negotiations appear to have been conducted simultaneously with embassies from France and Flanders, some of them in the presence of papal nuncios. They concerned the confirmation of the truce, the proposed peace conference and presumably Louis de Male's refusal to do homage to John until the towns of Lille, Douai, Béthune and Orchies were restored to him. It is clear from subsequent events that the truce was confirmed; but it was not prolonged and no arrangements were made for the proposed peace conference. Almost nothing is known about the negotiations with Louis de Male's council, but the conference to clear Enghien does not appear to have taken place.[25]

That Lancaster was the chief figure in all this is clear enough. Before he returned to London on 10 February he sent Ufford back to the city to report to the council, and one of his retainers, Sir Stephen de Cosington, and several others, including William de Burton, were sent to Flanders.[26] On 5 March these two arrived back in Westminster with a Flemish delegation and a fortnight later Lancaster, who had been elevated to the rank of duke on 6 March, John de Carlton and Andrew de Ufford were given a procuration to hear and determine complaints between the king's subjects and those of Louis de Male of activities contrary to the peace of Dunkirk.[27] On 23 March they left for Calais with several shiploads of troops under Lancaster's command.[28] The negotiations appear to have lasted about three weeks. Facilities offered to Spanish ships in Flemish ports may have been discussed, but if Edward was hoping that Louis would take the next step in implementing the secret treaty of Dunkirk he had sadly underestimated his man.

Since the beginning of the year enemy ships had been conducting hostile operations in the Channel and were apparently attempting to prevent the landing of supplies that were being ferried over to Calais from England. Cosington's return journey from Flanders had been menaced by French ships in February and the threat had by no means abated by May. On the 11th of that month, Ufford set out for Calais, where he was again due to treat with the Flemings on the 15th. When he arrived at Dover he was unable to secure a passage owing to the activity of enemy ships in the Channel. A shipment of horses had already been held up for over a week. He explained to the mayor and bailiff of Dover and to the constable of Dover castle that the negotiations were urgent, that he must have a speedy crossing and he showed them letters under the privy seal to that effect. To this they answered that they could not risk a ship in the Channel; they had already brought all ships then in the port ashore for fear that they might be set on fire by the enemy, and they had been obliged to put several untrustworthy sailors under lock and key in Dover castle. It was only after much persuasion and in view of the urgency of the negotiations that they finally agreed to provide him with a boat, a crew of ten of the best sailors and a bodyguard of archers.[29]

To secure supplies for the garrison of Calais and to prevent interference with shipments being sent over from England, after he had completed the negotiations with the Flemings around the middle of April, Lancaster led a raid through Artois and Picardy, made an unsuccessful attempt to capture Boulogne and set fire to the ships there and at Étaples.[30] The country was ravaged as far as Fauquembergues, Thérouanne and Saint-Omer and he returned to Calais with a large quantity of provisions. Shortly afterwards, Sir Walter Mauny and Sir Robert de Herle conducted a similar raid, which was followed at the beginning of June by another less fortunate foray of troops under the command of John de Beauchamp, Herle's successor as captain of Calais.[31]

Since the truce was due to expire on 1 August, on 27 June a procuration was issued to the bishop of Norwich, the earl of Huntingdon, Barthlomew de Burghersh and Robert de Herle to treat of its renewal.[32] Lancaster was not included on this embassy, but on the same day he was given a secret credential to treat with Louis de Male and he appears to have left for Calais with the English envoys two days later.[33] He was to try to arrange a marriage between John of Gaunt and the count's daughter, Margaret, to settle the question of the extradition of Flemish refugees settled in England (since this had been demanded by Louis), to negotiate on a sum (up to 10,000 écus), also demanded by Louis for the *chevauchée* into France first agreed upon in the secret treaty of Dunkirk, to work out the time and manner of the same and to endeavour to bring some of the count's council into the king's pay. This was to be the culmination of the long series of negotiations which appear to have begun in the previous autumn. Five days before the credential was issued to the duke two of his retainers, Sir Frank de Hale and Sir Stephen de Cosington, had been appointed to treat with the count and community and they were probably intended to prepare the ground for his arrival.[34]

There is no information on the discussion that followed, but by 21 July the envoys who had been appointed to extend the truce (with the exception of Herle) had returned to London having concluded only a short arrangement of a few weeks' duration.[35] They were unable to negotiate a longer extension without reporting to Edward and the council, and it is clear that their decision in turn depended upon the progress of Lancaster's negotiations with the count of Flanders; it must soon have become clear that these were not proceeding very well.

In effect, on 24 July 1351 Louis de Male came to terms with King John at Fontainebleau and did homage to him for the counties of Flanders, Nevers and Rethel.[36] John undertook to provide Louis with lands to the value of 10,000 *livres parisis* in Flanders, a cash payment of 15,000 gold *écus* in lieu of every 1,000 *livres* of land not so provided and a lump sum of 60,000 gold *écus* to be paid immediately. If, because of Louis' homage or the breaking of the treaties of Dunkirk, Edward or any of his allies made war on the count by sea or land or interfered with merchandise entering the county, John would give the count military and financial assistance. This was to consist of the wages of 1,000 men-at-arms, to be paid at Tournai or Lille as soon as he was notified of the aggression. If more troops were needed the French garrison forces on the frontier with Flanders would be placed at his disposal and if the situation became really critical John promised to lead an army in person. He also agreed to pay the wages of 200 men-at-arms to garrison the town of Gravelines (in order to meet possible attacks from Calais) and undertook not to make a truce of more than fifteen days without first consulting the count and making him a partner to the discussions. If Edward demanded that Louis should put forward his claim to the towns of Lille, Douai, Béthune and Orchies, or insisted on the execution of any clause of the secret treaty of Dunkirk, John would stand by the count; but if rebellion broke out in the county he was not to interfere.

For his part Louis, having done homage to John, surrendered his claim to the four disputed towns. He undertook to serve John loyally, not to make any alliances with Edward or other of John's enemies and to serve him in war when called upon to do so. He was to keep all the agreements made in the past between the kings of France and the counts of Flanders and to be a loyal vassal of John and his successors in the future. He undertook not to allow any foreign troops to be received in Flanders or to attack France by way of the county and he renounced all alliances made with the king of England to the detriment of the king of France.

French diplomacy had won the day. On 6 August 1354 Louis' four year old daughter Margaret was betrothed to the young duke of Burgundy, Philip de Rouvre, whose mother was King John's second wife.[37] Within two years the young couple were married in Paris.[38] Although Louis subsequently complained of the non-fulfilment of the financial clauses of the marriage agreement of 1350 and the treaty concluded at Fontainebleau in the following year,[39] it was but small comfort to Edward, for he had finally lost.

On 26 July the English envoys who had returned from the truce conference five days earlier were given a procuration to treat of peace.[40] As early as 13 June the pope had written to Edward and several other persons, including Lancaster, requesting them to receive Cardinals Gil Albornoz and Niccolò Capocci whom he was sending to England on the subject. He asked for a safe-conduct to be sent for them by way of Goffredo Truci and Dominic de Lucera, the bearers of the letter. Four days later the captain of Calais was requested to give the couriers a safe-conduct and Hugo Pelegrini, canon of London, was asked to receive them and to assist them in their business. The two cardinals joined the French and English envoys (probably whilst the truce negotiations were in progress) and they subsequently took part in discussions for peace, though not, it would seem, as mediators.[41]

Meanwhile, on 27 July, Sir Robert de Herle was empowered to extend the short truce drawn up earlier in the month by up to twelve days.[42] This arrangement was made in view of the possibility that the envoys appointed to treat of peace might be held up by contrary winds or some other fortuitous cause. In fact they left London on 4 August; but the discussions were of little consequence and they were back in the city on 1 September.[43] Three days later Michael de Northburgh was empowered to confirm the truce, which was published on 11 September and was to last for one year as from that date.[44] There was little chance that it would be strictly adhered to and, as the Leicester chronicler very fairly puts it, it was signed on the understanding that either king should be at liberty to disregard it if it suited him.[45]

# VIII  The expedition to Prussia (1352)

There was a knight, a most distinguished man,
Who from the day on which he first began
To ride abroad had followed chivalry,
Truth, honour, generous thought and courtesy.
He had done nobly in his sovereign's war
And ridden into battle no man more,
As well in christian as in heathen places
And ever honoured for his noble graces.

It is tempting to think that Chaucer might have had his patron's
father-in-law in mind when he devised his portrait of the knight in
the *Prologue* to the *Canterbury Tales*;[1] but although Lancaster had
much in common with Chaucer's pilgrim, the poet's knight merely
personified the chivalric concepts of the time and mirrored the ambitions and to some extent the achievements of other fourteenth-
century noblemen. Duke Henry was, in this respect, the perfect
example of the fulfilment of contemporary ideals. An expedition which
he led to Prussia in 1354 was in the best style of the knight errant and
his consequent visit to Paris to fight a duel with the duke of Brunswick
over a point of honour might have come straight from the romances,
even though more purely political motives appear to have lain behind
it.

Like his king and the aristocracy of his day, he shared a passionate
delight in tournaments which, being fought in the lists as series of
single combats or jousting, provided an opportunity for the display
of individual prowess and were celebrated amid great pageantry. In
the Christmas of 1341, before the truce had been concluded with the
Scots, he organized a tournament at Roxburgh, challenged Sir
William Douglas to tilt with him, wounded him and forced him to
give up the contest.[2] Upon the conclusion of the truce he took part in
the tournaments organized by the king at Berwick and on another

occasion challenged Sir Alexander Ramsay of Dalhousie to a joust and wounded him so severely that he died.[3] In 1344 he was elected captain for life of a group of knights who secured royal authorization to hold jousts yearly at Lincoln.[4] This was said to have been given upon the especial request of the earl, 'who delights in acts of war',[5] and it may have been this voluntary association of knights which first suggested to Edward III that he should found a knightly Order.[6] He organized jousts and tournaments on numerous occasions: at Leicester for the marriage of his daughter Maude to Ralph Stafford in 1344, at Lincoln when the county was conferred upon him by the king and possibly at Bristol in 1358.[7]

He was naturally present at the many festivities organized by the king: in honour of the countess of Salisbury in 1342 when, Froissart tells us, for fifteen days the nobility of England, Germany, Flanders, Hainault and Brabant confronted one another in the lists; at Dunstable and possibly at Northampton and Eltham during and before Easter 1342; at the celebrated festival at Windsor in 1344, when the Round Table was instituted and when he appeared (as his father's deputy) as steward of England; at Eltham in 1347, at Lichfield and Windsor in 1348 and again at Windsor ten years later, when before the captive King John single combats took place which were said to transcend everything since the days of King Arthur.[8] The costumes worn by the contestants on these occasions were all provided by the king and were very sumptuous. In 1342 Edward wore a velvet tunic covered with tiny Saracens of gold and silver, each containing a jewel 'with the king's motto' and embroidered with trees and birds and the effigies of two Saracens bearing shields of the king's arms.[9]

From the time of the king's return from Calais in 1347 to the end of December of the following year tournaments took place at Canterbury, Bury St Edmunds, Windsor, Reading, Eltham, Lichfield and Guildford, at some of which he was also present.[10] At the tournament at Eltham the king gave him a hood of white cloth embroidered with men dancing in blue habits, buttoned in the front with large pearls. Five of these hoods were made—for the king, Henry, Hugh de Courtenay, Sir John de Grey of Rotherfield and Sir John de Lisle of Rougemont—all of them Founder Members of the Order of the Garter.[11] In 1348 he received a harness covered with white taffeta surrounded by a blue border from the king.[12] Presents from the Black Prince included a pair of plates for the jousts, a breastplate and a pair of plates when he returned from Normandy.[13] The tournament at Lichfield (9 April 1348) was celebrated with great splendour, the prevailing dress being a blue robe with a white hood.[14] On this occasion the jousters consisted of the king (who wore the arms of Sir Thomas de Bradeston) with seventeen knights and Lancaster with thirteen knights. The king's daughter Isabella, subsequently countess of Bedford, six ladies of high rank and twenty-one other ladies (who wore coats and hoods of the same materials and colours as the knights, together with various masks and visors) took a conspicuous part in the festivities. At Canterbury the jousters included, besides the king, the Black Prince, Lancaster, the earl of Suffolk and five other knights (to whom Edward gave each a harness of cerulean sindon worked with the arms of Sir Stephen de Cosington). A number of ladies, who entered the city (along with the jousters) disguised in masks, again seem to have played a prominent part. Such occasions as these afforded Henry many opportunities for personal contact with the king and as a Founder Knight of the Order of the Garter his name appeared second on the list following that of the prince of Wales.

Crusading provided another outlet for knightly deeds. After the fall of Acre in 1291 crusades to Palestine were no longer possible and it became fashionable among the higher nobility and gentry to fulfil vows by joining the kings of Spain against the Moors or the Teutonic Knights against their pagan neighbours.[15] During his lifetime Lancaster did both. Like Chaucer's knight he had joined Alfonso of Castile at the siege of Algeciras and had accompanied Egidio Boccanegra in a descent on the African coast to attack the Benny Merrin Moors off Ceuta:

> Often, at feasts, the highest place of all
> Among the nations fell to him in Prussia.
> In Lithuania had he fought, and Russia,
> No christian man so often, of his rank.
> And he was at Granada when they sank
> The town of Algeciras, also in
> North Africa, right through Benamarin.

In the lull of fighting in 1351 he resolved to join the Teutonic Knights. Although the Order had no property in England, they did enjoy an annual subsidy from the king. Under Edward III payment was due at the house of the Order in Coblenz and although it had fallen into arrears, on the reminder of the Grand Master, Kniperodi (1351–82), Edward restored it and promised to pay the arrears.

Crossing to Flanders towards the close of 1351, together with other English knights and a considerable retinue, he was arrested in North

Germany and held to pay a ransom of 30,000 gold crowns.[16] A contemporary German chronicler, Heinrich von Herford, relates how the vanguard of the duke's army (which was conducting his treasury eastward through the territory of the bishop of Paderborn) had a sharp encounter with a gang of Westphalian knights who defeated and robbed them deplorably.[17] But despite this setback he continued his expedition to Prussia undeterred though, according to Knighton, on arriving there he heard that a truce had been concluded between the christians and their heathen enemies, and returned to England by way of Cologne.[18] We know, however, that he got as far as Stettin (where he promised the duke that he would inflict no damage upon the lands of Casimir III of Poland) and that he was then intending to continue into Poland.[19] Baker tells us that he did so and according to the *Chronique des quatre premiers Valois* he even reached Estonia, where the christians made him their captain.[20] According to this account the duke did have battle with the pagans and with the kings of Estonia and Cracow, who were said to have been allied with them. The author gives a somewhat idealized account of how, in a battle with their enemies in which there was 'great chivalry', 'the good duke' restored the christian standard which had fallen underfoot in the *mêlée*. Whatever the case, he was back in Cologne by 11 April and in England for the summer.[21]

According to Knighton (whose account is substantiated by a letter of King John of France) it was rumoured to Henry that Otto, duke of Brunswick, in connivance with John, intended to capture him as he made his way eastward. How far the suspected ambush in Westphalia saw the hand of Duke Otto is not clear, but certainly Lancaster took the matter seriously. On his return from Prussia, in the presence of the princes of Mark and Jülich and other notables in Cologne cathedral, he accused Brunswick of having attempted to capture him and his men and of having planned to hand him over to John. He also added that he found this action unworthy of a knight and that if Otto wished to challenge him to a duel he would be ready to take it up. Otto was not long in responding:

Otto, by the grace of God duke of Brunswick, lord of Thuringia, son of the grand duke of Brunswick, to the excellent and noble prince the duke of Lancaster. Know that the words which you uttered personally and with your own mouth in the sovereign church of St Peter's at Cologne on Friday after Easter last before the noble princes of Mark and Jülich and many honest knights and esquires and in the presence of the citizens of the same city, maliciously, shabbily and dishonestly, were lies and in no way the truth. The which things we will prove by challenging our body and goods against your body, as a good and loyal lord is bound and obliged to do with a wicked and dishonest and bad man. This we will do between the castle of Guines and St Omer, or wherever our lord the king of France sees fit. For we are not obliged to provide you and your men with a safe-conduct of the aforesaid lord to the place in question, on the which matter we beg you to send us a written reply under your seal with the bearer of these.[22]

Baker gives a lively account of the challenge:

Otto, son of the duke of Brunswick and in the pay of the Crown of France, sent letters to the duke of Lancaster, who was returned from Prussia, by the tenor of which he accused him, affirming that as he was returning from Prussia by Cologne he maliciously informed the Cologners that the said Otto went about by stealth to have him made prisoner and to have him presented to the king of France, adding that because he never made any such taking of him he was ready, in the declaration of his good name, by a singular combat in the court of the king of France, to prove the duke of Lancaster a liar touching the said article. The letters containing all this were not sealed and, therefore, since it might have been folly to have trusted in a letter delivered by a servant, the duke sent two knights to Otto to learn of the cause of the challenge and to demand thereof his letters patent, sealed with his seal of arms.[23]

It is clear from the subsequent letter of King John that, after the exchange of challenges, there was disagreement as to who was the offended party. Lancaster therefore secured letters of safe-conduct from John for three of his retainers—Sir Thomas Cok, Sir Stephen de Cosington and Stephen Rumbelow—to go to Paris on his behalf to discuss the matter with Brunswick. The meeting took place in the church of the convent of the Blessed Mary, where Lancaster's envoys produced a letter from Henry which contained the text of Brunswick's challenge, which they asked if he had sent. When Brunswick affirmed that he had, they produced a second letter which argued that since this was the case Lancaster was the offended party and that it was up to Brunswick to secure a safe-conduct for the duke and his retinue and to meet their costs in coming to Paris to settle the matter in the king's court.[24]

The hearing was fixed for 1 September. On 23 August Lancaster secured Edward III's authorization 'to go beyond the seas to excuse himself in respect of things wickedly laid to his charge by the duke of Brunswick' and for a retinue of an earl and sixty men to accompany him.[25] He did not, however, appear in court personally; but Cosington and Rumbelow acted as his proctors in the hearing before King John at Saint-Denis on 4 September. They argued that whoever was declared the plaintiff should bear the costs of the defendant and that the money should be handed over immediately upon judgement. Brunswick protested that he did not have the necessary money with him and that in any case he was the defendant. After much debate it was agreed that payment could be held over. John declared Lancaster the offended party and arranged for the combat to be held in the Pré-aux-Clercs at Saint-Germain-des-Prés on 4 December.

Knighton gives a fascinating account of the duke's journey to Paris and of his magnificent reception there.[26] He crossed to Calais at the beginning of December with a retinue of fifty knights and was met by the marshal of France, Jean de Clermont, at the time the king's lieutenant in Picardy, as he was approaching Guines. Conducted from there to Hesdin in great state, Jacques de Bourbon, subsequently constable of France, then accompanied him to Paris in equal honour. As he approached the city he was met by a multitude of people and the crowds on either side of the walls are said to have pressed so greatly upon his route that it was quite impossible to see him during the course of that day. As he made his way through the throngs John sent for him to come to the royal palace of the Louvre, where he was again received very honourably and his company sought after, especially, we are told, by Louis de Male.[27]

In an attempt to reconcile the two dukes, John gave King Charles of Navarre and count of Évreux, the dauphin and several others of his council the task of negotiating an agreement. Their approaches were, however, of no avail and no solution was reached before the day appointed for the combat. Everything was therefore prepared for the duel to take place at the Pré-aux-Clercs as scheduled.[28] Charles of Navarre, the duke of Burgundy and many French peers and notables were present along with John, who had a dais specially constructed for the occasion with velvet walls decorated with fleurs-de-lis and surmounted by a large canopy depicting a horse.[29] The duke of Brunswick was led into the lists by the king's sons and Lancaster was presented by Charles and Philip of Navarre;[30] but after the two dukes had sworn their oaths and were ready for battle, King John ordered the constable of France to lead them out of the lists in order that he might settle the quarrel himself. Knighton and Baker did their utmost to make the duke the victor in the situation.[31] According to Baker:

> ... in the lists, in the presence of the king of France, the king of Navarre and the duke of Burgundy and many peers and others of the realm of France, he mounted his horse in a seemly manner, ready in all signs without default to try the combat. And so he remained until his adversary was ready and the voice of the herald and the caution to be had by their common oath for the assurance of his word and to obey the law. On the contrary part the said Otto was scarcely seated upon his horse and was not able decently to put his helmet on or wield his lance—or else he feigned. Perceiving his inability, the king of France took the quarrel into his hands; whereupon Otto was commanded first to leave the lists and so went his way while the duke remained within them. After this, by command of the king of France, Otto swore that he would never after that day accuse the duke of Lancaster of that article ...

King John's letter of reconciliation says no more on the subject than that the contestants entered the lists in their armour and had their lances raised when, unwilling to see such valiant knights fight for so futile a purpose, he ordered the constable to lead them out of the lists and declared that since what Lancaster had said in Cologne cathedral was other than what had been reported to Duke Otto there was no cause for a duel and no cause for costs. The decision was taken by the king in council and the letters of reconciliation were drawn up and sealed in Paris on 9 December.[32]

On the evening of 4 December John gave a banquet in honour of the contestants at the Louvre, then in the course of reconstruction by his master mason Raymond du Temple, when the constable and one of the marshals of France waited on them at table. Knighton reports how, after the meal was over, the king offered Lancaster a choice of many presents, all of which he declined save one thorn from that half of the crown of Christ which lay in the Sainte-Chapelle and which he brought home and subsequently placed in his college of the Newarke at Leicester.[34]

Concern for his welfare was felt by many of his friends: the consuls of Bergerac sent a messenger to Paris for news of him, John of Paris brought news to the king and 'letters of the good expedition of the lord duke at Paris' to Leicester corporation. Abbot Clown of Leicester also had news of him and sent one of his servants to convey it to the corporation; a Welsh runner subsequently brought news of his safe return to Calais. He arrived back in England in time to join Edward who was spending Christmas at St Albans and whose congratulations were said to have been profuse.[35]

# IX  Guy de Boulogne and papal endeavours for peace (1352-1353)

Lancaster's expedition to Prussia and his visit to Paris had a decisive effect on the subsequent course of events, for they afforded him an opportunity to assess the reported divisions in the French court and to make a number of valuable personal contacts. Whilst he was in the French capital, Cardinal Guy de Boulogne, acting on instructions from Clement VI, approached him about a renewal of negotiations for peace. He discussed the matter with the duke and several of Edward's councillors who were then with him (Sir Reginald de Cobham, William FitzWarin, Sir John de Lisle and Bartholomew de Burghersh) and together they arranged for a conference to be held at Guines early in the following year. On 9 December, the day King John reconciled Lancaster and the duke of Brunswick, the cardinal wrote to Edward asking him to send Henry and other members of his 'secret council' to Calais for 2 February 1353 in order that negotiations could be conducted with the French and when, as he explained to Lancaster, he would do everything in his power to bring the two sides into agreement.[1]

Circumstances were in the cardinal's favour. On 6 December 1352, Pope Clement VI died at Avignon and the conclave of cardinals which assembled to elect his successor proclaimed Étienne Aubert (a distinguished jurist born at the village of Monts near Pompadour in Limousin) as Pope Innocent VI.[2] Almost immediately Guy de Boulogne returned to Avignon where his proposals were eagerly taken up by the new pope who was determined to bring the two great Christian kingdoms of the West into concord. On 26 January Innocent sent him back to Paris and on the same day he wrote to Lancaster and King John urging them to co-operate with him.[3] The stage was thus set for another round of top-level discussions for peace.

There were several newcomers to the subsequent conferences that were held at Guines, quite apart from the cardinal who acted as mediator. The English embassy, who were given their procuration on 19 February, included Simon Islip, archbishop of Canterbury, and Richard Fitzalan, earl of Arundel, along with the bishop of Norwich, Lancaster, Guy Brian and Michael de Northburgh. Nearly all the French envoys were new to the discussions: Guillaume Bertran, bishop of Beauvais, Robert le Coq, bishop of Laon, Pierre, duke of Bourbon, Charles of Spain, constable of France, and Robert de Lorris; only Pierre de la Forêt, archbishop of Rouen, and Jean de Boulogne, count of Montfort, had served before. There was thus some possibility of a fresh start to the negotiations and although for lack of time and other reasons an agreement was not concluded at their first meeting, the discussions appear to have gone well. On 10 March the truce was extended until 1 August and it provided for the envoys to reassemble 'between the castle of Guines and the *bastide*' on 20 May to continue the negotiations for peace.[4]

Innocent VI had great hopes for the forthcoming conference under the chairmanship of Guy de Boulogne. On 28 April he requested the English envoys to do everything in their power to arrive at a settlement with the French and during the first fortnight of May three procurations were issued to the cardinal which gave him extensive powers to bring about a peace treaty.[5] The first, issued on 4 May, empowered him to annul and revoke all pacts and confederations made by the two kings, their nobles, or others, which might hinder the conclusion of peace; the second, issued on 6 May, empowered him to confirm and ratify treaties of peace between John and Edward and their adherents; the third, issued on 13 May, empowered him to enforce observation of the same by ecclesiastical censure.

But the meeting arranged for 20 May did not take place. In a letter written to the cardinal towards the end of April, the English envoys related how Edward had called a council of prelates and barons to discuss the matters treated at Guines and how, owing to illness and for other unavoidable reasons, it had been poorly attended. He had therefore been obliged to postpone the discussions until 16 May and, they added, parliament was not due to assemble until 29 August. It was consequently impossible for them to be at Guines on the day arranged.[6] From this account, and in view of the procurations issued to the cardinal, it would appear that the negotiations of February–March had proceeded some way and that the envoys referred to meetings of council and parliament in which Edward proposed to secure assent to the conclusion of a formal treaty.

The cardinal received the envoys' letter on 3 May. In his reply, written in Paris two days later and sent with his familiar *Bernart*, he said that several of the French envoys who had attended the conference at Guines and several others of John's councillors suspected Edward's reasons for the delay. Some of them were astonished at it. He explained how John had called together his prelates and barons, together with the envoys whom he had sent to Guines, and how they had discussed the matters treated with the English envoys. However, he concluded that, for reasons which he could not reveal at the time of writing, the French envoys were themselves unable to reassemble at Guines before 29 August, but in the meantime arrangements would have to be made for the extension of the truce.[7]

To this end, on 10 July Lancaster and the other English envoys who had been sent to Guines in February were appointed to extend the truce until 11 November; but in the event they never left England.[8] On 15 July John de Welwick was sent from London with instructions from the king for the archbishop of Canterbury and other members of the king's council, very likely the other members of the embassy appointed five days previous. Having delivered Edward's instructions, whatever they were, he made his way to Paris and elsewhere to see Guy de Boulogne.[9] It was in the French capital that, on 26 July 1353, the truce was extended until 11 November and arrangements were made for the envoys to return to Guines before its expiry to negotiate further on a peace.[10] Welwick was back from Paris on 21 September, when he reported to the king and council; between then and 13 December he was sent on three further missions to the cardinal.

Fortunately, there is evidence to show why Edward did not send an embassy to Guines to continue the negotiations which were well under way in March. In effect, on 1 March, he had concluded an alliance with Charles of Blois, the French candidate in the Breton succession dispute, who had been a prisoner in England since his capture at La Roche-Dérien in 1347.[11] If, as has been suggested, this treaty was primarily concluded to secure an advantageous arrangement with France, it may be that Edward was not satisfied with the French offers discussed at Guines at the very time that the alliance was concluded with Blois and which, whatever it may have amounted to, appears to have raised considerable hopes at the time.

Instead of continuing with negotiations as arranged, Edward sent his confessor John de Woderone to Avignon with details of his conditions for peace to be delivered to the pope. Woderone was to begin by expressing to the pope the English king's desire for peace. He was then to convey his sovereign's demands for the conclusion of a treaty with the French, which were as follows: the restitution of the duchy of Aquitaine as fully as his ancestors had held it, the duchy of Normandy, the county of Ponthieu, all of the lands which he had conquered from his adversary in France, Brittany and elsewhere, and the obedience of Flanders which he claimed to possess. He demanded all of these territories in full sovereignty, to be held freely and without homage or other service; in return he would agree to give up his claim to the French throne. He was willing, however, to give up Normandy if it could be shown that John had an overt right to it. Woderone was to suggest that Innocent should sound the French king privately on these proposals, and he was to make it clear to him that Edward would not agree to a peace treaty on any other conditions.[12]

It is not clear at what point Edward sent his confessor to the curia with these instructions; but towards the end of July a memorandum was issued to the papal nuncio Raymond Pelegrini explaining how he was to promote negotiations for peace between the two kings.[13] When he arrived in France he was first to get instructions from Guy de Boulogne. He was then to secure an audience with John, to express to him the pope's desire for peace and to explain how Innocent had been intending to send nuncios to the two kings on the subject when he heard that the cardinal and Lancaster had already arranged a conference. To Edward, Pelegrini was to say that the pope was distressed that the negotiations were taking so long and that an agreement had not been reached within the prescribed time. He was not, however, to mention Innocent's annoyance that Edward had not sent his envoys to the meeting arranged for May, when it had been hoped a treaty would be concluded. He was to feel his way cautiously with the two kings and others as to whether the mediation of the cardinal would be agreeable for future peace talks, or whether they would prefer him to send other nuncios. On this point Innocent was willing to make considerable concessions to the English. Since the pope was not clear whether the truce had been extended until 11 November or until Easter, Pelegrini was to inquire into the matter. If it was only until 11 November he was to procure a prolongation until 24 June 1354, but if until Easter he was not to mention a further extension unless Guy de Boulogne saw fit.

It is clear from Welwick's expense account that negotiations were being pursued with the cardinal throughout the summer.[14] Meanwhile Edward, having received no news from Woderone, sent the archdeacon of Huntingdon, William de Witleseye, to the curia to request Innocent for an answer to the proposals made on his behalf by his confessor.[15]

A fairly clear idea of what followed may be had from a letter of the pope to the cardinal dated 2 August. Innocent began by relating how, after Pelegrini had left Avignon, Witleseye arrived at the curia to get a reply to the proposals put to him by Woderone. He told the archdeacon that, immediately after the confessor's departure, he had sent André de la Roche, abbot of Saint-Seine and Cluny, to John and to the cardinal touching the matters in question, but that he had not yet had an answer from the French king. Nevertheless, he must not be surprised if John refused to give way to Edward's demands as laid before him by the confessor, nor must he be surprised that John had not yet replied to him since it was not so long since the confessor had left Avignon. The Pope conferred with Witleseye touching the conclusion of peace and informed him of Pelegrini's mission. It was then that the archdeacon disclosed Edward's suspicions that the cardinal was partial to the French and that the king therefore refused to continue with negotiations under the chairmanship of Guy de Boulogne. Innocent immediately consulted with some of the cardinals then at the curia and with the constable of France, Charles of Spain, and requested the two kings to send solemn envoys to Avignon furnished with full powers to treat in his presence of a definitive peace. The cardinal was requested to do everything he could to obtain John's agreement to the project and to let the pope know the names of the French envoys and when they would arrive at Avignon. Pelegrini was to secure Edward's approval. Both were also to arrange another conference between Calais and Guines in order that the truce might be renewed for a year or two, since negotiations for peace could be expected to take a long time. The same day Innocent wrote to John, Edward and Pelegrini informing them of his proposals and requesting their agreement.[16]

Edward was unlikely to accede to the pope's plans unless John agreed to his terms. In an account of the negotiations given in the White Chamber on 7 October, Bartholomew de Burghersh explained that no positive answer had been given to the king's peace proposals and that it had therefore been agreed in council that preparations should be made for war.[17] Since money would be needed for the purpose the subsidy was renewed for a year—for a further two years if war broke out—but appropriated to the war. None the less, in accordance with the July truce extension, on 6 November English envoys were given their procuration to treat of peace and the extension of the truce.[18] Two days later Edward wrote to Innocent proclaiming his ardent desire for peace, pointing out that his envoys were already at Dover on their way to Guines and stating that Pelegrini would reveal the sincerity of his desire for a lasting settlement.[19] The English envoys left their various residences in England between 2 and 12 November, and once again crossed to Calais on board the *Tromphorn*.[20] Since the truce was due to expire on 11 November, an extension of two weeks had already been concluded for the Picardy region and once the envoys assembled at Guines this was extended until 30 December on the request of Guy de Boulogne.[21] Negotiations were thereby facilitated on the main truce, which on 13 December was extended until 7 April 1354, the envoys having agreed to meet again at the customary place on 23 March.[22]

# X  A mission in Holland (1354)

Upon the conclusion of the truce Lancaster went straight on from Guines to the Low Countries, where he was to negotiate a treaty of alliance with William, duke of Bavaria, count of Holland and Zeeland, whom he was also to reconcile with his mother the Empress Margaret, countess of Hainault.[1] As he explained in a letter to Charles of Navarre, the negotiations were of particular concern to him since two years earlier William had married his eldest daughter Maude.[2] He therefore had a personal interest in the settlement of a quarrel between mother and son which had begun on the death of Margaret's brother, Count William III d'Avesnes, at Stavoren in Friesland in September 1345. But much more was at stake than the happiness and well-being of Lancaster's daughter. Once again Edward's aim was to gain a foothold in the Low Countries, recently denied him by Louis de Male; Maude had been married as an instrument of English policy. Her father's mission to Holland and Zeeland was intended to see that it bore fruit.

William III had left behind him a disputed succession.[3] Since he died without heirs of his body, the nearest of kin were his sisters Margaret, wife of the Emperor Lewis of Bavaria, Philippa, wife of Edward III, and Johanna, wife of William, margrave of Juliers. William's lands were all fiefs of the empire, and the emperor could claim that Holland and Zeeland had fallen vacant and hence should revert to the sovereign. On the other hand, it could be argued that the patrimony of the house of Avesnes should be partitioned among the three sisters. The latter was apparently the view entertained by Edward, who actively pursued Philippa's claim in the winter of 1345–6 and who was thought to be making preparations to invade Zeeland. Philip VI, on the other hand, gave his support to Margaret's claim to the entire inheritance and it looked as if the succession would be dragged into the main stream of the Anglo-French conflict. For the moment, however, both kings were too preoccupied to think of active intervention.

In January 1346 the emperor was therefore able to grant the entire inheritance to his wife and in the following spring she made a tour of her possessions and secured recognition as sovereign. Before she returned to Germany she appointed her second son William governor or *stadtholder* of all these territories with a free hand in their administration during her absence.

Whatever hopes Edward may have entertained were for the moment dashed. But in the following year, when the Emperor Lewis died unexpectedly, he allied himself with the other disaffected party—the margrave of Juliers—and with the arch-enemy of the Bavarian family, the newly elected Charles IV of Luxemburg. Margaret's position was further weakened by the hostility of Brabant, also allied with Charles, and by a fresh outbreak of civil war in the provinces. All these circumstances induced her to resign Holland, Zeeland and Friesland to her son, but to retain Hainault, where William was only to remain governor. In return she was to receive certain sums of money in compensation and her friends were to be maintained in the offices which they held of her appointment. The government of the counties might then have been settled once and for all had not William, who assumed the title of count, failed to enforce his part of the agreement with his mother. Margaret therefore returned from Bavaria in 1350 and the counties divided into two camps.

Unable to turn elsewhere, Margaret now sought the assistance of her brother-in-law and rival claimant, Edward III. Edward immediately welcomed this opportunity to regain a foothold in the Low Countries. Without abandoning his claims to the inheritance he agreed to act as arbitrator between mother and son. He accepted the custody of Holland, Zeeland and Friesland, and in October Sir Walter Mauny, William de Burton, Sir William Stury, and Ivo de Glinton were commissioned to secure them in his name and were empowered to treat with both Margaret and William for an alliance.[4] It was hoped that an agreement might be reached within the year but, since this proved impossible, on 6 December Sir Nigel Loring, Stury, Glinton and Stephen Rumbelow were given a commission to discuss the government of the counties.[5] Glinton, who had only arrived back from Antwerp on 13 December, left for Zierickzee in Zeeland six days later.[6] But no solution seems to have been found and on 20 March 1351 Lancaster was given charge of an English embassy (which included the dean of Wells, John de Carlton, and Andrew de Ufford, archdeacon of Middlesex) again to arrange an alliance with Margaret and William.[7]

These attempts at negotiation failed; William allied with the bishop of Utrecht, the counties were divided into two parties and a major conflict was imminent. Less than a fortnight before the commission to treat was issued to Lancaster, he was appointed one of the two standing admirals.[8] A fleet was fitted out to assist Margaret and it advanced on Veer in the isle of Walcheren in May, when an indecisive victory was achieved. It seems fairly clear that Lancaster played no part in this, since on 12 May Sir Walter Mauny was given charge of the diplomatic mission and instructed to give Margaret all possible assistance if he failed to bring her into agreement with William.[9] After the engagement at Veer, the remainder of William's fleet retired to the Meuse to be re-equipped. On 4 July the Anglo-Dutch fleet which followed him to subdue Holland was defeated in a sanguinary battle which was fought between Vlaardingen and Brill. This was decisive. Margaret was forced to leave Zeeland and take refuge in Hainault. Her followers were banished, many of their castles destroyed and their property and offices redistributed. Since Edward's mediation was her only hope, she retreated to England and in December 1351 placed the three strongholds which her party still held in Holland in his hands: Geertrudenberg, the fortress of Vreeland on the Amstel and Heemskerk in Kennenmerland. But William was in a stronger position to negotiate with Edward than was his mother. On 18 July, a fortnight after his victory at Brill, letters of safe-conduct were issued to him and his retinue, also coming to England.[10] Both parties now agreed to the king's arbitration and in November Sir William Stury and Willam de Burton were appointed to assume control of all the castles and fortresses then under siege in Holland and Zeeland.[11] Edward pointed out, however, that he did not intend to use them against the dukes of Brabant and Guelders or the count of Flanders.

It was doubtless quite clear to Edward and the council that support for William was now the most profitable course to adopt. Some time before November 1351 arrangements were made for the marriage of Lancaster's eldest daughter to the count. On the 12th of that month letters of protection were again issued to William and his retinue coming to England, where his proctors were instructed to collect Maude for the marriage, which was duly celebrated in the King's Chapel at Westminster early in the following year, apparently after Lancaster had set out on his expedition to Prussia.[12] A settlement was then made whereby William was confirmed in the possession of Holland and Zeeland, provided that he paid an annual rent to his mother, who was to keep Hainault.[13] Bereft of English assistance Margaret returned to her faithful county in the spring.[14]

An alliance with William had, however, not yet been concluded. With this end in view, on 10 December 1352 Andrew de Ufford and John Avenel were appointed to treat with the count.[15] It was probably on the basis of the negotiations conducted by them that, on 17 February following, the day Lancaster left London for the first truce conference under the chairmanship of Guy de Boulogne, he was given the text of a treaty of alliance to take to William for his confirmation.[16] By the terms of this agreement either party was to provide the other with naval and military assistance whenever required, peace was not to be concluded with France without Edward's agreement and unless William was specifically included, merchants were to be free to come and go between the two countries and the subjects of either sovereign were not to be arrested whilst in the other's country.

It is clear that Lancaster did not go on to the Low Countries after the truce conference in the spring,[17] but on 14 October following he was again commissioned to negotiate a treaty of alliance with William and to bring him into agreement with his mother, with whom he was again in conflict.[18] On this occasion he went straight on to the Low Countries from Guines and early in 1354 he arranged a meeting with the councils of mother and son and several friends of either party at Antwerp.[19] The mission was absolutely without success. Even Lancaster was unable to mediate an agreement between his son-in-law and Margaret, and William refused to ratify the alliance.[20] It was not until 7 December following that mother and son were reconciled at Mons.[21] William agreed to pay his mother a large sum down and an annuity, he was recognized as count of Holland, Zeeland and Friesland and she as countess of Hainault. Prisoners of either side were to be freed and both were to forgive and forget. Thibaut Maulion, sergeant of Mons, was sent to Avignon by Maude to convey the news to her father, then involved in negotiations for peace with France.[22] But the quarrel did not really come to an end until July 1356 when Margaret died at Quesnoy in Hainault and for a short while William was able to enjoy the government of the entire disputed territories.[23]

For Maude it must have been a most unhappy marriage. Taken away from home at the age of thirteen, given as bride to William in Lancaster's absence, she only saw her father once again, in the Low Countries for the Christmas of 1353. After a visit to England in 1357 her husband began to show signs of insanity; in the following year he was confined to the Hague and was later removed to the strong castle of Quesnoy, where he dragged out a miserable existence for 31 years.[24] Contemporaries hinted at poison administered to him whilst in England and the Leicester chronicler tells us that when Maude died in 1362, it was popularly believed that she too had been poisoned in order that the entire Lancastrian inheritance might pass to John of Gaunt, Henry's second son-in-law.[25]

# XI Charles of Navarre and the abortive treaty of Guines (1354-1355)

On 8 January 1354 King John's son-in-law Charles, king of Navarre and lord of a number of fiefs in Normandy, had the constable of France, Charles of Spain (a cadet of the royal family of Castile of the House of La Cerda and favourite of King John) ambushed and murdered on his Norman lands at Laigle. Although he was then only in his early twenties (he was born in 1332), he was a plausible and ambitious young man, cunning, energetic, and he harboured several grievances which had led to a feud against the Valois dynasty.[1]

To begin with, his mother had been excluded from the succession to the throne of France and had he been born earlier he would have had a better claim to it than had Edward III. Nor had a dowry which had been promised to him on the occasion of his marriage to John's daughter Joan ever been paid. A more immediate grievance was his exclusion from the counties of Angoulême and Mortain and three castles in Poitou which should have been given to his mother, among other things, in compensation for the counties of Champagne and Brie. Shortly before her death in 1349 a new arrangement was concluded by which Angoulême and two of the castles were to be exchanged for three castellanies around Paris. But John had kept Angoulême without giving anything in compensation and it was the grant of the county to Charles of Spain that finally precipitated the murder at Laigle.

Two days later, on 10 January, the young king of Navarre wrote to Edward III, the Black Prince, Lancaster and others explaining the reasons for his action and seeking their protection from King John's wrath. 'Know that it was I', he insolently boasted, 'who had the constable killed.' He thanked Lancaster for letters in which the duke had offered to help him, and he requested him to collect forces at Calais and Guines for action when required. He sought the co-operation of Edward's captain and lieutenant in Brittany in order that the Breton forces might act in conjunction with Navarrese garrisons in the Cotentin. Eight days later, without awaiting replies to his first letters, he once more wrote to Edward and Lancaster, this time in more pressing terms, requesting the duke's assistance and insisting upon the imminent peril in which John's wrath placed him. He pointed out to Edward that he held strong, fully garrisoned and well-supplied castles —notably in Normandy—and that the Norman nobility was behind him to a man. Such an opportunity to renew the war was too good to be missed.

Little more than a year had passed since Lancaster had met Charles and his two brothers in Paris. He had obviously acquired a very clear picture of the divisions in the French court and he may have made overtures to Charles then.[2] It is not clear precisely what proposals he had put to the young king in his letters, nor is it clear when he had made them; but it is perhaps significant that Charles' letters of 10 January for the king and the Black Prince were sent to Lancaster, to be forwarded to England only if the duke saw fit, and that they were neither as long nor as specific as those which he wrote to Henry. It was of the duke alone, and not of Edward and the prince, that he requested forces to be sent to Calais and Guines. These were to be under the duke's personal command and it was the duke whom he proposed to meet there.

Lancaster was at Malines in Brabant, endeavouring to reconcile the Empress Margaret with his son-in-law when (probably on 18 January) he received Charles' first letter. He immediately sent Walter de Byntre —a household sergeant long in his service—direct to Évreux with a set of instructions and a written reply which completed them. The text of the reply does not appear to be extant but there is a copy of the *credence* given to Byntre—the set of instructions laying down just what he was to propose to Charles.

He was to begin by expressing Lancaster's sympathy, but was to point out that it was difficult for the duke to come to his assistance immediately since he was preoccupied in the Low Countries. He was, however, to add that if things became really critical he would postpone the mission on which he was then engaged in order to help right away. Since the forces which accompanied him amounted to no more than a few men-at-arms and no archers, to be of any real assistance he would need to return to England to assemble his troops and obtain Edward's permission to help him. To facilitate further negotiations he was to inform Charles that he would be at Bruges by 31 January or 1 February and would await the young king's envoys there. He was to request that these envoys should be given such powers as the duke would secure for himself—full powers to treat—and that they should be fully instructed in the way he could most help Charles. He was to recommend that the lord of Fricamps be included in the embassy, since he was already well known in England. He was to tell Charles that he had sent the letters for Edward, the Black Prince, the queen and the queen mother on to the king by way of one of his esquires and that he would shortly have news from them which should please him very much. He had instructed the esquire to be at Bruges by 1 February with the replies to these letters.

There were two reasons why he had chosen Bruges for the *rendezvous*: it was possible to get there just as quickly and more safely than it was to get to Calais and, in meeting there, he would be able to resume his former mission should Charles not require his services immediately. He was to caution the young king against coming to Bruges in person and was to tell him that Normandy was certainly the best place for the disembarkation of English troops. But he was also to point out that the matter would have to be determined by Edward, the prince and the council.

Meanwhile, Edward was in touch with Lancaster by way of John de Warrington, doubtless the esquire whom the duke had sent to England with Charles' and his own letters—a messenger bearing royal instructions for him and whom the duke subsequently sent to Bruges to secure a safe-conduct for Sir Walter Mauny, whom the king was sending out there.[3] On 26 January a procuration containing full powers to treat with Charles was issued to the duke.[4]

Lancaster was then at Malines. On the same day he received Charles' second letter and by way of reply he reiterated the position which he had previously stated. He did his utmost to dissuade Charles from negotiating with King John and once again promised his assistance. He pointed out that he could not come straight to Calais because he had bound himself on oath to see that the truce was observed and if he began operations in those parts, it would be obvious to everyone that he had committed a flagrant violation of its terms and perjured himself in the bargain. He concluded by pointing out that he could come to his assistance from England just as quickly as he could from Calais since the young king's possessions in Normandy were more accessible by sea.

Five days later, after Byntre had arrived at Évreux but probably before Charles received Lancaster's reply to his second letter, credentials were issued to the chancellor of Navarre, Tomás de Ladit, and to

Friquet de Fricamps empowering them to treat with Lancaster in Charles' name. The details of their journey to Bruges were subsequently recorded from a statement made by Fricamps during his interrogation in the Châtelet in Paris two years later. During the course of the questioning it transpired that the Navarrese envoys were accompanied by two of Charles' household officers called Pierre de la Tennerie and Gil de Bantelu. As a measure of safety the four of them travelled in pairs and did not meet again until they arrived in Flanders. Byntre, who appears to have left Évreux at the same time, was the first to arrive in Bruges, where the negotiations took place early in February. The duke is said to have received the Navarrese envoys with the greatest courtesy and to have offered to accompany Fricamps to England where he would arrange an audience with the king for him. He intimated to the chancellor that he might enter English service and become 'as good an Englishman as he had previously been a Frenchman'. Further details of their conversation were not recorded, since the two of them withdrew into the recess of a window where they could not be overheard.

Fricamps did not take up Lancaster's proposal to go to England, but on returning from Bruges he informed Charles of the duke's good disposition towards him and of his willingness to come to his assistance with a force of 200 men-at-arms and 500 archers. At least this is the story that was told during the interrogation. But was it the whole story?

It is unlikely that Charles was already aware of John's willingness to treat before he dispatched his envoys to Bruges, though this has been suggested. Arrangements were made and a date was fixed for the landing of English troops in Normandy under the duke's command and these were embodied in a projected treaty of alliance between Edward and Charles (cf. below, pp. 141–3). Upon the conclusion of negotiations Lancaster returned to England, where he arrived in London on 17 February.[5] Four days later the sheriff of Southampton was instructed to have delivered to him the equipment necessary for the embarkation of 1,000 horses and on 6 March John Gibbon was appointed admiral of a fleet destined for Normandy with an army under the duke's command.[6] But by the time the Navarrese envoys returned from Flanders—possibly around 10 or 12 February—the situation had changed abruptly. Guy de Boulogne, who had left Avignon for the north of France[7] and who had reason to believe from the discussions at Guines that the terms of a peace were at last within reach, had persuaded John to treat with Charles and to allow him to arrange a reconciliation between them.

On 8 February the cardinal was empowered, together with the duke of Bourbon, to grant Charles in lands and rents the inheritance of which he had been deprived and to issue letters of pardon to all those involved in the murder of the constable. Negotiations took place at Mantes in Normandy and it was there that, a fortnight later (22 February), an agreement was concluded between the two kings.

The terms were very generous. In return for the three castellanies around Paris, John ceded to Charles territories which, together with his hereditary lands, made him the lord of half of the duchy of Normandy and they included a large part of the Cotentin peninsula, including the port of Cherbourg. To surrender so much territory John had obviously been very frightened by the prospect of an Anglo-Navarrese alliance and had clearly been willing to concede anything that might put it off. But for Guy de Boulogne the issue at stake was above all else the peace for which he had been working for over a year and which the papacy had striven to bring about since the outset of the war. Only in the light of subsequent events did the terms which he had offered Charles seem too generous.

On 21 February, the day prior to the conclusion of the treaty, Charles dispatched two mounted valets to Lancaster with a letter informing him of the negotiations with the French. Was the duke to expect that these would be taking place? Whatever the case, he pointed out that the negotiations were taking longer than he had anticipated—longer than a term that had been agreed upon at Bruges. He therefore requested the duke to remain in a state of military preparedness until 12 March, intimating that by that date he would have good news of him in London. There could be no doubt that his intervention would be necessary. Not until 1 March, a week after the conclusion of the treaty of Mantes, did he again write to the duke to inform him of the agreement with John. In this letter he expressed his satisfaction with the entire French court: with the two queens—his aunt Joan and sister Blanche—who had intervened on his behalf, with the cardinal of Boulogne and other royal councillors, and even with King John whom he had found 'altogether reasonable'. He had been pardoned the murder of the constable and had been restored in his inheritance; the cession of almost half of the Cotentin had given him a particularly strong position in Normandy—it had been impossible to refuse such generous terms. The duke could therefore abandon all the preparations which he had made to come to his assistance. He thanked him profusely for all that he had done, undertook to serve him with equal devotion whenever his assistance might be required and concluded with a warning that 'all the Norman ports, especially those where the king's men think it most likely that you will disembark, have recently been well supplied and re-enforced with ships and men'. The following day he wrote a much shorter letter to Edward III informing him of the conclusion of the treaty with John.

Lancaster received Charles' letter in London on 11 March, but he had first heard the news from Guy de Boulogne in a sarcastic letter which had arrived the previous day. In his reply to Charles, written in the capital on 13 March, he did not attempt to hide his amazement at the treaty concluded with John, especially in view of the young king's communication of 21 February. On the point of completing this agreement, he should immediately have instructed the duke to abandon all military preparations in his favour. Lancaster complained that he had continued to maintain a fleet with 500 men-at-arms, and 1,000 archers on board until he had received Charles' letter of 1 March.[8] If Charles had trusted in his assistance he would not, the duke thought, have secured worse terms; that he had not abided by the arrangements which they had made he found far from pleasing. He reminded him of a letter which he had received from the young king at Malines, in which Charles had stated that he had many good friends by whom he was well protected, friends who had counselled him that if he attempted to conclude a peace with John it would lead to exile and destruction for himself and them. He hoped that those friends would now listen to and understand him and that he would be sufficiently well protected and secure in his possessions as to have no need to remember the counsel and the protection that the duke had offered. Before the year was out events were to prove both Charles and Lancaster right.

Guy de Boulogne's letter is only known to us from Lancaster's reply, written in London on 17 March. It is evident from this letter that he had written to the duke primarily to inform him of arrangements which he had made for the forthcoming conference at Guines. But he could not restrain himself from alluding to his diplomatic success at Mantes. He had prevented the threatened violation of the truce. 'The hole' by which the duke had planned to slip into France had been 'sealed'. He would have to seek another entrance to the kingdom.

In his reply Lancaster admitted that in reconciling Charles with John the cardinal had upset his plans. In this sense the hole had been sealed. 'Nevertheless', he warned him, 'we know of other holes which are not yet sealed and which we have not forgotten. And, although we do not doubt that your intelligence and your perception are very considerable, you cannot stuff up all the holes. For there is a saying which you know well, "A mouse which knows of only one hole is often in peril". Therefore, very reverend and very dear sir, on this day which is fast approaching [for the conference at Guines at the end of the month], you will need to be very diligent and take pains to see that all the holes are safely stuffed up and sealed. We pray God that he will give you the grace to honour and care for my lord the king and all his friends, and may Our Lord have you in His holy keeping.'

But the cardinal, who also prided himself in being a man of some wit, wished to have the last word. In a letter which he wrote to the duke three weeks later, he feigned astonishment at the sentiments which had led the duke to offer his assistance to Charles. Undoubtedly, he would find friends equally zealous and equally devoted should he ever murder one of Edward III's dearest friends; he was free to try it out—the joke could have been in better taste. Resurrecting the allusion to the mouse which needs to know of several holes in order to escape peril, he added that all the passages that gave access to the kingdom were well guarded. All the same, he greatly regretted that the duke had been unable to attend the conference which by that time had taken place at Guines. 'If God wishes it', he concluded, 'you will shortly see that, although we are now rebuking you in these letters, we shall certainly always willingly and with all our heart do what you wish.' The promise was not an empty one.

There can be no doubt that, in the immediate circumstances, Lancaster had suffered a serious diplomatic defeat and that it was bound to make itself felt in the negotiations at Guines. He had been taken in by Charles of Navarre and outmanoeuvred by Guy de Boulogne. It was the cardinal who, for the moment, held the trump cards. He had prevented a recourse to arms not only by the treaty of Mantes, but also by the terms of the truce concluded in December. It had been impossible for Lancaster to come to Charles' assistance immediately at Calais and by the time the Navarrese envoys had returned to Normandy from Flanders it was already too late. The cardinal was now in a stronger position to press the preliminaries of a peace. But Lancaster had done everything that he could in a difficult situation. The arrangements which he had made for the negotiations at Bruges, as laid down in the instructions given to Byntre, had been concluded prior to his receipt of powers to treat with Charles. He had thus kept the young king interested whilst he got into touch with Edward, but without committing himself or the king. He had acted independently in an emergency situation, neither having obliged Edward's support by acting beyond his powers, nor having surrendered the king's interests by failing to act at all. If Charles had double-crossed him it was hardly his fault. It was better to have tried and failed than never to have tried at all. For he had given the young king every reason to believe that he was a friend and, of however little value that might have been personally, it was to prove of great value territorially.

The climax to all this diplomatic activity came in the winter of 1354–5. On 6 April 1354 a draft peace treaty was 'initialled' at Guines.[9] For obvious reasons Lancaster had nothing directly to do with these preliminary negotiations. His name did not appear on the commission issued to the English envoys on 30 March[10] and in his letter of 17 March to Guy de Boulogne he had stated that the king did not wish him to be present. In view of the cardinal's recent diplomatic victory it was hardly advisable that he should be. But it is clear that, in more ways than one, he had a great deal to do with the turn which the negotiations took on this occasion.

It has always been a little hard to understand how the treaty of Guines got so far as a formal draft, particularly since it is generally assumed to have been concluded in a very short space of time. It represented a compromise in that both sides gave up what they had hitherto regarded as the essential element in their negotiating position. The French were to surrender less territory than had been demanded of them in the summer of 1353, and rather more than they eventually surrendered in 1360: the duchy of Aquitaine, Poitou, Touraine, Anjou, Maine, Ponthieu, Limoges (if it was found that it did not belong to the duchy), Calais, Marck, Oye, Cologne, Sangatte and Guines; and they were to surrender it without any reservation of sovereignty. There is no mention now of Normandy, of Brittany—where Edward's forces and those of his Breton allies were well established—or of Flanders. In return Edward agreed to give up his claim to the throne of France. The solemn renunciations were to be made and all final questions of detail settled in the presence of the pope at Avignon before October.

It has been suggested that this was the treaty that Edward had long been seeking and that John, 'shaken by the Breton defection' and 'aghast at the Navarrese intrigue', was 'now ready for the worst of surrenders', and accepted peace preliminaries. But by the time these were 'initialled' the treaty of Westminster with Charles of Blois was over a year old[11] and six weeks had passed since Charles of Navarre had made his peace. There could be no question therefore of 'panic fear' on the part of King John. In many ways France was a good deal stronger than she had been on the morrow of the fall of Calais. Her influence was predominant in the Low Countries and significant acquisitions had been made on her eastern frontiers—in the Dauphiné, Savoy, Franche-Comté, Verdunois, the duchy of Bar and the bishopric of Cambrai.[12] The work of Charles of Navarre, Charles of Spain and the count of Armagnac as John's lieutenants in the south of France had done much to restore French control in Aquitaine.

It was the English, not the French, who had been brought to a surrender. For Edward's prospects were a good deal gloomier in the spring of 1354 than they had been at any time since 1347. His influence in the Low Countries was virtually non-existent: he had lost everything that he had ever held in Flanders and his plans had been frustrated in Holland and Zeeland. His attempts to renew the war in Gascony in 1349 and 1352 had in no way advanced his cause. The alliance with Charles of Navarre had not been concluded and he had been losing heavily in the competition for allegiances which had been going on in the French provinces. There was now something to be said for a profitable peace—not a complete surrender—but a compromise on good terms.

This change in Edward's fortunes had not occurred suddenly, but slowly and imperceptibly during the years of truce. He had not been rushed into peace proposals by Lancaster's failure with Charles of Navarre, but had been seriously considering them for some time when the alliance with Charles had unexpectedly been offered to him and just as quickly lost. In effect, the negotiations of 1353 had come very near to a peace and, although nothing positive had been concluded at the December meeting of envoys under the chairmanship of Guy de Boulogne, discussions had taken place and a measure of agreement reached that made it likely for a treaty to be concluded at the conference convoked for 23 March. A letter written to Lancaster by the cardinal from Lyon on 1 February, in reply to a communication from the duke (presumably dispatched before he had word from Charles of Navarre) which he had received at Vienne on the previous day, makes it quite clear that arrangements had been made for a meeting of envoys in mid-March to discuss the terms of a settlement.[13] For this purpose the English delegates were to cross over to France on 9 March—a fortnight before the conference was scheduled to begin. One can therefore understand Guy de Boulogne's concern over the Navarrese affair. It had threatened to change the situation drastically by offering to

Edward the alliance which he had been seeking in northern France. But with the conclusion of the treaty of Mantes the English position was no better than it had been before the murder of the constable. It may even have been worse.

It is in fact quite clear that a peace had been decided upon before the spring conference began. The terms of the treaty had obviously been very fully considered before the envoys left for Guines—between 18 and 23 March[14]—since they were specifically empowered to renounce all Edward's claims to the French throne,[15] and such powers had not been given in any previous procuration. It is also clear that the French envoys had been empowered to surrender such territories as were in question without reservation of sovereignty: this was already on the books by 10 March.[16]

Ironically enough, the murder of the constable, who had been among the French envoys at the conferences in 1353, may have helped the cardinal to reach his goal. The French delegates at the spring gathering were all ecclesiastics, over whom the cardinal was likely to have more influence, and they included two other friends of Charles of Navarre—Robert le Coq and the king's chamberlain Robert de Lorris, who had also been among the negotiators of the treaty of Mantes.

It is unlikely that we shall ever know what actually passed between the envoys and the cardinal at Guines, but it is clear that everything was not above board. It looks as if preliminary discussions were to have taken place before the conference officially opened and, although the Navarrese intrigue prevented the English delegates from leaving for France as scheduled on 9 March, it is clear that they left between 18 and 23 March—before their procuration was issued to them. A letter which was subsequently written by the cardinal to Lancaster, Arundel and Huntingdon, makes it clear that secret discussions took place which concerned the manner in which the negotiations at Avignon were to be conducted and that any disclosure of what had been concluded would not only cause a terrific scandal, but was also likely to wreck the treaty. In view of Guy de Boulogne's subsequent loss of favour with King John and his behaviour at Avignon in the following December, it is not difficult to surmise what had been arranged at Guines.

Almost immediately upon the return of the English embassy preparations were set afoot for the forthcoming conference. At a meeting of parliament in May, the king's chamberlain Bartholomew de Burghersh described the state of the negotiations and declared that the king would not accept the treaty without the assent of the Lords and the Commons.[17] To this the Commons replied that they would approve whatever the king and the Lords decided. When the chamberlain pressed them for a direct answer to his question—whether they would accept a perpetual peace if it could be obtained—they replied with a general shout of 'Yes, yes'; whereupon Michael de Northburgh, keeper of the king's privy seal and who had been one of the English envoys at Guines,[18] instructed a papal notary called John de Swynleye to draw up a public instrument as formal evidence of their wishes.

It is in fact quite clear that Edward was anxious to hurry up the proceedings. Early in May, Lancaster, together with the earls of Arundel and Huntingdon, wrote to Guy de Boulogne requesting a safe-conduct for Edward's confessor, John de Woderone, and Sir Richard de la Bere, who were being sent to the curia in a retinue of 30 riders in connection with the treaty. Safe-conducts were also requested for prelates and barons (without naming any) and for retinues amounting in all to 500 riders and 100 extra horses who were to leave for Avignon by way of Gascony on 24 June. But, as the cardinal pointed out in his reply from Paris on 27 May, it had been agreed at Guines that the English ambassadors should leave for the curia at the beginning of August in order that they might arrive at Avignon in September. Their plan to leave earlier had caused a good deal of speculation in Paris and, if they persisted in it, it was likely to result in the disclosure of the secret discussions held at Guines, with all the consequences which that was likely to entail. In the meantime the cardinal undertook to see to it that safe-conducts were sent for the confessor and the knight, but requested the earls to send the names of the ambassadors whom Edward proposed to send to the curia, together with the number of horses which each of them required. This was necessary, not only so that he could send the conducts, but also to ensure that the French might send a delegation of equal size and standing. He enclosed a copy of the letters that would then be issued and requested the earls that, if envoys were sent other than those then mentioned, they were to make sure that they were 'sufficient persons'.

Mutual suspicion was already rampant. It is clear from a letter of the chancellor of France, Pierre de la Forêt, written to Lancaster and Arundel in Paris on the following day, that the earls had questioned the safety of the English envoys in travelling to Avignon. De la Forêt assured them that, as soon as he received the names of the English envoys, they would be given John's letters of safe-conduct and would be escorted to the curia by French notables.[19] To both the cardinal and the chancellor the earls complained that the count of Armagnac (then John's lieutenant in Languedoc) had laid siege to Aiguillon and that other captains were also acting contrary to the tenor of the truce. By way of reply, the cardinal maintained that on the conclusion of the conference at Guines he had written to all those concerned with the observance of the truce, instructing them to abide by its terms. In particular he had written to the count of Armagnac asking him to report to John, which had not made him very popular in some quarters in Paris. The chancellor, who pretended to be ignorant of any French violations of the truce, argued that John had issued instructions for its observance and that he had recently sent one of the marshals of France, Jean de Clermont, into Saintonge to see that it was observed. Both he and the cardinal complained of infringements committed in Brittany by Sir Thomas Holand, of the siege of a number of castles and towns in Saintonge by Anglo-Gascon forces and of violations committed at sea by English sailors.[20] If they expected anything to be done about French infringements, they must first have something done about their own.[21]

Quite why Edward sought to advance the departure of the English embassy for Avignon by some five weeks or more is something of a mystery; but that a plan was drawn up is quite clear.[22] This envisaged preliminary contacts at clerical level, to be completed with the arrival of two 'magnates of the council' under whose supervision the effective negotiations were to be carried on before the pope in his private capacity as Étienne Aubert. Already on 20 May—a week before Guy de Boulogne wrote to the three earls—Woderone and de la Bere set out from London for Calais on their way to Avignon to announce the arrival of the English embassy to Innocent,[23] and on 10 July papal letters of safe-conduct were issued for 500 riders who were to escort the ambassadors to the curia. The latter were now scheduled to arrive around 29 September or 1 October. Six days later, on 16 July, the pope wrote to Edward thanking him for his letters sent with the confessor and the knight, approving the king's decision to treat with John and send envoys to Avignon, and begging him to see that they came within the allocated time. De la Bere arrived back in London on 12 August, doubtless with Innocent's letters, the safe-conducts and a report from Woderone. It was on the basis of the confessor's findings that the first group of envoys set out for the curia.

On 28 August a procuration to treat before the pope was issued to William Bateman, bishop of Norwich, Michael de Northburgh, Lancaster, Arundel, Bartholomew de Burghersh and Guy Brian.[24] They were given three letters. The first, *De tractatu cum ambassiatoribus Franciae coram Papa continuando*, took the same form as the procuration which had been issued on 30 March to the envoys responsible for negotiating the treaty of Guines. It empowered them to treat with the French ambassadors for a final peace and truce, to issue letters on the subject and to renounce Edward's claim to the throne of France. The second letter, *De potestate submittendi Regem jurisdictioni Papae, super concordandis in tractatu, coram eodem cum adversario Franciae*, was strictly in accordance with the terms of the treaty of Guines. It gave them the power to treat before the pope with the French ambassadors for a final peace and all disputes and debates between the two kings, especially over Edward's right to the French throne, which they were to be able to renounce in return for territorial compensation. They could also conclude an alliance and perpetual friendship between Edward and John, treat of a truce and give every form of security demanded. Edward undertook to confirm under the great seal everything which they concluded. The third letter, *De potestate submittendi Regem arbitrio Papae, super debatis cum adversario Franciae*, was issued in conformity with clause ii of the treaty of Guines. It instructed them to submit to the pope's arbitration any disputes which might arise over the definition of the boundaries of the territories to be ceded to Edward.[25]

This first commission to the English ambassadors was not ineffective, as has been suggested. Already on 26 August arrangements had been made for the custody of the privy seal during Northburgh's absence abroad, and he was given four newly-written books 'touching the state of Gascony'.[26] The following day he and Guy Brian were given a prest on their wages for going to the curia to treat with the French, and Northburgh was also given an allowance for a number of horses to take 'muniments and divers other books' there for that purpose.[27] On 29 August they set out for Avignon, crossing to Calais in a retinue of 50 riders, probably together with Bartholomew de Burghersh, the archbishop of Canterbury and Welwick.[28] But it was not until five weeks later that, on 4 October, the bishop of Norwich left London for the curia with his retinue.[29] Towards the end of that month Welwick was sent back to England with further letters of safe-conduct for the remaining ambassadors and to report to the king on the progress of the negotiations; on 30 October another procuration, *De potestatibus super tractatu coram Papa*, was issued to the three English delegates then at the curia (Bateman, Northburgh and Guy Brian), together with four members of Edward's Gascon council:

Bernard Ezi, lord of Albret, Guillaume-Sanche, lord of Pommiers, Bertrand, lord of Montferrand, and the lawyer Gérard du Puy.[30] This was not, as has been suggested, a new commission replacing that of 28 August. It was issued in conformity with clause ii of the treaty of Guines which empowered the ambassadors named to treat before the pope with their French counterparts of disputes that might arise over the definition of the boundaries of the territories to be ceded to Edward. The four Gascons were included because it was over the boundaries of Gascony that difficulties were likely to arise. It was not issued to Lancaster and Arundel because they had not then left for the curia and because the business in question was expected to be under way before they arrived in Avignon.

However, the preliminary negotiations were obviously taking longer than had been anticipated, since preparations for the departure of the duke and the earl had been going ahead for the best part of a month.[31] But on the following day, 31 October, at a meeting of the council in the king's chapel at Westminster, these two were given secret instructions. As well as their formal Latin procuration of 28 August they received two documents in French. One was a secret credential or *credence secrée*, to be shown only if necessary; the other was a really secret set of instructions, laying down just what they might give away in order to secure a general agreement—a document which might be highly embarrassing if it got abroad and which was on no account to be revealed.[32]

The secret credential is a short document saying very little, the word *secrée* meaning only that it was not so very secret. It was drawn up so as not to reveal too much if it had to be shown and soon some 'confidants' may have seen it—'secretly' of course. We learn from it the very humble language which Lancaster and Arundel were to use when they first met the pope at the State Banquet on Christmas Day. They were to tell him that Edward recognized God's goodness to him and that he desired to exert his strength against God's enemies. He would willingly give up some of his hereditary rights in order to secure peace with France. If peace could be made on the terms offered he would be content; if not, matters were to stand as though no offer had been made. On account of his deep affection for the pope he had chosen him as arbitrator in the unsettled question of boundaries. The *lettre de credence* and the *credences sur cestes matires* were to be shown only of necessity.

The really secret set of instructions or *charge* provided that the ambassadors were to commend the king and queen and their children to the pope. They were to confirm the treaty of Guines but—the wording here is noteworthy—the duchy of Guyenne and the other possessions named in a *cedula* which had been sent to the pope through the king's confessor were to be given to the English king as compensation for the French Crown. No mention is made of this in the treaty itself, although it had been included in the procuration of 28 August issued to the English ambassadors. The contents of this *cedula*, namely the possessions claimed by the English, were to be given in the following order: the duchies of Aquitaine and Normandy, the counties of Ponthieu, Angers and Anjou, Poitiers and Poitou, Le Mans and Maine, Tours and Touraine, Angoulême and Angoumois, Cahors and Quercy, Limoges and Limousin, and all the lands, castles and towns acquired since the beginning of the war. To get a *bonne pees* they could give up Normandy (of which no mention had been made in the treaty of Guines), Cahors, Quercy and Angoulême, unless the last three were found to be part of the ancient duchy of Aquitaine, in which case they were not to be given up. Cahors, Quercy and Angoulême were to be claimed as demesne, unless it appeared that the king's ancestors only had feudal superiority. If the ambassadors had to renounce Angoulême and Angoumois, then to get a *bonne pees* they were to try to obtain other inland territories as compensation. But they were not to push matters so far as to cause the break-up of the whole conference. Concerning the boundaries of the possessions to be ceded by the French, they were to try to come to an agreement with the French ambassadors before they made use of their power of appointing the pope as an arbitrator. If that did happen they were to complete the whole business before 1 April 1355. They had to procure every kind of security from the French, since Edward was ready to give any form of security demanded. They could prolong the truce until the following Whit Sunday.

The duke and the earl had begun to draw the king's pay a few days earlier.[33] On 3 November they crossed over to Calais on their way to Avignon in a retinue of nearly 500 riders.[34] We do not know the names of the French notables who escorted them to the curia, nor the route which they took on the long journey south through France, but Knighton gives an engaging account of their arrival in Avignon and of the magnificent state that the duke maintained there:[35]

'Henry, duke of Lancaster, with the earl of Arundel and many others, arrived at Avignon on Christmas Eve in a convoy of 200 horses, and they stayed there for six weeks in great state. As they approached the city, about 2,000 persons, including bishops, magnates, citizens and others, came to meet them on horseback. Indeed the number of those who came out to welcome them was so great that from three in the morning until vespers it was scarcely possible to cross the bridge leading into the town. When Lancaster came into the city, he thanked them all and made his way to the papal palace. On reaching the gateway he got off his horse, went in, made his salutations to the pope with proper reverence and after a short conversation with him returned to his lodging. As long as he stayed in Avignon a vast quantity of food and drink was laid out for those who wished to refresh themselves and his hospitality was so splendid that all the curia marvelled. The wine alone which had been laid down in the cellars for his stay amounted to 100 tuns. In fact he showed such courtesy to everyone, and particularly to the pope and cardinals, that everyone said "There is no one like him in all the world".'

The essential truth of this account and the methods of diplomacy that we may deduce from it are confirmed by the expense accounts of the two ambassadors, which together amounted to £5,648—the cost of a short campaign. For not only were they given an extra £2,200 13s 11d towards their personal outfit and high daily expenses, but Lancaster's account allowed for an additional sum of £1,666 13s 4d for unspecified expenses.[36] His bills for this one mission alone amounted to more than twice as much as those for all his other diplomatic missions put together.

It is unfortunate that we know so little about the French delegation, but it is unlikely that it was any less impressive than its English counterpart.[37] It was headed by two well-known figures at the truce conferences—Pierre de la Forêt and Pierre duke of Bourbon—who appear to have left for the curia in November.[38]

Lancaster and Bourbon were lodged together in the rooms of Cardinal Audoin Aubert, a relative of the pope. The apartment had been richly refurnished for their arrival with hangings of red serge, two large red carpets, red chair covers, red cord and green material. The rest of the embassy were lodged at the palace, where a large quantity of carpets, chair covers, table-cloths, counterpanes, serge, linen, velvet and other materials had been purchased for their stay. Apart from the immediate entourages of the ambassadors the greater part of their retinues of knights, esquires, sergeants and others must have been billeted in the city, and it would be interesting to know what arrangements were made for them—whether or not they occupied different quarters of the city—since incidents could have arisen between the many armed men assembled there together.[39]

There can be no doubt about the magnificence of the occasion. The State Banquet which Lancaster and a good many others attended on Christmas Day appears to have been a very sumptuous affair, and the dinners that were given during the remainder of the ambassadors' stay at Avignon—there were two for Bourbon, another for Lancaster, and one for the two of them together—though not quite so sumptuous were nevertheless very splendid.[40]

According to Geoffrey Baker, who gives the fullest account of the conference, the discussions took place between the English and French ambassadors assembled together before the pope and cardinals in consistory.[41] But the treaty of Guines was not ratified. There is no direct evidence, such as exists for the negotiations conducted at the curia ten years earlier, to show which side was responsible for this breakdown. Most English chroniclers blame the French, who are said to have gone back upon what they had agreed at Guines by insisting upon the retention of suzerainty over Aquitaine and the other territories which were to have been ceded to Edward.[42] Innocent VI and the cardinals were accused of connivance with them, doubtless because —apart from Guy de Boulogne—they did not insist upon the ratification of the treaty as it stood.[43]

This appears to have been the official attitude adopted by the English ambassadors themselves. A credential or *lettre de credence* written shortly after the breakdown of the negotiations and given to an envoy, Thomas, whom Lancaster and Arundel sent to the Emperor Charles of Luxemburg to make arrangements for an alliance between him and Edward, begins by explaining how the treaty had failed because of the attitude adopted by the French ambassadors. Since the articles agreed upon at Guines had not been ratified, Innocent had urged the conclusion of a new agreement; but Edward had never agreed to this, neither had the English delegates, nor were they empowered to do so. The envoy was then to explain to the emperor how many times Edward had been persuaded to treat with the French, how he had always graciously inclined and consented and how on every occasion he had entered into negotiations in good faith and with honest intentions, but had always been deceived and cheated both by the papal court and by others. The grievances, wrongs and injuries which he had endured for a long time were notorious to the pope and the curia. And so it was that they showed very little favour towards him, as was quite clear from the fact that they increasingly encouraged the French in their wickedness.[44]

This is the explanation adopted—almost too faithfully—both by the majority of English chroniclers and in official pronouncements.[45] But the French chroniclers have little or nothing to say on the subject, and those who do make any comment—the monk of Saint-Denis, Froissart and the continuator of Lescot—place the blame upon neither side; agreement just was not reached.[46] Knighton, whose information may ultimately have come from Lancaster, says that the duke refused specifically to give up Edward's claim and title to the throne of France.[47] But he does not say why he did so.

At first sight this explanation of the Leicester chronicler appears to be contradicted both by the terms of the procurations issued to the English ambassadors and by the secret instructions given to Lancaster and Arundel. But by the time the duke and the earl arrived at the curia their instructions were nearly two months old; the first procuration had been issued four months previously and a great deal had meanwhile taken place. For there were two other factors in the diplomatic situation of the moment: the part played by Charles of Navarre and Cardinal Guy de Boulogne.

In November 1354 the young king of Navarre, having once again quarrelled with King John, fled the country to Avignon, where he had several meetings with Lancaster and concluded an arrangement with him. Delachenal in his great *Histoire de Charles V*, suggested that a document bound up into Cotton MS. Caligula D.III was a copy of a projected alliance drawn up on this occasion.[48] But he did not clearly make out why Charles had again quarrelled with John and whether the arrangement in question was concluded before or after the rupture of peace negotiations—whether, in fact, Edward's ambassadors had any intention of ratifying the treaty of Guines by the time they arrived at the curia.

For all of these questions there is no direct evidence from which we can draw a definitive answer. But an investigation of the time-table of events reveals several illuminating points. According to the monk of Saint-Denis Charles left his Norman lands for Avignon in November 1354. There seems to have been nothing sudden about his decision to go to the curia and he made his way there leisurely enough. As early as 16 November arrangements were put afoot to receive him there together with the English and French ambassadors and in these preparations Pierre de la Tennerie, who had played an important role in the negotiations with Lancaster at Bruges, appears to have taken a conspicuous part. Charles was to be lodged in the rooms of Arnaud Aubert, bishop of Carcassonne, which were specially refurnished for his arrival and included one room referred to as 'secret' in the papal accounts.[49] During the course of the same month—it is not clear at precisely what date—John issued instructions for the seizure of all the Navarrese lands and castles and proceeded to Caen to see that they were carried out. Already on 17 November he was in Rouen. Two days later he was at Bourg Achard, on the 22nd he crossed the Risle at Saint-Philbert and hurried on the following day to Cormeilles; by 30 November he had arrived in Caen.[50]

What exactly did John fear? Delachenal suggested that the king had discovered there was more to the murder of the constable than had initially been made known to him. But could the information which he received of an event then ten months old have resulted in such prompt action? It seems more likely that he was frightened of, or had received details of, Charles' present intentions and actions. For about this time Martín Enríquez de Lacarra, *alférez* of Navarre and one of the most devoted of Charles' partisans, secured the assistance of Edward's lieutenant in Brittany, Sir Thomas Holand, to conduct a raid into Normandy as far as Caen, the faubourgs of which, as those of Bayeux, they set on fire.[51] When John had arrived in Normandy he encountered a resistance which he had not anticipated. Six castles—Évreux, Pont-Audemer, Cherbourg, Gavray, Avranches and Mortain—were held firmly against him. Was it a coincidence that the storm blew up and that Charles departed for Avignon at precisely the point at which Lancaster and Arundel landed at Calais on their way to the curia? Whether premeditated or not it is certain that by the time the duke and the earl arrived at their destination—about the time that John arrived back in Paris—they were well aware of what had taken place and were doubtless in touch with Edward about it—for the king kept in close contact with the ambassadors. On 15 November Alan de Barley was sent to the duke, who could not have got very far by then since the messenger was only paid five shillings. On 5 December a clerk, John of Kent, was sent to the curia with letters for the bishop of Norwich and other 'magnates', and on the same day diverse valets were paid for taking letters under the secret seal to Lancaster and Arundel. On 20 February following another clerk, Master John de Branketre, was sent to Avignon with privy seal letters for Lancaster, Arundel and 'other magnates' and at least one esquire, Henry de Braybrok, was sent to the king at Woodstock with letters from Lancaster, Arundel, Bateman and Northburgh.[52] Edward's instructions on the matter could therefore not have been lacking. Moreover, in quite general terms, in view of the readiness shown by both Lancaster and the king to ditch the projected peace treaty after the murder of the constable in January 1354, it is unlikely that they would turn down Charles' request for assistance in order that it might be ratified a year or so later. It must have been quite clear that, after the turn of events in November, he was certain once more to seek English assistance—if he had not been assured of it already by that date.

Whatever John had discovered he had discovered by degrees. Already in September Guy de Boulogne, four times recalled to Avignon, finally departed for the curia having lost the king's favour.[53] In January he was joined there by Robert de Lorris who had also been among the negotiators of the treaties of Mantes and Guines and had similarly been obliged to exile himself from the king's court.[54] It was in Guy de Boulogne's rooms at Avignon, sometimes in those of the cardinal of Arras, that Charles and Lancaster met in ostentatious secrecy during the night and hatched a stupendous plot to partition France between Edward and the young king.[55]

How had this come about? According to the text of a 'projected treaty' published by Delachenal, Charles and Edward were to work together for the conquest of France. When that had been accomplished, Edward was to assume the French Crown, but Charles would be given a number of provinces amounting in all to about half the kingdom and including Normandy, where military operations were to begin. Delachenal believed this document to belong to 1354 or 1355, since it refers to grievances raised after the murder of the constable in the treaty of Mantes. But the only evidence for his conclusion that it was drawn up at Avignon is a note written at the head of the manuscript: *Ceste copie feust trovée entre les lettres de Navarre, escrite de la main l'evesqe de Loundres*, and, as he pointed out, Michael de Northburgh was one of the English ambassadors at the curia in the winter of 1354–5.

But is the document in question a copy of a 'projected treaty' as has generally been supposed? The manuscript begins *En noun de Dieu. Amen. Il sembleroit par manère de remembrance que pur treter de faire alliance et amour ferm(e) entre les deux seignurs (se) pourreit faire se qe s'ensuit*—it is a note of what might be conceded in treating of an alliance between Edward and Charles. It is not a projected treaty but a *charge* similar to that given to Lancaster and Arundel on 31 October for treating of peace with the French ambassadors at Avignon. Clearly it was written by Michael de Northburgh; but did he write it in the winter of 1354–5? According to clause iii Charles was to continue to enjoy all the possessions which he then held in Normandy together with everything else that John held in the duchy and he was to have them in compensation for the county of Angoulême and several rents due to him at the treasury. But by the treaty of Mantes Charles had been compensated for the county to an extent that was beyond even his wildest dreams. Is it likely, when he was to have virtually half of France by the new arrangement, that Normandy should be offered to him in these terms?

It seems more probable that the document was written after the murder of the constable, but before the conclusion of the treaty of Mantes—between 8 January and 22 February—and that it constitutes the basis of what Edward was offering Charles through Lancaster at Bruges at the beginning of the latter month. It was written by Michael de Northburgh in his capacity as keeper of the privy seal and, as it happens, we know that he was sent to Flanders some time after the truce conference at Calais in November-December 1353 when, along with Lancaster, he had been among the English ambassadors.[56] It is possible that this document (which is bound up into Cotton MS. Caligula D.III along with the letters relating to the negotiations between Charles and Lancaster of January-March 1354) was communicated to the duke at Bruges by him and that it is a copy of a *charge*, a list of instructions of what the duke could concede to the young king.

Then what was concluded at Avignon? For we know from a speech subsequently delivered to parliament by Sir Walter Mauny that an arrangement of some sort or other was concluded there.[57] Could it have been a treaty based on the document written by Northburgh? Geoffrey Baker, who gives a peculiarly full account of the events of 1354, says that an arrangement was concluded between Charles and Lancaster after the murder of the constable and before the treaty of Mantes. But in one of the manuscripts he also says that subsequently, at Avignon, Lancaster received Charles' homage.[58] A similar note was added in the manuscript of the *Anonimalle Chronicle*[59] and Sir Walter Mauny seems to have suggested as much. According to clause ix of the document published by Delachenal, Charles was to do homage to Edward as king of France at a date that was to be determined by him and the duke. It seems more likely, therefore, that the agreement concluded at Avignon in the winter of 1354-5 was based upon the terms which were offered to Charles at Bruges in February 1354.

The conclusions which are to be drawn from this tangled web of negotiations are as follows: Early in the year 1354 Charles of Navarre, having arranged the murder of Charles of Spain at Laigle, got into touch with Lancaster and (through him) Edward III and the Black

Prince, and a meeting was arranged to conclude an alliance at Bruges. A document containing the conditions that Edward was willing to offer Charles (Delachenal's 'projected treaty') was taken to Flanders by Michael de Northburgh, keeper of the privy seal, and was discussed at the conference at Bruges. There must have been some close and insincere bargaining on this, for the arrangement could not have been attained—France could never have held both Edward and Charles of Navarre. But from Edward's point of view, if Charles could be trusted for the moment, it might be exceedingly useful. Arrangements were made, which were based upon it, for the landing of English troops under Lancaster's command in Normandy. But at the last minute Charles was offered a particularly advantageous peace with King John and, for the moment, the project fell through.

That it happened this way was due to the influence which Cardinal Guy de Boulogne had with the French king and because, ambitious for promotion in the church—and maybe because he genuinely desired it—he was first and foremost determined to see that the terms of a peace, which were already within reach at the end of 1353, should be formally concluded. And so the treaty of Guines came about. It was Edward, not John, who had to give way on this occasion, for he had suffered some serious diplomatic and military setbacks during the years of truce and the defection of Charles of Navarre gave him the final push. But the treaty still had to be ratified at Avignon in the autumn.

At first Edward tried to speed up the business, but as the clauses of the draft agreement were discussed and debated over—there were difficulties over the boundaries of the territories which were to have been ceded to him—the months passed by and, in the event, the final stage was not reached until Christmas when Lancaster and Arundel arrived at the curia.

But at the beginning of November things had changed abruptly. King John, having slowly gathered together strands of information about what had taken place at Laigle, at Mantes, at Guines—and probably at Bruges—and having reason to distrust the latest Navarrese stratagems, threw over Guy de Boulogne, sought to stamp out Charles, and banished his chamberlain, Robert de Lorris, from his court.

All three made for Avignon, as if, it would seem, by intention. It must have been obvious that the treaty of Guines was on the rocks. Fearing that the French would refuse to ratify it, the cardinal tried to push them into it by allowing Charles and Lancaster to hold conferences in ostentatious secrecy in his rooms. How else can one explain his conduct? But his action had quite the opposite effect. For instead of ratifying the treaty of peace, the English ambassadors negotiated an alliance with Charles. In the course of all this twisted diplomacy Guy de Boulogne had brought about much more than he had intended to do.

Once the treaty had fallen through, Edward's ambassadors opened negotiations for an alliance with the Emperor Charles IV. The initial conversations took place with the bishop of Mende, who was then at the curia, and it was agreed that an envoy should be sent to present Edward's case to Charles. The credential or *lettre de credence* that was given to this envoy, Thomas, and which contained the official explanation of the break-down of peace negotiations, also instructed him to request the emperor for a meeting between his council and that of Edward to conclude an alliance between them. If Charles agreed, he was to arrange a time and a place for the negotiations and he was to secure the names of the envoys whom the emperor proposed to send.[60]

At first sight it would appear that these overtures could not meet with a great deal of success, for nearly all the early influences on Charles IV were French. He had been brought up in France; his father, the blind king John of Bohemia, like Louis de Male's father, had died fighting for Philip VI at Crécy; he had been tutored by the abbot of Fécamp, later to become Pope Clement VI, well known for his Francophile sympathies; he had married a French princess, Blanche of Valois, sister of Philip VI; and he was the brother-in-law of King John through the latter's marriage to his sister Bonne of Luxemburg. But the political realities of his house counted for more than these personal attachments. French territorial interests conflicted sharply with his own in the Dauphiné, Savoy, Franche-Comté, Verdunois, the duchy of Bar and the Cambrésis. An alliance with Edward could therefore be very advantageous to him in order to check French expansion eastwards. But he had to be careful not to become involved in the main-stream of the Anglo-French embroilment. His policy towards the king of France was therefore one of unfriendly neutrality which, if need be, could be turned into active hostility. He could threaten the French with an Anglo-Imperial alliance, and so state his terms in a settlement of the frontier territories.[61]

He had in fact already concluded an alliance with Edward at Prague on 24 June 1348; but this agreement, while it gave Charles everything he wanted, did not fully meet with Edward's wishes. For although the emperor undertook not to ally himself with any of Edward's enemies and agreed to allow Edward to raise troops in the empire for war against the French, he only undertook to participate directly in the Anglo-French conflict if the king of France usurped imperial rights. What Edward had wanted, as contained in his letters to Charles of 23 April previous, was a joint Anglo-Imperial offensive against France for their respective rights. This projected treaty was taken to the emperor by a chancery clerk, Thomas Brayton, and Sir William Stury, who were empowered to swear to it in Edward's name, and by another knight, Gorsorn de Zewele, who was to receive Charles' undertakings. Had it been signed it might have proved extremely useful to Edward in dealing with the situation in Flanders during the course of that year. As it was, the alliance concluded in June was of little immediate use to him, even in the disputed succession in Hainault, Holland and Zeeland, and when, in the following year, after the death of Blanche of Valois, he commissioned the margrave of Juliers to arrange the marriage of his daughter, Isabella, to Charles, his proposals were politely but firmly turned down. The emperor preferred to stay neutral and chose a German princess.

But there was every reason for Edward to hope that even the alliance concluded at Prague in June would sooner or later place the emperor firmly on his side. The annexation of the Dauphiné by Philip VI in 1349 could have brought it into full operation. Now, at the beginning of 1355, Charles IV, having arrived in Italy to assume the crown of the king of the Lombards at Milan and the imperial crown at Rome, was informed of the latest French proposals to encroach upon his rights in the frontier territories of the empire, notably in the counties of Savoy and Provence, the kingdom of Arles, Vienne and Franche-Comté, and was obliged to seek financial and military aid from Barnabo Visconti in order to resist them. The mission entrusted to Thomas Brayton by Lancaster and Arundel was therefore particularly well timed.

We know the details of this envoy's audiences with the emperor from a memoir or *ramenbrance* which he kept of his mission.[62] He found Charles in Pisa, where he arrived on Monday 2 March. It is clear from his account that he had several audiences with the emperor between 4 and 17 March and that Lancaster and Arundel also sent other envoys to Charles together with the cardinal bishop of Mende. These appear to have arrived at Pisa on 14 March, when the emperor verified that the peace negotiations had in fact fallen through, and two days later, notwithstanding his receipt of letters from Innocent VI and the cardinals giving contrary reasons for the rupture of the negotiations, he agreed to send some of his councillors to Lancaster and Arundel to see if an agreement could be concluded. On the morning of 17 March Thomas Brayton agreed to explain more fully to Charles the reason for his mission and the intentions of the duke and the earl therein. He spoke to this effect with the bishop, the marquess of Montferrat and a number of other persons, presumably Charles' councillors.

Of the subsequent negotiations we know very little; but by the time Charles agreed to send envoys to talk with Lancaster and Arundel, the duke and the earl were well on their way home.[63] It was not until August that other English envoys arrived in Prague to conclude the alliance which Edward had been seeking through his ambassadors at Avignon, and by then it was too late. In effect, the English overtures had served Charles' purposes: he had made good use of them to frighten the French with the prospect of an Anglo-Imperial alliance. On 26 August he concluded a treaty with King John whereby, in return for his friendship (not an effective alliance or anything like military aid), the towns of Verdun and Cambrai, together with Cateau-Cambrésis, were to be restored to him. The dauphin was to do homage for the Dauphiné and restore the town of Vienne and the duke of Burgundy was also to do homage for his county as a fief of the empire. He offered the English envoys nothing more than his mediation in the negotiation of a truce between Edward and John. But by that time preparations were well under way for the landing of English troops in Normandy and Gascony.

These negotiations with the emperor are significant in that they reveal Edward's plans and intentions, at the latest in February 1355. Already by that date his ambassadors at Avignon were engaged in diplomatic preparations for a recommencement of hostilities by way of alliances with Charles of Navarre and the Emperor Charles IV. The first plans for a series of campaigns scheduled for the summer were based upon them; English troops were to land in Normandy and imperial assistance was to be secured for military operations against France, presumably from the north-east. Bearing in mind the time it would have taken for English messengers to reach Avignon from London, Edward's instructions must have been given very early on in the diplomatic proceedings.

# XII  The Normandy campaign
## (1355-1357)

In spite of reported French attempts to ambush him on his return from
Avignon,[1] Lancaster arrived back in London on 28 March. During the
spring and summer at least two fleets were assembled at Plymouth,
Southampton and in the Thames estuary. One was bound for Gascony
with an army under the command of the Black Prince and another was
destined for Normandy with an army under the command of the duke.
In the short period of active warfare that followed, from the summer
of 1355 to the spring of 1357, the same general strategy of a group of
simultaneous campaigns was followed as ten years earlier; but this
time the plan is harder to follow because it had to be changed just as
it was being put into execution. The government's intention seems to
have been for two simultaneous campaigns starting in the summer of
1355. The Black Prince was to operate in Aquitaine and, on the basis
of the agreement concluded at Avignon, Lancaster was to co-operate
with Charles of Navarre in Normandy.

Preparations for the two expeditions were well under way by June
1355,[2] and at the beginning of August Charles arrived at Cherbourg
with a considerable force of men recruited from his Spanish domains.[3]
In mid-July a number of ships from Bayonne, which had transported
some of his troops to Normandy, arrived in the Channel Islands and
at Southampton and instructions were given for their transfer to the
fleet required for the Black Prince.[4] But, as in 1345, adverse winds
prevented Lancaster from leaving England at the appointed time.
Having sailed down to Greenwich from Rotherhithe on 10 July and
navigated the North Foreland, the fleet was held up at Sandwich until
15 August, unable to sail south and west down the Channel. It was
with considerable difficulty that it pulled into Winchelsea and then
made its way to the Isle of Wight, only to be forced into Portsmouth
harbour for shelter.[5] It had still not left the English coast when news

arrived that Charles had made peace with King John; the terms of their reconciliation were sealed at Valognes on 10 September.[6]

On this occasion it is probable that the young king of Navarre had little alternative but to seek terms with the Valois monarch, for despite the attempts which had been made to keep the destination of Lancaster's troops secret, the French had been aware of Edward's plans since at least the beginning of June and had alerted the coastal defences.[7] By the beginning of September considerable French forces had been built up in the Cotentin and they were sufficiently strong to make an English landing there a very dangerous venture.[8] Charles, who had commenced hostilities as soon as he arrived at Cherbourg at the beginning of August,[9] could not afford to await a change in the weather to bring the English reinforcements to his assistance. But by 7 September, three days before the conclusion of the agreement at Valognes, it had been decided to divert Lancaster to Brittany and 2,000 Navarrese forces had been sent into the duchy under the command of Martín Enríquez de Lacarra and Juan Ramírez de Arellano.[10]

On 14 September, the duke was given a commission as captain-general and lieutenant in Brittany; his patent of appointment was dated at Portsmouth.[11] Such a change of plan, made there and then, was clearly intended to preserve intact the military scheme for the year. The Black Prince had left for Bordeaux on 9 September[12] and from the strategic point of view it was essential that the two expeditionary forces should make more or less simultaneous landings in France.[13] Then the plan was once more changed: Edward determined to cross to northern France and engage King John in battle, and Lancaster and the troops who were to have served under his command in Normandy appear to have formed the main body of the royal army. The forces disembarked at Calais on 2 November and Edward advanced southward to meet King John who had long awaited him. At one point the two armies were only a few miles apart and an engagement seemed imminent, but in the event a battle did not take place and Edward withdrew to Calais where he received news that the Scots had taken Berwick. He had little alternative but to hurry back to England. The raid had lasted for ten days in all.[14]

But the intention to send Lancaster to Brittany had not been dropped.[15] For although, towards the end of November, he accompanied the king to Scotland to accomplish the recapture of Berwick and did not return south until the close of March, Thomas Dautre, one of the king's sergeants-at-arms, was in the meantime kept in residence in London awaiting the wishes of the king's council on the arrest

Map III.   The Normandy Campaign, 1356

of shipping for the duke's crossing to the duchy.[17] On Lancaster's return from Scotland, preparations were again put under way.[18] But when he eventually left England at the beginning of June it was not for Brittany, but for Normandy.

By one of those disastrous *coups d'état* to which the first two Valois kings too frequently descended, on 5 April 1356 King John arrested Charles of Navarre and several Norman lords at a dinner party given by the dauphin in Rouen castle and had some of his chief adherents executed without any form of trial. This brought to a head much smouldering discontent in Normandy and a considerable rebellion was led by Charles' brother Philip and a Norman seigneur called Godfrey d'Harcourt. Philip immediately put a number of Navarrese fortresses in Normandy into a state of defence and ignored the injunctions of King John to surrender them. Pont-Audemer, Évreux and Breteuil were then besieged by French troops and, when the dauphin arrived on the scene at the beginning of May, civil war broke out in the duchy. Meanwhile Philip and Godfrey sent Jean, lord of Morbecque, and Guillaume Carbonnel, lord of Brevands, as their envoys to England; the negotiations which they conducted were completed by 12 May. Just over a fortnight later (on 28 May) Philip and his associates issued letters of defiance to King John—something which they could not have risked without the assurance of English military assistance.[19]

The coincidence of timing between events in Normandy and military preparations in England is very striking. One set of preparations for Lancaster's crossing to Brittany began in mid-March—the payment of an advance on the wages of the troops, the issue of letters of protection, the arrest of shipping, arrangements for the embarkation of horses and the payment of the mariners. The process started again at the beginning of May—at the very time that the envoys of Philip of Navarre were in England. Every effort was made to keep the English military preparations secret; until the moment of departure of the expeditionary forces, all of them were said to have been made for a landing in Brittany. But on 4 May Richard of Derby was paid wages to distribute to the mariners at Southampton employed on Lancaster's passage to 'Normandy and Brittany'.[20]

According to the chronicler Robert of Avesbury, on hearing Philip's envoys Edward called a council and switched Lancaster to Normandy;[21] but it seems likely that this was the plan long before the arrival of the envoys and long before even 5 April. For if an Anglo-Navarrese link-up had not been intended all along it is difficult to understand why the council postponed its decision on the arrest of ships for the duke's passage to Brittany from Christmas until spring and why the arrangements made in the last fortnight of March were not succeeded by an embarkation until after the entire political situation changed in May; for the expeditionary forces appear to have been kept waiting for a landing in Normandy. The plan for operations to be based on Brittany had clearly proved impracticable. In the official explanation of the executions of 5 April King John claimed that Charles of Navarre and several Norman lords had plotted to deliver Normandy to the English.[22] Although, in a letter of 14 May, Edward III naturally denied any such complicity,[23] it would be foolish to take his words at face-value. Charles' 'defection' in September 1355 had saved Lancaster's troops a hot reception in the duchy; in June 1356 the Cotentin beaches were clear.

Once it began, the embarkation was carried out with remarkable rapidity—a rapidity made possible by long preparation. Inadequate shipping facilities and the urgency of the situation in Normandy necessitated the dispatch of an advance guard of 140 men-at-arms, 200 archers and 1,400 horses on board 48 ships. The flotilla left Southampton for La Hogue on 1 June; five days later it had returned to collect Lancaster and the remainder of his forces. On Saturday 18 June they also disembarked at La Hogue.[24]

The abbey of Montebourg in the Contentin had been chosen as the point of concentration. It was here that the duke (whose total expeditionary forces consisted of 500 men-at-arms and 800 archers and included John de Montfort) was joined by Philip of Navarre and Godfrey d'Harcourt with 100 men-at-arms and Sir Robert Knowles who brought a detachment of 300 men-at-arms and 500 archers from the Breton garrisons. His entire force stood at slightly more than 1,000 men-at-arms and 1,400 archers. The immediate object of the expedition appears to have been to raise the siege of a number of Navarrese towns besieged by the French: Évreux, Pont-Audemer and Breteuil. An excellent day-to-day account of the campaign was written on its conclusion by a soldier in the duke's company.

The march began on 22 June. The first night was spent at Carentan, the second at Torigny-sur-Vire. Saint-Lô was by-passed. The duke halted his troops a day before proceeding in an easterly direction to Évrecy on the 26th and (by-passing Caen) Argences on the 27th. The following day he reached Lisieux, having successfully crossed a marsh formed by the river Dives and its tributaries by way of a strongly fortified pass known as the bridge of Corbon. On the 29th he advanced north-eastward in the direction of Rouen to Pont-Audemer, which had been under siege from a force under the command of the master of the French crossbowmen, Robert de Houdetot, since the end of April. When the enemy heard that he had crossed the bridge of Corbon they withdrew during the night, abandoning both siege engines and other artillery. He halted his troops there over 30 June and 1 July in order to look to the future security of the town; mines, which had been driven within four feet of the walls, were filled up; the castle was victualled for a year and an Anglo-Navarrese garrison was established there under the command of a Brabançon knight, Jean de Luk.

From Pont-Audemer he turned south-eastward, marching down the eastern bank of the river Risle in the direction of Évreux, and spent the night of 2 July in the abbey of Bec-Hellouin. The next day he by-passed Évreux to the west and headed for Conches where he had the castle burned. On the 4th he moved south to Breteuil. A French force abandoned their siege of the castle as he approached. He had it re-victualled and on the same day continued to Verneuil and took the town by assault. But it was not until the 6th, after his forces had suffered some casualties, that a tower situated within the town capitulated. He had it burned. The troops were allowed to rest there the next day. On the 8th he began a rapid retreat, for King John, together with a large army (which included his eldest son, the duke of Normandy and his brother the duke of Orléans) were in pursuit.

Since the beginning of May the dauphin Charles, duke of Normandy, had been in charge of military operations in his duchy. King John had therefore been free to concentrate his attention on the major threat within his kingdom: the Black Prince's army in the south. At the beginning of June he left Paris for Chartres,[25] where he had summoned an army for 1 June.[26] The turn of events in Normandy prevented him from proceeding further. On 8 June he appointed his son John, count of Poitiers, lieutenant throughout the kingdom south of the Loire valley.[27] The commission, the first of its kind to embrace such extensive territories, gave him full responsibility for the prosecution of the war in those parts. By 22 June, the day Lancaster began his march from Montebourg, King John had moved his forces north to Dreux. From there he turned north-east in the direction of Mantes and passed down the Seine valley towards Vernon. As Lancaster began his march south-east to Bec-Hellouin and Conches he turned south-west to Évreux and Chanteloup, just to the east of the road from Conches to Breteuil.[28] The two armies had come very close. But John arrived too late to intercept the duke at Breteuil and Verneuil. It was not until 8 July, when the duke had begun his retreat to the Cotentin, that he succeeded in moving in upon him at Thubeuf, not far from Laigle. It was here that John sent two heralds to propose a battle. Lancaster declined the offer—in a manner fine enough to cover his retreat—and quickened his pace so as to arrive back at Montebourg in four days by way of Argentan, Thury-Harcourt and Saint-Fromond (9, 10 & 11 July), when he crossed the river Vire—though not without difficulty, for the French had destroyed the bridge and then tried to ambush his forces. He succeeded, however, in arriving at Carentan on the 12th and Montebourg on the 13th. It was at Montebourg, on 16 July, that the dispatch was written.

The campaign was undoubtedly a success. With a strong though not very large force he had made a lightning raid across Normandy and successfully re-victualled the Navarrese strongholds of Pont-Audemer and Breteuil. On his march he had made the greatest possible use of the cover afforded by the Navarrese lands in western and south-eastern Normandy, avoided such loyal French towns as Bayeux and Caen and taken great care, for all his fine words, to avoid a battle with the army led by the French king. Any attempt to take Évreux, had he even intended it, would certainly have involved him in such a conflict. His precipitate retreat, though perhaps not wholly in accord with chivalrous notions, was entirely the right thing to do. He had not the strength for a pitched battle: it was King John who missed a great opportunity in not forcing him to fight. He had successfully diverted the French king's attention from the south and returned to his base in the Cotentin with numerous prisoners, a sizeable booty and few losses to his forces. He had also accomplished something sufficiently impressive to strengthen the adherence of important men in the Navarrese party. Five days after his return to Montebourg, Godfrey d'Harcourt attached his seal to an important charter drawn up at his castle of Saint-Sauveur-le-Vicomte in the Cotentin.[29] By its terms he recognized Edward's right to the French throne and the duchy of Normandy, promised obedience, homage and service for all the lands which he held in the duchy and bequeathed them to Edward should he die without lawful heir of his body. On 1 August Edward took him into his protection.[30] Shortly afterwards Philip of Navarre crossed to England[31] and on 4 September a treaty of alliance was drawn up at Clarendon in which he recognized having done liege homage to Edward as 'king of France and duke of Normandy'.[32] On the basis of this recognition—which itself depended upon the success of Lancaster's campaign—an attempt was made to set up an administration in Normandy in the king's name.[33]

From Montebourg Lancaster, accompanied by John de Montfort and some 1,000 men-at-arms and 1,500 archers, made his way into Brittany to take up his appointment as captain and lieutenant of the duchy.[34] On 8 August a new commission was issued to him (in substantially the same form as the first but limited to a year's duration) commencing 29 September.[35] Little is known of his immediate movements on taking up this appointment. He appears to have begun a campaign in Penthièvre in August and was at Vannes on the 12th of that month.[36] Certainly he kept in close contact with the king by way of a royal sergeant-at-arms, William de Cornewaill.[37] For his part King John, having failed to force Lancaster to a battle, began a magnificent but archaic attempt to take Breteuil. Towards the middle of August news from the south obliged him to abandon the siege and offer the defenders favourable capitulation terms.[38] For on 4 August the Black Prince had begun the march northwards from Bergerac which brought him to the Loire valley early in September. On 28 August he crossed the river Cher and from 7 to 11 September halted on the outskirts of Tours.[39]

The reasons which lay behind the choice of the route have been the subject of much discussion. In his admirable study of the prince's expedition Dr Hewitt rejects the three explanations for the course of the campaign put forward by the prince himself in a letter which he subsequently wrote to the municipality of London: that it was determined by his wish to seek out the count of Poitiers at Bourges, to have news of his father should Edward venture a landing in northern France and to join Lancaster in the Loire valley.[40] He concludes that 'no dominant strategic plan determined the march', a view held by both H. B. George and General Köhler before him. Delachenal did not commit himself.[41] But the question deserves a little more attention.

The advance to Bourges, however slow, was carried out and it was not so pointless as at first it appears to have been. The count of Poitiers had been appointed John's lieutenant in all the provinces south of the river Loire and he had instructions to lead an army into Gascony, preparations for which dated back to 16 May.[42] It was at Bourges that he assembled his forces during the course of June and July.[43] He had a formidable council with him:[44] Jean de Clermont, marshal of France, Jean le Maingre (otherwise known as Boucicaut), the seneschals of Poitou, Saintonge and Toulouse, a royal secretary, Pierre de Labatut and several others—reason enough for the prince to seek him out. Although Edward III did not cross to France in 1356, there are grounds for believing that such a landing constituted part of the plan of campaign concluded in the previous year.[45] Certainly the duke intended to join the Black Prince. In his letter to the municipality of London the prince tells us that on leaving Tours he intended to join Lancaster who had made known his wish to draw towards him.[46] No less than six different chronicles refer to the duke's attempts to make such a juncture, to his advance to the Loire valley and his failure to cross that river;[47] the bridge had been destroyed at Les-Ponts-de-Cé just south of Angers.

It seems likely, therefore, that a very definite strategic plan had been formulated in 1355 and that it lay behind the preparations of the spring and summer of that year. The prince and Lancaster were to have made more or less simultaneous landings in France; it was for this purpose that the two fleets had been prepared together. Moreover, Lancaster was under a contractual obligation to aid the prince should he require his assistance. The prince's indenture of July 1355 included a clause to the effect that 'the king has promised that if it shall happen that the prince is besieged or beset by so great a force of men that he cannot help himself unless he be rescued by the king's power, then the king will rescue him in one way or another, provided that he can be rescued easily; and the duke of Lancaster, the earls of Northampton, Arundel, March and Stafford have promised and pledged their faith to give without fail all the help and counsel they can in making such rescue',[48] and the earls of Northampton, March and Stafford were to have accompanied the duke to Normandy.

This clause is to be read in the light of almost identical provisions included in the indentures drawn up with the king by Lancaster and Northampton in 1345.[49] In the indenture with Lancaster it was expressly stated that 'the king has agreed that if it shall happen that the said earl is besieged or beset by so great a force of men that he cannot help himself unless he be rescued by the king's power, then the king is bound to rescue him in one way or another, provided that he can be rescued easily'. In the indenture with Northampton it was agreed that 'in case the said earl or the aforesaid lords are beset or besieged by enemies whom they cannot meet, then the king is bound to rescue them by himself or by other sufficient rescue'. In 1345 the plan broke down when Edward, having crossed to Flanders with a large army, saw his hopes shattered by the opposition which culminated in the murder of James van Artevelde and was obliged to return to England. But in the following year, when a large French army under the command of the duke of Normandy had been drawn into the south of France, he had landed in the Cotentin, and under the guidance of that

Norman renegade Godfrey d'Harcourt, captured Caen, eventually defeated the main French army at Crécy and began the siege of Calais. He had done more. When the dauphin Charles heard of his landing he hurried to help his father, leaving the Anglo-Gascon forces with a free hand in Aquitaine. Edward had rescued Lancaster in the north of France. And so it was in 1355. In the initial stages the plan broke down owing to the contrary winds which prevented Lancaster from getting any further than Portsmouth before Charles of Navarre was obliged to make peace with King John at Valognes. But it is significant that, having crossed to Normandy in the following year, he refused the battle offered by the king of France only to come to meet the Black Prince in the Loire valley when King John moved south to stop his advance. He would have succeeded in joining forces with him had the French not destroyed the bridge at Les-Ponts-de-Cé. As things turned out the prince continued his retreat to meet glory alone at Poitiers.

Lancaster had nothing left to do but to return to his command, for he was still the king's lieutenant in Brittany and his commission had just been renewed. On his way back, however, he laid down a strong line of fortresses stretching northwards through Anjou and Maine into west and central Normandy between Angers and Caen: Villiers, Bois-du-Maine, Domfort, Messei, Tinchebray, Saint-Germain-du-Crioult, Condé-sur-Noireau, Martainville, Saint-James-de-Beuvron and Avranches. This incident has not received much attention and it would be interesting to know its purpose since the garrisons remained under his personal command and the places were treated almost as his personal conquest.[50]

It has been suggested that the fortresses were intended to render difficult communications between Brittany and the bordering provinces of Normandy, Maine and Anjou and thereby hinder French assistance to the city of Rennes, subsequently besieged by the duke.[51] Their control doubtless afforded some protection to the besieging force, while Avranches and Saint-James were strategically important to the defence of Brittany. For the Valois monarchy also appointed a lieutenant to look after its interests there and he usually established his military headquarters at Pontorson.[52] Or was Lancaster insuring himself against a change of front on the part of Philip of Navarre, whose allegiance to Edward was quite recent? Upon the conclusion of the Normandy campaign, the duke had been expected to look after Edward's interests there, for Philip had crossed to England and it was not until 30 October that he was given a commission as the king's captain and lieutenant in Normandy.[53]

Basically, his adherence depended upon the continuing French imprisonment of his brother. If Charles were given his liberty anything might happen. Edward had taken precautions. Lancaster was notified of Philip's appointment and instructed to assist him in both military and general matters.[54] The duke had, therefore, a continuing interest in Norman affairs. German mercenaries operated under his command there.[55] Avranches was taken from the Navarrese by his troops.[56] English troops were sent to operate in Normandy, but were not placed under Philip's command; a request that they should be, presented to the king's council on his behalf, was politely but firmly declined.[57] But in reply to a series of petitions sent to the king by Lancaster in the spring of 1357 Edward instructed the duke that he might appoint the captains of the fortresses in question, but insisted that they should be intendant to the guardian and lieutenant of Normandy.[58] Nevertheless, when the duke returned to England upon the termination of his command in Brittany he appointed Sir James de Pipe and Sir Robert Knowles (who had served with him in the duchy) to look after English interests in Normandy, in spite of the fact that Philip's commission had recently been renewed.[59]

# XIII The Breton lieutenancy (1355-1358)

Just over a year had passed since Lancaster had first been appointed captain and lieutenant in Brittany. It must have been a year full of exasperation for him. After all the pains which he had taken with Charles of Navarre at Avignon during the Christmas of 1354 and the preparations for war in Normandy in the following summer, the young king of Navarre had again made peace with King John. The subsequent raid around Calais and the relief of Berwick had kept him employed in the field, but these were no occasions to demonstrate his abilities as a commander. Only after three months of waiting had he and the forces under his command finally landed in Normandy and the campaign which he had conducted there, although highly successful, had only a limited objective. The main theatre of action was in the south and his failure to join forces with the Black Prince, which was probably an essential point in the military scheme for the year, appears to have annoyed him.[1] It must have been galling to have had no share in the glory and the profits of Poitiers. The impressive line of fortresses which he had taken on his way back from the Loire valley doubtless brought him considerable financial gain, but in view of the prince's victory contemporaries were not likely to be impressed. As autumn came to a close and he returned to his command in Brittany, he determined upon an ambitious military enterprise—to capture the town of Rennes for the young claimant to the duchy.

English occupation forces had then been present in Brittany for some fourteen years. When the succession dispute had broken out in the duchy in 1341 Edward III had found himself involved, quite apart from any immediate military preoccupation, by reason of the keen interest which the kings of England had shown in the affairs of the duchy since the time of the Norman Conquest and because the dukes of Brittany held the earldom of Richmond in England.[2] Between 1342 and 1345 Edward, allied to John de Montfort (and perhaps also his suzerain) enjoyed, in return for his military assistance, the right to collect the ducal revenues and to garrison such towns, ports and castles as he required. After 1345, when Montfort had done homage to him and entrusted him with the guardianship of his son, also called John de Montfort, the king assumed both the suzerainty and custody of the duchy. Nevertheless, he never secured possession of the whole of Brittany which, until 1364, remained divided between the partisans of John de Montfort and those of Charles of Blois.[3] The territories under allied control were for the most part situated in the Breton-speaking south and west. They included almost the whole of Léon and Cornouaille with their ports of Conquet and Brest, and the southern coast as far as the mouth of the Vilaine with the ports of Quimperlé, Hennebont and Vannes.[4] Most of upper Brittany, which was French-speaking, supported Charles of Blois; but English garrisons were established at Bécherel, Ploërmel, Fougerai and Châteaublanc, from which the countryside was ransomed over a wide area and which formed the frontier with the French who were firmly established at Pontorson, Rennes and Nantes.[5]

The government established by Edward III in those parts of Brittany in his control was primarily military in nature and the military personnel was for the most part made up of Englishmen placed under the authority of an English captain-general and lieutenant, who was the principal royal officer in Brittany. This was very different from the situation in Aquitaine where, as we have seen,[6] the military personnel was overwhelmingly Gascon, although the seneschals and lieutenants were usually, but not always, English. Since, however, the king only claimed the feudal suzerainty and the custody of the duchy, he was obliged to safeguard the traditional basis of government which he would sooner or later be required to restore to his ward. The principal royal officer in Brittany therefore received the more general title of guardian, in addition to the purely military titles of captain and lieutenant. From the beginning he appears to have exercised his office in the name of the king and of John de Montfort, and after 1354 this was specifically stated in his patent of appointment. In addition to his military responsibilities he was authorized to appoint and dismiss the ducal officers and was expected to supervise the civil as well as the military administration. To encourage support for John de Montfort, a 'secret' court was established in the newly-fortified town of Guérande[7] and the ducal council was maintained to advise the lieutenants. This council was largely Breton in composition and it included men who had advised Duke John III and the elder John de Montfort. Prominent among its members were Jean Coupegorge, Jean Barbu, Henri de Kaër, Bonabé de Callac, Jean de Bouelau and the archdeacon of Vannes, Jean de Lomene.[8] They gave the lieutenants the benefit of their local knowledge and experience in the affairs of the duchy and provided a measure of continuity throughout the administration.

Lancaster's successive commissions as captain and lieutenant in the duchy (14 September 1355, 8 August 1356 and 25 July 1357) gave him full military authority, with powers to lead an army and garrison the country, and over-riding administrative authority, with powers to dismiss and appoint local officials at his discretion.[9] He could receive rebels into the king's obedience, grant them letters of pardon and reward them with grants of land and revenues deriving from the war; conversely, he could confiscate the lands of those who deserted the king's allegiance and employ them as he thought best. His powers were thus similar in kind to those of the lieutenants in Brittany before him and to those which he had previously exercised in Aquitaine. The most notable feature of his command in Brittany was, however, the long siege which he conducted of the city of Rennes. Ostensibly, it was undertaken for John de Montfort who, on Edward's orders, had accompanied him on the Normandy campaign and who was with him in Brittany when he took up his command there.[10]

The young claimant to the duchy was then no more than fifteen years of age. Since his infancy he had been brought up in England, where he had been separated from his parents since before he was two years old. His father, who had been taken prisoner at Nantes in November 1341 and was subsequently held in custody at the Louvre in Paris until Easter 1345, when he escaped to England disguised as a merchant, had died suddenly before Hennebont in September of that year. His mother, the 'lion-hearted' Joan of Flanders, had been brought to England by Edward III in March 1343, but in October of that year she was put under close guard in the castle of Tickhill in Yorkshire, where she remained for the rest of her life, generally presumed to have been mad—though this is by no means certain. Her children, on the other hand, were installed in the Tower of London, then one of the royal residences with well-tended gardens and a menagerie which included several lions and a leopard, as well as being the chief military arsenal. It was there that the young John de Montfort was brought up, in his early years, under the guardianship of William de Wakefield; and as he grew older he may also have spent some time in the Lancastrian household.[11]

Montfort's cause had enjoyed success and suffered setbacks from both a military and a political standpoint, but his position would undoubtedly have been worse but for the capture of his rival, Charles of Blois, by Sir Thomas Dagworth at La Roche-Dérien in 1347; ever since then Blois had been held prisoner in England. Although an arrangement had been concluded for his release in the spring of 1353, it was not implemented and Charles had remained a prisoner. But in the summer of 1356 the situation changed. On 10 August, two days after Lancaster had been given his second commission in Brittany, another treaty was concluded for his release, a safe-conduct was issued to him on 7 August, and two weeks later he landed at Tréguier.[12] Lancaster, having laid siege to La Roche-Dérien and fortified Lannion, was then at Guingamp. On 2 October he began the siege of Rennes, which had remained constantly loyal to Charles of Blois.

Edward could not have chosen a more opportune moment to free Blois. The conditions of his release made it unlikely that he could make too much trouble: he had undertaken not to take any military action in the duchy until the completion of the agreement, which involved the payment of a huge ransom of 700,000 florins in gold écus. For his part Montfort came into Brittany as duke to secure his heritage, backed by a substantial force under Lancaster's command, and he was present with his lieutenant at the siege of Rennes.[13] Unable to participate personally, Charles of Blois had to appeal to Paris for the assistance of the dauphin.[14] The French were unable to give much help, but the lord of Rochefort was appointed captain in the duchy and given command of a force of 1,000 men-at-arms and 500 archers with which to relieve the city.[15] By 20 December he had established his headquarters at Vitré, some 36 kilometres due east of Rennes.[16] Early in the following year Guillaume de Craon was appointed lieutenant in Anjou, Maine, Poitou and Touraine and was given command of the relieving forces.[17]

Once begun, the siege lasted for more than nine months—from October 1356 to 5 July 1357.[18] It has been greatly studied, not for Lancaster's part in it, but because one of the captains in the defending force was the young Bertrand du Guesclin.[19] Most of the chroniclers devoted a few pages to the subject, but the principal account is in the *Chronique de Bertrand du Guesclin*, a poem by Jean Cuvelier.[20] This work, which has been described as one of the last of the *chansons de geste*, is both the most exhaustive and the least reliable. It was not written until after Du Guesclin's death, more than a quarter of a century later (between 1380 and 1387), by which time the constable's early deeds were already legendary. The author was one of the last minstrels;

he sought to emulate the heroic poets of the eleventh century and made good use of his imagination. He claimed, however, to have his evidence from Du Guesclin's companions and to have consulted the *Grandes Chroniques*; he is also known to have used the notes made available to the continuator of the chronicle of Richard Lescot. It is therefore possible that he was working from a fairly accurate written source and his controversial information mingles uneasily with well-established facts. Moreover, it should be remembered that Cuvelier wrote more to amuse than to instruct.[21]

Lancaster's forces are said to have been those with which he had conducted the raid in Normandy: some 1,000 men-at-arms and 1,400–1,500 archers. He deployed these troops around the ramparts, assigning detachments to guard the principal gates. The defending forces appear to have been under the command of the captain of the city, Bertrand de Saint-Pern, and the lord of Penhoet (known as Tort-Boiteux), who was castellan. Du Guesclin was not at the beginning among them. His name does not appear on any of the surviving musters of men-at-arms of the defending force or of any of the forces responsible for re-victualling the city. He played an important role, but was not well known at the time. He was neither castellan nor captain and commanded neither the castle nor the walls, at least in the initial stages. His part was to intercept Lancaster's convoys and supplies from the rear by way of ambushes, mostly carried out by night; but early in March he succeeded in entering the city with considerable supplies of food.

Lancaster's siege shows many curiously archaic features. As a method of conducting warfare it did not conform to the more advanced military notions of the day, which regarded challenges in open country to be eminently superior; raids, or *chevauchées*, conducted deep into enemy territory, by-passing centres of real resistance, had produced results out of all proportion to the effort put into them. Moreover, during the course of the siege there was a good deal of jousting and courteous visits between besiegers and besieged, which was very much in the tradition that regarded war as a large-scale tournament. Lancaster's methods were also rather old-fashioned. He began by attempting to mine the walls. When this failed he tried to induce the garrison to surrender by starving it out; but his blockade appears to have been far from complete. A gigantic *beffroi*, a huge wooden tower on wheels which he had rolled up to the battlements to enable the besiegers to enter the town over its walls, met the obvious fate which such machines had so often met with in the past—the defenders waited until it was just completed and then sallied forth and set it on fire.

All of this was, however, carried out in unfavourable circumstances. It was a particularly harsh winter and Lancaster's troops were camped in open country.[22] On 23 March a truce had been concluded at Bordeaux and one of its clauses provided for the immediate raising of the siege.[23] According to its terms, the Black Prince was to send letters to the duke requiring this to be done, together with a copy of the truce and the powers entrusted to the prince to make it. These appear to have been delivered to him by Sir Stephen de Cosington,[24] who had been in his service before entering that of the prince. The prince's requirement was not, however, effective and on 28 April the king was obliged to write to Lancaster ordering him to comply (Thomas Hoggeshawe was the bearer of these instructions);[25] but still Lancaster did not raise the siege. On 4 July Edward wrote to him again in more severe terms: 'You still have not raised the said siege, which surprises us much and displeases us greatly.' (These letters appear to have been delivered by Sir Richard Totesham.)[26]

Why did Lancaster not raise the siege? In his entire public career he had never before and was never again to be at cross purposes with Edward. According to Cuvelier the duke had sworn from the outset not to leave Rennes before he had placed his pennant on the battlements[27] and doubtless pride, honour and profit were at stake. The author of the *Chronique des quatre premiers Valois*, on the other hand, says that the duke had undertaken and continued the siege for John de Montfort.[28] The *Anonimalle Chronicle* of St Mary's, York, is more explicit:[29]

'. . . The aforesaid cardinals [mediating the truce of Bordeaux] humbly requested the prince of England [the Black Prince] that he would order his messengers with his letters to Duke Henry of Lancaster, who was besieging the city of Rennes in Brittany, to the effect that he would abandon and depart from the said siege; and the prince did so, and the king of England also sent letters ordering him to depart from the said city of Rennes on pain of forfeiture. To this order the duke humbly replied that he was not conducting the quarrel of his liege lord, but was conducting the quarrel of the duke, Montfort, and it would therefore not be honourable to so suddenly give it up; and for these reasons he stayed there and nobly continued, maintaining the said siege until the said city of Rennes had been surrendered to him and placed at his grace and wishes to do that which he pleased . . .'

As an explanation it is not out of line with the dual form of Lancaster's commission as lieutenant for the king and John de Montfort. The young claimant was present at the siege and we know him to have been making grants in the duchy in his own right as duke (albeit on Lancaster's advice).[30] It may account for the new form of Lancaster's appointment on 25 July: he received one commission, almost identical in form with the previous two, in the name of the king and John de Montfort, and another in the king's name alone, omitting all references to Montfort.[31]

It has been suggested that Edward's orders were insincere;[32] but Lancaster's intentions were well known to the king, as were those of the king to the duke. On 10 October 1356 Thomas Rede was paid £2 for bringing letters to Edward from Lancaster;[33] these may have contained news of the Black Prince's victory at Poitiers, which is known to have been sent to the king by the duke.[34] On 18 November Thomas Dautre was paid £4 5s od for a journey via Cherbourg with letters for the duke from the king[35] and in the following spring Lancaster sent Walter de Byntre to England with a complete dossier on the government of the duchy and in particular concerning the implementation of the truce in Brittany.[36] In his reply to the points raised by Lancaster, which was brought by Thomas Hoggeshawe, Edward made it quite clear that the truce was to be observed, provided that the opposing party in Brittany were for their part willing to implement it and there was no new impediment to its effectiveness. Unless there was, the duke was to raise the siege of Rennes immediately, as he had already been instructed to by letters under the secret seal. The real difficulty arose neither out of any insubordination on Lancaster's part nor from any insincerity on the part of the king; it arose out of the failure of those responsible for drafting the terms of the truce in Bordeaux to make the stipulations necessary to meet contingencies in Brittany.

Hoggeshawe left London on 7 May—shortly after the arrival of Byntre—and returned on 30 July.[37] By then Totesham had left Dover for Calais on his way to Rennes. He reached Gisors on 27 July and from there he was given a safe-conduct as far as Avranches by escorts provided by both King John and the dauphin.[38] By the time he arrived at his destination the siege had already been raised. This took the form of a truce between the opposing forces. For 100,000 crowns (60,000 from the city and 40,000 in ransoms from prisoners) Lancaster agreed to withdraw—but not until after he had been allowed to plant his banner on the walls and to hold the keys of the city for a few hours.[39] He entered with 10 knights, accepted wine from Du Guesclin and then retired.[40] Honour was saved, but the military significance of the entire episode was very little. Once again, the duke had been overtaken by affairs in the south.

After the conclusion of the truce at Bordeaux Lancaster had wished to return to England, but the king requested him to remain in Brittany until the autumn and if possible for a further year thereafter in order to carry out a major overhaul of the administration, and in particular to make a thorough investigation into the command and upkeep of the garrisons.[41] All of the duke's predecessors as lieutenant in the duchy had found it difficult to make their authority felt among the garrison forces. Basically the problem was financial. While the English government was able to pay the expeditionary forces, its resources were insufficient to meet the continuing needs of the allied garrisons in France.[42]

In any consideration of the financing of the English forces in France during the reign of Edward III a distinction must be made between expeditionary and garrison or occupation forces. The former operated on a short-service basis. They were made up of troops organized in companies under the command of the king and his lieutenants, with fixed rates of pay and conditions of service. They were not expected to remain in France beyond the period necessary for the conclusion of a campaign, when they returned to England and came off the king's pay roll. They were permanent only in so far as the troops were likely to serve again in future companies sent out from England. The position among the occupation forces was quite different. The effort required to finance and supply the garrisons in France, to sustain that effort over an indefinite number of years and to maintain central control at the same time was considerably greater than the effort required to finance, supply and control the expeditionary forces sent out from England for a limited period of campaigning. Edward III was unable to achieve in Brittany what Henry V and the duke of Bedford achieved in Normandy in the fifteenth century.

The problem of financing the occupation forces first became acute in Brittany. When Edward III returned from the duchy to England in 1343, part of the English expeditionary forces were assigned to garrison the towns and castles which had been brought into his control. Provision for their maintenance had already been made in the previous year in two agreements with Montfort's wife, Joan of Flanders.[43] According to the first of these, in return for English military assistance Joan agreed to provide the king with £2,000 in bullion and plate and to put at his disposal the towns, ports and castles which he required for his garrison forces and the conduct of military operations. By the terms of the second agreement, in place of the £2,000 all the ducal revenues were placed at the king's disposal.

Before Edward left Brittany in 1343 he appointed two captains-general and lieutenants (Sir John de Hardreshull and Ivon de la Roche, lord of Lohéak) to supervise the military situation, and a treasurer (John Coupegorge) to collect the ducal revenues and pay the troops serving under their command. In 1345 they were succeeded by the earl of Northampton, who crossed to Brittany with an expeditionary force which was to be paid for an initial three months by the English Exchequer and thereafter (together with the troops already serving in Brittany) by John Charnels, who was appointed to succeed Coupegorge as treasurer. When Northampton was in turn succeeded by Sir Thomas Dagworth, all the ducal revenues were handed over to him to keep the war going. But although the occupation of Brittany was theoretically to have been paid for out of the ducal revenues, in practice they proved inadequate and, owing to the continual fighting in the duchy, too difficult to collect. The accounts of Coupegorge, Charnels and Dagworth show that they had received none of the traditional revenues and that the troops serving under the lieutenants had to be paid from England. As early as 1344 a Breton merchant petitioned the king that the profits which had customarily been collected from the sale of ducal *brefs* should be handed over to the receiver of the duchy so that the troops could be paid.[44] The indiscipline typical of unpaid soldiers was already making itself felt.

In the absence of sufficient ducal revenues and an adequate system of supply, the garrisons were forced to live on the surrounding countryside. The accounts of the treasurer of the duchy, Giles de Wyngreworth, for the years 1359–62, and a large number of documents subsidiary to them, give a detailed picture of the situation during his term of office and that of Henry de Tatton who was the treasurer during Lancaster's period of office as lieutenant. By then, only the three principal fortresses of Vannes, Bécherel and Ploërmel accounted with the treasurer. The garrisons of these each had a captain, constable and receiver, and controlled extensive ransomed districts of as many as 124 parishes (divided into circuits, each with a collector) which provided money, food and labour services for the upkeep of the forces and the maintenance of the defences. These ransoms constituted by far the greatest single source of revenue received by the treasurer; they were scheduled to yield £14,735 a year.[45]

The most important revenues after ransoms were derived from the farms of the offices of receiver, constable and janitor at Bécherel and Ploërmel.[46] At Vannes, the revenues received by these officers were not accounted for by the treasurer, since they were assigned to him and the captain of the town to pay the wages of themselves and their retinues. In 1359–60 the town of Hennebont and the castles of Saint-Gwennolé and Ploëmeur were farmed out,[47] but thereafter the revenues were granted to their captains by the king for farms payable direct into the Exchequer. Other revenues (arising from customs on wine, corn and other merchandise, farms of mills, shipwrecks, confiscations and escheats) were collected at Vannes, but they amounted to a negligible proportion of total revenues.[48]

The revenues raised from these sources were expended on the wages of the lieutenant and treasurer of the duchy and their retinues and on the wages of the captains and garrisons of the three principal towns. In 1359–60 these amounted to £15,464.[49] Had the ransoms been fully paid, the total revenues would have been sufficient to meet all these expenses. As it was, expenditure was in excess of revenue by £2,591 which remained outstanding to Sir Robert de Herle, then lieutenant of the duchy.

The other towns, castles and fortresses in Brittany occupied by English troops were also commanded by a captain, assisted by a constable and a receiver, and ransoms and other revenues were levied there on the same pattern; but they were not paid in to the treasurer of the duchy. Some of these fortresses were farmed out to their captains for sums payable to the English Exchequer or the king's Chamber, but the majority were held for no payment whatsoever by the captains who had taken them and regarded them as their personal property, by grant of the king, or (in the case of Breton partisans of John de Montfort) by hereditary right. Here, the captains were directly responsible for the pay and upkeep of the garrisons and for the maintenance of the defences out of the revenues which their officers collected. The financing of occupation forces by means of reventions is particularly evident in Brittany owing to the survival of Wyngreworth's accounts and the documents subsidiary to them. It was not, however, unique to the duchy; the fortresses taken by Lancaster on his way back from the Loire valley in 1356 were financed by the same means, and the parishes ransomed to them extended the area under English control well beyond the Breton frontiers. After 1356 the practice became common for allied garrisons throughout France.

The problem of maintaining control over the English occupation forces in France was intimately connected with the problem of financing and supplying them. The importance of security of pay in maintaining discipline in the contract armies is well known. The haphazard and uncertain methods of finance and supply, and the financial impossibility of maintaining considerable forces in widely-scattered regions of France for an indefinite number of years, made this much more difficult for the armies of occupation. Moreover, in the absence of a sound financial organization and regular pay, no machinery of muster and review could be developed. It was a relatively simple matter to keep a check on the strength and quality of the expeditionary forces since they could be mustered at their port of embarkation in England or of disembarkation in France, and again on their return to England; but apart from Calais, where a serious attempt was made to ensure that the troops were paid from England, there is no evidence of regular mustering of the English occupation forces in France during Edward III's reign. In these conditions it was practically impossible for the king's captains and lieutenants to maintain control over the troops placed under their command; without regular wages it was impossible to maintain discipline in the ranks. The problem was already evident in Gascony in 1341;[50] in Brittany and Normandy in the 1350s it became acute.

This is well illustrated by a series of negotiations between Philip of Navarre and Edward III, prior to Sir Thomas Holand being sent out to join Philip as lieutenant in Normandy in 1359. On this occasion the king's council refused to give Philip command of all the English forces in the duchy. They argued that since the troops sent to Normandy had only been paid for an initial period and were thereafter fighting at their own expense, the king could not bind them to be obedient to Philip unless he paid them; but they preferred to be in Normandy at their own costs in order to be free to fight where they wished and for their own profit. The council would only go so far as to say that in an emergency (if, for instance, Philip was taken prisoner) the troops were to go to his assistance and he would be expected to help them when in difficulties. The soldiers could not even be expected to pay a third of their spoils to either Philip or the king as long as they were not paid. Nevertheless, the king had spoken to Holand on that matter and he had agreed that, provided Philip entrusted him with fortresses convenient for the lodging of his troops when they arrived in Normandy, he would give him such part of his profits as was agreed between them.

The situation in Brittany was, as one would expect, particularly acute because of the large number of towns and castles occupied by troops who, because of the relative strength of the English position there, were not always engaged in fighting. Soldiers without an enemy to attack found time hanging heavy on their hands. Unsupervised foraging offered ample opportunities for oppressing the country folk. The garrisons were small groups often set among a hostile people, whom they probably despised individually and feared collectively. The system of ransoming to meet upkeep costs aggravated relations with the local population. Instances of petty tyranny, clashes and rebellions were bound to, and often did, occur. Sir Walter Bentley, lieutenant of the duchy in the years 1350–1353, realized very clearly that as long as the troops there were inadequately paid not only would those Bretons loyal to the king go over to the French, but the lieutenant could have no real control over the garrisons in Brittany. A memorandum which he sent to the council, explaining his difficulties in detail, gives a clear picture of the kind of indiscipline with which he had to contend.

In the four principal towns (Vannes, Bécherel, Ploërmel and Hennebont), from which all the other fortresses and towns were supposed to be governed, the Bretons were going over to the enemy because of the extortions practised by large numbers of undisciplined soldiers not being properly paid. The troops did not want to live in the garrisons of these four towns unless they received very high wages, but preferred to be on the front, where they regarded the castles and fortresses which they won from the enemy as their own property, from which they put the surrounding countryside to ransom. Neither church nor poor people were spared. Fields went untilled. When they had extorted all they could from one district they moved on to another. They could not be mobilized when needed. Then, when they had enriched themselves sufficiently, they bought safe-conducts for a high price and made their way back to England.

The council could hardly fail to see the point of the memorandum, and they responded by giving Bentley extensive powers of supervision and inspection. He was empowered to remove all captains and men whom he regarded as unnecessary or undesirable; those he retained were all to receive the king's wages. Soldiers who captured a castle on the front might keep the movable goods found there, but the castle itself was to be handed over to the lieutenant, who was to appoint a captain who was to be on the king's pay roll and who was to be intendent to him. Only customary wages were to be paid, although captains were to receive an extra fee for their office. Troops were to be ready for mobilization when required and they were not to leave

Brittany without the permission of the lieutenant. The status and authority Bentley was intended to have was summed up by a paragraph stating that all keepers of castles and fortresses, and everyone else in the king's obedience, were to be intendent and obedient to the lieutenant as to the king himself on pain of loss of life and limb.

For these measures to be effective, not only would adequate financial resources have to be available to pay all the captains and garrison troops, but they would also have to be administered centrally; but this was never the case. In his memorandum Bentley requested that all captains should be on the king's pay roll so that he could enter the fortresses which they occupied and have authority over them. He claimed that the revenues were insufficient for this because the money which was supposed to be used for the upkeep of the towns, castles and garrisons had been alienated by the king. This, as we have seen, was precisely the case. He tried to augment the revenues, so as to pay the troops, by suggesting that Edward should resume all grants and confiscations. But the council, whilst they wished to have more information on the number of grants that had been made and wanted to know who the beneficiaries were, nevertheless seem to have been of the opinion that where the financial and other obligations were being fulfilled the owners should remain undisturbed; many grants had doubtless been made to buy support. The only concession they seem to have made was that such castellans as were subsequently appointed, whilst they were given the revenues of the castles they were to command, were also instructed to pay the lieutenant any balance that remained after the expenses of their garrisons had been met. Bentley's report goes to the heart of the matter: discipline could not be maintained through lack of regular pay. Despite repeated government pronouncements that all troops in Brittany should be on the king's pay roll such arrangements were just not feasible, and increasingly the authorities had to allow troops to live from the uncontrolled proceeds of ransom districts. By 1360 they had lost control of many of the garrisons themselves, and not only in Brittany, but in Normandy and far into the Loire provinces, in Picardy, Burgundy, Champagne and elsewhere in France.

These problems were far too great for Lancaster to solve on his own, but his task was also complicated by the conclusion of the truce at Bordeaux which, if it was to be made operative in Brittany, would leave the garrison forces unemployed although they still had to be paid. Moreover, its terms were clearly inadequate to meet contingencies in Brittany, since the troops depended on the occupied territories for their upkeep costs. On the question of ransoms they were evidently erroneous (*aweronses*). Lancaster had raised the matter with the king by way of Walter Byntre and Edward instructed the duke to discuss it with the Franco-Bretons but to make sure that the payments remained partially in force to meet the needs of the garrisons.[51] In this the duke was successful and he also went some way to solving the problem of indiscipline by giving his retainers and other trusted servants some of the key positions in the duchy.[52] The most important factor in his administration of Brittany was the facilities which his estates in England placed at his disposal. Unlike the majority of his predecessors as lieutenant in the duchy, he had behind him the resources of his enormous wealth.

# XIV The Lancastrian estates, household and entourage

Lancaster's estates, when at their greatest, extended into thirty English and three Welsh counties and included the lordships of Bergerac, Beaufort and Nogent in France, together with some property in Calais and, for a short time, in Saint-Jean-d'Angély.[1] In the letters issued in his name during the last year of his life he was styled 'duke of Lancaster, earl of Derby, Lincoln and Leicester, steward of England, lord of Bergerac and Beaufort',[2] and he enjoyed a gross income of around £8,380 from his English and Welsh estates alone.[3] He held twenty-three castles situated in the north and west: on the Welsh border, in the Midlands and the north. In Monmouthshire they included Grosmont, Skenfrith, Monmouth and Whitecastle. These four castles were flanked on the south by the strongholds of Carmarthen and Glamorgan: Kidwelly, Iscennen, Carreg Cennen and Ogmore. The castles of the Midlands stretched up into the north: Kenilworth, Higham Ferrers, Leicester, Melbourne, Tutbury, Newcastle-under-Lyme, Halton, Liverpool, Pontefract, Bolingbroke, Lincoln, Clitheroe, Lancaster, Hornby and, in Northumberland, Dunstanburgh.

By far the greater part of these possessions had come to him on the death of his father in 1345. He had held the castles of Kidwelly, Ogmore, Grosmont and Skenfrith since 1333 and that of Carreg Cennen since 1340; but other additions were made to his inheritance after he became earl of Lancaster.[4] The most important of these were the grants which he secured from the king before Calais in the summer of 1347 as reward for his work in Aquitaine—the castle and honor of Pontefract, Horston, Clitheroe, and Bergerac and Saint-Jean-d'Angély in France. It was also about that time that he was attempting to recover that part of the Lacy lands which his uncle Thomas had granted to John de Warenne, earl of Surrey, in 1319, and of which a reversionary interest was granted to the earl of Salisbury in 1337. On Warenne's death in 1347 he had a suit in chancery for these manors, and in September of that year, whilst he was with the king at Calais, Salisbury's son and heir, William Montagu, submitted a petition to Edward III for them, setting forth both his and Lancaster's claims.[5] Most of these lands were, however, delivered to the countess of Surrey, who subsequently leased them to the Black Prince, who in turn surrendered them to Salisbury after the death of the countess in 1361. Only the Norfolk manors in which Earl Thomas had been enfeoffed were delivered to Henry. But on 2 October 1348, when the countess of Lincoln died childless, he was heir to all the Lacy estates which had been the subject of dispositions in his grandfather's time (including Lincoln and Bolingbroke), and on 20 August of the following year he was created earl of Lincoln and added that title to his collection.

The greatest honour of all was, however, yet to be conferred upon him. On 6 March 1351 he was elevated to the rank of duke and the county of Lancaster was erected into a palatinate similar to that of Chester.[6] A number of views have been advanced as to the king's reasons for conferring this honour upon his 'cousin'. Only one such title had been conferred before—on the king's son and heir, Edward of Woodstock, the Black Prince, who became duke of Cornwall in 1337. It has been argued that Edward III's primary concern was to defend north-western England against the Scots, as the palatinate of Durham defended the north-east; but he may have intended nothing more than to honour Henry. Certainly there could have been no greater mark of the king's favour. It was at once the highest recognition of his services and an acknowledgement of his standing in the realm—next the Black Prince. Perhaps it was more. For a nobleman who was so much involved in negotiations with great territorial princes abroad and other foreign dignitaries, on truce, peace and other diplomatic missions, it was well that Edward should give him standing. His power to impress and persuade might be held in the balance by it.

The granting of palatine powers allowed Henry to exercise powers in Lancashire which were formerly the prerogative of the Crown. They enabled him to have a chancery there, with its own seal, under which he could issue a variety of instruments. He could appoint his own justices for pleas of the Crown and all other pleas touching the common law, and enforce their judgements by his writs and through his ministers in Lancashire. He had the power to make corporations and erect fairs and markets, and he could grant exemption from juries and assizes. The king did, however, reserve a number of rights in the county: to pardon life and limb and to reverse judgements made in error in the duke's courts; moreover, unlike the palatine lords of Durham and Chester, Henry was to send representatives of the shire and boroughs in the county to parliament.

Since the king's writ did not run in the palatinate it followed that, except in cases of treason and error, men of the county palatine could not be summoned to appear or answer any matter outside it. Mandates which the king issued to the sheriff in other counties were issued in Lancashire to Duke Henry or his deputy, sometimes his justice in the 'duchy'. Other writs were addressed to Henry or his chancellor in the duchy—the officer who had charge of his great seal, the authority of which was limited to the county palatine, as distinct from his personal or privy seal, which had no geographical limitations. Numerous instruments were, however, issued under the great seal and enrolled. Two such rolls of the Lancashire chancery are extant for Henry's time and the outgoing letters which they record are dated by the year of his *ducatus*, commencing on 6 March 1351—the date of his elevation to the position of duke. These letters were drawn up in much the same form as those issued under the great seal of the realm, the only difference being that the duke's name and style was substituted for that of the king. Although they were tested by the duke (normally at Preston, occasionally at Lancaster and for a few months—from December 1358 to April 1359—at Liverpool castle), Henry was not necessarily present when they were passed; they appear rather to have been dated according to the whereabouts of the chancellor. Letters under this seal were normally drawn up by order of the duke—often acting on the advice of his council—by warrant of a letter under his privy seal. In the rest of his lands Henry had no more than his existing rights. The title of duke was only a title and by itself conferred no new power on him. Thus, after the creation of the palatinate, grants relating to his other possessions continued to be made under his privy seal.

The granting of palatinate powers in the middle of the fourteenth century was indeed a mark of the royal favour, for the trend had previously been against the alienation of royal jurisdiction. It has been argued that Edward could afford to bestow such extensive powers on Lancaster, since the grant was made for the duke's lifetime only and Henry had no male heir;[7] but there seems to be no reason to believe that his wife could not have given birth to a son after 1351. It was not, therefore, altogether certain that (even if the king had already decided to marry John of Gaunt to Henry's daughter Blanche, which may be doubted) the reversion of at least a part of the inheritance would be secured for one of Edward III's children. In 1351 it was not inevitable that the Lancastrian inheritance would be divided between Henry's two daughters.

One final and mysterious honour was to be bestowed upon him. On 5 April 1359, David II of Scotland, lately returned into his kingdom after eleven years' captivity in England, created him earl of Moray.[8] The grant was made for himself and his heirs male with remainder, for their life only, to his daughters Blanche and Maude; but it is difficult to determine why it was made to him. Although his wife, Isabella, had Scottish blood in her veins (she was the daughter of Henry, first lord Beaumont, earl of Buchan through his wife Alice, first daughter and co-heir of Alexander Comyn),[9] there is no apparent claim which she could pass on to her husband to succeed Thomas Randolph in the earldom, although her father had numbered among the Disinherited who had a particular quarrel with the Randolphs and had led Balliol to his coronation. The reasons which lay behind the grant may in fact be hidden in the negotiations for the ransom and release of David II. In the course of these negotiations David had expressed his willingness to agree to the restoration of the Disinherited and, should he die childless, to the succession of one of Edward III's sons to the throne of Scotland; but these proposals were rejected by the Council General of Scotland both in 1351 and 1364. In the latter assembly, however, John of Gaunt was considered as a candidate and found acceptable to some of its members because he was not the heir to the English throne and because, it was argued, through his wife's connection with the earls of Buchan, the future king would thus be half a Scot.[11] The marriage between John of Gaunt and Blanche was celebrated on 19 May 1359—less than six weeks after Henry's creation as earl of Moray;[12] but Lancaster does not appear to have used the title in the two years before his death.

From the time he returned from his first expedition to Aquitaine Lancaster thus commanded estates which made him one of the richest men in England. But the inheritance which he then came into was a unit in social life as well as a unit in landownership and it supported, in addition to himself and his family, a host of receivers and auditors, soldiers and heralds, councillors and minstrels, menial servants and followers of all kinds who were fed and paid by him. Like the other great nobles of his day, he had a considerable body of men in his service: household officers and attendants to administer his affairs, maintain his state and dignity and protect his property and person; men who were bound by indenture to serve him for life in peace and war, who had received grants of land from him or who had taken his fees and wore his livery. The most important of these were his officers. In addition to the wardrober, treasurer, household steward, steward of lands and attorneys-general in his service as earl of Derby, as earl and then duke of Lancaster, he had a chamberlain, a chancellor or secretary who was in charge of his privy seal, a receiver-general, auditors and other officers.

Two esquires were prominent as his chamberlains: Simon Simeon (1354) and Robert de la Grene (1355).[13] Simeon began his career as a yeoman of the third earl and rose to prosperity in the service of the Lancastrian household.[14] One of the earliest mentions of his name is as a defender of Caerphilly castle against Queen Isabella. He accompanied the elder Henry abroad in 1329, first appears in the younger Henry's service as an esquire in his retinue in Scotland in 1336[15] and distinguished himself in the campaigns there and elsewhere in France, serving on no less than eleven missions in the earl's retinue. The place with which he seems to have been most closely connected was Grafton Underwood, near Kettering in Northamptonshire. One of the earl's *donzels* or household esquires in 1344,[16] he subsequently witnessed several of his charters,[17] was appointed master and keeper of his game in England and Wales in 1349,[18] was steward of Lincolnshire in 1361 and one of his feofees and executors. He was rewarded for his services with grants of the castle and manors of Castleford and Kilburn in Yorkshire and Ugley in Essex, with lands and tenements at Belper in Derbyshire and Sibsey in Lincolnshire, and sufficient housbote and heybote for his manor of Newstead in Lincolnshire and his house of Oulton near Rothwell, within the duke's parks of Pontefract, Rothwell and Ackworth in Pontefract honor.[19] After the duke's death he was active in the service of Henry's son-in-law: his steward in Lincolnshire and Bolingbroke, he was frequently employed in John of Gaunt's affairs. He founded and endowed a chantry in the chapel on the mount at Pontefract—the scene of the execution of Earl Thomas—and took an interest in other churches on the ducal estates. Long after his death (he disappears from view about 1385) he was remembered as *Simkyn* by the inmates of Henry's college at Leicester.

Not much is known about the functions of his various financial officers. Later practice would suggest that the surplus revenues from his estates and the casual receipts found their way to the receiver-general, but under his father and Thomas it was the wardrober who took this place.[20] The duke had at least three wardrobers[21] and four receivers-general[22] in his service; but he seems to have attached more importance to his treasurer. Of the five men who held this office,[23]

John Gynewell (1344–6) was already in Lancastrian service in 1329, when he accompanied Henry's father to France;[24] but shortly afterwards he entered the young earl's service. He acted as his treasurer-of-war in Scotland in 1336–7 and in the Low Countries in 1338–40,[25] served as one of his attorneys-general when Henry went abroad in 1340, 1344 and 1346,[26] and as steward of his lands in 1343–5.[27] His chaplain in 1343 and auditor of his accounts in 1344, he was one of his leading councillors.[28] Henry de Walton, who succeeded him as treasurer (1348–53) appears to have entered Henry's service in July 1345 when, together with William de Farley, he was responsible for receiving from the Exchequer the wages of the earl and his troops leaving for Gascony.[29] He served in Henry's retinue in the duchy—doubtless in some financial capacity—and later joined him before Calais.[30] In March of the following year he was appointed to prosecute the execution of certain recognizances made to the earl in chancery.[31] He frequently served as one of his attorneys-general, and as lieutenant of the county palatine of Lancaster when the duke was abroad in 1354 and 1359. Warden of his lands in 1352, he was naturally among the witnesses to his charters.[32] Nicholas de Colshull began his career in Lancastrian service with the earl's father; he was his receiver of Tutbury honor in 1329 and 1333 and served as his wardrober.[33] He continued in the earl's service, acting as his receiver-general in 1353–4, 1356 and 1358–9, as his treasurer in 1355 and 1358, as one of his attorneys-general during his absence on the Reims campaign of 1359–60[34] and as lieutenant of the county palatine of Lancaster during the same period.[35] He was among the witnesses to charters of both father and son.[36]

Besides these men, Henry also had a financial officer to look after his interests in Bergerac. Sir William Darampton and three clerks—Master Jean Vilet, William de Driffield and Adam de Everingham—acted as his attorneys in this respect,[37] and Everingham is specifically described as his 'treasurer of Bergerac'[38] and elsewhere as his 'receiver in Gascony'.[39] He accounted with the constable of Bordeaux for wages due to the garrison of the town upon receipt of a warrant from the seneschal of Aquitaine. In England, the steward of the lands, the auditors (who generally worked in pairs) and to a lesser degree the receiver-general, supervised the estates. They imparted a unity of control that was further exercised by the council.

Of the seven men known to have served as his steward,[40] only John Gynewell (1343–5) was a cleric; the subsequent stewards were all laymen, landowners who played an active part in local government—like Walter atte Bergh in Wiltshire or Sir Hugh Berwick in Lancashire and Yorkshire. Since these two men were stewards contemporaneously, it had evidently already been found necessary to divide the estates into two parts for administration purposes; in 1356 Walter atte Bergh is specifically called steward *citra Trentam*, while Sir Peter de la Mare seems to have confined his activities to the south parts.

No less than eighteen persons are known to have served as his attorney-general. They were normally appointed (always in pairs, but interchangeable) when Lancaster went abroad on military and diplomatic missions.[41] They acted for him in matters touching his estates and finances and requested letters of protection for those going to serve or serving in his retinue abroad.[42] He had at least fourteen valets or *donzels* in his service,[43] some of whom were very close to his person and so played a significant part in his affairs. John de Aldewyncle and Philip de Popham were among the more notable of them. Both were sent as his private envoys to Avignon and were employed on other diplomatic missions.[44] Aldewyncle appears to have been a native of the Lancastrian manor bearing that name in Northamptonshire and was among those yeomen who accompanied the elder Henry to France in 1329.[45] He secured a grant for life of the manor of North Standen in Wiltshire from the earl and two annuities, one of them a confirmation of a grant made by the elder Henry.[46] He served on at least five missions abroad in the duke's retinue.[47] Popham was granted a life annuity of £10 in the manor of King's Somborne in Hampshire, together with its bedelry.[48] He may have been the son of the elder Henry's *amé vadlet* John de Popham, to whom the third earl had granted a life annuity of £8 in the manor of Everleigh in Wiltshire.[49] He served in the duke's retinue on the Reims campaign of 1359–60.[50] Andrew Brauche, another of the earl's valets, also appears to have served the elder Henry.[51] A man of some property (he held the manor of Frome in Somerset),[52] he accompanied the earl abroad on at least three missions.[53] Thomas de Burton received an annuity of 20 marks for life in the manor of Gimingham in Norfolk from him, as well as the lordship and rent of Irchester in Northamptonshire.[54] He acted as the duke's messenger from Holland in 1354.[55] Thomas de la Mare, who was described as one of his valets in 1353, when he presented the king with two dextriers from the duke,[56] was the son of Sir Peter de la Mare;[57] he accompanied the earl abroad on at least two occasions.[58] Other men who were also described as his valets were John Blount, John Cockayn, Thomas Florak, Robert de la Grene, Roger Perot,

Nicholas Peyure, Richard Radcliffe, John Rithre and Simon Simeon. Apart from these men there were many others in his service: minstrels, pipers, tailors, armourers, sergeants-at-arms, carpenters, cooks, bakers, fishmongers and a host of other less important officers, in addition to the purely local officials who served on his estates.[59] There is also mention of Derby Herald coming from Prussia with Simon Simeon in 1352.[60]

About half of the household and central officers were ecclesiastics, including all three chancellors and five treasurers and at least two of the three known wardrobers. They were rewarded for their services with ecclesiastical benefices on the Lancastrian estates and, more important, through the duke's promotion of petitions to the pope. During his lifetime Henry requested sixty-six prebends and dignities and thirty-two lesser benefices—of which no less than eighty were for his clerks: only seven less than those asked for by the Black Prince and more than the number asked for by the king between 1342 and 1366.[61] All three of his known chancellors or secretaries were promoted by him. John de Welbourne, who held that office in 1348-9, 1351 and 1355,[62] secured a prebend in Salisbury, canonries and prebends in York and Lincoln, the treasurership of Lincoln and the church of Raunds (which was of the duke's advowson) and probably a canonry and prebend in Lichfield upon petitions promoted by him.[63] He also secured a dispensation to be non-resident while engaged in his service so that he could receive the fruits of his benefice for two years. William de Claville, who is first mentioned as his clerk and envoy in 1352, secured dispensation to retain the church of Burton-in-Kendal in the diocese of York and was provided to a canonry and prebend in Dublin and a canonry and prebend in Lichfield on petitions also promoted by him.[64] Roger de Burton, his chancellor in 1355, was parson of St Gregory's at Sudbury in 1355 and of Derford in 1360, and he owed a canonry and prebend in Lincoln to him.[65] Of the three known wardrobers, Peter de Wotton (1343-7), beginning as his chaplain and parson of Edmondthorpe in Leicestershire, secured canonries in Salisbury, Hereford and London and was provided to prebends in Salisbury and Hereford upon petitions made by him.[66] William de Horwich (1353-4) was provided to a canonry in Wells, with expectation of a prebend, upon his petition.[67]

Although little is known of John Gynewell's origin his earliest ecclesiastical preferments and his usual residence were in Leicestershire.[68] As early as 1334 he held the benefice of Foston in Guthlaxton hundred and deanery, six to seven miles south of Leicester, and was provided to a canonry of Salisbury with reservation of a prebend. Sometime between 1336 and 1338 he obtained the prebend of Bedwin. Meanwhile, in 1337, he exchanged Foston for a canonry and prebend in St Mary's in the castle at Leicester, where he was conveniently near his work in the Lancastrian household. He obtained the prebend of Staunton in the conventual church of Wilton in the diocese of Salisbury, which he exchanged for the prebend of Caistor in Lincoln early in 1344. He continued to hold the prebend of Salisbury and, sometime before June 1343, was presented to the rectory of Llanelly which lay upon the Lancastrian estates in Carmarthenshire. He was provided to canonries in Wells and York on petitions of the earl; by April 1344 he held prebends at Tamworth and St Martin's-le-Grand in London, in addition to his prebends in Lincoln and Salisbury, his canonry at Wells and the rectory of Llanelly. After 1347, when he became bishop of Lincoln (an office which he held until 1362) he was seldom employed in the earl's service; but it is clear that the two men remained close friends. Lancaster drew upon his advice and counsel at every step in his great project of Newarke College at Leicester; he chose him as one of his executors and enjoyed his assistance when making his will.

Of his other treasurers, Henry Walton held the chaplaincy of St Michael's in the Castle at Clitheroe by grant of the earl and by 1348 was in possession of the rectory of Llanelly in succession to Gynewell.[69] He had secured the rectory of Preston (which was also in gift of the earl) by February of the following year and by April, when he is referred to as of the diocese of Coventry and Lichfield, he held the prebend of Yetminster in Salisbury in addition to the rectory of Preston. He was provided to canonries and prebends in York, Hereford and Leicester, canonries in Chichester and Hereford and secured the archdeaconry of Richmond and a canonry and prebend in Exeter on petitions by Lancaster. By 1355 he held the archdeaconry of Richmond, canonries and prebends in Lincoln, Salisbury, Exeter, Wells; he was in expectation of a prebend in York and held the rectory of Preston. William de Driffield, who held office as the duke's treasurer from 1354–7, was provided to a benefice (valued at £30) in the gift of the abbess and convent of Wilton upon a petition by him.[70] He subsequently secured the archdeaconry of Coventry and a provision to exchange his canonry of Salisbury and prebend of Roften (both of which he had resigned) with the canonry of Lichfield and prebend of Tervyn. In 1357 he had a grant for life of the hospital of the Holy Innocents without Lincoln. Nicholas de Colshull was provided to a canonry and prebend in Lincoln on petition by him and secured the churches of Collingbourne-Ducis (which lay upon the Lancastrian estates) and Stockton, and a canonry and prebend in Wells. In 1348 he acquired farms of the earl in Tutbury honor.[71] Richard de Walton, his receiver-general in 1353, was provided to a canonry of Salisbury, with expectation of a prebend, on a petition made by him.[72]

The duke exercised this ecclesiastical patronage to reward the leading clerks in his service in much the same way as he granted lands and annuities to the more important of his lay officers and soldiers. That it was intended in such a way is made clear in the case of one of his clerks, Thomas de Buxton, who accompanied him on the Reims campaign of 1359–60 and who was granted an annuity of 20 marks until he should be promoted to an ecclesiastical benefice in the earl's patronage.[73] But Henry was also able to promote the men in his service by drawing the king's attention to them. Both Gynewell and Henry de Walton enjoyed the royal favour.[74] Both are referred to as the king's clerks, Gynewell in 1338 and 1346, and Walton in 1351 and 1354. Walton may have been a clerk of the Exchequer as early as 1345. He secured grants of two prebends in the king's gift: Hagworth in Salisbury cathedral and Nassington in Lincoln cathedral. He was confirmed in the quasi-episcopal powers which he exercised as archdeacon of Richmond, 'by reason of his [the king's] affection for him' and in November 1354 he was ratified in his estate as archdeacon of Richmond, prebendary of Lincoln and Wells and parson of Preston. He possessed a lodging in London by 1357 and in December of the following year was put in charge of the royal wardrobe as William Retford's successor. Plunged into preparations for the Reims campaign, assisted by William de Farley as controller (his colleague in organizing the financing of Lancaster's first expedition to Aquitaine) he was, however, incapacitated by illness before Edward crossed to Calais and he died at Sandwich sometime before 21 November 1359.

To reconstruct the duke's retinue is not so simple, since the contracts for service concluded with him were not systematically preserved. Only five men are known to have drawn up indentures with him: Sir Edmund de Ufford and Sir Ralph de Hastings (who were both retained for life during war and peace with a fee of 40 marks), Sir Norman de Swinford, William Bracebridge and a London carpenter called Richard de Felstede.[75] All of them received fees tied to specific manors in return for some form of service—in the cases of Ufford, Hastings and Swinford, for military service. Ufford was to serve him with three men-at-arms in war time and one in peace time, each of whom was to wear the earl's livery, be paid and fed by him and come to his service at his command. He was also to have ten horses, nine pages to attend them and a chamberlain dining in the earl's hall (although these were to be reduced to four horses, three boys and the chamberlain during peace time). Ufford and Hastings served, or were intended to serve, on no less than six separate military and diplomatic missions in Lancaster's retinue and Swinford on four.[76] Ufford subsequently acquired the manor of Passenham in Northamptonshire for life from him and acted as his steward in Suffolk in the 1350s.[77] Bracebridge secured a similar grant of the manor of Barlow in Yorkshire[78] and Hastings, who had served the third earl as steward of the honor of Pickering in 1334,[79] brought news of the progress of the first expedition in Aquitaine to Leicester corporation in 1346.[80]

There are, however, other ways of determining the composition of the duke's retinue. Since his career was so largely spent in the king's service abroad it is not unreasonable to suppose that the majority and perhaps the most important of his retainers were soldiers like Ufford and Hastings who undertook to serve him in war and peace and who appear most frequently among the names of those who accompanied him abroad on military and diplomatic missions. Of 538 men known to have served with him in this way forty-six also received grants of land and annuities from him.[81] Fifteen of these forty-six were witnesses to his charters and nine of them were his officers in England and Wales.[82] Clearly they were among his leading retainers. Although another fifty-three persons are known to have received lands and annuities from him, the grants made to the soldiers in his retinue were un-questionably the most important.[83] Only three of the donees who did not serve with him abroad were among his household and central officers.[84]

Apart from these men there were others who served sufficiently frequently in the duke's retinue and who, although there is no evidence that they received grants of lands or annuities from him, were clearly closely connected with him.[85] Of the eighteen knights who served on upwards of four missions at least five witnessed his charters and five were entrusted with important responsibilities during his commands abroad. Of the twenty-six who served or were intended to have served on at least three separate missions twenty are known to have been knights. Only one, John Blount, was an officer and witnessed one of his charters. Of the sixty-five who served or were intended to serve on at least two missions thirty-five are known to have been knights. Five of them were among the witnesses to his charters and one, Sir William Scargill, appears to have been both an officer and councillor of the earl. For the remaining 380 who served or were intended to have served with him on one mission there is very little evidence of connection. Only 88 of them are known to have been knights and only one was among the witnesses to his charters.

It has been suggested that life engagements for war and peace strengthened the royal contract armies of the fourteenth century at their weakest point by providing some continuity of service. The number of donees who served in Lancaster's company or *comitiva* on military and diplomatic missions was not, however, very large in proportion to the total size of the troop. Only five of the sixteen knights and eight of the eighty-three esquires named on his pay roll for service in Scotland in 1336 and one of the eight bannarets and fourteen of the eighty-seven knights named on his pay roll for service in Aquitaine in 1345–6 are known to have been his donees.[86] Full lists of the names of those who made up his retinue on other occasions do not appear to be extant, but it is clear that the donees formed no more than a nucleus of their number.[87] Similarly the number of those who served in his retinue on several occasions, both donees and non-donees, amounted to no more than a small proportion of the total troop.

But although the number of possible retainers—the donees and those who served on a more permanent basis—was not very large in proportion to the total size of his *comitiva*, they did form a nucleus around which others who served on a more temporary basis could collect. It was the men of this nucleus who were given posts of responsibility in Lancaster's commands in France. This is particularly true of his administration of Brittany. Prevented by more immediate matters from taking up his appointment for almost a year, it was one of his annuitants, Sir Thomas de Uvedale—a soldier who had done service with him during his first command in Aquitaine and who subsequently served in his *comitiva* on the Reims campaign—who was appointed his lieutenant during his absence and who continued to hold the office once he had taken up his commission.[88] Uvedale was assisted in his duties by Sir Philip de Lymbury (who served on seven missions, witnessed several of his charters and held property in Lincolnshire)[89] and Sir Alexander Aunsel (who served on eight occasions and held property in Lincolnshire), who had previously been given responsibilities in Aquitaine.[90] He dispatched his ducal treasurer, William de Driffield, to arrange the payment of the troops.[91] Another soldier and annuitant, Sir Thomas Florak (a member of a Wiltshire family of tenants who had benefited from the patronage of Earl Thomas) and one of his clerks, Richard de Walton (one time receiver-general of his lands), acted as his receivers at Bécherel.[92]

The same is true of his commands in Aquitaine. The three men whom he appointed to appraise the horses of his troops in the duchy in 1350—Sir Robert de la Mare, Sir Stephen de Cosington and Sir Thomas Cok[93]—were all men upon whom he could rely. Both de la Mare and Cosington were certainly his donees, and probably Cok was too.[94] A soldier of some repute,[95] he was marshal of the army during his first expedition to Aquitaine, and in that capacity he was responsible for mustering the troops.[96] Appointed captain of Villefranche and one of those subsequently sent to take charge of Aiguillon,[97] he was among the duke's council of war, and his capabilities singled him out for succession to Ralph Stafford as seneschal of the duchy—an appointment made by Lancaster himself.[98] Together with Cosington he acted as one of the nuncios and proctors sent to Paris by the duke to deal with his quarrel with Otto of Brunswick in 1351.[99]

Others served as captains and castellans—soldiers like Sir Frank de Hale who was a bannaret in his retinue during the first expedition to Aquitaine, a donee, given command of Auberoche by the earl and in charge there during the siege.[100] One of the marshals of the army along with Sir Walter Mauny, he was rewarded for his services with a grant of the strategically important castle of Rochefort in Saintonge and he subsequently played an important role as captain there.[101] Similarly Sir Hugh Meignill of Hornby (who served on five missions in his retinue and was appointed captain of Aiguillon during the long siege by the duke of Normandy)[102] or Uvedale, Thomas Fogg and Richard Sholl (whom he entrusted with the fortresses taken on his way back from the Loire valley in 1356)[103] all held important positions during his commands in France. The devolution of responsibility to men who had a strong tradition of service with him was of fundamental importance for the effective prosecution of the war, particularly when the primary difficulty facing a king's lieutenant in France was the control of men placed under his command.[104] There are many more examples of such men: Sir Richard de Hebden (who served on four missions and held lands in Lincolnshire) was among those specially selected to serve with him during his first command in Aquitaine, a member of his council of war and among those sent to take charge of Aiguillon after the duke of Normandy had raised the siege.[105] And there were others of whom Froissart speaks—soldiers like Sir Stephen de Gumby, Sir John de Neville and Sir John de Lenedale who distinguished themselves in one way or another.

No less important was the part played by his ducal officers. Although the accounts of his treasurers-of-war do not appear to have survived, it is fairly clear that one of his clerks, his wardrober or his treasurer, dealt with the financial side of his missions abroad. John Gynewell (his treasurer in 1344–6) acted in this capacity in Scotland in 1336 and in the Low Countries in 1338–40.[106] Peter de Wotton (his wardrober in 1343–7) accompanied him to Brittany in 1342–3 and Aquitaine in 1345–6 when he drew up the account of his expenses.[107] John de Welbourne (his chancellor and secretary in 1348–9, 1351 and 1355) also appears to have been acting as his treasurer-of-war in the duchy in 1346: he accompanied him on the diplomatic mission of 1348 (possibly in his capacity as secretary) and on his second expedition to Aquitaine in the following year.[108] Richard de Walton (his receiver-general in 1353) served in his retinue in Aquitaine in 1349–50 and drew up the expense account for his command there.[109] William de Horwich, acting in his capacity as wardrober, accounted with the Exchequer for the wages of the earl and his retinue during the preparations for his expedition to Normandy in the spring of 1354.[110] He had previously been employed in the financing of the diplomatic mission to Hainault, Holland and Zeeland.[111] William de Driffield (his treasurer in 1354–7) acted as his treasurer of war in Brittany in 1356.[112] And there were others whose co-operation he could rely upon—soldiers like Sir Bernard Brocas, an annuitant who held office as the king's controller of Bordeaux during his two commands in Aquitaine,[113] and clerks like Henry de Walton, one of his leading officers and who was put in charge of the royal wardrobe at the time of the Reims campaign.[114]

There are not a few examples of generations of the same family who successively served Thomas, the first duke and John of Gaunt.[115] There was, however, surprisingly little continuity of service from his father's lifetime. Sir William Trussell and Sir Thomas de Verdoun (whom we know to have served in his retinue on at least two military and diplomatic missions) had each been granted annuities of £20 in Leicester honor by the third earl and the grant to Verdoun was subsequently confirmed by Henry.[116] Trussell was also one of his father's officers[117] and his son Theobald served on no less than ten missions in Henry's retinue. Verdoun's son, John, served on one. Only the families of Twyford, Blount and Walkington were otherwise prominent in the service of both father and son.[118]

This in itself is perhaps not so surprising. Lancaster was thirty-five by the time his father died. He had, by then, estates and property of his own with officers and a council to administer them. An entourage distinct from that of his father was therefore growing up around him. It is perhaps significant that several of his most prominent donees—Sir Peter and Sir Robert de la Mare, Sir Hugh Berwick, Sir John de Walkington, Sir Frank de Hale, Sir Stephen de Cosington, Sir Hugh de Camoys, Sir Thomas Florak, John de Aldewyncle and Philip de Popham—held manors or annuities tied to manors which he inherited by way of his mother, Maude Chaworth, in Hampshire and Wiltshire, several of which were granted to him and his wife in or before 1337.[119] With his successor there is much stronger continuity. John of Gaunt inherited some of Lancaster's leading men. It is possible to cite no less than fifty families, members of which served in his retinue and in that of Henry, and there are examples of individuals who did service with the first duke and who subsequently served in Gaunt's retinue.[120]

It is not, therefore, difficult to understand why Lancaster was given so many important commands in France; for, besides enjoying the king's favour, he was, which was no less important, from the time of his father's death and next to the king, perhaps the richest man in England, with broad lands and liberties well distributed over much of the country. Though he drew the king's pay when serving abroad it was his landed inheritance which gave him the wherewithal to support a sizeable personal retinue, enabled him to call out his tenants to do service in the wars and helped the king to finance them. Possibly more important, it supported a machinery of government that could be placed at the king's disposal—men who could promote the king's affairs by promoting those of their lord: personal retainers who served as his lieutenants, marshals, captains and castellans, and household officers who acted as paymasters to the troops, as secretaries and receivers. A noble who could wield such power in England could also wield it abroad in the king's service. For the domestic peace of England it was perhaps as well that he did.

# XV  A devout layman

Not all of the wealth derived from the Lancastrian estates was spent on the duke's person, his family and his entourage. Like his father and grandfather before him, Henry was a generous benefactor to the church. In addition to maintaining the charities and endowments begun by his ancestors, he founded a great collegiate church at Leicester, a chantry in St Mary's at Liverpool and a monastery of Grey Friars at Preston,[1] and he was the author of a remarkable devotional treatise which, in addition to giving some clear insight into his personality, provides ample evidence that he was a deeply religious man. To Whalley abbey (in want of money to pay for their new buildings) he granted the manor of Standen and the advowson of St Michael's chapel in Clitheroe castle, lands in Blackburn chase and Castleton, one quarter of the bailiwick of Blackburn and property in Blackburn chase, Pendleton and Clitheroe.[2] Out of friendship for the sporting and much-loved Abbot Clown, he granted the great abbey of St Mary de Pratis at Leicester permission to enclose and impark their wood beside the road to Anstey and he stocked it with game from his own park on the other side of the way. The churches of Humberstone and Hungarton were appropriated to them as a result of his personal supplication to the pope.[3] He confirmed a number of his ancestors' charters to Furness abbey and granted them some property in Lancaster.[4]

The Dominican Friars also benefited from his generosity; at Leicester they received fishing rights in the Soar and at Thetford the site of the hospital of Maison-Dieu.[5] He granted St Leonard's hospital at Lancaster to the nuns of Seton, a house in East Garston and the advowson and right of appropriation of the church there to the nuns of Aumbresbury (where his sister Isabella was prioress) and the advowson and right of appropriation of the church of Tunstead and the chapel of St James within the manor there to the nuns of Campesse.[6] To the anchorites of St Helen's at Pontefract he assigned a livery in the hospital of St Nicholas and provided for a chaplain to celebrate divine service in the chapel of the house.[7] He was also interested in the chapel in Pontefract castle, which was well endowed and where he provided for a fourth chaplain.[8] To the parson of St Mary's in the Strand he granted a plot of land for the enlargement of the church and churchyard and another plot (by the Thames outside New Temple Bar) with a chamber built upon it for a vicarage.[9] As a Founder Member of the Order of the Garter he granted the advowson and right of appropriation of the church of Uttoxeter to the warden and chaplains of St George's chapel at Windsor,[10] and he intervened on behalf of numerous religious foundations to secure royal licences to alienate or acquire property or rights of appropriation.[11] He also had some claims as a part founder and benefactor of Corpus Christi College at Cambridge. As alderman of the Guilds of Corpus Christi and the Blessed Virgin Mary there he used his influence to obtain the necessary licence from the king and granted the college the manor of Barton and the advowson of Grantchester.[12]

Provisions for divine service were attached to some of these benefactions. The Dominican Friars at Thetford were to find an altar, vestments, chalice, candles and other necessaries for a canon chaplain to chant mass daily for the soul of his father as founder of the hospital of Maison-Dieu. The prioress and nuns of Campesse were to find a chaplain to celebrate divine services daily in the chapel of St James and to support other works of piety. The prioress and nuns of Seton were to maintain chantries and other charges on St Leonard's hospital 'as the duke shall ordain' and similarly the anchorites of St Helen's were to find a chaplain to celebrate divine service in the chapel 'according to the duke's ordinances'. At St Mary's in Liverpool a priest was to celebrate for the souls of himself and his ancestors. One of his grants to Whalley abbey was conditional upon the abbot and monks finding sufficient sustenance to support a recluse and two women servants in a place within the churchyard of the parish church in order that they might perpetually pray for himself and his ancestors and providing that they found a chaplain to chant mass for himself, his ancestors and heirs in the chapel of the recluse, together with the necessary vestments, a chalice, bread, wine and other ornaments which he would require.[13]

But by far the most important was his foundation of a college in honour of the Annunciation of St Mary in the Newarke at Leicester.[14] In 1331 his father had founded a hospital there with the same dedication, and which housed a warden, four chaplains, fifty poor folk and five women attendants. The warden and chaplains, though secular clerks, led a common life. The warden was elected by the chaplains, and then presented by the patron to the bishop. They all wore a habit with a white crescent and a star. Of the fifty poor folk, twenty were permanent inmates of the hospital and lived in a house by the hospital's church; the remaining thirty, who were only admitted on a temporary basis, were housed on beds in the body of the church. The original endowment consisted of the site of the hospital, four carucates at Leicester and the advowson of Irchester, Northamptonshire, with certain common rights in the founder's woods around Leicester. In 1331 Earl Henry had added the advowson of Duffield in Derbyshire to the possessions of the hospital and the rectories of Irchester and Duffield were both appropriated to it when they fell vacant. The buildings seem to have been begun in 1350 and work was well under way by March of the following year under the direction of Brother Thomas of Gloucester as 'master of works', assisted by other members of the Dominican Friars at Leicester.[15] In addition to the central buildings a laundry was begun, which was completed in 1335 when new gates to the hospital were constructed.[16]

It was during the years of truce which followed the fall of Calais that the project of transforming the hospital into a college of secular canons was forming itself in Duke Henry's mind. In 1353 he obtained papal permission for his plans and in the following year he provided that it should be staffed by a dean, twelve canons, thirteen vicars, three other clerks and a verger, and that it was to accommodate a hundred poor folk and ten women attendants to care for them. To provide the necessary funds for this, in 1355 the endowment was increased by a grant of the manors of Inglesham and Hannington in Wiltshire, Wollaston in Northamptonshire and Kempsford and Chedworth in Gloucestershire, with the advowsons of Edmondthorpe and Wymondham in Leicestershire, Higham Ferrers and Raunds in Northamptonshire and Hannington in Wiltshire. Shortly afterwards the advowsons of Edmondthorpe and Wymondham were exchanged for those of Llandefeilog and Pembrey, together with their chapels in Carmarthenshire and 1,000 marks rent from the duke's manors of Gimingham, Methwold, Thetford, Tunstead, King's Somborne and the lordships of Kidwelly, Carnwyllion, Iscennen, Ogmore and Morgyng, although the payment of this rent was only contingent.

That Henry had the advice and counsel of his friend and late servant, John Gynewell, bishop of Lincoln, at every step in this great project is clear enough; but the general shape of the foundation and perhaps some of the statutes in detail derive almost certainly from his own ideas. On 24 March 1356 the charter of foundation and endowment was delivered in the church of the New College. The statutes provided that the dean, canons and vicars should all be priests. When the office of dean fell vacant, the canons were to nominate two persons to the duke, to his lieutenant if he should be abroad, or to the duke's heirs after his death, and one of the two was then to be chosen for presentation to the bishop. New canons were to be chosen by the duke or his heirs. The dean, canons and vicars were to be allowed to be absent for up to two months every year, provided that no more than three canons and three vicars were absent at any one time.

The poor folk were all to live together in one house, containing a chapel where masses were to be said daily for the poor. The dean and canons were each to have a separate house and each vicar was to live in the house of one of the canons until a separate house (to include a hall, kitchen, bakehouse, brewhouse and a great chamber where they were all to dine and sleep) was constructed for them within the gates of the close. The provost was also to have a separate dwelling house and a suitable house was to be constructed within the close for six choristers to dine and sleep. Three chests were to be placed in the church—one for ornaments, money for copes and the like, another for jewels and relics and the third for the books of the chapter.

During services the dean and canons were to wear black copes, white surplices and almuces of grey fur, and the vicars white surplices, black copes and almuces of black cloth furred with black budge. At other times when they were in residence the dean and canons were to wear tunics and supertunics reaching to their heels and fastened close; only black hose was permitted. The serving women were to have a coat and hood. Of the three clerks other than the thirteen vicars, one (who was to wear a surplice and black cope) was to be about the High Altar to kindle lights, fold up the vestments and the like; the other two were to ring bells and help the priests (who celebrated at the altars in the nave of the church) when they said masses. The six chorister boys were to wear black copes and surplices. The verger was to carry the white rod and open and shut the gates of the close. One of the canons was to be elected almoner. The sacrist was to find candles, bread, wine, water and other things necessary for the services, to look after the sacred utensils, books, bells and vestments, and to see that the church was cleaned.

The dean, canons, vicars and other ministers were to say matins, vespers and other canonical hours according to the Use of Sarum.

They were to sing mass each day and recite that of the Blessed Virgin Mary (except on such feast days as high mass was celebrated in her name) and (save on double feasts) matins and vespers of the Virgin in company without song. The rest of the canonical hours were to be recited throughout both day and night. A mass in special without song was also to be said; in the first place that which was wont to be said in the chapel of the Blessed Mary on the south side of the church for the souls of his father and mother, of his departed kinsfolk and all those to whom he was bound; in the second place a special mass, *Salus populi*, during the lifetime of the duke for himself and for all his friends and well-wishers, at the north altar next to the altar of the chapel of the Blessed Mary. After the duke's death the mass that was wont to be said for the departed was to be said at the same altar for his soul. When the dean was present in church he was to say *Confiteor*, *Misereatur* and the absolution every day throughout the whole year, both at prime and compline. As they entered and left the church all the canons, vicars and ministers were to bow to the dean in his stall and they were all to rise reverently when he entered choir or chapter or when he passed through either. The obits of the duke's father and mother and of Henry after his death were to be celebrated every year upon their several anniversaries, solemnly and with music in masses and funeral offices and the dean, canons and vicars were bound each day in their masses to say a special collect for Edward III and Queen Philippa, their children and heirs while they lived, and for their souls and their successors as king and queen after their death. No other yearly masses or trentals for the souls of deceased persons were to be celebrated by the canons and vicars, who were to rest content with their stipends. The regulations also provided for the maintenance of the morals of the clergy. The canons, vicars and ministers were not to be haunters of taverns, forbidden public assemblies or lawless spectacles; they were not to sleep out and women could not be lodged with the dean, canons and vicars.

As established by Duke Henry the college was adequately endowed and the buildings of the hospital founded by his father were greatly extended. John Leland, who saw them on the eve of the Reformation has left us this description of them:[17]

'The collegiate chirch of Newarke and the area of it yoinith to another peace of the castelle ground. The college chirche is not very great, but it is exceding fair. There lyith on the north side of the high altare Henry Erle of Lancaster, withowt a crounet, and 2 men childern under the arche nexte to his hedde. On the south side lyith Henry first Duke of Lancaster; and yn the next arch to his hedde lyith a lady, by likelihod his wife.'

On the south side of the choir stood the chapel of Saint Mary and another chapel on the south cross-aisle.

'The cloister on the south weste side of the chirch', he continues, 'is large and faire; and the houses in the cumpace of the area of the college for the prebendaries be al very praty. The waulles and the gates of the college be stately. The rich Cardinal of Winchester gilded all the floures and knottes in the voulte of the chirch. The large almose house stondith also withyn the quadrante of the area of the college.'

In its day the foundation was not unusual. William Edington, bishop of Winchester and successively the king's wardrober, treasurer and chancellor, founded a similar college at his native village of Edington in Wiltshire in 1347 and the duke of Gloucester founded another at Pleshey in 1394. It was of much the same type as Edward III's colleges at Westminster and Windsor: it was intended for a resident body of dean and canons with a common fund. Although it was therefore a step in the direction of the chantry college, on the other hand the prebends were not (as in the ordinary college of chantry-priests) mere fellowships held by appointment of the head of the foundation, but freehold benefices in the presentation of the patrons, to which the bishop instituted. But the college, well endowed with land and churches, also enjoyed a dignity which placed it on a level with older foundations. It quite outstripped the ancient college of Saint Mary in Leicester castle in importance. Its staff were for the most part drawn from the neighbourhood: its deans were local men of affairs, often connected by interest with the noble families of Leicestershire and sometimes holding offices under the Crown; its canons, who frequently held rectories in Leicestershire and the adjoining counties, were seldom well known in the world outside. In this respect the chapter differed from the great cathedral and some collegiate chapters, which were habitually reinforced by prominent clerks in the service of the Crown. On the other hand it was distinct from groups of poorly-endowed priests bound to perpetual residence who were the chaplain-fellows of chantry colleges in the later Middle Ages.

But the devout streak in Henry's personality is not only evident from his reputation, his crusading, his great religious foundation at Leicester and his endowment of numerous religious bodies; it is also demonstrated by his authorship of a rather remarkable devotional work which argues the genuineness of his piety. The *Livre de Seyntz Medicines*, written in 1354, possibly as a task set him by his confessor, is not remarkable as a work of literature, but it is remarkable in coming from a man in his position and in showing a lively imagination, some traces of originality within a conventional framework and a gentleness of spirit and humility which cannot be a literary pose if only because he did not have the literary skill for such an artifice. The book is an allegory in which the author, after taking stock of himself, reveals to the Divine Physician and his assistant the *Douce Dame* the wounds of his soul, that is his five senses, each of which is infected by the seven deadly sins (pride, envy, wrath, covetousness, gluttony, lechery and sloth) and then suggests and prays for the remedies appropriate to each cause of infection. As a wounded man needs a physician, so mankind, wounded with various wounds of sin, wounds of ears, eyes, nose, mouth, hands, feet and heart, needs Christ as a physician to apply remedies. There is an allegorical treatment of the various remedies required: beverages, lotions, bandages, ointments and so forth. The theme is one which could well provide the material for an arid academic exercise; but Duke Henry's illustrations are taken from his personal experiences, they reflect his personal feelings and the book rings true.[18]

The chief source which Henry drew upon was the folk-lore of the Middle Ages in the widest sense. In its medical content his work shows that he was conversant with the practical remedies used by the people rather than the knowledgeable treatises of the doctors of the time; in matters of belief and devotion it reveals that the didactic works and sermons of the period had left their imprint on him. But for the most part Henry exploited a richer and more personal source: the experiences of his varied career livened by a keen sense of observation. Whether or not he had read the *Château d'Amour* of Robert Grosseteste before comparing his body to a fortified castle, he adapted the metaphor to his subject in an altogether independent way, drawing upon his military experiences in Scotland and in France. His hands and his feet are the walls of the castle, his heart is the dungeon; all are assaulted by the seven deadly sins. He also compares his heart to a whirlpool in the sea, a fox's hole and a market place. The latter description may well have been based directly on his observation of the market held at

Leicester. He tells us what precautions the lord took to prevent illegal sales and the infraction of regulations, to ensure fair sales and the collection of seigniorial dues. We learn of the excesses to which the market day gave rise—of the habitual drunkenness which the tavern-keepers encouraged, of the cooks who praised their foodstuffs, of the young ladies dressed up like Easter Cakes and the shame of those who spent their money in evil places. Nothing is lacking in this description, nor in the allegorical interpretation of the incidents.

Perhaps most interesting of all are the passages which give some insight into the duke's personality. He was a good-looking youth in his own estimation. Tall, fair and slim, he took a pride in, amongst other things, the fine rings on his fingers, the elegance of his foot in the stirrup, his shoes, his armour, his ability as a dancer and the garters which he thought befitted him so well. Froissart tells us how, after his first victorious raid in Aquitaine, he and his army returned to Bordeaux, where they amused themselves with the citizens and their wives and how at Saint-Jean-d'Angély he made handsome presents to the ladies and damsels of the town, and held dinners and suppers for them almost every day.[19] The duke himself tells us more: how he stretched out his stirrups in the jousts for the ladies, sang love songs and danced elegantly 'out of great desire to be praised, then loved, then lost'[20] and we know that there was a *daunsyngchambre* in Leicester castle and a troop of minstrels in his service.[21] He even confesses that he had a particular fondness for kissing ordinary women rather than women of rank and beauty, since they did not disapprove of his conduct. And he lets us know that his sensuality did not stop at that. These were, however, the reflections on youth of a middle-aged man suffering from gout. Now in his forties he liked rich food, well spiced and with strong sauces, and wine 'to put myself and my friends out of our senses, for it is a good feeling to be merry'.[22] Sometimes he over-indulged himself so that at feasts his legs were 'neither so good nor so ready to bring me away as they were to get me there'.[23] Contemporary accounts speak of his fondness for food. When he came back from Aquitaine, his father's heir, he was given a dinner in his honour by Leicester corporation which included salmon (his favourite dish) and lampreys brought all the way from Gloucester at an enormous cost and kept alive in fish locks in the Soar to await his arrival.[24] The town watched his career with pleasure and would seem to have been very proud of him. When he was at home the burgesses' relations with him were far more intimate than they had ever been with his father; when he hunted in the Frith the town sent wine; when messengers brought news of his welfare in distant countries they were rewarded.[25] He was undoubtedly fond of the hunt and the country.[26] He gives an elaborate description of the digging and smoking out of foxes (even though it is an allegory of a good confession with the shrift-father digging out the penitent's sins). He tells us how he liked to hear the barking of the hounds, the song of a nightingale, the smell of roses and violets, musk and lily of the valley—to say nothing of scarlet cloth. It was doubtless through a mutual interest in the hunt that he got on with Abbot Clown, who was also a man of sporting instincts.[27]

But it must not be thought that Henry was proud to record those aspects of his personality which he himself found unbecoming. Nor was he unaware of the social abuses to which the prerogatives of his class often gave rise, as when, being overcome by wrath, he had brought about the injury or death of his fellow-men, 'my neighbour, my brother'.[28] He reproaches himself for ruthlessly extorting money from the poor and for acquiring lands and other property which he coveted by threats or the exercise of undue influence in his courts. He was ashamed of recoiling from the stench of sick and poor people and of grudging that any food left over from a feast should be handed to them. But he nevertheless accepted the conventions of his class; although he deplored his own gluttony and self-indulgence, he saw nothing wrong in the aristocracy enjoying a moderate amount of feasting, dancing and jousting.

The date and the authorship of the *Livre de Seyntz Medicines* are given in a kind of postscript—'This book was begun and finished in the year of our Lord Jesus Christ 1354. And it was made by a poor miserable sinner called *Henri Duc de Lancastre*. May God pardon his sins'—with the words *Henri Duc de Lancastre* written backwards.[29] There is no reason to doubt the authenticity of this statement. There is too much of Lancaster's own life and experiences in the book to credit some other person with its authorship. The passages on the art of sieges recall his numerous campaigns; he himself tells us 'as is very often apparent in these wars'.[30] He alludes to the jousts and tournaments in which he had so often taken part and to the heavy responsibility of an 'admiral of a great fleet'[31]—a responsibility he had known. The description of the digging and smoking out of foxes was composed within weeks, perhaps days, of his writing to Guy de Boulogne on the subject of stopping up holes:[32] 'The second manner is to catch them in their holes. All the outlets are stopped up, but one; upon the latter a fire is lit, so that the smoke goes into the hole, where it destroys all the foxes and any other vermin that may be inside.'³³ This entire section may contain more specific allusions to the twisted diplomacy of January to April 1354. Towards the end of the book, he offers three excuses for its defects—that he was not qualified for such a work, that being English he had little acquaintance with French and, perhaps most revealing of all, that he was a poor writer, having learnt late and by himself. This says as much of Lancaster's modesty as it does about the nature and extent of his education, for it is clear that he was fluent in French. The work itself was written in that language—not in English or in Latin—and it is perhaps significant that the year of its writing was the year of the negotiations with Charles of Navarre and the huge display at Avignon.

# XVI  The Reims campaign (1359-1360)

Edward III's last great expedition to France was also Lancaster's last. The campaign of 1359-60 was intended to deliver the *coup-de-grâce* and its destination was a great coronation ceremony in Reims Cathedral. With the king of France a prisoner in London, after capture by the Black Prince at Poitiers, and France torn by civil strife, with Anglo-Navarrese forces swarming in Normandy and up to the gates of Paris, with half Brittany and most of Aquitaine in English hands, with English garrisons establishing themselves in Anjou, Maine, Touraine and even Burgundy, it finally seemed as though Edward III's great moment had come. The strategy of provincial opportunism had done its work and the time had come to revert to the single grand army marching straight to its goal, a goal that could now be defined.[1]

When Henry returned from Brittany in 1358, King John (who had been brought from Bordeaux to London in the previous year) was staying at the duke's manor of the Savoy, situated on the road from the City to Westminster at Temple Bar.[2] Henry may have passed some time with him there, but he appears to have spent most of the next year at Leicester and elsewhere on his estates.[3] He may have taken part in the jousts put on for John at Windsor on St George's Day and was doubtless present at the marriage of his younger daughter Blanche to John of Gaunt at Reading in May 1359 and at the festivities organized to celebrate the occasion;[4] but some of his time must also have been taken up with the negotiations which were proceeding in the capital.[5]

The truce concluded at Bordeaux in March 1357 was to last for two years. After the Black Prince and his royal captive arrived in London on 24 May, negotiations for John's release (which had begun in Gascony) were continued, and a year later these resulted in a ransom treaty (8 May 1358) which Delachenal called the first treaty of London. By the terms of this agreement Edward was to acquire an enlarged Aquitaine, Ponthieu, Calais and the county of Guines, all in full sovereignty, the suzerainty of Brittany and a sum of 4 million gold *écus*, of which 600,000 florins, due by 1 November, were to be paid before John could be released. Edward's territorial demands were less than those which he had made in 1353–4 since no concessions were required of him; the lands were to be conceded to him in return for John's release. But by 12 December this treaty had failed—apparently on Edward's initiative[6]—and preparations were immediately put under way for what was intended to be the decisive campaign in France. During February and March mobilization was in full swing and the truce of Bordeaux was due to expire on 9 April.

Why Edward then agreed to extend the truce until 24 June and to negotiate a new agreement with John (Delachenal's second treaty of London, dated 24 March 1359) is not altogether clear; but this time he demanded far greater territorial concessions from the French. He now wanted Touraine, Anjou, Normandy and the county of Boulogne in addition to the lands stated in the agreement of the previous May. Moreover, although the ransom remained at the same figure as in 1358, the French were now given four months in which to raise a first instalment of 3 million florins instead of six months in which to raise 600,000. Edward was asking for nothing less than the old Angevin empire, together with the counties of Ponthieu, Boulogne and Guines and the town of Calais, all in full sovereignty and completely detached from the kingdom of France, and a sum of money five times larger than one which the French had previously been unable to raise in two-thirds of the time. In return he would renounce his claim to the French throne. These demands were so outrageous that it is difficult to believe that they represented a sincere proposal for peace on Edward's part. And so it seemed to the French Estates when on 25 May they courageously rejected the treaty as neither acceptable nor practicable.

Edward received the news from Paris during the first half of June and his military preparations, which had been proceeding since the close of the previous year, were rapidly speeded up.[7] During the course of August and September a vast expeditionary force of about 11,900 men—surpassed in size only by the Crécy-Calais armies—was assembled for the campaign,[8] and an immense convoy of wagons was got together to transport the military stores—weapons, ammunition, equipment, clothing, tentage and the like—which were required for the expedition.[9]

In the event Edward was not ready to move until late in the autumn and by then the situation in France was a good deal less favourable

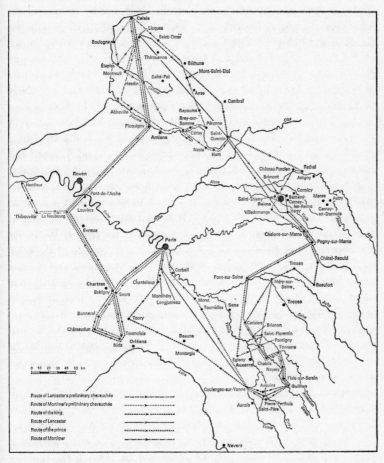

Map IV.   The Reims Campaign, 1359–1360

to him than it had been a year earlier. Ever since King John's capture at Poitiers the government of the kingdom had fallen to the dauphin Charles, first as lieutenant and then as regent for his father. But from the beginning it had been difficult for him to make his authority felt. Early in 1358 a revolution took place in Paris, led by the *prévôt des marchands*, Étienne Marcel, and during the course of which the dauphin was obliged to flee the capital; in May a peasant rising known as the *Jacquerie* broke out and Charles of Navarre (who had escaped from the imprisonment in which he had been held since his capture at Rouen in April 1356) was elected captain of Paris and popularly acclaimed. But the *Jacquerie* was soon put down and by the summer Marcel had been murdered, the rebellious Estates had been brought to order and the regent was beginning to make his authority felt; a year later the Navarrese war had been brought to an end. Edward had either ignored Charles of Navarre in his military plans or had decided that it was time to abandon the tenuous connection with him, since he had made much of his claims to the French throne during the Parisian revolution of the previous year.[10] Or had Charles once again decided that he had more to gain from an agreement with the regent? Whatever the case the young king made his peace with the dauphin at Pontoise in August and he subsequently remained non-participant and neutral when he might have been useful.[11] Moreover, Edward's security was very bad in 1359. As early as 10 July it was known that he would make for Reims and the citizens consequently had time to complete and strengthen the new defences of the city. When Edward arrived there in December he faced the prospect of a long siege in the depths of winter and many miles away from base. In the event he was more than a year too late.[12]

Edward and his generals were not unaware of the difficult task which lay ahead of them. Provisions were made to meet the rigours of winter and a march across a landscape denuded of food by war, the *Jacquerie* and the regent's express command. The army would for once have to subsist upon its own commissariat. Among the supplies loaded on to the baggage-wagons were hand-mills to grind corn and ovens to bake it, falcons and dogs for the chase and small portable boats for fishing.

There is no direct evidence bearing upon Edward's military plan for this campaign and no surviving dispatch relates its progress. Before he left England he is said to have sworn never to return until he had put an end to the conflict either by war or a peace. Judging from subsequent events he had decided upon a peaceful progress to

Reims for his coronation, but was fully prepared to meet opposition from the regent should Charles choose to give him battle. He hoped to secure the support of the archbishop of Reims, Jean de Craon, and to persuade the citizens to open the gates of the city to him. If the plan miscarried he would try to force the regent to battle.

This hypothesis would appear to be borne out by the way in which the campaign progressed. During the course of the summer a swarm of troops from Flanders and the empire assembled at Calais to join the expeditionary forces. They were causing Edward some embarrassment since they not only left little room for lodging or stables for horses and used up supplies of food, wine, hay and oats then in the town, but they were also expecting to enrich themselves from the spoils of France.[13] It was therefore decided to send Lancaster across to Calais in charge of an advance-guard to rid the town of these new-comers.[14] The plan also had the merit of facilitating the transport of the expeditionary forces (whose crossing might otherwise be further delayed by a shortage of transport vessels)[15] and of providing for a reconnaissance of the route subsequently to be taken by the king on his way to Reims.

Around 1 October the duke disembarked at Calais and collected together the troops who had gathered there for the campaign. The total strength of his forces is not known, but his personal *comitiva*, which was over 1,000 strong, was the largest he ever took to France.[16]

The route of his preliminary *chevauchée* across Artois and Picardy is well enough known.[17] By-passing Saint-Omer and Béthune, he halted four days at the abbey of Mont-Saint-Eloy (situated nine kilometres to the north of Arras) to refresh the troops and their horses and then advanced to Bapaume and Péronne, destroying the surrounding countryside. From Péronne he swung westward down the Somme valley in the direction of Amiens, where there was a panic among the citizens, who believed the town threatened on 18 October. An attempt to take Bray-sur-Somme (which would have got him across the river) met with a stiff resistance and some casualties. His troops had to wade shoulder-deep through the moats to the foot of the walls and were attacked in the rear by a small force commanded by Guy de Châtillon, count of Saint-Pol, then lieutenant in Picardy, Beauvaisis and Vermandois, and Raoul de Renneval, who had recently been given joint charge of Amiens.[18] Unable to take the town he was obliged to move downstream to Cérisy, where he finally crossed the Somme on 1 November. He could not have proceeded much further when

Edward, who had disembarked at Calais with the main body of his army on 28 October, recalled him to that town.

Edward spent about a week in Calais organizing and arraying his forces before departing on 4 November.[19] He divided his troops into three columns: one remained under his own command and included his sons Lionel of Antwerp and Edmund of Langley, John de Montfort and the earls of Warwick, Suffolk, Salisbury and Oxford; another was placed under the command of the Black Prince and included John of Gaunt and the earls of Northampton and Stafford; the third, temporarily under the command of the earl of March, was intended for Lancaster.[20]

Roger Mortimer, earl of March and constable of England, had crossed over to France six days in advance of the king and had conducted a raid down the coast by way of Boulogne to Étaples, which was burnt, doubtless as a precaution against possible French naval attacks on the English transport vessels.[21] It is likely that Lancaster, who was returning to base by way of the Somme valley, joined forces with him to the south of Calais, when he made contact with the other two columns and when general policy was discussed, presumably after he had given a report.[22] It was at this juncture that most of the foreigners who had served with the duke were discharged. The work of devastation and looting had achieved the desired results and, with possible resistance eliminated, Edward was now able to begin his progress to Reims in the manner befitting a king who had come to take up his inheritance and to secure the allegiance of his subjects. From this point his army advanced to its destination in three parallel columns, a formation it kept until the end, doubtless for reasons of supply.[23]

The itineraries of the forces under the command of the king and the Black Prince are known in some detail.[24] The troops under Edward first made for Saint-Omer, crossed Artois (by-passing Arras), Cambrésis (by-passing Cambrai), Vermandois, Thiérache, Laonais (by-passing Laon), entered Champagne towards the close of November and crossed the Aisne to arrive before Reims on 4 December. The route of the troops under the prince is particularly well documented since the author of the *Scalacronica*, Sir Thomas Gray of Heton, was among them and noted the principal stops: Montreuil, Hesdin, through Ponthieu and Picardy then (after crossing the Somme at some unknown point) Nesle, Ham, Saint-Quentin and finally, before Reims, two places in Champagne—Rethel (where the French burned the town to prevent him from crossing the Aisne) and Château-Porcien (where he succeeded in crossing the river). The interesting thing about these two itineraries is that, as far as the river Somme, they roughly correspond with that of Lancaster's preliminary *chevauchée*. The route of the duke's forces is not known in detail, but they proceeded at more or less equal distances from those of the king and the prince, by-passing Saint-Quentin on 26 November.[25] It was probably at this point that the three columns, which had lost contact during the course of the march, rejoined one another on 28 November.[26] Another council was then held with Lancaster and the other military leaders before they continued their descent on Reims through new country on the following day.[27]

The ancient city of Champagne, which guarded the bones of Saint-Rémy and the holy oil, brought to him by a dove from heaven, with which kings of France had been anointed since the time of Clovis, was not unprepared. The great *enceinte*, begun in the time of Philip Augustus but only recently completed, now encircled the entire city and large supplies of armaments and victuals had been purchased in anticipation of a long siege. At the beginning of December the expeditionary forces took up quarters at a number of places encircling the walls: Edward at the abbey of Saint-Basle and subsequently at Verzy, the Black Prince at Villedomange, the earls of Richmond and Northampton at the abbey of Saint-Thierry, Lancaster at Brimont, the earl of March at Cernay-les-Reims and John de Beauchamp at Bétheny.[28]

The siege, if it can properly be called that, lasted for more than five weeks (4 December 1359–11 January 1360).[29] During this period no attempt was made to take the city by assault and the operations were confined to a simple and not very effective blockade.[30] The headquarters of the army were situated between five and ten miles outside the city, where the king awaited the news that the gates had been opened for his entry. The Italian chronicler Matteo Villani relates how every consideration was shown to the citizens and how offers were made to persuade them to accept Edward as their king.[31] According to Henry Knighton, Edward issued strict injunctions that the inhabitants were to be treated as friends and the troops behaved as if they were on their own soil.[32]

What action there was took place in the environs of the city—most of it over thirty miles to the east—and was probably occasioned by the need to keep troops employed. Several detachments were sent out. Whilst the celebrated partisan Eustache d'Auberchicourt ravaged the banks of the Aisne, and Bartholomew de Burghersh and contingents from the retinues of John of Gaunt and the Black Prince besieged Cormicy (20 December), Lancaster, Gaunt, the earl of March, Sir John Chandos and James Audley took and burned Cernay-en-Dormois and (having joined up forces with d'Auberchicourt) Autry and Manre, which suffered a like fate. There had been plenty of room for individual prowess, but the profit of this enterprise went to d'Auberchicourt who ransomed the surrounding countryside and then sold Autry to the duke of Bar for 7,000 gold florins and Manre and Attigny to the count of Flanders for 25,000 gold *deniers*.[33]

These diversions in no way advanced Edward's cause; Reims still held out. Moreover, it was a particularly wet winter and the rain, which had slowed down the army on the march across northern France, still continued to pour; the horses suffered severely from lack of shelter and were badly in need of forage; the morale of the troops was rapidly declining. Edward and his generals were clearly aware of all this; but the gates of the city were still held against them and it was therefore decided to put the army on the move. On 11 January the siege was raised; the troops departed during the night and in good order.[34]

On abandoning Reims Edward's plan was to proceed into Burgundy in order to secure the support of the young duke Philip de Rouvre—perhaps the most important of the twelve peers of France—for his coronation at some future date.[35]

The army first made for Châlons, which it did not attempt to take, but proceeded up the Marne to Pogny (where it was obliged to halt for over a week whilst the bridge across the river was repaired) before proceeding into southern Champagne.[36] Once again the troops moved in three columns for reasons of supply. They crossed the Aube and then the Seine, the latter in two places—at Pont-sur-Seine and Méry. By-passing Troyes (where the remaining German contingent left) they turned due south into Burgundy. The right column under Lancaster's command may have advanced as far as Provins, by-passing Sens *en route*. The Black Prince (badly in need of forage for his horses) descended to Auxerre and lodged at Égleny, where his troops suffered more from the enemy than they had done at any other time hitherto during the expedition. The earl of March (now in command of a separate detachment of the army) made his way to Saint-Florentin, whilst Edward, passing near to Cerisiers and Brienon l'Archevêque, rejoined him at nearby Armançon.[37] From here they made their way to Pontigny, where the entire army reassembled.[38] The story of the king's pilgrimage to the shrine of St Edward there and his severe orders against pillage, which is told by the anonymous chronicler of St Mary's, York, requires at least to be weighed against the general assumption that the abbey was plundered.[39]

The troops were shown the way down the Serein valley from Pontigny to Chablis by one Jean Pounteney.[40] From there diverse fractions of the army made for Tonnerre, which was taken by assault, whilst Edward followed the course of the Serein to Noyers (where the castle was likewise taken), l'Isle-sur-Serein (where he rested his troops awhile) and Guillon (where he arrived on the night of 19 February and where the army once again reassembled).[41]

Edward spent the best part of a month at Guillon.[42] He passed his time there neither disagreeably nor unprofitably. In addition to the tents and pavilions, hand-mills, ovens, forges, dinghys and small boats which the army had brought with them on their baggage-wagons, for his own diversion Edward had brought thirty mounted falconers, hawks and sixty couple of hounds and as many greyhounds with which he hunted and hawked each day by the river.[43] Neverthe-less, there was more serious business to be attended to. Whilst the marshals of the army conducted foraging raids into the surrounding country (on one of which Roger Mortimer was killed) Edward and some of the chief nobles who accompanied him were busy negotiating a treaty with the Burgundians—their main purpose in the duchy.[44]

Since the death of Eudes IV (1349), who had reunited the county of Burgundy (which lay within the empire) with his hereditary lands, the duchy of Burgundy had been in the hands of the infant Philip de Rouvre, who was married to Louis de Male's daughter Margaret, heiress to the counties of Flanders, Nevers and Rethel.[45] But since Philip was still a minor real authority rested in the hands of his mother, the duchess Joan, who remarried to King John early in 1350. The resulting French influence in Burgundian affairs was resented by a people used to a large measure of independence and particularly by the nobles of the county some of whom, like Jean de Neufchâtel, had been brought into either English or Navarrese pay to conduct raids and seize castles in the duchy. With the arrival of the English army in the winter of 1359-60 they sought out Edward III before Reims and proposed an arrangement with him which they were instrumental in concluding at Guillon.[46]

For a ransom of 200,000 gold *moutons*, payable in three terms, Edward undertook to restore the fortress of Flavigny (taken by an English esquire called John Harleston in January 1359) and agreed to a three years' truce or *patis* whereby all hostilities in the duchy and county were to cease. But if during this time he secured the support of the majority of the twelve peers of France to his coronation and the young duke refused to lend his voice, then the truce was no longer to hold good and Burgundy would again be prey to English troops.[47] From Edward's point of view the most important clause of the treaty was that whereby Philip obliged himself to assist at the king's consecration. The promise of a respite from hostilities, the threat of their recommencement and the ransom demanded for immunity were all intended to persuade him to stand by it. A similar ransom had been demanded from the duchy of Bar and others were subsequently demanded from the county of Nevers and the barony of Donzy;[48] all of these arrangements were intended to build up support in the French provinces for Edward's coronation.

Up till this point the king had been pursuing a perfectly logical policy. Having failed to persuade the citizens of Reims to open their gates to him and in view of the privations which winter forced upon his army he had been temporarily obliged to abandon his primary objective. But he had secured the support of a section of the Burgundian nobility and others to his coronation at some future date. He now had to force the regent to an engagement in the field and if he proved successful in battle not only Reims but the kingdom of France would be his. Towards the end of March, having achieved his purpose in Burgundy, he left Guillon for Paris.[49] The regent had, however, assembled his forces within the city walls and (since he had so far refused to meet Edward in battle) it would be necessary to bring him out or to force him into a surrender. To achieve this Edward may have hoped for assistance from within the capital, for in December a plot had been laid to assassinate the regent, apparently at the instigation of Charles of Navarre.[50]

The English army left the valley of the Serein for that of the Cure, where it was again divided into three columns.[51] The troops with Edward assembled at Asquins, those under Lancaster and the Black Prince moved into formation some two to four leagues away, at Saint-Père and Pierre-Perthuis. After a halt of several days they proceeded into the valley of the Yonne, the majority of them crossing the river at Coulanges. Edward himself went upstream to the village of Asnois, where the ransom treaties with Nevers and Donzy were probably concluded. The army could now approach Paris by a march north between the Loire and the Yonne and south of the Seine. The routes taken by the three columns are not known in detail. Both the king and the prince went through the Gâtinais; Edward apparently to the west, by way of Montargis, Beaune and Boëse, his eldest son to the east, by way of Tournelles and Moret.[52] Nothing is known of the route taken by Lancaster, but it probably lay between the other two. The troops now turned to destroying the countryside on their way to the capital, according to Knighton, burning, killing and devastating everything around them.[53] During the last days of March they took up quarters some twelve to twenty miles south of the city: Edward in an old residence of the dukes of Burgundy at Chanteloup, his sons and the rest of his army in the surrounding villages between there and Corbeil and Longjumeau.[54]

Edward remained at Chanteloup throughout Easter week. It was at this point that peace negotiations were opened with the French. Innocent VI had been pressing these for some time. As early as 18 November of the previous year he had entrusted a mission to Simon de Langres, general of the order of Friar Preachers, and William de Lynn, dean of Chichester. On 4 March following André de la Roche, abbot of Cluny, and Hugues de Genève, lord of Anthon, were given charge of another.[55]

Papal efforts at mediation may have begun whilst Edward was at Guillon.[56] As a result of the endeavours of Simon de Langres arrangements were made for their resumption and a conference was held in the leper house at Longjumeau on Good Friday (3 April). Lancaster was at the head of the English delegation, which included the earls of Northampton and Warwick, Sir John Chandos and Sir Walter Mauny. The regent was represented by Robert de Fiennes, constable of France, marshal Boucicaut, the lord of Garencières, Ainard de la Tour, lord of Vinay, Simon de Bucy, Guichard d'Angle and several secretaries and councillors. No record exists of the discussions, but it is unlikely that Edward took them very seriously since they were not resumed the following day. According to the continuator of Richard Lescot's chronicle his demands were still too great.[57]

There was no truce during the conference and, with no enemy forces to engage, skirmishing and pillaging proceeded ruthlessly and unrestricted. The chronicler Jean de Venette records a sad story of that fateful Easter week.[58] While the peace discussions were in progress the fortified church of Orly was taken and later that of Chastres, where the inhabitants had taken refuge and suffered a horrible fate. On Good Friday and Easter Saturday Montlhéry and Longjumeau were burned. The smoke and flames rising from the fires were clearly visible in Paris, where the inhabitants of the faubourgs and the surrounding countryside had fled for protection. On Easter Saturday the two famous butcheries of Saint-Marceau and Saint-Germain were moved inside the city walls and orders were given for these two faubourgs and that of Notre-Dame-des-Champs to be burned as a measure of defence. Venette tells us how lamentable it was to see men, women and children so desolate and how on Easter Sunday he saw priests of ten country parishes communicating their people and keeping Easter in various chapels or any spot they could find in the monastery of the Carmelite friars in Paris.

Edward's forces were in fact rapidly encircling the city.[59] The bulk of his army took up position along the heights to the south-west, between the left bank of the Seine and the Bièvre. He appears to have established himself at Châtillon, above Montrouge, whilst his lieutenants occupied Issy, Vanves, Gentilly, Cachan and Vaugirard. The intention, fairly clearly, was to bring the French out to fight. But the regent had given strict orders that no resistance was to be shown to the English provocations.[60] The arrival of the abbot of Cluny resulted in further peace discussions on 10 April; but once again no agreement was reached and two days later Edward therefore arrayed his forces before the walls of the city and sent Lancaster to one of the gates to demand battle of the regent, with the assurance that if the king was defeated he would never again claim the French throne.[61] But Charles prudently declined, for there was little that Edward could then do. A demonstration on the part of several detachments of the English army covered its withdrawal during the course of the same day.

It is not at all clear what Edward's plans were at this juncture. His failure to secure a favourable peace or to force the French to fight had determined the withdrawal from Paris; but where was he heading for now? According to Froissart he intended to pass into Beauce and then down the Loire valley into Brittany, where he would rest and recuperate his army until the late summer and then return to besiege Paris.[62] Gray, in his *Scalacronica*, asserts that he had to find fodder for the horses, since it was lacking outside Paris.[63] Both the weather and the itinerary of the army appear to bear this out. On Monday 13 April there was a terrible storm, mentioned by nearly all the chroniclers, notable for the heavy rain and large hailstones and during the course of which both men and horses died. According to the *Chronicle of London* the day became known as Black Monday.[64] In point of fact it was a particularly bad day of a particularly wet winter.[65] We know that over 1,200 war-horses were lost by the troops during the course of the campaign, to which must be added the loss of those drawing the baggage-wagons.[66] Knighton says that so many perished on that one day that the army was immobilized, making it necessary to return to England.[67] But the storm occurred near Chartres and the troops continued to march south towards the Loire by way of Bonneval and Châteaudun, apparently with Vendôme as their objective.[68] From Châteaudun they swung east in the direction of Orléans and only the arrival of the abbot of Cluny, once again endeavouring to conclude a peace, brought them to a halt at Tournoisis and Nids.[69] Edward was then moving south by much the same route by which he had come north from Burgundy.

This time the abbot's overtures were taken seriously and Edward agreed to treat. According to Froissart Lancaster was now urging him to accept the French proposals. 'My lord', he is reputed to have said to the king, 'this war which you are waging in the kingdom of France is a wondrous thing, but too costly for you. Your men profit by it, but you are losing time and money. Everything considered, if you continue to pursue it according to your opinion it will last for your lifetime and it is very doubtful that you will even then secure what you want. I would therefore counsel you, whilst you can still bring it to an honourable conclusion, to accept the proposals which are offered to you; for, my lord, we could lose more in one day than we have gained in twenty years.'[70]

It seems likely that the duke had been an advocate of peace for some time.[71] What weight his advice bore with the king is another matter; but essentially he was right. It was not that Edward had been beaten in the field, for the French had wisely refused to meet him in battle;[72] it was not that his army was demoralized by the storm on Black Monday, for it had continued its progress south; it was the fact that he, the Black Prince, Lancaster and all those commanders who had been so successful on their own, had taken over to France one of the largest armies ever seen there and achieved nothing. It was, in fact, a failure of strategy and if we may believe Froissart it may have been Edward's own.[73] Either the duke or the chronicler was right, for the king had not been the chief gainer from the war, over which he was losing control. It was from peace that he was to have his return, even though he was to surrender his claim to the French throne which, according to Froissart, was what he had wanted.[74]

Negotiations began towards the end of April, probably while Edward was at Tournoisis and Nids. The regent responded to the king's overtures by sending some of his councillors to Chartres with full powers and a special mandate to represent him. There were sixteen delegates in all, led by the bishop of Beauvais and accompanied by two secretaries or notaries. They left Paris and arrived in Chartres on 27 April, but were obliged to come further south, doubtless to Tournoisis and Nids, where Edward and his council were encamped. Upon requesting the king where the conference should take place, he replied that he was returning to Chartres. In fact he established his quarters at Sours, about two leagues from Chartres, and it was at Brétigny, a tiny hamlet of the parish of Sours, that the negotiations took place.[75]

The English delegates, again led by Lancaster, opened discussions with the French on 1 May and an agreement was reached within a few days. Delachenal thought that this was possible only because the treaty which was now concluded at Brétigny and dated 8 May was no more than a revival of the First Treaty of London of 1358, of which only the details needed to be modified.[76] The negotiators were doubtless not starting from scratch; the ground had been worked over many times since the beginning of the war and particularly during the last three years; but the total effect of this treaty was very different from either of its two predecessors.

Edward now had to give way on almost every major point. For while, at first sight, the territorial concessions demanded of the French, though much less than those of 1359, do not seem to differ greatly from those of 1358, and although Aquitaine was defined rather more generously, this did not compensate for the loss of the sovereignty of Brittany, which he had very largely been exercising during the past eighteen years. More important, whilst in 1358 King John's promise to renounce his sovereignty over the lands to be ceded appears to have been balanced by no comparable renunciation on Edward's part, Edward now undertook to renounce (after John had made his renunciation) the crown and kingdom of France, the homage, sovereignty and domain of Normandy, Touraine, Anjou and Maine and the sovereignty and homage of Brittany and Flanders. These were not empty words, for in many ways he had possessed all these things and had even gone a long way towards establishing his claim to the French throne. John's ransom was reduced from four to three million florins, of which 600,000 were to be paid before his release (or within seven months) and the remainder in annual instalments of 400,000—a more realistic schedule than hitherto. Edward was to give up his alliance with the Flemings (in so far as it still held good) in return for John's abandonment of the Scots; the castles which the English had occupied in territories which were to remain French were to be evacuated.

Only the fear of imminent disaster and the realization that the vast effort put into his last campaign had brought him no nearer to his goal can have persuaded Edward to negotiate such a treaty. But it was provisional; it still had to be ratified by the two kings at Calais. Several matters—mostly concerned with the practical application of the principles which had been agreed upon—were left for discussion when they were to meet and the French had to find the first instalment of the ransom and do several other things. On 8 May the delegates for either side exchanged the ratifications and oaths that concluded their missions. The regent and the Black Prince had still to give their approval and to this end some of the French delegates, together with six English knights, left for Paris on 9 May and secured an oath from the regent on the following day; that of the prince was registered in the church of Notre-Dame at Louviers on 15 May.[77]

Louviers was one of the places at which Edward stopped on his return to England by way of Honfleur. He seems to have had no part in the negotiations at Brétigny. On the conclusion of the treaty he left Sours with his entire army for Le Neubourg, where he stayed for eight days leaving for Honfleur with his four sons, John de Montfort, the earls of Northampton and Suffolk and several others.[78] From Le Neubourg he was conducted to Thibouville (where he halted on 12 and 13 May) by Robert de Vipount, Mapinus Marell and Pierre de Morance.[79] On 18 May he crossed from Honfleur to Rye and made post haste for Westminster, where he arrived the following day.[80]

The main body of the army returned from Le Neubourg by way of Calais, crossing the Seine at Pont-de-l'Arche and the Somme at Picquigny.[81] Once again the troops were divided into three columns. The first, under Lancaster's command, took the most easterly route; the second, made up of the forces previously in the king's column, was in the centre; and the third, made up of the forces previously in the Black Prince's column, took the most westerly route.[82] Having embarked at Calais they arrived back in England during the last week of May.[83] Only the earl of Warwick, who was appointed the king's lieutenant in Normandy,[84] remained in France to attend to the execution of the treaty, to prevent violations of the truce and, doubtless, to keep an eye on Charles of Navarre.[85]

Nothing is known of Lancaster's movements during June and July. He appears to have been at Leicester in the middle of August, but before the month was out he once again left his palace of the Savoy for Calais.[86] It was to be the last time he would make that now familiar crossing to France.

There was a good deal of business to be transacted at Calais before the treaty concluded at Brétigny was formally ratified by the two kings and before John could be released.[87] A decision had to be taken on how and when the renunciations should take place, on when and in what manner the hostages were to be released and on how a settlement of the Breton dispute might be reached. According to the timetable prescribed at Brétigny John was to be brought to Calais by 15 July, the first instalment of his ransom was to be paid within four months of that date and when this had been done, when certain of the hostages had surrendered themselves and when the town and fortresses of La Rochelle and the county of Guines had been handed over, all within the same four months, he would be released.

On 22 May, three days after Edward had returned to Westminster, John published his acceptance of the treaty and on 14 June following the two kings exchanged promises of ratification. Arrangements were soon put in hand for transferring John to Calais, where he landed on 8 July after a leisurely journey. Before the end of the month a complete plan and time-table appears to have been drawn up for the discussions which lay ahead. This provided for preliminary contacts at clerical level, to be followed by a delegation of 'magnates of the council' under whose supervision the effective negotiations would be carried out before the king arrived. In France, the regent left Saint-Omer for Boulogne on 23 August and on the following day the English 'magnates of the council', headed by the Black Prince and Lancaster, left their respective castles and palaces for Calais, where they remained until early in November. Evidently the discussions were protracted, for the business took a long time and Edward, who seems to have thought that a fortnight would suffice for the work, did not arrive in Calais until 9 October. But either before or after this date the articles concerning the renunciations were taken out of the main treaty and legislated for separately.

The *littere cum clausula c'est assavoir*, which embodied the agreement on the occasion and the procedure of the renunciations, provided that the king of France should transfer the lands and rights in question —if possible by 24 June 1361—and that letters recording that the renunciations had been duly made should be sent by either side to Bruges and exchanged there by 15 August or, if this were impossible, by 1 and 30 November respectively. Had Edward's policy been to secure the French king's renunciations in advance of the transfer of territories? It looks suspiciously as if he was hoping to secure the territories assigned to him soon, or at once, with, or even without, the French king's renunciations, and then to find reasons why he should not make his own. Even now he may not have been reconciled to the abandonment of his dynastic claims; but events were no longer moving in his favour. Companies of independent troops—the *Free Companies* —which had spread throughout France since the battle of Poitiers were no longer operating in his name. Some of them were in the pay of Charles of Navarre, who was now a serious rival. Moreover, the dauphin Charles, who was to succeed his father as king of France within four years, had already demonstrated his mettle. Time was to show that the future lay with him.

The final peace ceremonies took place on 24 October, when the solemn ratification of the treaty took place in the church of Saint-Nicolas at Calais. Lancaster was naturally present on this occasion; he swore to abide by the various instruments of which it was composed and played the leading part in reconciling Charles of Navarre with John.[88] The same day he did homage to the king of France for those lands which his father had held in Champagne before the outbreak of the war[89] and he was present at the great banquet given by the two kings before John was released on the following day.[90] On 3 November he arrived back at his palace of the Savoy.[91]

# XVII  The duke's last months

For over twenty-five years Lancaster had played a leading part in almost all of Edward III's enterprises abroad or, as we might say, in all foreign affairs, military, diplomatic and administrative; so much so that it is not easy to find many months together when he can safely be located at home. Since entering public life in 1333 he had spent approximately half of his time on the continent or in Scotland and no year had elapsed which he passed entirely in England. Even when he was there, much of his time was taken up with affairs of state in London—attending meetings of the king's council and parliament, being briefed for or reporting on military and diplomatic missions— and it was probably the need for a residence near to the centres of government and administration which led him to have a palace erected in his manor of the Savoy. Reputed to have been built from the profits of his first campaign in Aquitaine at an estimated cost of £35,000,[1] work appears to have started on it in the summer of 1349. In April 1350 he purchased a good deal of land and property adjoining the manor in the parishes of St Clement and St Mary-le-Strand outside Temple Bar;[2] but although most of the new buildings had been completed by the summer of 1357 when, during his absence in Brittany, they were assigned to the captive King John,[3] he can have spent relatively little time there.[4] It was his son-in-law, John of Gaunt, who was to enjoy the fruits of his labours in the twenty years that elapsed before the palace was sacked in the Great Revolt of 1381.

Henry had, however, numerous other residences at his disposal. In 1351 he spent a good deal of his time at his manor of Kingston Lacy in Dorset,[5] doubtless because it was conveniently situated for his duties as admiral to the west and warden of the sea coasts of Somerset, Dorset, Hampshire and Wiltshire, to which offices he was appointed during the course of that year.[6] But Leicester castle was undoubtedly his favourite residence and the numerous presents which he received from the borough corporation indicate frequent sojourns there.[7] His longest period of residence appears to have been in the first half of 1356, before the embarkation for Normandy, when he was settling the final details of his great foundation of the Newarke.[8] After his father's death in 1345 he never lived for very long at any of his other castles.

By that time Leicester castle was more of a private residence than a fortified position.[9] The main buildings, which were situated around a courtyard, included a great chamber and a suite of private apartments for the duke, his family and guests, a hall (which formed the communal living room and dormitory for the majority of the castle residents), a chapel, a dancing chamber and a kitchen block with its buttery, pantry, bakehouse, scullery, larder, saucery, spicery, chandlery and cellar. Another group of buildings was reserved for the officers concerned with the administration of the estates and included a treasury, which acted as a muniment room for the duke's charters and other important documents, as well as being a strong-room for his money and other valuables. There was a house for the chief forester near to the castle, the castle prison and prison house, stables and miscellaneous buildings, the remaining space within the castle enclosure being taken up by gardens. The furnishings were meagre since, despite the growth of a money economy, Henry still needed to move round his estates with his various household departments, their effects and equipment, staying at one or other of his numerous residences; he was never at Leicester for a very long time. His father had been a considerable expense to the borough during the fifteen years prior to his death in 1345, most of which were spent at Leicester.[10]

The popularity of Leicester forest as a hunting place doubtless accounted for much of the duke's partiality for Leicester castle. Here he could hunt the fallow deer with his pack of greyhounds and smoke and dig out foxes. In 1352 he had a new hunting lodge erected in the Frith (that part of Leicester forest adjacent to the town of Leicester) at a well known site which was then called *Briddesnest*, and this lodge was pre-eminent as a centre of sporting activity.[11]

The little time which Henry could have devoted to his family was probably spent at Leicester, but there is not a great deal which can be said about them. His wife, Isabella, was probably considerably younger than himself, since their first child was not born until 1341,[12] but it is not known when she died—only that she survived him. In their thirty years of married life she hardly appears on record at all. But she evidently accompanied him to France on some of his military and diplomatic missions: to the Low Countries in 1341 and Gascony in 1345–7.[13] He appears to have seen more of Eleanor than of any of his other sisters after they were married, doubtless because she was first married to his wife's brother and then, in 1343, to his friend and companion-in-arms Richard Fitzalan, earl of Arundel, known to contemporaries as 'Copped Hat'.[14] They spent much time together in their youth and two years after Beaumont's death in 1342 Eleanor accompanied him and Arundel to Spain.[15] Of the other sisters there is little to add. Two of them were dead by 1349: Isabella, who had entered the alien priory of Amesbury in Wiltshire and who subsequently became prioress there, and Joan, who was married to John Lord Mowbray.[16]

Henry's greatest tragedy was his failure to secure a male heir. According to one account he had a son who died in infancy at Kempsford in Gloucestershire, which was said to be why he granted the manor to the dean and canons of his collegiate church at Leicester;[17] but it is a solitary account. Of his two daughters, Maude was born in 1341 and Blanche in 1347. Both of them were contracted to marry early, Maude to Ralph, son and heir of Ralph Lord Stafford, on 10 October 1344 and Blanche to John, son of John de Segrave, on 3 May 1347.[18] A number of manors were settled on Maude and Ralph, but Henry was to have control of them and the guardianship and upbringing of both daughter and son-in-law until they were of age. They were married on 1 November 1344, but Ralph died three years later.[19] Both daughters were destined to have more eminent husbands.

Of the two, Blanche was perhaps more like her father; she took after him in many ways. Both Froissart and Chaucer, who knew her well, tell us that she was tall and fair.[20] If Chaucer's picture is true to the original, the White Lady of the *Book of the Duchess* was a tall and graceful blonde, whose looks appealed to fourteenth-century fashion. He tells us of her 'goodly softe speeche', of her eyes 'Debonair, goode, glade, and sadde', of her beautiful dancing, sweet singing and happy disposition.[21] From his testimony and that of Froissart we know that she shared Henry's personality; she was simple, benign, and not given to malice.[22] There is much in their portraits of Blanche of Lancaster that rings true to the author of the *Livre de Seyntz Medicines*.

Not much is known about Henry's movements after his return to England in November 1360. He may have been at Whalley for Christmas and the New Year and was possibly again in London for the parliament convoked on 24 January and which sat until February following;[23] but it is clear that he was suffering from ill-health. In addition to Richard of Ireland, his doctor in 1359, he was now attended by two Italian physicians then resident in London: John Gouche of Florence, who was subsequently surgeon to Edward III, and Pascal of Bologna, a prebend of St Paul's.[24] When he returned to Leicester at the beginning of March he was seriously ill, apparently suffering from a further outbreak of the plague. On the 15th of that month he made his will.[25]

He wished to be buried on the south side of the high altar of the college which he had founded (on the opposite side to his father) within three weeks of his death. If he died at Leicester, which now seemed likely, his body was to be carried to the parish church three days before his funeral and divine service was to be performed there with twenty-three torches. Twelve torches and two cloths of gold were to remain to the church and the curates were to have his best horse or its value in money. From the parish church he was to be carried to the college. The *cortège* was to be without vanity or parade; there were to be no armed men, horses with trappings or other vain things. Fifty poor men, half of them dressed in white and the other half in blue, and each bearing a lighted torch, were to walk by his body. The hearse was to bear five great candles, each of them weighing 100 lb, and four great funeral lights. The king and queen, the Black Prince and his royal brothers, his wife Isabella, his sisters and their husbands and other great folk of his blood were to be notified of the funeral. He bequeathed fifty linen cloths to be divided among poor needy folk. No cost was to be spared in giving food to the country people and the commons of the town; clerics were to be treated generously. All the wax, cloths of gold, his private altar-furniture, hangings, ornaments and other relics of his chapel were bequeathed to the collegiate church.

He appointed John Gynewell, bishop of Lincoln, William Clown, abbot of Leicester, his sister the Lady Wake, Sir William de Walkington, Sir Robert de la Mare, Sir John Buckland, John Charnels, Walter Power, Simon Simeon and John Newmarch his executors. All his goods, silver plate and furniture were placed at their disposal to pay debts, to reward those of his poor servants who had never been rewarded and to finish the collegiate church and all the houses which he had planned to build around it. Anything which then remained they were to put to the profit of his soul. If they could be honestly informed that he held lands which were not his by right, so that his estate therein could not honestly be held by his heirs, they were to persuade the heirs to return such lands to their rightful owner or owners. If they were informed that he had received wrong of others, they were to forgive it in discharge of his soul. If anything was in doubt or undeclared in his will, they were empowered to interpret it.

He did not make any of the detailed and specific bequests so beloved of medieval testators. He could not by law dispose of his lands in his testament, but he adopted the expedient, then becoming common, of enfeoffing his executors, or some of them, in part of his lands. Accordingly, on the day after he had made his will he obtained licence from the king to enfeoff some of the executors named in it in certain of his possessions in Lincolnshire, Norfolk, Staffordshire and Northampton-shire—including the honors of Bolingbroke and Tutbury.[26] The trust was evidently intended to provide funds for the additions to St Mary's College and for the payment of his debts.[27]

On the morning of Tuesday 23 March he died at Leicester.[28] Edward appears to have received the news in Windsor Park on the 25th. In a letter under the secret seal bearing that date he instructed the chancellor to issue briefs *diem clausit extremum* as quickly as he could.[29] The custody of his lands was entrusted to his son-in-law John, earl of Richmond.[30] On 30 March the will was proved at Leicester before John Gynewell. On 14 April he was buried in the church of Newarke College as he had wished. The royal family were present at the funeral and the Black Prince placed two cloths of gold on his bier.[31]

*Conclusion*

That Henry of Grosmont had played such a large part in the public affairs of Edward III's reign is perhaps not altogether surprising. Clearly he had ability and he had charm; he was closely related to the king and about the same age. His father had taken so large a part in the revolution of 1327 and the removal of Mortimer in 1330 that Edward could have felt his throne had been secured for him by the elder man. It is not unreasonable to suppose, since both the king and the younger Henry shared a passionate interest in tournament and display, all the magnificent ritual of chivalry, and since they doubtless agreed on Edward's rights and opportunities in Scotland and in France, that one may divine, even in the conventional phrases of state documents, the real affection and respect in which Edward held his 'cousin'. This is evident from Henry's creation as earl of Derby, his elevation to the rank of duke, the grants made to him on these occasions, when he came of age, and in acknowledgement of his services in Aquitaine; but it is perhaps most clearly demonstrated by his imprisonment in the Low Countries for the king's debts to the Malines and Louvain creditors, in sums for which he was personally bound. The day-to-day details of Edward's attempts to get his 'dear cousin' out of prison are as revealing as is Henry's action in itself. Similarity of interests, companionship in arms, the bond of shared experiences, all this strengthened their friendship as the years passed by, and throughout their lives there is no evidence of serious discord between them. That Henry, unlike his uncle Thomas, used his resources in the king's service is part of the wider theme of Edward III's harmonious relations with the magnates of his realm; but that the duke was given the highest place in the kingdom outside the royal family is a striking indication of the high esteem in which Edward held his 'cousin'.

In the nature of things, it is difficult to reach any firm conclusions about Lancaster as the king's intimate and trusted counsellor, although it cannot be doubted that he held that position. For while the court, being an informal body, has left behind no records; while virtually no council minutes have survived to indicate the part he played in shaping military and diplomatic policy; nevertheless, there can be little doubt that his influence was often decisive. He was the prime mover in the diplomatic overtures of 1344 and the renewal of the war in 1345; the expedition which he led to Aquitaine in the latter year was from beginning to end very much a Lancastrian affair and it marked the apogee of his career as a soldier. He was almost certainly the principal architect of the secret treaty of Dunkirk and of the campaigns of 1349–50 that were to have resulted from it. The naval battle off Winchelsea may have been fought as a result of his reports, and the part which he played at Avignon in the winter of 1354–5 was decisive to the subsequent course of events. It is possible that he became an advocate of peace—though not at any price—after his visit to Paris in 1352. He had the confidence of both pope and king, he promoted the negotiations with Guy de Boulogne which were intended to lead to a general settlement, and he may have been moved by conscience. For it was during these years that the *Livre de Seyntz Medicines* was written, that his great collegiate church was founded, that middle age drew on. He tired of the Breton lieutenancy and, amid the fiasco of the Reims campaign, he was finally successful in urging Edward to make peace at Brétigny in 1360.

With Lancaster's work as a soldier and administrator we are on rather firmer ground. There can be no doubt that he was a very competent military leader, and one who could attract able men to serve under him; though judging from his reputation, his fondness for the showiness of the tournament, the degree of success he achieved in one type of operation, his failure, relatively, in others, he was somewhat old-fashioned in his methods. The most notable feature of his campaigns was the speed with which they were carried out. The raids which he conducted deep into enemy territory with relatively small forces that could move quickly, picking off places that could be carried by assault, by-passing centres of real resistance, planting allied garrisons wherever possible and returning to base before an effective intercepting force could be brought up, produced results out of all proportion to the effort put into them. In Aquitaine in 1345–6 and 1349–50 they had the desired effect of impressing those whose security depended upon choosing rightly between an English and a French suzerain, and they substantially restored English authority there. In Normandy in 1356, where the object was to re-victual and strengthen certain castles belonging to Charles and Philip of Navarre then besieged by loyal French forces, and also, no doubt, to impress such as might tend to win over important men in the duchy to English allegiance, his task was successfully accomplished and his avoidance of the engagement offered by King John on that occasion was altogether prudent. But it is significant that he failed to join up forces with the Black Prince on the Loire—an operation calling for a higher degree of planning and which was an essential point in the military scheme for the year—and that he subsequently wasted his energies before Rennes, the siege of which demonstrated several curiously archaic features. No doubt it was a matter of chance, but it so happened that he was given so many independent commands that, unless he fought at Halidon Hill, of which we cannot be sure, he missed all the noteworthy battles of his time in which the English used their new tactics—Morlaix, Crécy, Mauron, Poitiers—tactics that were regarded by the more conservative French knights as offending against all the rules of war. His real achievement as the king's lieutenant in Aquitaine and Brittany was above all as an administrator who could draw upon the resources of his enormous wealth, both in the organization of the expeditions and in his daily work as governor of these overseas territories; although it should be noted that his work in redistributing lands and revenues in Aquitaine aggravated rather than alleviated the financial problem in the duchy.

It is not possible to judge the quality of his diplomacy in the same way as his military methods, since for so much of fourteenth-century diplomatic affairs there is no evidence beyond the formal documents appointing envoys, the texts of the final agreements and sometimes the envoys' expenses accounts. We can often know fairly exactly where and when the envoys met and how much it cost them to get there and back; but of what passed between them, save such as may be deduced from subsequent events, we can have very little idea at all. The very unusual survival of documentation connected with the two treaties of Dunkirk and the abortive treaty of Guines strongly suggests that Lancaster was duped on more than one occasion by both Louis de Male and Charles of Navarre; but it would certainly be wrong to conclude from these tortuous dealings with two slippery individuals that he was a failure as a diplomat. Indeed, perhaps the most significant factor in Lancaster's diplomacy was the reputation which he secured during his own lifetime, the figure which he cut in Europe and his knowledge of European affairs. He was universally respected for his bravery, his piety and the regard which he paid to the rules of fourteenth-century chivalry. His expedition to Prussia, which was emulated by his grandson Henry Bolingbroke, struck the imagination of his times, and the extraordinary affair in Paris that followed it, while it was to have important diplomatic consequences, might have come straight from the romances, even to his acceptance of no prize but one thorn from the Crown of Thorns and his bringing this home to the Lancastrian *Sainte-Chapelle* at Leicester. No other English nobleman had figured so large upon the European stage before. In his public career, in his familiarity with the contemporary European scene, Henry of Grosmont was the king's lieutenant for foreign affairs, and he foreshadowed the role that was subsequently to be taken up by his son-in-law John of Gaunt who, living in more troubled times, was to play for higher and more selfish stakes.

## The assembling and financing of Lancaster's first expedition to Aquitaine, 1345–1346

According to the terms of Lancaster's indenture, of the 2,000 men he undertook to take to Gascony, 500 (250 men-at-arms and 250 mounted archers) were to be in his personal retinue and the remaining 1,500 (250 men-at-arms, 250 mounted archers, 500 foot archers and 500 Welsh foot) were to be provided by the king.[1] To secure these troops, on 11 April 1345 Edward made an indenture with Laurence Hastings, earl of Pembroke, whereby Pembroke agreed to go to Gascony in Lancaster's company (also for six months in the first instance) with a retinue of 80 men-at-arms and 80 mounted archers.[2] Lancaster arrived at Southampton on 22 May with the retinue envisaged in his indenture and which included many of the soldiers who had served in his retinue on previous campaigns and who were to serve with him again in the future—men retained by him for life, some of them his councillors and officials.[3] Pembroke arrived on the following day with a retinue of 2 bannerets, 56 knights and 80 mounted archers which had partly been assembled at Tenby on the Pembrokeshire coast.[4] A retinue of 40 men-at-arms and 40 mounted archers mustered in Staffordshire by Sir James Audley in Staffordshire was brought down to Southampton by Sir John Tromwyn and joined Lancaster's forces there on 22 May.[5] The remaining 130 men-at-arms and 130 mounted archers were placed in two retinues under Sir Walter Mauny and Ralph Stafford.[6] The 500 Welsh foot were raised by commissions of array in North and South Wales, were formed into groups of 20 under 24 *vintenars*, and brought down to Southampton for 8 June by Geoffrey de Wrightington (subsequently Henry's escheator in Lancashire) and Richard Sholl, who were appointed *ductores*. They were accompanied by 6 constables, 2 chaplains, 2 surgeons, 2 criers and 6 standard-bearers. The majority of the foot archers were raised by commissioners of array in Lancashire, Derbyshire and Staffordshire, and brought to the port of embarkation by *centenars* appointed for the purpose by Lancaster. William de Whitton, who had previously served in the earl's retinue in Scotland, brought 125 from Lancashire, John Meynell brought 124 from Derbyshire and John Lesing of Barton, alias John de Duffield, brought 124 from Staffordshire. They were paid 15 days' wages for their journeys to Southampton, where they were assembled with the rest of Lancaster's forces on 12 June. Finally, 24 miners from the Peak District and the Forest of Dean joined the forces at Southampton on 26 May.[7]

Responsibility for the arrest and preparation of the shipping technically rested with Richard, earl of Arundel, in his capacity as admiral of the fleet west of the Thames. In fact, he delegated his powers to his lieutenant Phillip de Whitton. Whitton was responsible for the direction of the entire naval preparations and all disbursements in connection with them required his consent. Day-to-day organization was entrusted to John de Watenhull who, on 9 April, was appointed receiver of the sums necessary for payment to the mariners and others in charge of the ships. He left London on 19 April and between then and 19 September—when he reported to the council in London—he executed this business at Southampton, Portsmouth, Sandwich and Dartmouth. He received some of his funds direct from the Exchequer, but the majority of the financing was done by way of intermediaries—Exchequer officials like John de Baddeby, William de Waverley, Thomas de Aldham, John de Houton and William de Farley, and merchants like John de Wesenham. Watenhull was also responsible for delivering victuals for the sea-passage to Gascony—flour, cider, pigs, cheese, fish and other goods. Waverley and Aldham took up residence at St Cross near Winchester, where they paid the wages of the mariners commanding the fleets bound for both Gascony and Brittany.[8]

Lancaster's indenture had provided that he and his retinue were to begin to receive their pay on the evening of 14 May, when they were to be at Southampton ready for their passage to Gascony, or on whatever subsequent date they arrived there. They were to be paid at the current rate (6s 8d a day for himself, bannerets 4s 0d, knights 2s 0d, esquires 1s 0d, mounted archers 6d), but were also to receive a bonus or *regard*. An advance of £7,825 14s 0d (£4,492 7s 4d wages and £3,333 6s 8d *regards*) for himself and his personal retinue for six months was to be paid to him in three instalments: £5000 within a month after Easter (i.e. before 27 April), £1,825 14s 0d from the clerical tenth for St Barnabas term (11th June) and the remaining £1,000 on 15 November. Edward undertook that, if the earl wished to remain in Gascony beyond the initial term of six months, he would appoint deputies to see that the same wages and *regard* were paid to him in the duchy. The horses of the earl and his retinue were to be appraised in the customary manner before embarkation, but if any of the troops preferred to purchase their horses in Gascony they were to be appraised there by the constable of Bordeaux. The entire shipping costs of both the outward and the return voyages were to be met by the king.[9]

Lancaster arrived at Southampton on 22 May. By that date two Exchequer officials, Henry de Walton and William de Farley, had advanced £6,825 14s 0d to him. When the fleet put in at Plymouth on its way down the Channel coast from Southampton to Falmouth, they were sent up to Westminster to collect the remaining £1,000 wages and *regard* for the initial six months. By the time they returned to Plymouth Lancaster had already embarked, but on 19 July they followed him to Gascony with the money.[10] Pembroke was to receive wages and *regard* under the same condition as the earl[11] and an initial sum of £1,989 5s 4d was paid to him before he left England.[12]

Lancaster's indenture with the king also provided for the payment of the infantry not organized in retinues. William de Farley was appointed paymaster of these troops and he disbursed sums to them both before they left England and during their service in the duchy. He had a ready supply of money to make the necessary payments which, however, could only be made upon receipt of a mandate from Lancaster. During the month of June, while the troops were being assembled at Southampton, he was in residence at Winchester, disbursing sums to the *centenars* entrusted with conducting the foot archers from the North and the Midlands.[13] Once the forces had arrived in Gascony, he acted as treasurer-of-war to the troops not serving in the larger retinues.[14]

John Gynewell, Lancaster's treasurer in England, received the wages, *regard* and other sums due to the earl during his command in Aquitaine[15] and he had at least two clerks in his service in the duchy who appear to have acted as his treasurers-of-war. John de Welbourne, one of the earl's clerks as early as 1343 and subsequently his chancellor and secretary, appears to have acted as paymaster of the troops.[16] Peter de Wotton, already in his service in 1342, his chaplain in 1343, wardrober in 1343–4 and subsequently his receiver-general, served with him during his command in the duchy and recorded his daily expenses.[17] During these years he is described as clerk of his treasury.[18] Mauny, Stafford and Audley do not appear to have received any advances, but Pembroke and Mauny also had attorneys and lieutenants to receive those sums due to them from the Exchequer in England. Robert de Elleford acted in this capacity for Pembroke and Hugh de Walkan for Mauny.[19] Doubtless they also had treasurers-of-war in the duchy. In December 1345 Peter Gretheved received £10,200 from the Exchequer: £3,000 for delivery to Lancaster, Pembroke and Mauny in respect of their *regards*, and £7,200 to be used as Lancaster, the seneschal and constable saw best for furthering the king's interests in the duchy.[20] He was also given considerable supplies of victuals—flour, wheat, oats—for delivery to the troops.[21]

There was some change in the composition of the forces during the course of the expedition. Sir John Tromwyn returned to England with Audley's retinue on 30 November 1345.[22] On 27 March following the sheriff of London was instructed that the archers going to Gascony to serve with the earl were to be assembled at Tothill near Westminster on the following day,[23] and 300 Welsh foot archers were raised in South Wales and sent out to Bordeaux from Carmarthen.[24] A further four hundred foot left Portsmouth during May.[25]

# Appendix II

## Lancaster's income

In the absence of comprehensive central accounts for Duke Henry's time—such as the accounts of wardrobers and receivers-general, and auditors' *valors*, from which the incomes of Earl Thomas, Henry's father and John of Gaunt have been calculated[1]—it is not possible to say precisely what Henry's income from his estates amounted to. *Inquisitions Post-Mortem* are available,[2] but in general the *valors* attached to them cannot be trusted as a source for incomes.[3] However, an abstract of charges in his ministers' accounts survives for the year ending Michaelmas 1348[4] and this puts the gross value of his estates in Lancashire and the honors of Tutbury, Bolingbroke and Leicester at £3,506 8s 1d,[5] viz:

| | Lancashire | | | Tutbury Honor | | | Bolingbroke Honor | | | Leicester Honor | | |
|---|---|---|---|---|---|---|---|---|---|---|---|---|
| | £ | s. | d. | £ | s. | d. | £ | s. | d. | £ | s. | d. |
| Gross Values | 528 | 8 | 6½ | 750 | 16 | 9½ | 643 | 11 | 5¼ | 786 | 0 | 1½ |
| Casuals | 84 | 9 | 1½ | 220 | 2 | 7 | 184 | 8 | 3 | 308 | 11 | 2¾ |
| Total Charge | 612 | 17 | 8 | 970 | 19 | 4½ | 827 | 19 | 8¼ | 1,094 | 11 | 4¼ |

Only reprises—fees and liveries of officers and annuities paid to retainers—are listed on the discharge side, and these amounted to no more than £241 17s 6¼d.[6] These figures can be supplemented from two surviving honor accounts and a valuation of the majority of the estates made shortly after the duke's death in 1361 to facilitate their partition between his two daughters, Maude and Blanche. One of these accounts, made by his auditors John Cockayn (also steward of his lands) and William de Blaby for Pontefract honor in the year to Michaelmas 1357,[7] supplements one gap in the abstract of 1348 and reveals the extent of Edward's appreciation of the earl's work in Gascony. The gross charge amounted to £1,696 0s 1¼d (including £269 7s 5d arrears), the discharge to £1,375 6s 6¾d, leaving £320 13s 6½d unexpended. The profit which Henry derived from the honor was, of course, considerably greater than the figure given as unexpended would at first sight appear to suggest. Medieval accounts must not be read as if they were cast in modern form.

This is well illustrated by the second surviving account, which was drawn up by John Hayward, receiver of Leicester honor, for the year to Michaelmas 1352.[8] Total revenue was put in charge at £635 9s 5d (including £26 3s 10d arrears). Much of this was, however, at the duke's disposal, for although the discharge amounted to £652 4s 9¼d, of this sum £478 6s 9¾d was spent on building (£286 7s 2¼d on Newarke hospital and £181 19s 7½d on a new hunting-lodge in the Frith at Leicester) and £102 18s 0d was made over to his treasurer, Henry de Walton in London on 6 February.[9]

The valuation of 1361, although incomplete, is by far the most comprehensive.[10] His possessions in Yorkshire, Lancashire and Wales were valued at £1,187 3s 3d, £982 0s 4½d and £1,180 0s 0d respectively; in Hampshire, Berkshire, Wiltshire and Dorset at £597 9s 3½d; in Staffordshire, Warwickshire, Leicestershire, Northamptonshire and Rutland at £372 14s 10½d; in Cheshire at £312 11s 5½d; in Northumberland at £220 15s 8½d; in Huntingdonshire at £183 4s 0d; in Gloucestershire at £121 19s 4½d; and in Warwickshire at £72 4s 6d. Beaufort and Nogent in France were valued at £400. The total valuation thus stood at £5,630.

The figure excludes those possessions in Lincolnshire, Norfolk, Staffordshire and Northamptonshire—including Bolingbroke and Tutbury honors—in which the duke enfeoffed some of his executors shortly before his death, Bergerac and Calais in France and a number of manors granted for life to retainers who survived him.[11] Since Bolingbroke and Tutbury honors were put in charge at £1,798 19s 0¾d in the year to Michaelmas 1348[12] these, together with the other possessions in which he enfeoffed the executors, could not have been much less than £2,750 gross annual value.[13] He would thus appear to have been assured of over £8,380 gross from his English and Welsh possessions alone.

This figure may be compared with those which we possess for Henry's father, uncle and son-in-law.[14] In the year to Michaelmas 1331, Earl Henry's possessions were put in charge at £8,073 16s 10½d (£6,408 12s 7¼d, not including £1,665 4s 3¼d arrears), of which a net amount of £6,876 11s 8d was at the earl's disposal. The total charge of John of Gaunt's estates stood at £12,335 4s 3½d and £12,473 17s 0½d in the years to Michaelmas 1394 and 1395 respectively; Thomas of Lancaster had an income of £6,661 17s 11d from his lands.

# Appendix III

## Lancaster's retinue

The following tables are based on (*a*) a nominal roll of the men who served in Lancaster's personal retinue or *comitiva* on military and diplomatic missions and (*b*) a list of those who received grants of land and annuities from him.

The nominal roll has largely been compiled from:

(1) Exchequer records, which include two surviving pay-rolls containing soldiers' names preserved among the Accounts Various, one for the Scottish expedition of 1336 (E 101/15/12), the other for the expedition to Aquitaine of 1345–6 (E 101/25/9); a list of the names of those who were compensated for horses killed in action in the Low Countries in 1338–40, preserved in Norwell's Wardrobe Book among the collection of Miscellaneous Books (E 36/203, fo. 125v); a number of debentures issued to those who sold their horses before leaving Bordeaux in 1350, preserved among the Writs and Warrants for Issue (E 404/508/51–72, 74, 76–9) and listed on the Issue Roll for that year (E 403/355, m.19); writs of exoneration from service in the king's army in 1346–7 enrolled on the Memoranda Roll (King's Remembrancer) for 1347 (E 159/123).

(2) Chancery records, which include letters of protection and general attorney enrolled on the Scottish, Gascon and Treaty Rolls (C 71/21; C 61/56–8, 61–2; C 76/12–27, 29, 32–8, 40); surviving requests for these letters preserved among the files of Warrants (C 81/1724, 1730); surviving warrants for the issue of writs of exoneration from service in the king's army in 1346–7, also preserved among the files of Warrants (C 81).

The nominal roll is not exhaustive. The financial records are confined to four campaigns (1336, 1338–40, 1345–6, 1349–50), only two of them are pay-rolls (1336, 1345–6), and one of these (1345–6) is deficient in the names of the esquires. The Chancery records, although available for most of the missions, are not always reliable for evidence of service. Letters of protection and general attorney were only requested for and issued to a small proportion of Lancaster's *comitiva*. Occasionally, they were not issued at all. Moreover, those which were requested and issued prior to the commencement of a mission (as opposed to during its course) only provide evidence of intended service. Doubtless this was almost always performed, but circumstances sometimes arose which prevented its performance, as was the case in 1350 when the troops who were given letters of protection and general attorney to join Lancaster in Gascony never left Plymouth, or in 1355 when those who were given similar letters to accompany him to Normandy and Brittany were likewise held up at Portsmouth.

The list of donees has largely been compiled from:

(1) Duchy of Lancaster Records, including original grants preserved among the series of Ancient Deeds (DL 25, 27), enrolled on a Duchy Chancery Roll

(DL 37/1) and evident from mandates and confirmations in *John of Gaunt's Register*; payments of annuities recorded among the Accounts Various (DL 28), Ministers' Accounts (DL 29) and Miscellanea (DL 41).

(2) Royal chancery enrolments of licences for and confirmations of such grants, pardons for their acquisition without royal licence and licences for the beneficiaries to retain them, to be found in the *Calendars of Patent Rolls*, and evidence of possession at the time of the duke's death available in the *Calendar of Inquisitions Post Mortem*, vol. XI.

Table 1. *Number of missions on which donees and non-donees served in Lancaster's comitiva*

| | Number of missions on which served | | | | | | | | | | | Total |
|---|---|---|---|---|---|---|---|---|---|---|---|---|
| | 11 | 10 | 9 | 8 | 7 | 6 | 5 | 4 | 3 | 2 | 1 | |
| *Donees* | | | | | | | | | | | | |
| Knights | | | | | 2 | 3 | 2 | 4 | 7 | 7 | 5 | 30 |
| Esquires | 1 | | | 1 | 1 | | 2 | | 1 | 2 | 8 | 16 |
| Total | 1 | | | 1 | 3 | 3 | 4 | 4 | 8 | 9 | 13 | 46 |
| *Non-Donees* | | | | | | | | | | | | |
| Knights | | 1 | | 2 | 3 | 4 | 4 | 4 | 20 | 35 | 88 | 161 |
| Esquires | | | | | | | | 3 | 6 | 30 | 292 | 331 |
| | | 1 | | 2 | 3 | 4 | 4 | 7 | 26 | 65 | 380 | 492 |

Table 2. *Distribution of grants of lands and annuities between those who served in Lancaster's comitiva and those who did not*

| Grant | | Soldiers | Others |
|---|---|---|---|
| Manors | | 16 | 6 |
| Annuities: | £40 | 2 | |
| | 40 marks | 3 | 1 |
| | £20 | 13 | 2 |
| | 20 marks | 4 | 3 |
| | £10 | 5 | 5 |
| | 10 marks | 4 | 4 |
| | £5 | 1 | 6 |
| | 5 marks | | 6 |
| | £1 10s 0d | | 3 |
| | £1 | 1 | 6 |
| | 1 mark | 1 | 3 |
| Other annuities | | 3 | 9 |
| Other grants | | 5 | 2 |
| Totals | | 58 | 56 |

Table 3. *Number of donees who served in Lancaster's comitiva on individual missions*

| Mission | | Total men-at-arms | Total men-at-arms known by name | Total of donees who served |
|---|---|---|---|---|
| 1336 | Scotland | 100 | 94 | 13 |
| 1338–40 | Low Countries | 93 | 70 | 14 |
| 1340 | Low Countries | | 6 | 1 |
| 1341 | Scotland | | 11 | 1 |
| 1342–3 | Brittany | 182 | 48 | 11 |
| 1343 | Spain | | 3 | |
| 1344 | Aquitaine-Spain-Avignon | | 40 | 10 |
| 1345–6 | Aquitaine | 250 | 173 | 23 |
| 1347 | Calais | | 81 | 18 |
| 1348 | Calais-Flanders | | 17 | 2 |
| 1349–50 | Aquitaine | | 41 | 15 |
| 1354–5 | Avignon | 317 | 9 | 2 |
| 1355 | Normandy-Brittany | | 72 | 7 |
| 1356–8 | Normandy-Brittany | | 80 | 15 |
| 1359–60 | Reims campaign | 582 | 78 | 13 |

Appendix IV

# Unpublished documents

1. *Indenture of war between Edward III and Henry of Lancaster, earl of Derby, concerning an undertaking by Lancaster to go to Gascony as the king's lieutenant, Westminster, 13 March 1345* (Exchequer enrolment, Public Record Office, E 159/123, m.254).

Ceste endenture faite entre nostre seigneur le roi d'une parte et monsieur Henri de Lancastre, conte de Derby, d'autre parte, tesmoigne que le dit conte, par comaundement nostre seigneur le roi, ad empris d'aler en Gascoygne a y demorer come lieutenant le roi pur un demy an, si guerre soit, et a faire le bien q'il poet ove cink centz hommes d'armes, milles archers, dont cink centz serront a chival et cink centz a pie, et outre cink centz Galeys a pie. Et du noumbre susdit deux centz et cinquante hommes d'armes et deux centz et cinquante aultres a chival serront a la retenance propre du dit conte, c'est assavoir soi, oytisme a banere, quatre vintz et douze chivalers et cent et cinquante esquiers. Et nostre seigneur le roi lui perfournira des gentz d'armes, archers et gentz Galeys tanque au noumbre susdit. Et le dit conte ove sa retenance susnomee serra au port de Southamptoun le veille de la Pentecost proschein avenir pour passer versus les dites parties de Gascoigne. Et meisme la veille de Pentecost soit le primer jour de demy an avantdit pour acompter des gages et pour touz autres covenances composes en ceste endenture, s'il ne soit garni par maundement du roi par covenable temps de prendre autre jour par defaute de navie que ne soit mye pleynement venue. Et est l'entencion toutes voies que le jour q'il vendra a la meer sur son passage il commencera d'aconter. Et le dit conte prendra pour lui meismes sys soldz et oyt deniers le jour, pour chescun baneret quatre soldz, pour chescun chevaler deux soldz, pour chescun esquier douze deniers, et pour chescun archer a chival sys deniers; les queux gages pour sa retenue propre pour le demy an avantdit amontent a quatre mille quatre centz quatre vintz douze livres sept soldz et quatre deniers, et ovesque ce il prendra pour regard pour meisme le temps troys centz trente et trois livres sys soldz et oyt deniers; les queles summes amontent en tout a sept mille oyt centz vint et cynk livres quatorze soldz, dont il serra paie dedeinz un moys apres la Pasque proschein avenir de cynk mille livres.

Item, il avera assignement sur la disme de Seint Eglise du terme de Seint Barnabe proschein suant de mille oyt centz vint et cynk livres quatorze soldz.

Item, sur la quinzisme de la commune du terme des Touz Seintz proschein suant, mille livres.

Item, le dit conte avera eskippeson pour lui, ses gentz, chivaux et vitailles en alant et venant as custages nostre seigneur le roi.

Item, les chivaux du dit conte et de sa retenance serront prisez a covenable pris devant lour eskippeson en manere acustumee; et en cas q'aucuns des ses gentz d'armes ne se voillent monter des chivaux decea la meer, mes faire le pourveance par delea, que adonques meismes ceux chivaux soient prisez illoeques par le conestable de Burdeux en la manere suisdite et a quel heure que nul homme d'armes perde chival avant prise que de temps lour chivalx q'ils pourvoierent soient prisez par le dit conestable en convenable manere come desus est dit.

Item, est ordene que un clerc suffisant soit assigne pour paier gages a les communes qi serront en la compaignie du dit conte, aussibien decea la mer come delea; et serra meisme clerc covenablement estuffe d'argent pour faire meisme les payementz, et si ne ferra nul payement saunz l'avis et comaundement du dit conte.

Item, le roi voet que en cas que prisons soient pris es dites parties par le dit conte ou les soens, q'il puisse faire d'eux sa volente et q'il puisse avoir toutes autres avantages de guerre, forspris villes, chastelx, terres, rentes et homages, a quiconque q'ils soient; pour queux choses le dit counte avera pleyn poair par commission de les doner ou lesser selonc ce q'il verra que mieux soit pour le profit nostre seigneur le roi.

Item, il avera pleyn poair par commission de seisir en la mein le roi toutes terres, tenementz, villes, chastelx, franchises, custumes, profitz des monoies et toutes autres choses en queconque manere a la duche de Guyenne, en nul temps regardantz en qi meins q'il soient devenuz, par la ou il verra q'il le puisse faire par bone et juste cause, et de les tenir ensi en pees en la mein nostre seigneur le roi tanque il lui eut eit certifie, issint que par son avis il eut puisse ordener ce que mieux soit.

Item, il avera poair par commission de prendre treives et soeffrances en les parties susdites quant il verra que busoigne soit pour l'onour du roi et la sauvete de lui et de ses gentz et du pays.

Item, il avera poair par commission a surveer les faitz de touz les ministres le roi es dites parties, et de les nient covenables remuer et autres mettre en lour leux a toutes les foitz q'il verra q'il soit affaire, reservant neproquant au roi les offices du seneschal et du conestable.

Item, il avera poair par commission de granter vie et membre et de faire mise de rebealx et disobeissantz aussibien par meer come par terre es dites parties durant le demy an avantdit, et aussint q'il puisse receivre a la pees nostre seigneur le roi les rebealx et desobeissantz en celles parties et a eux pardoun faire de lour trespas; et les covenances q'il ferra ovesque eux serront tenuz et perfourniz par nostre seigneur le roi et par touz autres qi y serront apres le dit conte.

Item, le roi voet que si nul poair soit grante a aucun autre acordant a nul des pointz compris en ceste endenture, que meisme cel poair soit repelle et anienty.

Item, en cas que apres le demy an susdit il plese a nostre seigneur le roi que le dit conte demoerge en les dites parties de Gascoigne come son lieutenant ove tut sa retenance et les gentz d'armes et archers susditz a faire le bien q'il poet pour le demy an ensuant, que adonques soient gentz suffisantes assignez par comission d'aconter ovesque lui aussibien de ses gages come de restor de ses chivalx perduz, et de lui paier quant que lui serra duz par meisme l'aconte et aussint ses gages et regard devant la mein pour le temps q'il demora illoeques, et q'il eit touz autres covenances sicome est dit plus pleynement pour le primer demy an.

Item, voet le roi que en cas que nul des covenances susdites ne soit tenuz au dit conte, que adonques au chief du primer demy an il soit de tut descharge et ove toutes ses gentz puisse venir en Engleterre ou aler par aillours queu parte

231

que il plerra saunz empechement de nostre dit seigneur le roi ou de nul autre en son noun. Il est acorde que le treives nadgaires prises en Bretaigne soient susrendues par covenables temps, issint que le dit conte ent puisse estre certifie en Gascoigne devant q'il chivauche de guerre.

Item, le roi ad grante que en cas que aucunes terres ou tenementz puissant avenir droiturelement au dit conte, par descent d'eritage ou en autre quecunque manere resonable durant le temps q'il demorra issint en service nostre seigneur le roi, que par defaute de homage ou foialte ou aucun autre service tieux terres et tenementz ne soient retenuz en la mein le roi par eschetour ne par autre ministre, einz soient delivres par duz proces as attornez le dit conte, franchement, pour faire ent son profit saunz contredit ou empeschement de nullui; et soient les homages et foialtees respitees tanque a sa venue en Engleterre.

Item, le roi ad grante que s'il aviegne que le dit conte soit assiege ou prisse par si grant force des gentz q'il ne se pourra eider saunz estre rescous par le poair du roi, que le roi soit tenuz de lui rescoure par une voie ou par autre, issint q'il soit rescous convenablement.

Item, en cas que ceste viage du dit conte soit par aucune cause chaunge ou destourbe, le roi ad promis q'il avera regard a les custages queux le dit conte covient faire par ceste cause, come en retenance des gentz, pourveances faire et en autre manere, et ferra ensi devers lui q'il s'agreera par reson. En tesmoignance de queu chose a ceste partie de l'endenture demorrante devers nostre seigneur le roi le dit conte ad mys son seal.

Donne a Westminstre, le xiii jour de marz, l'an du regne nostre seigneur le roi d'Engleterre disnoefisme et de France sisme.

2. *Indenture between Henry of Lancaster, earl of Derby, lieutenant of Edward III in Aquitaine and Languedoc, and Bernard Ezi, lord of Albret, and his brother Bérard d'Albret, lord of Vayres, touching the custody of the town of Bergerac, Bergerac, 10 September 1345* (Original parchment, Archives départementales des Basses-Pyrénées, E 131; eighteenth-century copy, Bibliothèque Nationale, Collection Doat, vol. 189, fos. 167–70).

Haec indentura, facta apud Brageracum die sabbati, decima die mensis septembris anno Domini millesimo trecentesimo quadragesimo quinto, inter egregium virum dominum Henricum de Lancastria, comitem Derbi, locum tenentem serenissimi principis domini nostri Angliae et Franciae regis in ducatu Aquitaniae et lingua occitana, ex parte una, et nobiles viros dominos Bernardum Ezii, dominum de Lebreto, et Berardum de Lebreto, dominum de Vayriis, milites, fratres, ex altera, testatur conventiones habitas et concordatas inter ipsos super custodia villae Brageraci ejusdem domini nostri regis, quae sunt tales.

Primo, quod dicti fratres erunt capitanei dictae villae, illamque custodire, salvam facere domino nostro regi praedicto tenebuntur a dicto die usque diem nonum sequentis mensis octobris; et pro custodia dictae villae habebunt et tenebunt cum ipsis ducentos octoginta decem et octo homines equites armorum et mille ducentos servientes pedites, tam balisterios, sive archerios quam lancerios cum taulachis, videlicet, per primos quatuordecim dies dicti termini et per residuos quatuordecim dies ejusdem termini, ducentos quinquaginta homines equites armorum, ipsis fratribus computatis; et dictos mille ducentos servientes ad vadia regia, videlicet, pro quolibet ipsorum fratrum quatuor solidos, pro quolibet milite equite duos solidos, pro quolibet scutiffero equite duodecim denarios, pro quolibet balesterio seu archerio tres denarios et pro quolibet lancerio duos denarios sterlingorum vel eorum valorem per diem, secundum consuetudinem Patriae alias usitatam et antiquitus observatam; et finito dicto termino dictus dominus comes et locum tenens ponat alium vel alios capitaneum sue capitaneos in dicta villa, si ipsi fratres plus custodire noluerint eandem.

Item, dicti fratres facient monstram dictarum gentium equitum et peditum et equorum de octo in octo diebus durante termino predicto coram illo quem dictus dominus comes et locum tenens duxerit deputandum.

Item, quod dicti fratres poterunt, vocato deputato per dictum dominum comitem et locum tenentem et per visum ejusdem, opera et reperationes necessarias in dicta villa faciendas fieri facere, suburbia sive barria munire vel destruere et reparari facere, secundum quod discretioni videbitur faciendum et commodius fuerit pro utilitate regia et salvatione villae predictae.

Item, dictus dominus comes et locum tenens per suum deputatum faciet providere de arcubus sive balestris unius pedis et duorum pedum springallis et quadrellis necessariis pro custodia et defensione villae predictae quae tamen in villa predicta presenti reperiri poterunt et aliunde commode haberi; quam artillariam dicti capitanei dividere custodibus dictae villae, et in fine termini praedicti dicti capitanei illam reddere et restituere dicto deputato tenebuntur, exceptis illis quae, si necessario contigerit, fuerint devastata.

Item, quod finito dicto termino dicti capitanei capitaniam et custodiam villae praedictae, cum eadem benivolentia dicti domini comitis et locum tenentis qua easdem receperunt, dimittere possint ipso prius certiorato legitime et requisito.

Item, si forsan vellet dictus dominus comes et locum tenens dictos fratres in capitania et custodia praedictis ulterius moraturos, finito termino praedicto, quod solvantur eis, prae manibus, vadia pro ipsis et dictis gentibus ut est dictum per tempus quod ipsos voluerit ultra remansuros et moraturos; et, in casu quo dicta vadia sic non solventur, quod cum eadem benivolentia dimittere possint capitaniam et villam praedictas, ipso tamen ut supra requisito.

Item, equi ipsorum capitaneorum et gentium suorum armorum praedictorum appretiabuntur si et quando monstrabuntur, de die in diem, et si qui in servitio regio perdantur, illi qui eos perdent habeant vadia sicut est fieri consuetum in ducatu in tali casu; et nihilominus emenda eis fiat de restauro equorum condigna perditorum quam cito fieri poteri bono modo.

Item, quod dicti fratres et quilibet ipsorum, tamen cum magistro Johanne Wawayn, constabulario Burdegalae, per dictum dominum comitem et locum tenentem deputato et eis adjuncto, habeant potestatem reappellandi et convocandi gentes Bregeraci de redeundo ad villam praedictam, perdonandi, graciam faciendi, et homines equites et pedites ad vadia regia in locis si quae ipsos capere vel domino regi adquirere contingeret, et eis expediens videatur ponendi conventiones et pacta faciendi eisdem gentibus et aliis quae venire voluerint ad obedientiam dicti domini nostri regis, et quod dictus dominus comes et locum tenens ordinata, tractata, promissa, contenta et facta per dictos fratres et quemlibet ipsorum, simul cum dicto adjuncto deputato, ad commodum et honorem dicti domini nostri regi strata et grata habeat et confirmet. In quorum omnium testimonium sigilla dominorum praedictorum his indenturis alternatim sunt appensa.

Datum Bregeraci undecima die septembris anno praedicto.

3. *Indenture of retainer between Henry, earl of Lancaster, and Sir Edmund de Ufford, London, 1 March 1347* (Original parchment, Public Record Office, DL 27/155).

A touz ceux qui cestes lettres verront ou orront, Henri, counte de Lancastre, de Derby et de Leycestre, seneschal d'Engleterre, saluz en Dieux. Come nostre tres chere cousyn monsieur Esmon de Ufford, filz a monsieur Thomas de Ufford, soit demorre ovesque nous de nous servir a toute sa vie en guerre et en pees, par manere que s'enseust; c'est assavoir, en temps de guerre, soi, tiercz hommes d'armes bien armez et mountez comme appent, et avera mounteour pour lui meismes de nostre lyveree, et avera dis chyvalx pour lui et ses gentz a liveree, de fein, avein, clowes et ferres, neof garsouns as gages, un chamberlein mangeant en sale. Et les chivalx sur queux ses esquiers serront mountez serront covenablement preisez par noz gentz, et avera restor resonable de ceux qui serront perduz ensi en nostre service. Et en temps de pees quele heure q'il soit par nous maunde il vendra ove un esquier la ou nous soioms, et avera quatre chivalx a lyveree, un chamberlein mangeant en sale et trois garsouns as gages. Et toute foitz quant nous fesoms liveree as autres chivaliers de robes et seales nous ferroms devers lui auxi come as autres de sa condicion. Et pour le bon et greable service que le dit monsieur Esmon nous ad avant ces heures fait, et auxi pour le bon service q'il nous ferra en manere susdit, avoms donez et grauntez au dit monsieur Esmon quarrante marcz d'annuele rente a prendre d'an en an en nostre manoir de Heigham Ferrers as termes en nostre dit manoir usuels par les meyns des prevostz q'illoeques sont et serront en temps avenir a avoir et tenir l'avant dite annuetee de quarrante marcz de nous, noz heirs et nos assignez a l'avantdit monsieur Esmon a toute sa vie, liberalment, bien et en pees, sanz destourbir ou contredit de nous ou nul des noz, fesant toute foitz a nous le dit service de pees et de guerre de manere susdite. Et voloms et grauntoms pour nous et noz heirs que si la dite rente soit arere a nul terme avantdit, qe bien lise au dit monsieur Esmon ou a son attorne a destreindre noz tenantz de Heigham Ferrers susdit et noz fermers illoeques, et la destresse amenir et detenir taunque gree lui soit fait de touz les arrerages de la rente avantdit. Et nous Henri, counte de Lancastre avantdit, et noz heirs, l'annuetee de quarrante marcz susdite a l'avantdit monsieur Esmon en manere come desus est dit garrantiroms et defendiroms countre toutes gentz. En tesmoigne de queu chose a la partie de l'endenture demouraunt devers le dit monsieur Esmon nous avoms mys nostre seal, et a la partie de l'endenture demouraunt par devers nous le dit monsieur Esmon ad mys son seal. Par yceux tesmoignes monsieur Reygnaud de Mohun, monsieur Johan de Seyton, monsieur Richard de Rouclyf, chyvaliers, Simon Symeon, Payen de Mohun et autres.

Donne a Loundres, le primer jour de marcz, l'an du regne nostre seigneur le roi Edward tiercz puis le conquest, vintisme primer.

4. *Agreement concluded between the envoys of Edward III and those of Louis de Male, count of Flanders, Dunkirk, November 1348* (Original parchment, British Museum, Additional Charter, 59142).

Il fait a ramembrer que accorde et consenti est par reverent pere en Dieu, Guillaume, evesque de Norwicz, Henry, conte de Lancastre, de Derby, de

Leycestre, seigneur de Bragerak et senescal d'Engleterre, Robert de Ufford, conte de Suffolk, Gautier, signeur de Mauny, et mestre Jehan de Carleton, doctour en loys, commis et deputez de par tres noble et tres poissant prince monsigneur Edward, par la grace de Dieu roy de France et d'Engleterre d'une part, et Henry de Flandres, seigneur de Nieneve, Sohier, seigneur d'Ainghien, et Jaqueme Metteneye, commis et deputez de par tres noble prince monsigneur Loys, conte de Flandre, de Nevers et de Rethel, d'autre part, pour bien de pais, tranquillite et amour norrir, accroistre et procurer entre les dessudis signeurs roy et conte de Flandres, leurs subgetz et adherentz a tous jours mais, que dedens le premier jour de septembre prochain venant le dit conte envoiera soffissanment ses messages par devers l'adversaire de France dou dit roy de France et d'Engleterre, et fera requerre et demander son droit et heritage de la conte d'Arthoys, des villes de Lille, Douay, Bethune et Orchies, les chasteleries et appendances d'ycelles. Et ou cas que le dit adversaire dou dit roy de France et d'Engleterre la dicte requeste fesist et acordast, que le dit conte par tant seroit content en sa personne, et que le dit roy de France et d'Engleterre, ne ses adherentz, par les gentz de le dicte conte d'Arthoys, des villes de Lille, Douay, Bethune, Orchies, des chasteleries et appendances d'ycelles, ne seroient de riens empeschie, moleste, ne greve. Et soufferroit le dit conte que son pays de Flandres tenist et acomplist devers le dit roy de France et d'Engleterre, ses hoirs et successeurs, toutes les alliances et promesses faites a lui orez et en temps passe. Et en cas que la dicte requeste dou dit conte ne fust acceptee et acomplie et a lui rendu son dit heritage, que le dit conte, apres ceste requeste soffisanment fait, feroit le dit son adversaire de France deffier et lui rendroit sus tous les hommages qu'il tient de luy, trois semaines devant le premier jour de septembre prochain venant. Et adonc le dit roy de France et d'Engleterre et contes de Flandres, pour yaus, pour leur hoirs et successeurs, feroient une certaine alliance ensamble durant la guerre le meisme premier jour de septembre, et promettront l'un l'autre a aidier et conforter de tous leurs povoirs a conquerre le droit sur le dit adversaire de France sur ses hoirs et successeurs, loyaument et en bonne foy.

Item, en cest accort et alliance, le dit roy de France et d'Engleterre et le dit conte prometteront loyaument et en bonne foy, li uns a l'autre, pour yaus et pour leur hoirs et successeurs, que il ne aucuns d'yaus jamais ne feroient ne ne soufferroi a faire aveuques le dit son adversaire de France, ses hoirs et successeurs ne encontre ses adherentz, pais, acord, trieuwes ne souffrance, sans le sceu, volente, assent et consent de l'autre.

Item, se le dit conte en temps a venir ne peust paisivlment joir de ses contes de Nevers et de Retheslz et de ce que y appartient, que li dis roys de France et d'Engleterre, en recompensation de ce, paiera au dit conte ou a son commant, aussi longuement qu'il sera en deffaute de ce, quarante mille escutz d'or, de poys et de loy tels comme il keurent a present, ou autre bonne monnoye aussi proffitable a l'avenir, chascun an, l'une moitie a le Pasque et l'autre a le Saint Michiel, et de ce lui donra ses lettres ouvertes, bien seellees, le dit premier jour de septembre as alliances faire. Et de ce fera le dit roy de France et d'Engleterre bonne seurte au dit conte a payer dedens la ville de Bruges en la manere qui s'ensieut, assavoir est que en celi cas li dis roys prommettera au dit conte de Flandres et ses hoirs et successeurs ou a son certain commant payer loyaument, fermement et en bonne foy, sans enfraindre au lieu et as termes dessus nommez as propres perilz et despens dou dit roy les quarante mille florins d'or a l'escu dessus ditz cascun an en la manere dessus dicte; et quant a ce il obligera li, ses hoirs et successeurs, ses biens et les leur quelconques. Et pour plus grande seurte de ce, li dis roys de rechief promettra loyaument, veritablement et en bonne foy que ou cas q'il seroit en aucune manere en deffaute de payer le somme de quarante mille florins d'or a l'escu, as termes, au lieu et en la manere dessus dicte, il envoireroit, dedens un mois prochain apres la premiere deffaute de paiement, dedens la ville de Bruges, deux chevalers bannerez et wyt chevalers bachelers en leurz estatz, sans fraude et malengien, liquel jurront par leur foys et seremenz, si tost qu'il seront entrez en la dicte ville, en la main dou dit conte ou de son certain depute, que d'ycelle il ne se partiront jusques a tant que la dicte deffaute sera entierement paye si que dit est, se donc ne fust que le dit conte de Flandres et non autres leur donnast eslargissement ou respit. Et en samblable manere, ou cas que uns ou pluiseurs termes eskeissent de la dicte rente payer par le dit roy, si que dit est, apres le dessus dicte premiere deffaute, le dit roy de France et d'Engleterre dessus dits de rechief envoieroit deux autres chevalers bannerez et wyt chevalers bachelers en la manere dessus escripte par cascun terme et a cascune fois que la dicte deffaute ou deffautes seroient ou dit roy, avecques les autres qui y seroient, sans yceux a retourner par nulle voye tant et si longuement que li dis roys auroit entierement paye la dicte deffaute ou deffautes au lieu, as termes et en la manere dessus ditz, et tout as propres cousteuges et despens dou dit roy. Et en cas que aucun ou aucunes des chevalers que le dit roy auroit ensi envoyes au lieu dessus dit, trespassassent tenantz les dictes couvenences, li dis roys seroit tenuz de y renvoyer, en lieu de celi ou ceux, un chevaler ou tant que la faute seroit, de tele condition comme li trespassez ou trespasse auroient este, si tost qu'il venroit a la cognissance dou dit roy, sans malengien. Et de rechief, il est acorde et prommis par les dessus ditz tracteurs de par le dit roy de France et d'Engleterre, en la main dou dit conte, que se il avenoit que avant les dictes trieuwes faillons, en quel temps que ce fust, les dessus dictes conteez de Nevers et de Rethel, et ce que y appartient, fussent arrestez ou calengies, par quoi li dis contes n'en peuist joir pour cause de ces presens traitiez et accors, que tantost que ce avenroit, li dis roys de France et d'Engleterre sera tenuz de faire au dit conte de Flandres, en restor des dictes deffautes, les paiementz des quarante mille florins d'or a l'escu a l'avenant dou temps et des termes sans malengien sur les obligations dessuz dictes. Et en quelconques temps le dit conte aura ariere et joira paisivlement de ces deux conteez devant dictes, ou l'une d'ycelles, sans fraude et malengien, qu'il rabatera de la dicte somme a l'avenant et value de che.

Item, le dit roy de France et d'Engleterre et conte promметteront, l'un a l'autre, par seremenz, foy et loyautez de aider a tout leur povoir a conquerre le droit de chascun d'yaus sur le dit son adversaire de France et les siens. Et se en temps a venir le dit roy de France et d'Engleterre peust acquerre par pais, conquest ou autrement la dicte conte d'Arthoys, entierement ou partie (de ce hors mis Calays, Marc et Hoye, lesquelz sont desja au dit roy), la cyte de Tournay, les villes de Lille, Douay, Bethune et Orchies, avecques les chasteleries et appendances d'ycelles ou aucune d'ycelles, que il les donra et baillera tantost apres ce q'il les aura conquis au dit conte a posseder perpetuelement par lui et par ses hoirs contes de Flandres comme leur propre heritage, sauve le droit dou dit roy Edward quant temps sera. Et se la dit conte, en temps a venir, peust conquerre aucune autre terre, ville, chastel ou chastelerie ens ou royaume de France ou ailleurs, touchant la quarelle du dit roy Edward, q'il le baillera en le meisme manere au dit roy de France et d'Engleterre et a ses hoirs.

Item, que la dicte alliance soit fait par le dit conte sur les paines d'estre perjures et de deux chentz mille livres de gros tournois a la value de tielz comme courent dedens le dit pays de Flandres, au jour de la faisance de cestes. Et le dit conte obligera lui, ses hoirs, successeurs, leurs biens moebles, non moebles, presentz et a venir, la dicte somme a payer, ou cas q'elle fust encourue et forfaite veritablement par lui, par ses hoirs et successeurs, la guerre durant, dedens sys ans prochains ensuians, par ywelles porcions, dedens la ville de Londres a le Saint Michiel. Et quant la dicte alliance ensi sera faite et confremee, que li premiers articles contenuz ou premier rolle des traitoies, dont li dessus dit roy et conte ont baillie lettres li uns a l'autre, sera quassez et mis au neant.

Item, en la dicte alliance, quant elle se fera, doievent estre contenuz et expressez les trois articles prochains ensiewans, le dessus dit premier article contenuz en la lettre de la dit conte a baillies au roy a tenir sur les painnes d'estre CONJOINT, d'estre parjurs et de deux chentz mille livres de gros comme dessus. Et outre ce le dit conte, aveuques le dit roy de France et d'Engleterre, priera ses bonnes villes de son dit pays de Flandres, Gand, Bruges et Yppre, et fera son loyal povoir sans enforchement faire sur yaus que nuls de ses hoirs ou successeurs serra rechus comme contes dedens le dit pays de Flandres, la guerre durant entre les deux roys, ains qu'il aura ou auront fait les seremertz en telle manere que dit est.

Item, que en toutes les choses dessuz escriptes soient sauves les alliances que le conte de Flandres, pere au dit conte de Flandres, qui Dieux absoille, et son pays de Flandres firent au duc de Brabant et a son pays de Brabant, lesquelles alliances furent faites devant les alliances d'Engleterre, et lesquelles alliances de Brabant li contes de Flandres qui ores est a promises et confremees selonc la fourme et contenu d'ycelles. Et le dit roy de France et d'Engleterre fera jurer et promettre en noun de lui et de par lui aucune soffisant personne de son sanc et linage de tenir et garder la dicte alliance et acomplir toutes les choses dessus dictes fermement et veritablement, et ce par le manere que le dit conte le jurrera, sauf le paine et parjur, sauves aussi les alliances que le dit roy de France et d'Engleterre ha au dit pays et gens de Flandres.

Et soient es dictes lettres des alliances expresse de par le dit conte de Flandres tout li proesme fait es premieres lettres dou dit conte au roy de France et d'Engleterre dessus dit sur les premiers articles dou traitiet.

Et tesmoign des choses dessus dictes nous roys et contes dessus nomme avons plaquies nos seaulz secrez a ces ramembrances changiement. Rex.

## 5. *Memorandum touching Lancaster's lieutenancy in Poitou, 1349* (Original parchment, C 81/343/20741)

Memoire d'avoir lettres du roi nostre seigneur pour Johanne, dame de Belleville.

Premiere, que monseigneur le counte de Lancastre ait commission d'avoir la garde de tout le heritage de la dite Johanne et de ses enfantz, taunt en fie qe en domaine, et de tout le sel qui y est en Peito.

Item, que Gautier de Bentele, aient cause de la dite Johanne son espouse, et la dite Johanne, pour le et pour ses heirs, eient lettres pendentes seallees en saye et cire vert que nostre seigneur le roi ad donne et octroie a la dite Johanne et ses heirs a touz leurs vies, perpetuelement, le heritage de la dite Johanne taunt en fie que en dommaine; c'est assavoir, Beauvoir et la forteresce ove toutes ses appourtenantz, Ampaut, La Barre, o toute La Baiee entierement, le chastel et l'isle de Nermoustier ove lour appourtenauntz, l'isle Chaunet et la forteresce, et Chastel Neuf ov toutes lour appourtenantz, la moite de l'isle de Boign ove ses appourtenaunces, et tout le sel qui y est ou dit heritage, taunt en fie que en demoiagne, pour sustenir et eider et garder les dites forteresces et pour refaire et amender les chaucees du paiis qe la mere a rompues et minees. Et que cest demieison et octreiaunce viegne et tiegne noun obstaunt lettres empetriees ou a empetrer au contraire de monsieur Raoul de Caours ou d'autres et cause aient de lui sur la dit heritage, taunt en fiee, en domoine, que sur le dit sel, les queles soient repellees et anullees par la tenour des lettres au dit Gautier et a la dite Johanne et a ses heirs.

Item, a monsieur Raoul de Caours maundement et commaundement q'il soit obeissaunt et entendaunt a tout ce qe le dit monseigneur le counte de Lancastre ou ses desputez li commaunderont touchaunt les choses desusdites, etc.

Item, a Mouniquot de Fraunce ou a cellui ou a ceux q'auront la garde du chastel de Nermoustier, par semblable maniere.

Item, a Thoumelyn de Bentele ou a cellui ou a ceux q'auront la garde de La Barre, par semblable maniere.

Item, a cellui ou a ceux qui ount garde de la forteresce de l'isle Chaunet, par semblable maniere.

Item, a cellui ou a ceux qui ount garde de la forteresce de Boign, par semblable maniere.

Item, lettres du dit nostre seigneur le roi de priere, seoller souz son privie seal, adrecentes a monseigneur le counte de Lancastre q'il preigne la garde de toutes les choses desusdites, etc.

Item, lettres a touz ceux des forteresces desus dites q'ils facent toute ce qe le dit monseigneur le counte ou ses desputez lour commaunderount sur quant que ils se puet forfaire vers le roi nostre seigneur en corps et en biens.

Item, lettres a Guillaume Dubigny, capitain de Guerrande, que lui et ses subgiez ne facent chose que soit encountre la garde desusdit.

6. *Letter of Pierre de la Forêt, archbishop of Rouen and chancellor of France, to the duke of Lancaster and the earl of Arundel, touching infringements of the truce and the forthcoming conference at Avignon, Paris, 28 May 1354* (Late fourteenth-century copy, Edinburgh University Library, MS. 183, fo. 53v).

A nobles hommes et puissans le duc de Lencastre et le conte d'Arondell.

Chiers amys. Nous avons aujourduy receu voz lettres par monsieur Bociqaut et oy ce qu'il nous a dit de par vous. Si vous plaise savoir que sur les choses contenues en voz lettres monsieur le cardinal vous avoit nadgairs escript et envoie certain message sur ce. Et encore vous escript a present et nous en raportens a ce qu'il vous en escript. Et vraement il n'est venu a nostre cognoissance que de la partie de par deca ait este aucune chose attemptee contre les trieves, mais a le roy nostre seigneur demande et comande par ces lettres que elles soient tenues et gardees. Et encore de novel a ordenee le marchal de Clermont pour les aler faire tenir et garder en Xaintonge. Et toutevois les gentz de vostre partie les ont mal gardees, quar monsieur Thomas de Hollande fait grant chevauchies en Bretaigne contre les gentz du roy nostre seignour et le pais du duc de Bretaigne. Et avec ce ont mys les gentz de vostre partie siege en Xaintonge devant plusours villes et chasteaux, et ne tiennent en rien les trieves. Si veulliez sur ce purveoir a fin q'elles soient bien tenues de vostre partie, et en fera de la partie par deca q'elles seront fermement tenues. Et quant as conduiz de ceux qui doivent aler a Avignon sur le fait de traitie, il nous a doubter, quar il auront sauf et seur conduit et par lettres du roi nostre seigneur et par personnes notables qui lour seront baillees pur les conduire seurement et en bonne foy. Si nous envoiez les nouns des messages et l'en lour fera lettres de sauf conduit teles comme il appartient. Chers amys, le Saint Espirit vous ait en sa garde. Escrit a Parys, le xxviii jour de May.

L'ercevesque de Rouan, chancelier de France.


**7.** *Instruction concerning the government of Brittany given to Thomas Hoggeshawe for the duke of Lancaster, May 1357* (Eighteenth-century copy of an indented charter formerly in the British Museum, Bibliothèque Nationale, collection Moreau, vol. 700, fos. 73r–5v).

La charge donee a monsieur Thomas de Hoggeshawe pur monstrer a monsieur le duc de Lancastre.

Primer, il lui doit monstrer coment le roi ad receu et entendu les lettres et la credence queles mon dit seignur le duc lui ad envoie par Wauter de Byntre, et devant la venue du dit Wauter le roi avoit ordene d'envoier le dit monsieur Thomas par devers lui pur lui monstrer sa entencion et volente, si bien endroit des trieves come d'autres choses.

Et quant a les trieves, plest au roi q'il l'en face publier, garder et tenir en due manere en cas que eles soient acceptees et tenues par l'autre partie et que novelle cause ou empeschement ne y soit pur quoi elles ne se puissent ou ne deivent resonablement tenir, et que le duc se leve du siege de Renes selonc l'effect de meismes les trieves selonc ce que le roi lui ad escrit par ses secrees lettres, si tiel empeschement ne y soit come desus est dit.

Item, quant a les ranceons du paiis le roi ne son conseil ne scierent declarer l'entente des trieves en ce cas devant la venue monsieur le Prince et de ceux qi les pristrent, mes par causes que les paroles des trieves semblent estre aweronses en ce cas si semble il au roi que monsieur le duc se taille d'avoir parlance et tretee ovesques les Britons franceis sur celle matire en la meilloure manere q'il verra que soit affaire, et preigne sur ce l'avantage q'il purra par voie de tretee endroit de meismes les ranceons, c'est assavoir d'avoir tout ou partie en eide de garder et maintenir les villes et chasteux esteantz en la main du roi es dites parties.

Item, por ce q'il semble au roi et a son conseil que grant damage et peril purront avenir a les chasteux et villes qi sont en la main du roi, et grant empesche-ment a l'exploit de sa guerre en cas que monsieur le duc departist du paiis devant que meisme le paiis feust duement establi, si prie le roi au duc molt especialment que devant son departir du paiis il voille ordener conevenablement pur l'estat et governance de meisme le paiis et pur l'establissement des villes et chasteux illoeques a mieulz q'il purra, et q'il voille ordener pur la garde de mesme le paiis tanque a la Seint Michel et entre lui prie q'il voille emprendre meisme la garde pur un an proschein ensuant et ordener ses gentz a y demorer en la meilloure manere q'il verra que soit a faire, car il serroit bien fort au roi de y envoier ore autres gentz pur la garde avantdite.

Item, quant a Ploermel, plest au roi que le duc eit la garde et le governement d'ycel et de quanques y appartient en manere come monsieur Wauter de Bentele l'avoit, selonc ce que sire Henri de Walton ad requis au roi de par le duc, et si come le roi lui ad certifie par ses lettres.

Item, quant a Danfront et les autres lieux de Normandie qi sont pris et conquis par les gentz du duc sur les ennemys, plest au roi que le duc eit la garde et governance de meismes les lieux par ceux queux il vorra a ce deputer, selonc ce que le dit Wauter ad prie au roi depar le duc, issint toutes voies que les capitans de meismes les lieux et ceux qi y demorront soient entendantz et obeissantz a celui qi serra gardein et lieutenant le roi pur le temps en parties de Normandie, si come il appartient de reson.

Item, quant a l'enfant de Montfort, duc de Bretaigne, semble au roi et son conseil pur le meillour pur touz perils eschure que quele heure que le duc viegne as parties d'Engleterre que le dit enfant y viegne ovesques lui ou devant, si lui semble que soit a faire.

8. *Letter of Edward III to Henry, duke of Lancaster, requesting his presence at Westminster for the conclusion of a peace treaty with King John, 4 November (? 1358), together with the duke's reply* (Fifteenth-century copy, British Museum, Harley MS. 4971, fos. 13v–14r)

Edward, par la grace de Dieu roi d'Engleterre et de France, seigneur d'Irlande, a nostre tres chere cosyn Henri, duc de Lancastre, conte de Derby, Leicestre et Notingham (*sic*) et seneschal d'Engleterre, saluz et nostre amour. Purceo que nous sumes en propos de treter de la pes entre nous et nostre aversarie Johan de France, qele nous prions en tot puissant que bien soit de ambedeaux parties, et ne poons sanz l'acent de pluis grauntz de la tere faire l'acorde, vous prions si cherement come pluis poons q'al jeosdy prochein apres la feste de Pasches prochein avenir soiez a Westminstre pur ent faire la trete a bon fyn. Et si avons mande nos lettres as altres de la terre q'ils y soient. Tres chere cosyn Nostre Seigneur vous eit en sa garde.

Done soutz nostre seal le quarte jour de novembre.

Responcio:

A tres noble et tres reverent seigneur Edward, par la grace de Dieu roi d'Engleterre et de France, seigneur d'Irlande, ove totes maneres de reverences et honours et prest come a son lige seigneur de faire sez pleisers et commandementz en touz pointz selonc son poair, assez bien ay entenduz voz reverentez lettres a moy directes, as quelles jeo mettra tute la force et haste que jeo pourra pour estre a vostre tres graciouse persone a jour en vostre lettre assys come principalment suy tenuz. Meais endroit dul consail que vous entenduz avoir jeo prie a vostre seigneurie q'en tel manere y conseillent que bien pourra estre pour vous et vostre roialme. Tres douce seigneur le tot puissant en Trinite vous doyne bon conseil avoir du maintenance de vostre droit.

Le vostre en quant q'il peot. Henri, duc de Lancastre.

# Sources and bibliography

## I MANUSCRIPT SOURCES

### Public Record Office (London)

The principal documents upon which this study is based are among the records of the Chancery, Exchequer and Duchy of Lancaster in the Public Record Office in London. The most important of the first class of documents were the *Gascon Rolls* (C 61) and the *French*, now called *Treaty Rolls* (C 76), which were consulted for the years 1344–58 (C 61, nos. 56–70) and 1337–60 (C 76, nos. 11–43) respectively. Enrolled upon them are the majority of writs concerning the English dominions in France: commissions and mandates addressed to the king's officers there, royal confirmations of grants made by them, letters of protection and general attorney issued to people going abroad, safe-conducts for foreigners coming to England, and other letters concerned with political, military, administrative and diplomatic affairs. They provided much information upon the preparation and composition of the expeditionary forces commanded by the duke, and upon his work as an administrator of overseas territories, not to be found in the published selections in Rymer's *Foedera*, which are mostly concerned with the appointment of ambassadors, truces and alliances. The *Scottish Rolls* (C 71, nos. 13, 15–17, 21), by contrast, were only consulted for letters of protection issued to soldiers going to Scotland with Lancaster, which are omitted from the published volumes.

A considerable number of *Warrants* (C 81) for these and other letters under the great seal, which were issued under the privy seal (files 270–384), the signet and other small seals (files 1330–8), and which include signed bills and other warrants (file 1538) and warrants for letters of protection and general attorney (files 1657, 1720–1, 1723–5, 1727, 1730, 1747–8), being written nearer to the sources of decisions, often contain information not to be found in the final instruments in which they resulted. The collection of *Chancery Miscellanea* (C 47) and the *Parliament and Council Proceedings* (C 49) also contain documents once among the records of the privy seal office. The former produced a number of letters and memoranda relating to Gascony and Brittany (files 24/7; 28/6). The latter yielded some fragmentary but valuable communications between the king and council which throw an interesting light upon Edward III's financial predicament in the Low Countries in the summer of 1339 (file 7, no. 7) and upon the political and military situation in Gascony and Brittany at the close of 1341 (ibid. no. 15). They also include a series of petitions sent to the king and council from Gascony after 1346 which are concerned with grants of land, money, offices and privileges made by Lancaster and other royal officers in the duchy (C 49, file 66, no. 27).

Undoubtedly the richest of the Exchequer records were the extensive series of *Accounts Various* (E 101), which consist of more than thirty sections.

Of these, the section concerned with the *Army, Navy and Ordnance* provided accounts of soldiers' wages (some of which include retinue lists), and accounts for their provisioning and supply, the fitting out of ships and the payment of mariners' wages for their passages to France (nos. 15/12; 24/18, 20; 25/5, 7, 9, 17–20; 26/25; 27/26). A sub-section contains a number of relevant indentures of war (no. 68, files 3–4). The most important documents in the section on *France* were the accounts of the constable and controller of Bordeaux and documents subsidiary thereto (nos. 166/11–12; 167/2–3, 10, 12, 17; 168/3; 170/12, 20; 171/4–5; 172/1–4) and similar accounts and documents of the treasurer of Brittany (nos. 174/4–6, 10–12; 175/1, 5–7; 176/9–10), which provided invaluable information on the situation in these two provinces in the time of Lancaster's lieutenancies there. The accounts of the treasurer and controller of Calais (nos. 167/8; 170/16; 171/1, 3; 173/6–7; 174/1, 8) were distinctly less rewarding. The section *Nuncii*, on the other hand, provided numerous accounts for diplomatic missions in which the duke was involved (nos. 312/33, 36–40; 313/1–19, 21–5, 27, 32–3, 37, 41; 314/2–5); that headed *Miscellaneous* produced an account for soldiers' wages of the lord of Albret (no. 507/22) and the *Recent Additions* yielded an important account for diplomatic expenses which helped to fill in a gap in the negotiations with Cardinal Guy de Boulogne in 1353 (no. 620/7) and more documents subsidiary to the accounts of the constable of Bordeaux (no. 650). Unquestionably the most important of the *Household Accounts* consulted (nos. 389/8, 11; 391/15; 393/11) was that of the keeper of the king's wardrobe for the Reims campaign of 1359–60 (no. 393/11).

Abstracts of these accounts, and of other relevant original accounts which are now lost, are to be found on the *Enrolled Foreign Accounts* (E 372), which were consulted for the years 1342–62 (nos. 187–207), and among the payments entered on the *Issue Rolls* (E 403), which frequently record more details than might be expected. The *Receipt Rolls* (E 401), by contrast, although they were consulted together with the *Issue Rolls* for the years 1330–61, proved of little value. The *Memoranda Rolls* (E 159), of which seven were consulted (nos. 120–3, 125–6, 132–3), were chiefly used for the enrolments of mandates issued to the treasurer ordering the payment of wages and expenses; one of them yielded the text of Lancaster's indenture for service in Gascony in 1345–6. More important were the Treasury of Receipt *Writs and Warrants for Issue* (E 404), of which parcels 3–6, files 15–42 (which cover the years 1332–61) and boxes 486–510 and 620–1 (for the fourteenth century) were consulted. They contain a large number of debentures issued by the king's wardrober (boxes 486–99) and several boxes of vouchers (500–8) of which the last, which relates to affairs in Gascony, proved most rewarding. The *Exchequer Miscellanea* (E 163) produced little of note (no. 5/38), but the series of Miscellaneous Books (E 36) contains two extremely valuable accounts of the king's wardrober (nos. 203–4) for the payment of the English forces in the Low Countries in 1338–40 and 1341–2, and in Brittany in 1342–3, similar to those for the expeditions to Scotland in the years 1334–7 (BM, Cotton MS. Nero C VIII) and for the Reims campaign of 1359–60 (E 101/393/11). One series of *Ancient Deeds* (E 43) proved to contain a considerable number of worthwhile documents (indentures, ransom agreements, mandates for payments, debentures, bills, receipts) relating to affairs in France which are similar in kind to the *Writs and Warrants for Issue* and the documents subsidiary to the accounts of the constable of Bordeaux. The other series of *Ancient Deeds* (E 40–2, 44, 210, 212–13, 326–30, 354; LR 14) were of marginal interest. The Treasury of Receipt *Diplomatic Documents* (E 30) were equally disappointing.

A unique source for this study was provided by the archives of the Duchy of Lancaster which, because the estates were incorporated into the Crown lands with the accession of Lancaster's grandson to the English throne in 1399, have survived better than most family archives. The *Returns of Knights' Fees* (DL 40/1, no. 11) and the series of *Miscellanea* (DL 41), which contains writs, warrants and receipts subsidiary to the financial accounts of Lancaster and his father (9, nos. 1–7; 10, no. 34), made possible an almost day-to-day reconstruction of Henry's activities and those of other members of his family in 1328 and during the two years (1330–2) before he entered public life. The latter class of documents also furnished information on his imprisonment at Malines for the king's debts (10, nos. 32, 36). By far the most rewarding, however, were the collections of *Ancient Deeds* (DL 25, 27), which contain a considerable number of grants made by and to Henry, many of which were copied into registers now among the series of *Miscellaneous Books* (DL 42, nos. 1–2, 11). These contain information on almost every aspect of the duke's activities in England and made it possible to trace his movements there. An extensive sampling of this class of records and his *Ministers' Accounts* (DL 29) provided invaluable evidence on the composition of his household and retinue. The latter were also used in conjunction with the series of *Accounts Various* (DL 28) to calculate the income he derived from his estates. The *Chancery Rolls* (DL 37, nos. 1–2), while containing valuable information on the functioning of the palatinate, were of only marginal interest for this study.

Another class of documents consulted were the Special Collections, of which a sampling of several volumes of *Ancient Correspondence* (SC 1), although it produced several letters from Lancaster, proved disappointing. The series of *Ancient Petitions* (SC 8) was more rewarding, in particular volumes 281–93 of the Gascon Petitions, which contain much interesting material relative to Lancaster's work as lieutenant of the duchy. Among the series of *Transcripts* (PRO 38/8), volumes 133–4 provided useful references to documents among the *Trésor des Chartes* (série J) in the Archives nationales, which were subsequently consulted in the original, and volume 142 to a number of documents in the town archives at Ghent connected with the negotiations with Louis de Male in 1348.

## British Museum (London)

Much the most valuable documents consulted here were *Cotton MSS. Caligula D III* and *Nero C VIII*. The former contains a large number of documents concerned with Anglo-French affairs in the fourteenth century which were once among the records of the privy seal office; they include a considerable correspondence with Charles and Philip of Navarre of which only a part was published by Lettenhove in his edition of *Froissart* and by Delachenal. The latter is the controller's copy of the wardrobe book of Richard Ferriby, referred to above. One of the two originals of the secret treaty of Dunkirk, formerly among the archives of the *chambre des comptes* at Lille, is now preserved among the *Additional Charters* (no. 59142) and, unlike the text published by Lettenhove from the other original in *MS. Caligula D III*, this is an intelligible text. An undated correspondence between Edward III and Lancaster, which appears to be connected with the negotiation of the second treaty of London in 1359, is preserved among the *Harleian MSS* (no. 4971).

## *Archives nationales* (Paris)

The principal documents consulted here were among the *Trésor des Chartes*: (i) *Layettes* (série J), nos. 188B, 190B, 241B, 362, 365, 370, 571, 637, 864; (ii) *Registres* (série JJ), nos. 68, 72–90 (1326–61). The former, which are divided by the French provinces to which they relate (Guienne, Brittany, etc.) or by subject matter (e.g. relations with England, ransoms of prisoners) are original letters which include a large number of diplomatic documents, ransom agreements, submissions and pardons. The latter are chancery copies of royal letters and they provided information on the French lieutenants similar to that furnished by the *Gascon* and *Treaty Rolls* for their English counterparts: the texts of their commissions, royal confirmations of their letters recording grants, pardons and appointments to offices; they were also useful in dating the movements of both the king and his lieutenants. Among the *Monuments historiques*, the *Cartons des rois* (série K), boxes 42–52 (1328–80) furnished a number of financial documents relative to the conduct of the war, and among the series of *Comptes* (série KK) one account (no. 8) provided information on Lancaster's reception in Paris for the duel with the duke of Brunswick. The records of the *Parlement de Paris* (série X), of which registers Xla, nos. 9–22 (1338–72), and X2a, nos. 4, 6, 7 (1340–3, 1352–67), X1b, no. 9532 (1352–1586) and X1c, no. 4 (1348–9) were consulted, contain a large number of cases concerning prisoners-of-war and their ransoms; they provided information on the fortresses taken by Lancaster's forces in Anjou and Maine in 1356, and on the ransoming of the duchy of Burgundy in 1360.

## *Bibliothèque nationale* (Paris)

The most important documents consulted here were among the collection of *Pièces originales* and the collection *Clairámbault*, which contain a large number of documents subsidiary to the accounts of the French treasurers-of-wars (letters retaining troops, mandates for their payment, muster rolls, receipts) formerly among the archives of the *chambre des comptes*. Whereas a fairly extensive sampling of these volumes was made, the collection *Doat* (copies of letters and some originals relating to Languedoc) and the collection *Moreau* (copies of documents in London made by Bréquigny), the *MSS. françaises* and the *Nouvelles acquisitions françaises* were only consulted for a few specific documents to which reference was found in the catalogues and elsewhere.

## *Archives départementales*

The departmental archives were not a very rich source of documentation for this study. Those of the Basses-Pyrénées (Pau) and the Gironde (Bordeaux) furnished a few original letters and other documents relating to Lancaster's work as lieutenant in Aquitaine (série E, nos. 31, 131, 188, at Pau; série E supplément, nos. 2774, 3968, at Bordeaux); those of the *département du Nord* (Lille) contain a number of documents relating to the Anglo-Flemish negotiations in which he was involved (série B, nos. 414, 1316), and those of the Côte d'Or (Dijon) contain a very full documentation on the treaty of Guillon (série B, nos. 11922–5).

*Edinburgh University Library*

The only manuscript consulted here was MS. 183 (formerly MS Laing 351), a formulary apparently compiled for the use of an active and influential clerk of the privy seal called John Prophet. It yielded a letter addressed to Lancaster and the earl of Arundel by the chancellor of France, one of the few documents from this MS. not already published by Professor Perroy.

# II  PUBLISHED DOCUMENTS

*Actes normands de la chambre des comptes sous Philippe de Valois, 1328–1350*, ed. L. Delisle, Société de l'histoire de Normandie, Rouen, 1871.

*Archives historiques de la Saintonge et de l'Aunis*, 48 vols, Société des archives historiques de la Saintonge et de l'Aunis, Saintes and Paris, 1874–1930.

*Archives historiques du département de la Gironde*, 58 vols, Société des archives historiques du département de la Gironde, Bordeaux, 1859–1932; new series, 1 vol, Bordeaux, 1933–6.

*Archives historiques du Poitou*, 34 vols, Société des archives historiques du Poitou, Poitiers, 1872–1905.

*Calendar of Charter Rolls*, vols. iii–v, H.M.S.O, London, 1908–16.

*Calendar of Close Rolls*, Edward I, vols. ii–v; Edward II, vols. i–iv; Edward III, vols. i–xi, H.M.S.O, London, 1893–1910.

*Calendar of Documents Relating to Scotland*, ed. J. Bain, vols. iii–iv, H.M.S.O, Edinburgh, 1887–8.

*Calendar of Entries in the Papal Registers Relating to Great Britain and Ireland*, vol. i, *Petitions to the Pope*, ed. W. H. Bliss, H.M.S.O, London, 1896; vols. ii–iii, *Papal Letters*, ed. W. H. Bliss and C. Johnson, H.M.S.O, London, 1895–7.

*Calendar of Fine Rolls*, vols. v–vii, H.M.S.O, London, 1915–23.

*Calendar of Inquisitions Post Mortem*, vol. xi, H.M.S.O, London, 1935.

*Calendar of Patent Rolls*, Edward I, vols. ii–iv; Edward II, vols. i–v; Edward III, vols. i–xii, H.M.S.O, London, 1891–1912.

*Calendar of Plea and Memoranda Rolls Preserved Among the Archives of the City of London at the Guildhall, 1323–1482*, ed. A. H. Thomas and P. E. Jones, 6 vols, Cambridge, 1926–61.

*Cartulaire de Louis de Male, comte de Flandre, 1348 à 1358*, ed. T. de Limburg-Stirum, 2 vols, Bruges, 1898–1901.

*Cartulaire des comtes de Hainaut, de l'avènement de Guillaume II à la mort de Jacqueline de Bavière, 1337–1436*, ed. L. Devillers, 6 vols, Brussels, 1881–96.

*Clément VI (1342–1352). Lettres closes, patentes et curiales se rapportant à la France*, ed. E. Déprez, J. Glénisson and G. Mollat, 3 vols, 5 fascs, Bibliothèque des Écoles françaises d'Athènes et de Rome, Paris, 1925–59. Cited as *Clément VI: lettres closes, etc.* (1).

*Clément VI (1342–1352). Lettres closes, patentes et curiales intéressant les pays autres que la France*, ed. É. Déprez and G. Mollat, vol. i, fasc. i, Bibliothèque des Écoles françaises d'Athènes et de Rome, Paris, 1960. Cited as *Clément VI: lettres closes, etc.* (2).

*Collection générale des documents français qui se trouvent en Angleterre*, ed. J. Delpit, Paris, 1847.

*Corps universel diplomatique du droit des gens*, ed. J. Dumont, 8 vols. in 16, Amsterdam, 1726–31; supplement by M. Barbeyrac and M. Rousset, 5 vols. in 8, Amsterdam, 1739.

*The Coucher Book of Furness Abbey*, ed. J. C. Atkinson, 3 vols, Chetham Society, new series, vols. ix, xi and xiv, Manchester, 1886–8.

*The Coucher Book or Chartulary of Whalley Abbey*, ed. W. A. Hulton, 4 vols, Chetham Society, vols. x, xi, xvi and xx, Manchester, 1847–9.

*Documents parisiens du règne de Philippe VI de Valois extraits des registres de la chancellerie, 1328–1350*, ed. J. Viard, 2 vols, Paris, 1899–1900.

*Expeditions to Prussia and the Holy Land Made By Henry Earl of Derby*, ed. L. Toulmin-Smith, Camden Society, second series, vol. lii, London, 1894.

*Foedera, Conventiones, Litterae, etc, or Rymer's Foedera, 1066–1383*, ed. A. Clarke, J. Caley, J. Bayley, F. Holbrooke and J. W. Clarke, 4 vols. in 7 parts, Record Commission, London, 1816–69.

*Innocent VI (1352–1362). Lettres closes, patentes et curiales se rapportant à la France*, ed. É. Déprez, vol. i, fasc. i, Bibliothèque des Écoles françaises d'Athènes et de Rome, Paris, 1909. Cited as *Innocent VI: lettres closes, etc.*

*Innocent VI (1352–1362). Lettres secrètes et curiales*, ed. P. Gasnault and M. H. Laurent, vol. i, fasc. i, Bibliothèque des Écoles françaises d'Athènes et de Rome, Paris, 1959. Cited as *Innocent VI: lettres secrètes, etc.*

*Inventaire des archives communales de la ville de Toulouse antérieures à 1790*, ed. E. Roschach, vol. i, Toulouse, 1891.

*The Itinerary of John Leland In or About 1535–1543*, ed. L. Toulmin-Smith, 5 vols, London, 1906–10.

*John of Gaunt's Register*. Part I (1371–1375), ed. S. Armitage-Smith, 2 vols, Camden Society, 3rd series, vols. xx–xxi, London, 1911; Part II (1379–1383), ed. E. C. Lodge and R. Somerville, 2 vols, Camden Society, 3rd series, vols. lvi–lvii, London, 1937.

*Jurades de la ville d'Agen, 1345–1355*, ed. A. Magen, Archives historiques de l'Agenais, vol. i, Agen, 1894.

*Jurades de la ville de Bergerac,* ed. G. Charrier, 12 vols, Bergerac, 1892–1903.

*Mémoires pour servir de preuves à l'histoire ecclésiastique et civile de Bretagne,* ed. P. H. Morice, 3 vols, Paris, 1742–6.

*Ordonnances des roys de France de la troisième race,* 23 vols, Paris, 1723–1849.

'Papers Relating to the Captivity and Release of David II', ed. E. W. M. Balfour-Melville, *Miscellany of the Scottish History Society,* 3rd series, vol. ix, 1958, 3–56.

*Preuves de mémoires pour l'histoire de Navarre et de Flandre,* ed. A. Gallard, Paris, 1648.

*Records of the Borough of Leicester,* ed. M. Bateson, 4 vols, London, 1899–1923.

*Recueil de pièces servant de preuves aux mémoires sur les troubles excités en France par Charles II, dit le Mauvais, roi de Navarre et comte d'Evreux,* ed. D. F. Secousse, Paris, 1755.

*Recueil des documents concernant le Poitou contenus dans les registres de la chancellerie de la France,* ed. P. Guérin, 4 vols, Archives historiques du Poitou, vols. xi, xiii, xvii, xix, Poitiers, 1881–8.

*Recueil des guerres et traictez d'entre les rois de France et d'Angleterre,* ed. J. Du Tillet, Paris, 1588.

*Register of Edward the Black Prince, 1346–1365,* 4 vols, H.M.S.O, London, 1930–33.

*Rotuli Parliamentorum ut et Petitiones et Placita in Parliamento, 1278–1503,* 6 vols, London, 1783; index, London, 1832.

*Rotuli Scotiae in Turri Londinensi et in Domo Capitulari Westmonasteriensi asservati,* ed. D. Macpherson, J. Caley, W. Illingworth and T. H. Horne, 2 vols, Record Commission, London, 1814–19.

*Scriptores Rerum Prussicarum. Die Geschichtsquellen der preussischen Vorzeit bis zum Untergange der Ordensherrschaft,* ed. T. Hirsch, M. Söppen and E. Strelkhe, 5 vols, Leipzig, 1861–74.

*Scriptorum Brunswicensia Illustrantium,* ed. G. G. Leibnitz, vol. ii, Hanover, 1710.

'Some Documents Regarding the Fulfilment and Interpretation of the Treaty of Brétigny, 1361–1369', ed. P. Chaplais, *Camden Miscellany,* vol. xix, London, 1952, 1–84.

'Some New Documents Illustrating the Early Years of the Hundred Years War, 1353–1356', ed. F. Bock, *Bulletin of John Rylands Library,* vol. xv, Manchester, 1931, 60–99.


## III NARRATIVE SOURCES

*The Anonimalle Chronicle, 1333–1381,* ed. V. H. Galbraith, Manchester, 1927.

Avesbury, Robertus de, *De Gestis Mirabilibus Regis Edwardi Tertii,* ed. E. M. Thompson, Rolls Series, no. 93, London, 1889.

Baker, Galfridi Le, de Swynebroke, *Chronicon*, ed. E. M. Thompson, Oxford, 1889.

*The Brut, or The Chronicles of England*, ed. F. W. D. Brie, 2 vols, Early English Text Society, London, 1906–8.

Capgrave, Johannis, *Liber de Illustribus Henricis*, ed. and trans. F. C. Hingeston, Rolls Series, no. 7, London, 1858.

*Chronica Monasterii de Melsa ab anno 1150 usque ad annum 1506*, ed. E. A. Bond, 3 vols, Rolls Series, no. 43, London, 1866–8.

*Chronicle of London from 1089 to 1483*, ed. N. H. Nicolas, London, 1827.

*Chronicles of London*, ed. C. L. Kingsford, Oxford, 1905.

*Chronicles of the Reigns of Edward I and Edward II*, ed. W. Stubbs, 2 vols, Rolls Series, no. 76, London, 1882–3.

*Chronicon Angliae, 1328–1388*, ed. E. M. Thompson, Rolls Series, no. 64, London, 1874.

*Chronicon Briocense, 377–1415*, ed. P. H. Morice in *Mémoires pour servir de preuves à l'histoire ecclésiastique et civile de Bretagne*, vol. i, Paris, 1742, 7–102. See P.-A. de Berthou, 'Analyse sommaire et critique de la chronique de Saint-Brieuc', *Bulletin archéologique de l'Association bretonne: Mémoires*, vol. xix, 1900–1.

*Chronicon Britannicum, 211–1356*, ed. P. H. Morice in *Mémoires pour servir de preuves à l'histoire ecclésiastique et civile de Bretagne*, vol. i, Paris, 1742, 1–8.

*Chronicon Britannicum alterum, 593–1463*, ed. P. H. Morice in *Mémoires pour servir de preuves à l'histoire ecclésiastique et civile de Bretagne*, vol. i, Paris, 1742, 101–18.

*Chronique de Bazas, 1299–1355*, ed. M. E. Piganeau in *Archives historiques du département de la Gironde*, vol. xv, Bordeaux, 1874.

*Chronique de Guyenne*, ed. from the Livre de Coutumes of Bordeaux by H. Barckhausen in *Archives municipales de Bordeaux*, vol. v, Bordeaux, 1890.

*Chronique des quatre premiers Valois (1327–1393)*, ed. S. Luce, Société de l'histoire de France, Paris, 1892.

*Chronique des règnes de Jean II et de Charles V*, ed. R. Delachenal, 4 vols, Société de l'histoire de France, Paris, 1910–20.

*Chronique du Mont-Saint-Michel (1343–1468)*, ed. S. Luce, 2 vols, Société des anciens textes français, Paris, 1879–83.

*Chronique françoise (1341–1450)*, ed. P. H. Morice in *Mémoires pour servir de preuves à l'histoire ecclésiastique et civile de Bretagne*, vol. i, Paris, 1742, 155–7.

*Chronique normande du XIVe siècle*, ed. A. and É. Molinier, Société de l'histoire de France, Paris, 1882.

*Chroniques de London dépuis l'an 44 Hen. III jusqu'à l'an 17 Edw. III*, ed. G. J. Aungier, Camden Society, vol. xxviii, London, 1844.

*Chronographia Regum Francorum*, ed. H. Moranvillé, 3 vols, Société de l'histoire de France, Paris, 1891–7.

*Corpus Chronicorum Flandriae*, ed. J. J. de Smet, 4 vols, Recueil des chroniques

de Flandre publié sous la direction de la commission royale d'histoire; collection de chroniques belges inédites, Brussels, 1837–65, viz:
*Chronicon Comitum (sive forestariorum) Flandrensium*, vol. i, 1837, 34 ff.
*Chronica Aegidii Li Muisis*, vol. ii, 1841.
*Breve Chronicon Comitum Flandriae (1333–1356)*, vol. iii, 1856, 5–30.

*Crónica del rey Don Alfonso XI*, ed. Francisco Cerdá y Rico, Biblioteca de autores españoles, vol. lxvi, Madrid, 1875.

Cuvelier, Jean, *Chronique de Bertrand du Guesclin*, ed. E. Charrière, 2 vols, Collection de documents inédits sur l'histoire de France, Paris, 1839.

*Eulogium Historiarum*, ed. F. S. Haydon, 3 vols, Rolls Series, no. 9, London, 1858–63.

*Fragments d'une chronique inédite relatifs aux evénéments militaires arrivés en Basse-Normandie de 1353 à 1389*, ed. L. Delisle, Saint-Lô, 1895.

'Fragments inédits de la chronique de Jean de Noyal', ed. A. Molinier, *Annuaire Bulletin de la Société de l'histoire de France*, vol. xx, Paris, 1883, 246–75.

'Fragments inédits d'une chronique de Maillezais', ed. P. Marchegay, *Bibliothèque de l'École des Chartes*, vol. ii (1840–1), 148–68.

Froissart, Jean, *Chroniques*, ed. S. Luce, G. Raynaud and L. and A. Mirot, 14 vols, Société de l'histoire de France, Paris, 1869–1966; *Oeuvres*, ed. Kervyn de Lettenhove, 25 vols. in 26, Brussels, 1867–77.

*Grandes chroniques de France*, ed. J. Viard, 10 vols, Société de l'histoire de France, Paris, 1920–53; ed. P. Paris, 6 vols, Paris, 1836–8.

Gray, Sir Thomas of Heton, *Scalacronica*, ed. J. Stevenson, Maitland Club, Edinburgh, 1836; ed. and trans. H. Maxwell, Glasgow, 1907.

Hervordia, Henricus de, *Liber de rebus memorabilioribus sive chronicon*, ed. A. Potthast, Göttingen, 1895.

Knighton, Henricus, *Chronicon*, ed. J. R. Lumby, 2 vols, Rolls Series, no. 92, London, 1889–95.

Lancaster, Henry of, *Le Livre de Seyntz Medicines*, ed. E. J. Arnould, Anglo-Norman Texts, vol. ii, Oxford, 1940.

Lescot, Richard, *Chronique de Richard Lescot, religeux de Saint-Denis (1328–1344) suivie de la continuation de cette chronique (1344–1364)*, ed. J. Lemoine, Société de l'histoire de France, Paris, 1896.

López de Ayala, Pero, *Crónica del rey Don Pedro*, ed. E. Llaguno y Amirola, Crónicas de los reyes de Castilla, vol. i, Madrid, 1779.

Murimuth, Adae, *Continuatio Chronicarum*, ed. E. M. Thompson, Rolls Series, no. 93, London, 1889.

'Petite chronique de Guyenne, jusqu'à l'an 1442,' ed. G. Lefèvre-Pontalis, *Bibliothèque de l'École des Chartes*, vol. xlvii, 1886, 53–79.

*Poema del rey Don Alfonso XI*, ed. F. Janer, Biblioteca de autores españoles, vol. lvii, Madrid, 1864.

Reading, Johannis de, *Chronica, et Anonymi Cantuariensis, 1346–1367*, ed. J. Tait, Manchester, 1914.

Venette, Jean de, *Chronicle*, trans. J. Birdsall, ed. R. A. Newhall, Columbia University Press, Records of Civilization, Sources and Studies, no. 50, New York, 1953.

Villani, Giovanni, *Cronica*, ed. F. G. Dragomanni, 4 vols, Florence, 1844–5. *Historie fiorentine*, ed. L. A. Muratori, *Rerum Italicarum Scriptores*, vols. xiii–xiv, Milan, 1728–9.

Villani, Matteo, *Istorie*, ed. L. A. Muratori, *Rerum Italicarum Scriptores*, vol. xiv, Milan, 1729.

Walsingham, Thomas, *Historia Anglicana*, ed. H. T. Riley, 2 vols, Rolls Series, no. 28, London, 1863–4.

## IV SECONDARY AUTHORITIES

Alis, R. L, *Histoire de la ville d'Aiguillon et de ses environs*, Agen and Sainte-Radegonde, 1895.

Armitage-Smith, S, *John of Gaunt*, London, 1904; reprinted 1964.

Arnould, E. J. F, *Étude sur le Livre des Saintes Médecines du duc Henri de Lancastre*, Paris, 1948.
'Henry of Lancaster and his "Livre des Seintes Medicines",' *Bulletin of John Rylands Library*, vol. xxi (1937), 352–86.

Baines, E, *History of the County Palatine and Duchy of Lancaster*, 4 vols, London 1836.

Balfour-Melville, E. W. M, *Edward III and David II*, The Historical Association, General Series, G 27, London, 1954.

Bertrandy, M, *Étude sur les chroniques de Froissart: guerre de Guienne*, Bordeaux, 1870.

Blok, P. J, *History of the People of the Netherlands*, trans. O. A. Bierstadt and R. Putnam, 5 vols, New York and London, 1898–1912.

Blomefield, F, and Parkin, C, *An Essay Towards a Topographical History of the County of Norfolk*, 5 vols, Fersfield, Norwich and Lynn, 1739–75.

Boutruche, R, *La crise d'une société; seigneurs et paysans du Bordelais pendant la guerre de cent ans*, Publications de la Faculté des Lettres de l'Université de Strasbourg, fasc. 110, Paris, 1947.

Cazelles, R, *La société politique et la crise de la royauté sous Philippe de Valois*, Paris, 1958.

Chaplais, P, 'Documents concernant l'Angleterre et l'Écosse anciennement conservés à la chambre des comptes de Lille (XIIe–XVe siècles)', *Revue du Nord*, vol. xxxviii (1956), 185–210.

Clemesha, H. W. A, *A History of Preston in Amounderness*, Manchester, 1912.

Cokayne, G. E, *The Complete Peerage*, 13 vols, in 14, London, 1910–59.

Communay, A, *Essai généalogique sur les Montferrand de Guyenne*, Bordeaux, 1889.

Daumet, G, *Étude sur l'alliance de la France et de la Castille au XIVe et au XVe siècles*, Bibliothèque de l'École des Hautes Études, fasc. 118, Paris, 1898.

Delachenal, R, *Histoire de Charles V*, 5 vols, Paris, 1909–31.
'Premières négociations de Charles le Mauvais avec les Anglais (1354–1355)', *Bibliothèque de l'École des Chartes*, vol. lxi (1900), 253–82.

Delisle, L, *Histoire du château et des sires de Saint-Sauveur-le-Vicomte*, Valognes, 1867.

Déprez, E, 'La conférence d'Avignon (1344). L'arbitrage pontifical entre la France et l'Angleterre', *Essays in Medieval History Presented to Thomas Frederick Tout*, ed. A. G. Little and F. M. Powicke, Manchester, 1925, 301–20.

'La "Querelle de Bretagne", de la captivité de Charles de Blois à la majorité de Jean IV de Montfort (1347–1362), i: Pendant la captivité de Charles de Blois (1347–1356)', *Mémoires de la société d'histoire et d'archéologie de Bretagne*, vol. vii (Rennes, 1926), 25–60.

*Les préliminaires de la guerre de cent ans. La papauté, la France et l'Angleterre, 1328–1342*, Bibliothèque des Écoles françaises d'Athènes et de Rome, fasc. lxxxvi, Paris, 1902.

'Une conférence anglo-navarraise en 1358', *Revue historique*, vol. xcix (1908), 34–9.

Devic, C, and Vaissete, J, *Histoire générale de Languedoc*, 16 vols, Toulouse, 1872–1904.

Drouyn, L, *La Guienne militaire (histoire et description des villes fortifieés, forteresses et châteaux construit dans le pays qui constitue actuellement le département de la Gironde) pendant la domination anglaise*, 3 vols, Bordeaux and Paris, 1865.

Dupont-Ferrier, G, *Gallia regia, ou état des officiers royaux des bailliages et des sénéchaussées de 1328 à 1515*, 6 vols, Paris, 1942–61.

Elton, J, 'The Chapel of Saint Mary del Key, Liverpool', *Transactions of the Historic Society of Lancashire and Cheshire*, vol. liv, new series, xviii (1904).

Eubel, C, *Hierarchia catholica medii aevi*, Munich, 1898–1900.

Fournier, P, *Le royaume d'Arles et de Vienne, 1138–1378*, Paris, 1891.

Fowler, K. A, *Henry of Grosmont, First Duke of Lancaster, 1310–1361*, Leeds University Ph.D. thesis, 1961, Leeds University Library.
'Les finances et la discipline dans les armées anglaises en France au XIVe siècle', *Les Cahiers Vernonnais*, no. 4 (1964), 55–84.

Fox, L, *Leicester Abbey*, Leicester, 1949.
*Leicester Castle*, Leicester, 1944.

Fox, L, and Russell, P, *Leicester Forest*, Leicester, 1948.

Galbraith, V. H, 'The Chronicle of Henry Knighton', *Fritz Saxl, 1850–1948. A Volume of Memorial Essays*, ed. D. J. Gordon (London, 1957), 136–48.

Gallard, A, *Mémoires pour servir à l'histoire de Navarre et de Flandre*, Paris, 1648.

Galway, M, 'Froissart in England', *University of Birmingham Historical Journal*, vol. vii (1959), 18–35.

Hewitt, H. J, *The Black Prince's Expedition of 1355–1357*, Manchester, 1958.

Holmes, G. A, *The Estates of the Higher Nobility in Fourteenth-Century England*, Cambridge, 1957.

'The Rebellion of the Earl of Lancaster, 1328–9', *Bulletin of the Institute of Historical Research*, vol. xxviii (1955), 84–9.

Honoré-Duvergé, S, 'L'origine du surnom de Charles le Mauvais', *Mélanges d'histoire du moyen âge dédiés à la mémoire de Louis Halphen* (Paris, 1951), 345–50.

Hossart, Abbé, *Histoire ecclésiastique et profane du Hainaut*, 2 vols, Mons, 1792.

Jeulin, P, 'L'hommage de la Bretagne en droit et dans les faits', *Annales de Bretagne*, vol. xli (1934), 380–473.

'Un grand "Honneur" anglais. Aperçus sur le "comté" de Richmond en Angleterre, possession des ducs de Bretagne (1069/71–1398)', *Annales de Bretagne*, vol. xlii (1935), 265–302.

La Borderie, A. Le Moyne de, *Histoire de Bretagne*, 6 vols, Rennes, 1896–1914.

La Roncière, C. de, *Histoire de la marine française*, 6 vols, Paris, 1899–1934.

Lauzun, P, 'Le château de Duras', *Revue de l'Agenais*, vol. xlviii (Agen, 1921), 1–9, 89–98.

Lemoine, J, 'Du Guesclin, armé chevalier', *Bibliothèque de l'École des Chartes*, vol. lvi (1895), 84–9.

Le Patourel, J, 'Edouard III, "roi de France et duc de Normandie", 1356–1360', *Revue historique de droit français et étranger*, 4e série, vol. xxxi (1953), 317–18.

'Edward III and the Kingdom of France', *History*, vol. xliii (1958), 173–89.

'L'administration ducale dans la Bretagne montfortiste, 1345–1362', *Revue historique de droit français et étranger*, 4e série, vol. xxxii (1954), 144–7.

'The Treaty of Brétigny, 1360', *Transactions of the Royal Historical Society*, 5th series, vol. x (1960), 19–39.

Leroux, A, *Recherches critiques sur les relations politiques de la France avec l'Allemagne de 1292 à 1378*, Paris, 1882.

Lewis, N. B, 'A Certificate of the Earl of Lancaster's Auditors, 1341', *English Historical Review*, vol. lv (1940), 99–103.

'The Organization of Indentured Retinues in Fourteenth-Century England', *Transactions of the Royal Historical Society*, 4th series, vol. xxvii (1945), 29–39.

Lucas, H. S, *The Low Countries and the Hundred Years' War, 1326–1347*, University of Michigan Publications, History and Political Science, no. 8, Ann Arbor, 1929.

Luce, S, 'Du Guesclin au siège de Rennes', *Bibliothèque de l'École des Chartes*, vol. lii (1891), 615–18.

*Histoire de Bertrand du Guesclin et de son époque. La jeunesse de Bertrand, 1320–1364*, Paris, 1876.

Marboutin, J. R, 'Le château de Castelnoubel (commune de Bon Encontre)', *Revue de l'Agenais*, Bulletin de la société d'agriculture, sciences et arts d'Agen, vol. xxxviii (Agen, 1911), 285–303, 398–408, 477–93; vol. xxxix (Agen, 1912), 35–55, 141–63, 197–226.

McKisack, M, *The Fourteenth Century*, Oxford, 1959.

Ménard, V, *Histoire religieuse, civile et militaire de Saint-James de Beuvron*, Avranches, 1897.

Mendl, B, and Quicke, F, 'Les relations politiques entre l'empereur et le roi de France de 1355 à 1356', *Revue belge de philologie et d'histoire*, vol. viii (1929), 469–512.

Mirot, L, and Déprez, E, 'Les ambassades anglaises pendant la guerre de cent ans. Catalogue chronologique (1327–1450)', *Bibliothèque de l'École des Chartes*, vol. lix (1898), 550–77; vol. lx (1899), 177–214.

Molinier, A, *Les sources de l'histoire de France des origines aux guerres d'Italie*, 6 vols, Paris, 1901–6.

Mollat, G, 'Innocent VI et les tentatives de paix entre la France et l'Angleterre (1353–1355)', *Revue d'histoire ecclésiastique*, vol. x (1909), 729–43.
'La diplomatie pontificale au XIVe siècle', *Mélanges d'histoire du moyen age dédiés à la mémoire de Louis Halphen* (Paris, 1951), 507–12.

Monier, R, *Les institutions centrales du comté de Flandre de la fin du IXe siècle à 1384*, Paris, 1943.

Moranvillé, H, 'Le siège de Reims, 1359–1360', *Bibliothèque de l'École des Chartes*, vol. lvi (1895), 90–8.

Morice, P. H, *Histoire ecclésiastique et civile de Bretagne*, 2 vols, Paris, 1750–6.

Nichols, J, *The History and Antiquities of Leicester*, 4 vols. in 8, 1795–1815.

Nicholson, R, *Edward III and the Scots*, Oxford, 1965.

Nicolas, N. H, *A History of the Royal Navy*, 2 vols, London, 1847.
'Observations on the Institution of the Most Noble Order of the Garter, Illustrated by the Accounts of the Great Wardrobe of King Edward the Third', *Archaeologia*, vol. xxxi (London, 1846), 1–163.

Pantin, W. A, *The English Church in the Fourteenth Century*, Cambridge, 1955.

Perroy, É, 'France, England and Navarre from 1359 to 1364', *Bulletin of the Institute of Historical Research*, vol. xiii (1935–6), 151–4.
'Quatre lettres du cardinal Guy de Boulogne (1352–1354)', *Revue du Nord*, vol. xxxvi (1954), 159–64.
*The Hundred Years War*, trans. W. B. Wells, London, 1951.

Petit, E, 'Séjours de Jean II (1350–1356)', *Bulletin historique et philologique du comité des travaux historiques et scientifiques* (Paris, 1896), 587–612.

Pirenne, H, *Histoire de Belgique*, 7 vols, Brussels, 1900–32.

Pocquet du Haut-Jussé, B.-A, *Les papes et les ducs de Bretagne. Essai sur les rapports du Saint-Siège avec un état*, 2 vols, Bibliothèque des Écoles françaises d'Athènes et de Rome, fasc. 133, Paris, 1928.

Prince, A. E, 'The Strength of English Armies in the Reign of Edward III', *English Historical Review*, vol. xlvi (1931), 353–71.

Queller, D. E, *The Office of Ambassador in the Middle Ages*, Princeton University Press, 1967.

Quicke, F, *Les Pays-Bas à la veille de la période bourguignonne, 1356–1384*, Brussels, 1947.

Raynaldus, O, *Annales ecclesiastici ab anno MCXCVIII*, 15 vols, Lucca, 1747–56.

Ribadieu, H, *Les campagnes du comte de Derby en Guyenne, Saintonge et Poitou*, Paris, 1865.

Russell, P. E, *The English Intervention in Spain and Portugal in the Time of Edward III and Richard II*, Oxford, 1955.

Secousse, D. F, *Mémoirs pour servir à l'histoire de Charles II de Navarre*, 2 vols, Paris, 1758.

Somerville, R, *History of the Duchy of Lancaster, 1265–1603*, London, 1953.

Sturler, J. de, *Les relations politiques et les échanges commerciaux entre le duché de Brabant et l'Angleterre au moyen âge*, Paris, 1936.

Thompson, A. H, 'Notes on the Colleges of Secular Canons in England', *Archaeological Journal*, vol. lxxiv (1917).

*The Abbey of Saint Mary in the Meadows, Leicester*, Leicester Archaeological Society, Leicester, 1949.

*The History of the Hospital and New College of the Annunciation of Saint Mary in the Newarke, Leicester*, Leicester Archaeological Society, Leicester, 1937.

'The Registers of John Gynewell, Bishop of Lincoln, for the Years 1347–50', *Archaeological Journal*, vol. lxviii (1911).

Tout, T. F, *Chapters in the Administrative History of Medieval England*, 6 vols, Manchester, 1920–33.

Wilkinson, B, 'A Letter to Louis de Male, Count of Flanders', *Bulletin of John Rylands Library*, vol. ix (Manchester, 1925), 177–87.

Wolff, P, *Commerces et marchands de Toulouse*, Paris, 1954.

Wrottesley, G, *Crécy and Calais*, Reprinted from the William Salt Archaeological Society, London, 1898.

# Notes

## Introduction

1. E. Déprez, *Les préliminaires de la guerre de Cent ans* (Paris, 1902), 400; E. Perroy, *The Hundred Years War* (London, 1951), 69. For a convenient discussion of the origins of the war, see G. Templeman, 'Edward III and the Beginnings of the Hundred Years War', *Transactions of the Royal Historical Society*, 5th series, II (1952), 69–88; P. Wolff, 'Un problème d'origines: La guerre de Cent ans', *Eventail de l'histoire vivante: homage à Lucien Febvre*, II (1953), 141–8.

2. See R. Cazelles, *La société politique et la crise de la royauté sous Philippe de Valois* (Paris, 1958), 133–48.

3. See J. Le Patourel, 'The King and the Princes in Fourteenth-Century France', *Europe in the Late Middle Ages*, ed. J. R. Hale, J. R. L. Highfield and B. Smalley (London, 1965), 155–83.

4. J. Le Patourel, 'Edward III and the Kingdom of France', *History* XLIII (1958), 180 ff.

5. For the ensuing remarks on the treaty of Paris and its consequences, see M. Gavrilovitch, *Étude sur le traité de Paris de 1259* (Paris, 1899); G. P. Cuttino, *English Diplomatic Administration, 1259–1339* (Oxford, 1940), and 'The Process of Agen', *Speculum*, XIX (1944), 161–78; P. Chaplais, 'Reglement des conflits internationaux franco-anglais, 1293–1377', *Le Moyen Age*, LVII (1951), 269–302; W. Ullman, 'The Development of the Medieval Idea of Sovereignty', *English Historical Review*, LXIV (1949), 1–33.

6. For the ensuing remarks on the succession question, see R. Cazelles, *op. cit*, 35–52; Le Patourel, 'Edward III and the Kingdom of France', *cit. supra*, 173–6, and the sources cited on p. 173, n. 5.

7. P. Chaplais, 'Un message de Jean de Fiennes à Édouard II et le projet de démembrement du royaume de France (janvier 1317)', *Revue du Nord*, XLIII (1961), 145–8.

8. Perroy, *op. cit*, 69, 116 and *passim*; Templeman, *op. cit*, 87.

9. Le Patourel, 'Edward III and the Kingdom of France', *cit. supra*, 176 ff.

10. See Cazelles, *op. cit*, 151–63, 176–7, 204, 247–52.

11. See below, p. 205.

12. For the legal theory of just war, see M. H. Keen, *The Laws of War in the Late Middle Ages* (London, 1965), 63–81.

13. For the latest discussion of this question, see D. E. Queller, *The Office oj Ambassador in the Middle Ages* (Princeton, 1967), 76–84.

## Chapter I

1. For these and the ensuing remarks on the Lancastrian inheritance, see R. Somerville, *History of the Duchy of Lancaster, 1265–1603* (London, 1953), 11–12, 15, 17–19, 22, 31–2.

2. *GEC*, VII, 401, note b.

3. E. J. F. Arnould, *Étude sur le Livre des Saintes Médecines du duc Henri de Lancastre* (Paris, 1948), ix, n. 1.

4. For the following account of the elder Henry's career, see *GEC*, VII, 397–9; T. F. Tout, *Chapters in the Administrative History of Medieval England* (6 vols, Manchester, 1920–33), III, 4, 10, 15, 23; M. McKisack, *The Fourteenth Century* (Oxford, 1959), 83–7, 90–1, 100–2; *CPMR*, I, 68–9, 81, 85; G. A. Holmes, 'The Rebellion of the Earl of Lancaster, 1328–9', *BIHR*, XXVIII (1955), 84–9.

5. *CPR, 1321–4*, 69.

6. *Knighton*, I, 450.

7. *CCR, 1327–30*, 528–30; *CPR, 1327–30*, 472, 484, 519, 546–7, 553, and *1330–4*, 26, 97, 177.

8. Rosselin and Wyther had been retained by Lancaster: G. A. Holmes, *The Estates of the Higher Nobility in Fourteenth-Century England* (Cambridge, 1957), 68–9. While in exile, Rosselin's fee was paid from the earl's French estates: *Documents Parisiens du règne de Philippe de Valois, 1328–1350*, ed. J. Viard (2 vols, Paris, 1899–1900), I, 84–5, no. lvi.

9. Edward III was born on 13 November 1312 (J. Barnes, *The History of that Most Victorious Monarch Edward III*, Cambridge, 1688, 1; McKisack, *op. cit*, 29).

10. *Le Livre de Seyntz Medicines*, ed. E. J. F. Arnould (Oxford, 1940), 15–16, 67, 72, 94, 239; see below, pp. 193–6.

11. *Capgrave*, 161–4.

12. *GEC*, VII, 400.

13. *Records of the Borough of Leicester*, ed. M. Bateson (4 vols, London, 1899–1923), I, 345.

14. They were married before 24 June 1330 (DL 41/10/34, m. 44; cf. *CPL*, II, 343). For Beaumont, cf. *GEC*, II, 59–60.

15. They were married at some date between 1 September and 6 November 1330 (DL 41/10/34, m. 40; DL 40/1/11, fo. 46v). On John de Beaumont, cf. *GEC*, II, 60–1.

16. Blanche was married before 9 October 1316 (*GEC*, XII, ii, 304). De Burgh's marriage to Maude was granted to Earl Henry on 3 February 1327 (*CPR, 1327–30*, 8), a papal dispensation for it to take place was issued on 1 May following (*GEC*, XII, ii, 179) and it was celebrated before 16 November 1327 (DL 41/9/1, m. 13). Mowbray's marriage to Joan was granted to Earl Henry on 28 February 1327 (*CPR, 1327–30*, 26) and took place before 4 June 1328 (DL 41/9/1, m. 19). Mary was married on or before 4 September 1334 at Tutbury castle (*GEC*, X, 463; cf. *CPR, 1334–8*, 6). On Isabella, cf. *CPR, 1334–8*, 430; *1343–5*, 225; *CCR, 1346–9*, 428; *1349–54*, 5.

17. DL 40/1/11, fos. 46r–v & 52v; DL 41/9/1 & 10/34.

18. DL 41/9/1, m. 18. De Burgh was born on 17 September 1312 (*GEC*, XII, ii, 178). For his possible upbringing in the Lancastrian household, cf. *CPR 1327–30*, 8.

19. *Froissart*, ed. Luce, I, ii, 94; *Chronographia*, II, 12.

20. DL 41/9/1, ms. 19, 20 & 34; DL 41/10/34, ms. 40–45. On Simeon, cf. below, pp. 176, 179, 217.

21. DL 40/1/11, fo. 46v.

22. His father went blind in 1329 or 1330 (*Baker*, 106; *Knighton*, I, 460).

23. DL 40/1/11, fos. 46v & 52v.

24. Ibid, fo. 46r.

25. Ibid, fos. 46v & 52v.

26. Ibid, fos. 46r-v & 52v.

27. *CPR*, *1330–4*, 265, 397.

28. Somerville, *op. cit*, 38 & n. 2 (lands in South Wales, etc); *CChR*, *1327–41*, 390 & 401 (creation as earl of Derby); *CPR*, *1334–8*, 400, 538; *1350–4*, 524–5 (annuity of 1,000 marks); DL 42/2, fo. 179v & *CPR*, *1334–8*, 473 (Chaworth manors); Somerville, *op. cit*, 35 (Pontefract honor); C 81/316/18058 & E 159/123, ms. 124d & 170d (Abergavenny); *CFR*, *1337–47*, 263–4, 335 & Somerville, *op. cit*, 38, n. 6 (Carmarthen, etc.).

# Chapter II

1. For a full discussion of the background to and the conduct of Edward III's Scottish campaigns, see R. Nicholson, *Edward III and the Scots* (Oxford, 1965), *passim*, and E. W. M. Balfour-Melville, *Edward III and David II* (London, 1954), 6–13.

2. *Rot. Scot*, I, 253, 764; *Foedera*, II, ii, 864–5.

3. BM, Cotton MS Nero C VIII (Ferriby's Wardrobe Book), fos. 233v, 252v.

4. Ibid; *GEC*, VII, 401.

5. Nicholson, *op. cit*, 201.

6. BM, Cotton MS Nero C VIII, fo. 236r.

7. *Rot. Scot*, I, 414–15; *Foedera*, II, ii, 936; BM, Cotton MS Nero C VIII, fo. 240r.

8. BM, Cotton MS Nero C VIII, fos. 240r, 259r; E 101/15/12.

9. Ibid; *Rot. Scot*, I, 473; *Foedera*, II, ii, 953.

10. *Rot. Scot*, I, 472.

11. *Ibid*, 474–5.

12. *Murimuth*, 77; he was party to an indenture at Berwick on 15 May 1337 (DL 25/330).

13. BM, Cotton MS Nero C VIII, fo. 263; H. S. Lucas, *The Low Countries and the Hundred Years' War* (Ann Arbor, 1929), 240–2; cf. *Froissart*, ed. Luce, I, ccxiv–ccxv, 135–7.

14. He was with the king at Walton on 6 July 1338; Edward left for Harwich on the 12th and set sail on 16 July; Lancaster appears to have been in charge of a fleet assembled at Great Yarmouth and to have joined him at sea (*Foedera*, II, ii, 1047, 1050; *CCR*, *1337–9*, 519, 522; cf. *Knighton*, II, 4; *Anonimalle Chronicle*, 13; *Historia Anglicana*, 200). Wages were due to him for the period from 12 July 1338 to 19 February 1340 (E 36/203, fos. 131, 142). For his presence at Antwerp, Ghent, Brussels and Marquion, see *Foedera*, II, ii, 1055–6, 1063, 1068,

1081–4, 1104; *CPR*, *1338–40*, 311, 371, 374, 378, 383–4, 391, 393–4, 396, 407; for his presence at Coblenz, Arnould, *Étude*, xv, n. 2; and for his part in the Thiérache campaign and at Buironfosse, Lucas, *op. cit*, 335, 337; *Froissart*, ed. Lettenhove, XVIII, 86, 91; *Chronographia*, II, 67, 77–8; *Froissart*, ed. Luce, I, i, ccxliii, II, 178.

15. *Foedera*, II, ii, 1104; *CPR*, *1338–40*, 407; Lucas, *op. cit*, 364; E. Déprez, *Les préliminaires de la guerre de cent ans* (Paris, 1902), 276.

16. *Foedera*, II, ii, 1100, 1115; *CPR*, *1338–40*, 374; *CCR*, *1339–41*, 451.

17. Wages were due to him and his retinue from 7 June to 29 September 1340 (E 101/389/8, m. 11). For his departure from Orwell, see *Foedera*, II, ii, 1129; *CCR*, *1339–41*, 482; *Anonimalle Chronicle*, 16. For his presence at Sluys, see *Froissart*, ed. Luce, II, 37, 222, and for his part in the Tournai campaign, *Chronographia*, II, 139; *Grandes Chroniques*, ed. Viard, IX, 205; *Chroniques de London* 79–80.

18. *Froissart*, ed. Lettenhove, XVII, 104–5; *Chronographia*, II, 150.

19. The principal source on Lancaster's imprisonment at Malines is E 101/127/40, which is to be seen in conjunction with DL 41/10/32 & 36; DL 25/983, 3566 & 3582; DL 27/322, ms. 1–8; E 372/191, m. 54.

20. C 81/278/14259 & 14260A; E 101/389/8, m. 7; E 372/191, m. 54.

21. E 101/389/8, m. 7; DL 27/322, m. 1.

22. C 81/269/13359.

23. Ibid.

24. C 81/270/13463.

25. Hastings served or was intended to serve abroad in Henry's retinue in 1336 (E 101/15/12), 1338–40 (C 76/12, m. 8), 1340 (C 76/15, m. 21), 1345–6 (*Froissart*, ed. Luce, III, 48), 1355 (C 76/33, m. 8), 1356–8 (C 76/34, m. 15) and 1359–60 (C 76/38, m. 16), and was among the witnesses to his charters (DL 25/248 & 2302). For Peter de La Mare, see below. pp. 178 & 287 n. 119. For Bohun and Favelore, see Holmes, *The Estates of the Higher Nobility* (1957), 69–70, 75.

26. E 101/389/8, ms. 7 & 25, and E 404/490/338 (the earl's expenses); DL 25/983 (jousts at *Le Bure*).

27. E 404/501/302; *CPR*, *1340–3*, 483, 512, 531; *CCR*, *1341–3*, 225.

28. *Rot. Scot*, I, 617–8; *Foedera*, II, ii, 1179. On 8 October William de Kellesey, receiver of moneys arising from the sale of wool in Flanders, was instructed to pay him an advance on the wages of himself and 200 men-at-arms retained with him for a quarter of a year upon the safe custody of the march (*CCR*, *1341–3*, 286).

29. *CCR*, *1341–3*, 354. The earl was still in London on 18 October (*CPR*, *1340–3*, 304), at Leicester and Pontefract during the first week of November (*CCR*, *1361–4*, 200; DL 25/75). He only came into the king's pay on 25 November (E 36/204, fo. 102) and *Murimuth*, 122–3, almost suggests that he accompanied the king to Scotland.

30. *CDRS*, III, 251, no. 1378; *CPR*, *1340–3*, 382.

31. *Knighton*, II, 23; *Murimuth*, 123.

32. *Rot. Scot*, I, 623–4; *Foedera*, II, ii, 1191; *Knighton*, II, 23.

33. On Edward's intervention, see J. Le Patourel, 'Edward III and the Kingdom of France', *History*, XLIII (1958), 186–7, and for the dates of the expeditions of Mauny and Northampton, E 36/204, fos. 105v–6r; E 404/5/30; E 43/202, no. 1; A. Le Moyne de La Borderie, *Histoire de Bretagne* (6 vols, Rennes,

1896–1914), III, 464–5. Wages were due to Lancaster and his retinue from 21 August 1342 to 8 February 1343 (E 36/204, fos. 106r & 108v). The king left Portsmouth on 24 or 25 October 1342, returned from Brittany on 27 February 1343, and arrived at Weymouth on 1 March (ibid, fo. 37 ff.).

34. E 404/5/30; C 81/1331/2–4. He was ready to leave England as early as 15 July, but was with Edward at Sandwich on 4 October (*CCR, 1341–3*, 660). Both *Froissart*, ed. Luce, II, 225, and, by implication, the *Chronique normande*, 56–7, say he crossed to Brittany with the king.

35. *Grandes Chroniques*, ed. Viard, IX, 231; *Avesbury*, 348.

36. See below, pp. 45–6.


## Chapter III

1. Arch. nat, JJ 74, nos. 109, 125, 131, 150, 178, 190, 412, 418–19, 481; JJ 75, no. 217; Bibl. nat, Pièces originales, vol. 231, Des Baux, no. 8; *Arch. hist. Gironde*, V, no. clviii; XXXIII, no. lvi.

2. É. Perroy, *The Hundred Years War* (London, 1951), 67; Déprez, *op. cit*, 22.

3. G. Dupont-Ferrier, *Gallia regia* (6 vols, Paris, 1942–61), I, 1–2, 13–16, 19–27, 466 ff.

4. Déprez, *op. cit*, 154, n. 1.

5. R. Boutruche, *La crise d'une société* (Paris, 1947), 196–7.

6. Blaye was taken on 20 April 1339 (E 101/166/11) and Bourg on 6 February 1340 (*Arch. hist. Poitou*, XIII, 165–7), but were again in English control in 1343 (E 101/167/3, ms. 17, 23, 24). For the French attempt to take Bordeaux, see E 101/166/12, m. 7d.

7. Arch. nat, JJ 68, fo. 60; *Arch. hist. Gironde*, XXXIII, no. lxiv.

8. Arch. nat, JJ 68.

9. E 101/167/3, ms. 1–2, 6–7, 9.

10. For the commissions to Ingham, Diens, Albret and Genève, see *Foedera*, II, ii, 975, 1047, 1105.

11. The following details concerning the organization of the Gascon forces in the years 1337–43 are taken from the accounts of the constables and controllers of Bordeaux (E 101/166/11 & 12; E 167/3) and documents subsidiary to them (E 404, box 508). On average, there were 4,820 Gascon troops on the king's pay roll during these years. Bernard Ezi's retinue alone stood at between 500 and 1,000 men during the years 1341–7 and at as many as 1,500 to 2,000 at certain periods during these years, and sometimes more. His brother Bérard, lord of Vayres, had 424 men in the king's pay in 1338–9; Raymond, *vicomte* of Fronsac, had 1,060 in 1341–2; Jean de Grailly, captal of Buch, had 765 men and the lord of Lesparre 182 men in 1337–40; Alexander de Caumont maintained 160 men in 1342–3 and Arnaud Garsie de Got, lord of Puyguilhem, 224 men in 1337–8 and 120 men in 1341–3.

12. For a full discussion of the financial problem, see K. A. Fowler, 'Les finances et la discipline dans les armées anglaises en France au XIVe siècle', *Les Cahiers Vernonnais*, no. 4 (1964), 55–61. Already during the financial year ending 29

September 1339 the revenues received by the constable of Bordeaux amounted to only 59½% (£8,332) of total expenditure (£13,963) and 22% of this was received from the Wardrobe in England. No less than 54% (£7,339) of expenditure was in the form of wages paid out to the troops; but this represented only 12% part payment of sums due to them during that year. The position was basically the same in the year ending 29 September 1341. Although receipts had almost doubled (£16,692), and were 12% in excess of expenditure, this was largely due to the contracting of loans which amounted to 42% of revenue. No less than 57% (£8,168) of expenditure was in the form of wages paid to the troops; but this represented only 29% part payment of a new series of debentures.

13. £13,850 to Jean de Grailly, £11,690 to Alexander de Caumont, £6,488 to Guillaume Sanche, lord of Pommiers, and no less than £14,692 to Bernard Ezi, lord of Albret.

14. Arch. dép. Basses-Pyrénées, E 31.

15. Ibid; C 49, File 7, no. 15; E 101/507/22.

16. *Foedera*, II, ii, 1204–5; C 81/272/13622.

17. In the year ending 29 September 1343 only 15% (£9,674) of new bills for wages to the troops amounting to £66,643 was paid.

18. C 81/291/15587. He ceased to draw pay for service in Brittany on 8 February 1343 (E 36/204, fo. 108v).

19. *Crónica del rey Don Alfonso XI*, 541–69; *Poema del rey Don Alfonso XI*, 543, 545–6; López de Ayala, *Crónica del rey Don Pedro*, 6.

20. *Foedera*, II, ii, 1232–3; III, i, 19–20, 22–3.

21. C 81/288/15239.

22. P. E. Russell, *The English Intervention in Spain and Portugal* (Oxford, 1955), 5–6.

23. *Knighton*, II, 28.

24. C 81/301/16586. For Trussell, see below, p. 185.

25. *Foedera*, III, i, 8–10.

26. *Ibid*, 11; *CPR, 1343–5*, 224.

27. *Murimuth*, 156; *Knighton*, II, 29.

28. SC 1/38, no. 10; *Foedera*, III, i, 19–20, 22–3.

29. *CCR, 1343–6*, 456.

30. *Foedera*, III, i, 21–3, 25–7, 58; *CCR, 1343–6*, 492; E 101/312/11 & 16.

31. *Foedera*, III, i, 20, 22–3, 58–9; *CCR, 1343–6*, 456; Russell, *op. cit*, 7–9.

32. He was to have accompanied Joan to Spain (*Foedera*, III, i, 154), but appears to have delegated the task to one of his retainers, Sir Thomas de Uvedale (E 43/462). For her death, see *Foedera*, III, i, 171, and *Baker*, 97, 269.

33. While, between 1338 and 1343, grants by the seneschal remained at little more than £1,000 a year, those made by the king and council in England rose from just short of £570 in 1338–9 to £2,347 in 1340–1 and no less than £8,800 in 1343–4—over a quarter of total expenses, including the wages of the troops (E 101/166/11 & 12; E 101/167/3; Fowler, *op. cit*, 60).

34. SC 8/293/14613 & 14603. This is to be seen in conjunction with *Foedera*, II, ii, 1235.

35. *Foedera*, III, i, 8–10.

36. E. Déprez, 'La conférence d'Avignon (1344)', *Essays in Medieval History Presented to Thomas Frederick Tout*, ed. A. G. Little and F. M. Powicke (Man-

chester, 1925), 305; *Clément VI: lettres closes, etc.* (1), II, fasc. 3, nos. 864, 899, 2726; *CPL*, III, 9–11, 13.

37. Lancaster is said to have gone 'causa devotionis' (*Foedera*, III, i, 54; *Clément VI: lettres closes, etc.* (1), II, fasc. 3, p. 24. Certainly the government believed him to be in Spain in May. On the 15th of that month a royal valet, Ive de Cornwaille, was sent there with a letter under the signet for him, but on arriving in Bordeaux he was informed that the earl was at Avignon—this had clearly not been anticipated. On 5 July another valet, Nicholas of Ireland, was sent to Bordeaux with another letter for him, but by then Lancaster was already on his way back to England (E 403/501/300).

38. *Murimuth*, 158–9.

39. *CPL*, III, 10–11; Déprez, *op. cit*, 305.

40. *Froissart*, ed. Lettenhove, XVIII, 202–56; Déprez, *op. cit*, 301–20.

41. On 10 December the treasurer was instructed to pay wages to him and Bartholomew de Burghersh for a mission to Avignon (E 404/5/31) and a papal safe-conduct was issued to him three days later (*CPL*, III, 18); but the mandate to the treasurer bears the following note on the dorse: 'Nichil fiat per hoc breve quia infrascriptus Henricus et Bartholomus hunc viagium infrascriptum non assumpserunt.'

42. *Murimuth*, 160–1.

43. *CPL*, III, 15–16.

44. *Murimuth*, 164, 168, 170; E 101/25/7 & 9; E 372/190, m. 41; E 372/191, m. 54d. The crew of the Southampton flotilla consisted of 148 masters, 44 constables, 2,380 mariners and 295 boys (E 372/191, m. 54d).

45. 500 men-at-arms, 500 mounted archers, 500 foot archers and 500 Welsh foot. Of these 2,000 men he agreed to provide a personal retinue of 250 men-at-arms and 250 mounted archers including himself, 8 bannarets, 92 knights and 150 esquires, and Edward undertook to provide the remaining 1,500 men (E 159/132, m. 254).

46. Ibid. The decision to send Lancaster to Gascony with an expeditionary force had been taken by the king and council at the latest by 25 February when commissions were issued to raise and array 600 foot archers in Staffordshire, Derbyshire, Lancashire and Cheshire, and 500 Welsh foot (half archers and half lances), to equip them with bows and arrows and lances, and to have them ready for 10 April; on 12 March instructions were given for them to be at Southampton for 14 May (C 76/20, ms. 32 & 34).

47. *Foedera*, III, i, 32. Thirteen ships were fitted out for his passage there (E 101/24/18) and letters of protection were issued to him on 20 April (*Foedera*, III, i, 36).

48. C 61/57, ms. 7–8.

49. *Foedera*, III, i, 34–5, 37–8.

50. See Appendix I.

51. E 101/68/4, no. 72; *Foedera*, III, i, 37.

52. Northampton was still at Portsmouth on 1 June (E 404/501/372), but had left by 11 June, when the instructions concerning those leaving for Gascony with Lancaster were issued to the sheriffs (*Foedera*, III, i, 44; *CCR*, *1343–6*, 573).

53. *CCR*, *1343–6*, 588.

54. E 101/25/9, ms. 4 & 5.

# Chapter IV

1. R. Boutruche, *La crise d'une société* (1947), 378; *Foedera*, II, ii, 1047, 1105; E 404/508/130 & 132.

2. Boutruche, *op. cit*, 390–1.

3. E 101/25/9.

4. L. Drouyn, *La Guienne militaire pendant la domination anglaise* (3 vols, Bordeaux and Paris, 1865), I, 58–60, 63.

5. Boutruche, *op. cit*, 79–80, 358.

6. A. Communay, *Essai généalogique sur les Montferrand de Guyenne* (Bordeaux, 1889), *passim;* Bibl. nat, Moreau, vol. 650, p. 241, for the Blaye grant.

7. J. R. Marboutin, 'Le château de Castelnoubel', *Revue de l'Agenais*, XXXVIII (Agen, 1911), 288–9, 398–408.

8. *Chronique de Guyenne*, 400–1; Villani, *Historie fiorentine*, XIII, 928; *Foedera*, III, i, 123. Another group of knights who served in the earl's retinue were Fergaunt de Stysak, Gérard de Tartas, Hurtaud de Burgoyne, Vascomede d'Espaigne, three knights of the lord of Pommiers and a *compagnon* of the mayor of Bordeaux (E 101/25/9).

9. The following account of the siege of Bergerac is based on the following chronicles: *Chronique de Baças*, 43–4; *Chronique normande*, 66–7; *Chronique de Guyenne*, 400; *Froissart*, ed. Luce, III, xiii, 47–51, 262, 268. For the date of its surrender, see also *Petite Chronique de Guyenne*, 61, 99; M. Bertrandy, *Étude sur les chroniques de Froissart* (Bordeaux, 1870), 31–4.

10. Walter de Herewelle, a king's sergeant-at-arms who had been appointed to go to Gascony with Lancaster to determine the number of ships to be sent to the earl 'ad certum locum' (E 372/190, m. 41), may have been in charge of this operation.

11. *Murimuth*, 249, 251; *Avesbury*, 356; *Chronique de Guyenne*, 400.

12. Arch. nat, J 190B, no. 63; JJ 82, nos. 601 & 662.

13. *Knighton*, II, 32, 118.

14. He was there on 2 September 1345 (Bertrandy, *op. cit*, 33), and on 10 September following (Arch, dép. Basses-Pyrénées, E 131).

15. Bertrandy, *op. cit*, 33 n. 1, 43–6 & 44 n. 1 & 2, 56–8, 67, 75; Arch. nat, JJ 68, no. 147; C 61/63, m. 9; C 61/60, m. 9; *Avesbury*, 356; *Chronique de Baças*, 44. See map II.

16. Arch. dép. Basses-Pyrénées, E 131.

17. *Chronique de Baças*, 43.

18. For the details set forth in this paragraph, see Bertrandy, *op. cit*, 41, 47, 61, 68–77 & 77 n. 1 & 2, 97, 106–8; *Avesbury*, 356; C 61/60, ms. 6 & 14; SC 8/243/12138.

19. Villani, *Historie fiorentine*, XIII, 927; *Chronique de Baças*, 44; *Petite Chronique de Guyenne*, 61; *Chronique de Guyenne*, 401; *Avesbury*, 356.

20. Bertrandy, *op. cit*, 156–8, 189, 191–2, 196 & n. 1, 241, 247–9; *Jurades de la ville d'Agen, 1345–1355*, ed. A. Magen (Agen, 1894), 61; C 61/60, ms. 5, 6 & 32. See map II.

21. For the following account of Duke John's movements, see the itinerary in K. A. Fowler, *Henry of Grosmont, First Duke of Lancaster, 1310–1361* (Leeds University Ph.D. thesis, 1961. Leeds University Library), Appendix no. C 4.

22. Arch. nat, JJ 81, no. 234. For his movements to 8 October, see C. Devic and J. Vaissete, *Histoire générale de Languedoc* (16 vols, Toulouse, 1872–1904), III, 246–57; *Ordonnances des rois de France* (23 vols, Paris, 1723–1849), III, 154 ff.; Arch. nat, JJ 76, no. 334. He was in Agen by 15 October (Arch. nat, JJ 76, fo. 155r) and remained there until 28 December (*Ordonnances des rois de France*, III, 154; see Fowler, *op. cit*, Appendix B, IIa, no. 13, for the intervening dates).

23. *Froissart*, ed. Luce, III, 71, 73, 294; *Murimuth*, 190, 249–52; *Avesbury*, 356–7; E 159/123, m. 254 (Lancaster's indenture); E 101/68/3, no. 60 (Pembroke's indenture); Villani, *Historie fiorentine*, XIII, 927. For further details, see Fowler, *op. cit*, Appendix C 5.

24. Lancaster had taken La Réole by 2 November (E 159/123, m. 327), although the castle was not taken until after a long siege lasting into early January (*Chronique de Baẓas*, 44; *Chronique normande*, 69–60; *Froissart*, ed. Luce, III, xxii, 87, 308; *Baker*, 77; C 61/59, m. 10; *Arch. hist. Gironde*, I, 302–3, no. clii). His letters continued to be dated there until 12 August, save only on 2 and 22 April 1346, when they were dated at Bordeaux (C 61/59, ms. 6 & 7; 60, m. 41).

25. Fowler, *op. cit*, Appendix C 8, and C 61/60, ms. 5 & 6 for the submission of Aiguillon.

26. *Chronique normande*, 69; *Grandes Chroniques*, ed. Viard, IX, 258–9; C 61/59, m. 10; *Arch. hist. Gironde*, I, no. clii.

27. For the grants to the burgesses (26 January 1346) and ratification of customs there (5 February 1346), cf. C 61/59, ms. 6, 7 & 10; *Arch. hist. Gironde*, I, nos. clii & cliv; *Foedera*, III, i, 125. The town's petitions for royal confirmation have been preserved (SC 8/243/12134). For the grant of the castle to Pommiers, cf. C 61/60, m. 14 & SC 8/243/12134. Edward instructed the chancellor to meet the town's petitions 'par cause . . . nostre chere cousin et foial le comte de Lancastre ad tesmoigne des gentz avantdites' (C 81/319/18388). The royal grants to La Réole are recorded in C 61/59, ms. 7, 9 & 10; *Foedera*, III, i, 125; C 61/57, m. 2; *Arch. hist. Gironde*, II, no. cclxiv (the promise to Seguin); SC 8/243/12134 (its execution by Lancaster).

28. For these grants, cf. SC 8/243/12141 & 12154–5; C 61/59, ms. 5–8, 10 & 12; *Arch. hist. Gironde*, VI, no. lxxii.

29. J. R. Marboutin, 'Le château de Castelnoubel', *Revue de l'Agenais*, XXXVIII (Agen, 1911), 403; Boutruche, *op. cit*, 235 & n. 3, 240; P. Lauzun, 'Le château de Duras', *Revue de l'Agenais*, XLVIII (Agen, 1921), 1–9, 89–98.

30. Bibl. nat, Doat, 189, fos. 238–43; C 61/60, m. 7.

31. Notably of Raymond Bernard de Durfort, lord of Fenolhac and Gaynhac, who was rewarded with grants of four *bastides* in the Sarladais and Quercy, and Gaillard's brother Bertrand de Durfort, lord of Gaiac, who was granted the castle of Sauveterre in the Agenais and an annuity of £100 (C 61/60, ms. 17 & 18). Arnaud de Durfort, lord of Castelnoubel, on the other hand, served in Lancaster's retinue and conducted a heroic defence of his castle of Bajamont in the summer of 1346. As long as Agen was loyal to the Valois monarchy it was not profitable for him to choose a French suzerain (Marboutin, *op. cit*, 405–6; see above, p. 54).

32. *Avesbury*, 373.

33. *Chronique normande*, 67.

34. R. L. Alis, *Histoire de la ville d'Aiguillon et de ses environs* (Agen and Sainte-Radegonde, 1895), 117.

35. C 61/60, ms. 5 & 6. Arnaud Garsie du Fossat was subsequently thanked for his assistance to Lancaster (*Foedera*, III, i, 123), and was maintaining troops in English service in 1348 (E 101/167/12, m. 14v) and again in 1352, by which time he was seneschal of the Agenais (E 101/170/12, fo. 57r).

36. E 372/204, m. 44.

37. Arch. nat, JJ 74, nos. 232 & 754–6; C 61/67, m. 15.

38. *Arch. hist. Gironde*, III, nos. lxvii & lxviii.

39. C 61/60, m. 27.

40. C 61/60, m. 34; E 101/167/17, m. 3.

41. *Jurades de la ville d'Agen*, ed. A. Magen (Agen, 1894), 98.

42. C 61/60, ms. 18, 19, 25–7; SC 8/243/12127.

43. C 61/60, ms. 23–4, 27; *Arch. hist. Gironde*, II, no. cxxix. There were many others whom Lancaster rewarded for coming into the king's obedience. Cf. the grants to Élie Prévot, Bertrand de Clairac, Guillaume de Guarland and Blanche de Foix recorded in Bertrandy, *op. cit*, 33; C 61/60, ms. 14, 19; C 61/69, m. 6; E 101/170/12, fo. 51. Among the loyalists rewarded by the earl were Bernard Ezi (Arch. dép. Basses-Pyrénées, E 188; Bibl. nat, Doat, 189, fos. 251r–3v; C 61/67, m. 5; E 43/741) and Bertrand de Pommiers, brother of Guillaume-Sanche, lord of Pommiers (C 61/60, m. 6; SC 8/243/12138).

44. Large numbers of these grants are recorded on C 61/59, ms. 2–4; C 61/60, ms. 1, 5–6, 27, 30, 32, 39, 41; C 81/324/18824, 325/18969 & 18975, 329/19372; E 101/171/4, file 1, part 2, no. 20; *Rot. Parl*, II, 208, no. 14, 216, no. 45 & 222, no. 66.

45. For the following remarks on the composition and functions of the king's council in Gascony, see *Histoire des institutions françaises au moyen âge*, ed. F. Lot and R. Fawtier, I (Paris, 1957), 173; E. Pole Stuart, *Aspects of the Political and Administrative History of Gascony, 1303–1327* (University of London, Ph.D. thesis, 1927), 214–17; P. Chaplais, *Gascon Appeals to England, 1259–1453* (University of London, Ph.D. thesis, 1950), 171. Its role during Lancaster's lieutenancy is evident from the notes of warranty on his letters (e.g. Arch. dép. Basses-Pyrénées, E 188; Arch. dép. Gironde, série E, supplément no. 3968, fo. 19r; E 101/171/4, file 1, part 2, no. 20) and from the terms of some of the grants made by him (e.g. E 43/741; Arch. dép. Gironde, série E, supplément no. 3968, fo. 31r; C 61/59, m. 3; C 61/60, m. 41; C 81/319/18362 & 325/18969; *Rot. Parl*, II, p. 222, no. 66).

46. In the spring of 1346 he dispatched letters by way of Simon Simeon; Edward kept in touch by way of Richard de Cardoil (E 403/336, m. 48).

47. See Appendix I.

48. His letters were dated at Châtillon-sur-Indre on 1 February 1346 (Arch. nat, JJ 76, no. 398), at Cahors on 13 March (Bertrandy, *op. cit*, 288), Montauban on 22 and 30 March (*ibid*, 228 & n. 1; Devic and Vaissete, *op. cit*, III, 259), Agen on 5, 7 and 10 April (Devic and Vaissete, *op. cit*, IV, Preuves, cols. 205 & 220; Arch. comm. Toulouse, AA 4), and from 16 April to 18 June, 'in our tents before Aiguillon' (Arch. nat, JJ 75, no. 423; JJ 68, no. 170. For the intervening dates, cf. Fowler, *op. cit*, Appendix C 4).

49. *Froissart*, ed. Luce, III, xxx, 111, 329.

50. Lancaster's letters were dated at Bordeaux on 2 and 22 April (C 61/59, ms. 6 & 7, C 61/60, m. 41), and at La Réole on 1 and 16 May (E 43/741; C 47/24/7, no. 3), 23 June (E 404/508/47), 3 and 26 July (Arch. dép. Basses-Pyrénées,

E 188; C 61/59, m. 10; C 61/67, m. 5), and on 7 August (C 61/60, m. 25; *CPR, 1348–50*, 24). After 18 June the duke of Normandy's letters were dated 'in our tents between Tonneins and Aiguillon' (Arch. nat, JJ 68, no. 286; JJ 76, no. 299; JJ 77, no. 79; JJ 81, no. 226, etc.).

51. *Murimuth*, 170.

52. *Avesbury*, 372–4. I have annotated the text of this, to establish its extreme accuracy (Fowler, *op. cit*, Appendix C 6).

53. The route of his return from Poitiers to Saint-Jean-d'Angély is given by the *Chronique de Maillezais*, 166–7; cf. *Froissart*, ed. Luce, IV, 13–14.

54. *Clément VI: lettres closes, etc.* (1), II, fasc. 3, no. 2894; *CPL*, III, 29.

55. *CPR, 1345–8*, 562; *Clément VI: lettres closes*, etc. (1), II, fasc. 3, no. 2901.

56. *Chronique de Maillezais*, 166–7.

57. *Arch. hist. Poitou*, XIII, xxx–xxxvii.

58. *Knighton*, II, 46.

59. *Arch. hist. Poitou*, XIII, xxviii.

60. *Froissart*, ed. Luce, IV, 16.

61. *Avesbury*, 373–4.

62. Arch. nat, JJ 68, fo. 451; JJ 76, no. 175.

63. C 61/60, m. 39.

64. *CPR, 1345–8*, 560. On him, cf. below, p. 184.

65. C 61/60, ms. 12 & 16.

66. C 61/60, m. 41.

67. C 61/60, ms. 19, 20 & 41.

68. C 61/60, ms. 1 & 3; C 81/332/20638 & 20639.

69. C 61/60, ms. 7 & 17.

70. *Avesbury*, 374; *Chronique de Maillezais*, 166–7; C 61/60, m. 36.

71. *Arch. hist. Poitou*, XIII, xxxvii–liii. The castle was in French control again on 25 May 1351 (Bibl. nat, Pièces originales, vol. 774, Clerambaut, no. 827).

72. His letters were dated there on 31 October and on 5, 8, 12, 13, 20 and 28 November (*CPR, 1345–8*, 474, 558; C 61/60, ms. 1, 7, 14, 30; C 61/69, m. 7).

73. E 101/25/9; E 372/191, m. 54d; E 43/78.

74. *Foedera*, III, i, 104; *CPR, 1345–8*, 526.

75. *CFR, 1337–47*, 494.

76. *Foedera*, III, i, 120–1. He was with the king on 1, 3, 10 and 14 June (C 81/319/18383B & 18388; C 81/320/18409 & 321/18545; DL 41/10/34, no. 2), and had been informed of Philip VI's intention to relieve Calais as early as 14 May (*Foedera*, III, i, 104; *CPR, 1345–8*, 526).

77. *Froissart*, ed. Luce, IV, xxii, 47–8, 276–7.

78. *Avesbury*, 392; *Foedera*, III, i, 129; but cf. *Froissart*, ed. Luce, IV, xxiii–xxiv, 51–2, 281–3, and *Baker*, 90.

79. *Anonimalle Chronicle*, 50; *Baker*, 91.

80. *Avesbury*, 396–402; *Foedera*, III, i, 136–8; *CPR, 1345–8*, 562.

81. *Knighton*, II, 54.

82. DL 10/305; *CPR, 1345–8*, 542; *Foedera*, III, i, 123; C 81/319/18383B.

83. C 81/320/18405 & 18410.

84. *CPR, 1345–8*, 538

85. C 81/321/18545.

86. *CCR, 1346–9*, 610; *CPR 1348–50*, 217; C 81/334/19893.

87. *CChR, 1341–1417*, 70; C 81/326/19006; *CCR, 1346–9*, 447.

88. R. Somerville, *History of the Duchy of Lancaster* (1953), I, 34–5 & 35, n. 2.
89. *CPR, 1345–8*, 562, 566.
90. DL 42/1, fo. 419 (published by J. Delpit, *Collection générale des documents français qui se trouvent en Angleterre*, Paris, 1847, p. 83, no. clxxxv); C 76/42, m. 3.
91. For these and the following remarks on military and financial reorganization, see K. A. Fowler, 'Les finances et la discipline dans les armées anglaises en France au XIVe siècle', *Les Cahiers Vernonnais*, no. 4 (1964), 59–60, and the sources cited there.
92. During the years 1350–4 they constituted 55% of the total number of troops in the king's pay (29% men-at-arms, 21% mounted sergeants and 5% mounted archers), 50% of the total garrison forces (30% men-at-arms, 13% mounted sergeants and 7% mounted archers) and 67% of the troops maintained in retinues and which operated in the field (31½% mounted sergeants and 2½% mounted archers).
93. This is amply demonstrated in a large number of warrants and other documents subsidiary to the accounts of the constable of Bordeaux, e.g, E 101/650/85–92, 115, 123–32, 153, 157–9; E 101/171/4, file 2, no. 27; file 3, part 1, nos. 10 & 11; part 2, no. 26.
94. 52% of total income in 1348, 72% in 1348–9, 81% in 1349–50, 71% in 1350–1, 49% in 1352–4 and 46% in 1354–61.
95. 51% of total expenditure in 1348, 33% in 1348–9, 78% in 1349–50, 91% in 1350 and 49% in 1354–61.


Chapter V

1. For a full account of his diplomatic setbacks, see H. S. Lucas, *The Low Countries and the Hundred Years' War* (1929), 425–578.
2. The political situation in Flanders during these years is dealt with in *ibid*, 362–3, 525, 560–5, 578; H. Pirenne, *Histoire de Belgique* (7 vols, Brussels, 1900–32), II, 129–33; B. Wilkinson, 'A letter of Louis de Male, Count of Flanders', *Bulletin of John Rylands Library*, IX (1925), 177–87.
3. *Corpus Chronicorum Flandriae*, I, 224; II, 282 ff.; III, 20.
4. *Ibid*, III, 21.
5. *Foedera*, III, i, 174; E 372/193, m. 34d.
6. He had returned from Calais in November (*Knighton*, II, 54) and was in Lincoln on 19 and 27 November (DL 27/127; *CChR, 1341–1497*, 444–5).
7. See below, pp. 104–5.
8. *Foedera*, III, i, 136–8; *Avesbury*, 396–402.
9. *CCR, 1346–9*, 496; *Rot. Parl*, II, 164–5, 200.
10. *CPL*, III, 36–8; *Foedera*, III, i, 161, 165–6.
11. *Baker*, 101–2, 271–2; *Knighton*, II, 60; *Chronique normande*, 282 n. 4.
12. *Foedera*, III, i, 166.
13. *Ibid*, 170–1, 173.
14. *Ibid*, 172–3, 177.
15. R. Cazelles, *La société politique et la crise de la royauté sous Philippe de*

*Valois* (1958), 247–51. He was executed in Paris on 19 November 1350 'pour certain traisons et meffais qu'il avoit commis' (Arch. nat, X2a, 4, fo. 166).

16. *Corpus Chronicorum Flandriae*, III, 21; cf. *Baker*, 272.

17. *Foedera*, III, i, 174.

18. *Corpus Chronicorum Flandriae*, III, 21.

19. E 372/193, ms. 34r–d, 45r; E 101/312/33.

20. *Corpus Chronicorum Flandriae*, II, 285.

21. *Foedera*, III, i, 175.

22. Arch. dép. Nord, B 1316 (published in *Froissart*, ed. Lettenhove, XVIII, 324–7).

23. It is clear from the contents of the treaty that it was concluded before the truce of 13 November, which was to last until 1 September 1349 (*Foedera*, III, i, 177–8). According to Li Muisis (*Corpus Chronicorum Flandriae*, II, 285) it was concluded around 11 November.

24. E 372/193, m. 34r–d; E 372/194, m. 45r; E 159/125, ms. 46d, 63r.

25. BM, Additional Charter 59142; Cotton MS Caligula D III, fos. 39r–40r (published in *Froissart*, ed. Lettenhove, XVIII, 319–24); *Corpus Chronicorum Flandriae*, I, 225; II, 285; III, 21–2; PRO 31/8/142, fos. 147r–8v, and *Froissart*, ed. Lettenhove, XVIII, 318 (ambassadors from Ghent and Ypres). For the pro-English tendencies of the ambassadors, see Lucas, *op. cit*, 323, 351, 434, 552, 554, 569, 571 (Henry of Flanders, lord of Enghien, and William van Vaernewije, one of the ambassadors from Ghent).

26. BM Additional Charter 59142 (the upper part of the chirograph sealed with Edward III's privy seal and formerly in the chambre des comptes at Lille) and Cotton MS Caligula D III, fos. 39r–40r (the lower half, formerly sealed with Louis de Male's seal) are the projected alliance. Cf. P. Chaplais, 'Documents concernant l'Angleterre et l'Écosse anciennement conservés à la chambre des comptes de Lille (XIIe–XVe siècles)', *Revue du Nord*, XXXVIII (1956), 193, no. 7.

27. Arch. dép. Nord, B 1316 (published in *Froissart*, ed. Lettenhove, XVIII, 327–8).

28. *Foedera*, III, i, 178–9; *Froissart*, ed. Luce, IV, xxxvi, n. 2 (Arch. dép. Nord, fonds de la chambre des comptes de Lille, orig. parch.).

29. *Baker*, 98; *Corpus Chronicorum Flandriae*, I, 225.

30. In a procuration issued in February 1349, Edward referred to agreements 'nuper apud Caleys initae et concordatae' (*Foedera*, III, i, 181). The secret treaty concludes 'En tesmoignage des choses dessus dictes, nous roys et contes dessus nommé avons plaquiés nos séauls à ces ramembrances'.

31. R. Monier, *Les institutions centrales du comté de Flandre de la fin du IXe siècle à 1384* (Paris, 1943), 107.

32. Pirenne, *op. cit*, II, 184–5.

33. *Foedera*, III, i, 178.

34. The envoys sent to England on Louis' behalf in 1348 are said to have been sent by the 'consilio sapientium comes Flandriae' (*Corpus Chronicorum Flandriae*, III, 21).

35. Lucas, *op. cit*, 559–65.

36. *Froissart*, ed. Lettenhove, XVIII, 326–7.

37. PRO 31/8/142, fo. 304r–v (transcript of a letter of Louis dated at Dunkirk on 13 December 1348, in the Archives de la ville de Gand, Register Blanc, fo. 129v).

38. E 372/193, ms. 34r–d, 45r; E 101/312/33.

Chapter VI

1. *Foedera*, III, i, 188–9; *CPR, 1348–50*, 373–4.
2. *Foedera*, III, i, 181, 189; E 101/312/40.
3. *Foedera*, III, i, 177.
4. *Ibid*, 182.
5. *CPL*, III, 39; E 101/312/33, 37–9; E 372/193, ms. 34r–d & 45r–d.
6. E 101/312/39.
7. *Baker*, 100.
8. *Foedera*, III, i, 184–5.
9. *CPL*, III, 41.
10. *Knighton*, II, 57; *Baker*, 108.
11. K. A. Fowler, *Henry of Grosmont, First Duke of Lancaster* (Leeds University Ph.D. thesis, 1961), Appendix B, Ia, no. 16; C. de La Roncière, *Histoire de la marine française* (6 vols, Paris, 1899–1934), I, 495.
12. *Foedera*, III, i, 190.
13. Attempts were again made to get Louis to implement the secret treaty of alliance in October 1349 (*ibid*, 190; E 101/312/36), but were of no avail.
14. He drew wages for himself, 2 bannerets, 23 knights, 54 men-at-arms and 87 mounted archers returning with him from Gascony (E 372/195, m. 46).
15. Letters of protection were still being issued for those 'going to Gascony in his company' on 28 October 1349, but 'staying in Gascony in his company' on 10 November following (C 61/61, m. 1). According to *Baker*, 108, he crossed around 1 November. There are two letters issued by him in Bordeaux on 3 and 6 November (E 43/293, nos. 2 & 3).
16. *Actes normands de la chambre des comptes sous Philippe de Valois, 1328–1350*, ed. L. Delisle (Rouen, 1871), 409, no. 235.
17. *Avesbury*, 412. Nesle was appointed captain-general on 9 August 1349 (Bibl. nat, français 20684, fo. 314r). Cf. *Baker*, 109.
18. De la Roncière, *loc. cit.* See map.
19. Bibl. nat, Clairambault, vol. 40, p. 3011; vol. 47, p. 3517; vol. 54, p. 4069; vol. 80, no. 121; français 20683, fo. 337.
20. E 43/293, nos. 2 & 3.
21. *Knighton*, II, 66.
22. C 61/61, m. 5.
23. *Clément VI: lettres closes, etc.* (1), III, fasc. 5, nos. 4339–40, 4399; E 404/508/123.
24. *Jurades de la ville d'Agen*, ed. A. Magen (Agen, 1894), 187.
25. Arch. nat, JJ 78, no. 114.
26. *Chronique normande*, 92–3, 283–4; Arch. nat, JJ 80, no. 231. On his orders, Sir Robert de Beverley and John de Asprode garrisoned Laplume with their retinues from 20 December 1349 to 22 February 1350 (E 404/508/73 & 75; E 403/355, m. 19).
27. Arch. nat, JJ 80, fos. 221r–4v; *Inventaire des archives communales de Toulouse*, ed. E. Roschach, I (Toulouse, 1891), 463 (Arch. comm. Toulouse, AA 35, no. 76); P. Wolff, *Commerces et marchands de Toulouse* (Paris, 1954), 37. See map II.
28. *CPL*, III, 42; *Clément VI: lettres closes, etc.* (1), III, fasc. 5, no. 4317.
29. *CPL*, III, 43; *Clément VI: lettres closes, etc.* (1), III, fasc. 5, nos. 4333–4, 4336–40.

30. C 61/67, m. 15.

31. *Clément VI: lettres closes, etc.* (1), III, fasc. 5, nos. 4401, 4403, 4426; *CPL*, III, 44–5; Roschach, *op. cit*, 464 (Arch. comm. Toulouse, AA 35, no. 82); C. Douais, 'Le frères prêcheurs en Gascogne au XIIIè et au XIVe siècle', *Archives historiques de la Gascogne*, VIII (1885), 281.

32. C 61/61, m. 3.

33. *Foedera*, III, i, 188.

34. His letters were dated there on 14 February, 2, 4 and 5 March (C 61/63, ms. 5, 8, 11; C 61/64, m. 1; C 61/65, m. 6).

35. Auch was at Toulouse on 26 October and at Carcassonne on 21 November (Arch. nat, JJ 80, no. 325, JJ 78, no. 195). The French army was not assembled until 26 January at Moissac (Devic and Vaissete, *op. cit*, IX, 618). Bourbon was there on 22 February, but at Toulouse on 1 March and Carcassonne on 3 March (Arch. nat, JJ 78, no. 217; JJ 80, nos. 195 & 765).

36. *Chronique normande*, 92–3, 282–5; Devic and Vaissete, *op. cit*, IX, 618, n. 4. See map II.

37. He made grants to Amanieu du Fossat, Bertrand de Montferrand, William de Arenton, Raymond Guillaume, lord of Caupene, Pierre de Saint-Martin, Raymond Seguin and Jean Guitard (C 61/62, m. 5; C 61/63, ms. 5, 8 & 11; C 61/64, m. 1; C 61/65, m. 6; C 61/67, m. 15; *CPR, 1348–50*, 541).

38. He drew wages for himself and his retinue returning from Gascony for the period 5 March 1350, when they set out from Bordeaux, to 10 May following, when they arrived in London (E 372/195, m. 46). There is a letter of his dated at Chastillon on 20 March 1350 (C 61/62, m. 5; *CPR, 1348–50*, 541), which I have taken to be Chastillon-de-Médoc (comm. Saint-Christoly, arr. and cant. Lesparre) rather than Castillon-sur-Dordogne (arr. Libourne, ch.-l. cant.). Payments for the horses are recorded in E 403/355, m. 19; E 404/508/51–72, 74 & 76–9; C 61/62, m. 3.

39. *Foedera*, III, i, 192–4; cf. *Baker*, 108.

40. C 61/61, m. 2. Pursuant upon a royal mandate of 23 January, the sheriff of Lincoln purchased 500 quarters of wheat and sent it to Boston, where it was delivered to John Spicer, the earl's attorney and provisioner in the county, so that he could take it to Gascony for the maintenance of the earl and others in the king's allegiance there (E 372/195, m. 39v; *CCR, 1349–54*, 131). By 4 February following the *Gode Beyete* of Lancaster had been laden at Bristol, *La Trinité* at Boston, *La Dieu Garde* of Bayonne (which had been arrested by royal order) at Sandwich, *La Isabelle* at Lynn, and were ready to put out for the duchy (C 61/62, m. 6; *CCR, 1349–54*, 158).

41. E 404/5/32; E 159/126, m. 91; E 372/195, m. 4; E 403/355, m. 19. On 10 February the sheriff of Gloucestershire was instructed to purchase the necessary equipment for the embarkation of the horses of men-at-arms and other troops being sent out to join the earl in Gascony as quickly as possible, and to have them transported to Bristol, where a flotilla of 15 ships was being prepared for their crossing (C 61/62, m. 6). Throughout February and March letters of protection and general attorney were being issued to those going to join him in the duchy, another large batch was issued on 12 April and a final letter of general attorney on 13 April—over five weeks after the earl had set out on his return voyage from Bordeaux (ibid.).

42. As early as 12 February the sheriffs were instructed to provide arrows and

to have them sent to London for 5 April. On 20 March instructions for the provision of men-at-arms were sent out to some 110 towns. The sheriffs were to ensure that they arrived at Sandwich for 23 May and Phillip de Whitton (who had been in charge of the preparation of the fleet which took Lancaster to Gascony in 1345) was appointed lieutenant of John de Beauchamp, admiral of the fleet east of the Thames, and he once again supervised naval organization. On 1 May sheriffs, mayors and bailiffs were required to array mariners for the king's crossing to France (*Foedera*, III, i, 192–5).

43. *Baker*, 108.

44. Arch. nat, JJ 75, no. 154; JJ 80, no. 6. See R. Blanchard, *Le pays de Rays et ses seigneurs pendant la guerre de Cent ans, 1341–1372* (Vannes, 1898), 5–6.

45. S. Luce, *Histoire de Bertrand du Guesclin et de son époque* (Paris, 1876), 89.

46. *Foedera*, III, i, 101–2; C 81/316/18025. He was empowered to admit enemies into the king's obedience, to take their homage and grant them letters of pardon, and he secured an additional commission to carry out the transfer of Nantes to English allegiance. He was paid 1,500 gold écus for the expenses of 100 men-at-arms and 200 mounted archers to make war on the king's enemies and undertake the custody of the castle of Prigny (C 81/316/18025; E 43/209).

47. C 47/28/6, no. 10. For Dagworth's commission as lieutenant, see *Foedera*, III, i, 100.

48. He was to serve the king in his other wars, but on such occasions he was to enjoy the royal pay whenever summoned. In the wars in Brittany and Poitou he was to have all the advantages of war which fell to him, saving to the king all castles, towns, lands and a moiety of his share in prisoners taken by him and his men; he undertook not to liberate any great person thus captured without first securing the king's consent (C 81/332/19684; *Foedera*, III, i, 164, 168).

49. *Foedera*, III, i, 204.

50. Arch. nat, X2a, 4, fos. 186r–7r, 203v–4r, 206v, 209r.

51. C 76/27, m. 6; C 81/339/20344.

52. C 76/27, m. 6. See map II.

53. Arch. nat, JJ 80, no. 6. On Laval, cf. Bibl. nat, Pièces originales, vol. 1668, nos. 10, 11, 13, 14.

54. C 81/343/20741.

55. *Foedera*, III, i, 190.

56. C 81/342/20641; C 61/61, m. 1.

57. *Foedera*, III, i, 190.

58. C 61/61, m. 2.

59. C 76/27, m. 1.

60. Arch. nat, JJ 80, nos. 6 & 9.

61. G. Daumet, *Étude sur l'alliance de la France et de la Castille* (Paris, 1898), 16–18; P. E. Russell, *The English Intervention in Spain and Portugal* (1955), 7–9.

62. *Foedera*, III, i, 195–6.

63. *Ibid*, 200.

64. C 76/28, m. 6; cf. *Avesbury*, 412.

65. N. H. Nicolas, *A History of the Royal Navy* (2 vols, London, 1847), II, 102.

66. *Froissart*, ed. Luce, IV, xxxvi–xxxvii, 88, 90, 320–1; *Avesbury*, 412; *Knighton*, II, 66–7.

67. *Foedera*, III, i, 201–2.

68. Nicolas, *op. cit*, II, 104.

69. This account is based on Nicolas, *op. cit*, II, 104–13; *Froissart*, ed. Luce, IV, xxxvi–xxxviii, 88–98, 320–8; *Avesbury*, 412; *Chronicon Angliae*, 28; *Knighton*, II, 67; *Baker*, 109–11.
70. Cf. *Foedera*, III, i, 207, and *CPR*, *1350–4*, 9.
71. *Rot. Parl*, II, 311.
72. For the following details, see *Foedera*, III, i, 202–3, 206, 210, 228–9.


# Chapter VII

1. *Clément VI: lettres closes, etc.* (1), III, fasc. 5, nos. 4426, 4442–6; *CPL*, III, 44–5.
2. *Clément VI: lettres closes, etc.* (1), III, fasc. 5, no. 4506; *CPL*, III, 46.
3. *Foedera*, III, i, 196; Arch. nat, J 918, no. 26.
4. E 101/313/1; E 372/194, m. 45d.
5. *CPL*, III, 46.
6. *Foedera*, III, i, 197–8; J. Dumont, *Corps universel diplomatique du droit des gens* (8 vols. in 16, Amsterdam, 1726–31), I, ii, 254–7, no. cccxxii.
7. E 101/313/1; E 372/194, m. 45d.
8. *Clément VI: lettres closes, etc.* (1), III, fasc. 5, no. 4684; *CPL*, III, 47.
9. *Foedera*, III, i, 201.
10. *CPL*, III, 47.
11. *CPL*, III, 46, 48, 49; E 101/313/1.
12. *Clément VI: lettres closes, etc.* (1), III, fasc. 5, no. 4684; *CPL*, III, 47.
13. *Clément VI: lettres closes, etc.* (1), III, fasc. 5, nos. 4701–4, 4707; *CPL*, III, 47–8.
14. *CPL*, III, 47–8.
15. *Foedera*, III, i, 207.
16. E 101/313/4.
17. *Foedera*, III, i, 210.
18. *CPL*, III, 48.
19. *Ibid*, 49.
20. E 372/198, m. 38.
21. A. Gallard, *Mémoires pour servir à l'histoire de Navarre et de Flandre* (Paris, 1648), 275.
22. Arch. nat, J 365, no. 8.
23. *Froissart*, ed. Luce, IV, 88, 90, 320–1.
24. *Corpus Chronicorum Flandriae*, I, 227.
25. *Foedera*, III, i, 219.
26. E 101/313/4 & 6.
27. *Foedera*, III, i, 216.
28. E 101/313/7.
29. E 101/313/6 & 7.
30. *Baker*, 114–15, 283–4; *Knighton*, II, 68.
31. *Ibid; Chronique normande*, 101–2, 291–2; *Froissart*, ed. Luce, IV, xlvi–xlvii, 115–22, 341–5; *Foedera*, III, i, 236.
32. *Foedera*, III, i, 197, 225.
33. *Ibid*, 224; E 101/313/8, m. 1.

34. *Foedera*, III, i, 224.
35. *Ibid*, 227; E 101/313/8, m. 1.
36. A. Gallard, *Preuves de mémoires pour l'histoire de Navarre et de Flandre* (Paris, 1648), 156–8, no. xxix; *Froissart*, ed. Lettenhove, XVIII, no. lxxv.
37. F. Quicke, *Les Pays-Bas à la veille de la période bourguignonne, 1356–1384* (Brussels, 1947), 44–5.
38. Gallard, *Mémoires*, 278.
39. *Froissart*, ed. Lettenhove, XVIII, no. lxxv; Gallard, *Preuves de mémoires*, 159–60, no. xxx.
40. *Foedera*, III, i, 227.
41. *CPL*, III, 49–50.
42. *Foedera*, III, i, 227.
43. E 101/313/8, m. 2.
44. *Foedera*, III, i, 230, 232–3.
45. *Knighton*, II, 68.


Chapter VIII

1. For this and the ensuing quotation from Chaucer, see *The Canterbury Tales*, ed. and trans. into modern English by N. Coghill (Penguin Books, 1951), 26.
2. *Knighton*, II, 23.
3. *Ibid; DNB*, IX, 553.
4. *CPR, 1343–5*, 196.
5. C 81/294/15900 & 301/16577; *Foedera*, III, i, 5.
6. M. McKisack, *The Fourteenth Century* (Oxford, 1959), 251.
7. *Knighton*, II, 30; *Baker*, 97; E. J. F. Arnould, *Étude sur le Livre des Saintes Médecines du duc Henri de Lancastre* (1948), lvii.
8. *Froissart*, ed. Luce, III, i, 3; *Murimuth*, 123–4, 232; N. H. Nicolas, 'Observations on the institution of the Most Noble Order of the Garter, illustrated by the accounts of the Great Wardrobe of King Edward the Third', *Archaeologia*, XXXI (London, 1846), 109, 113, 115–18, 125; E 101/391/15; *Reading*, 130, 273–4; *Eulogium historiarum*, 227; *Knighton*, II, 99.
9. Nicolas, *op. cit*, 113.
10. *Ibid*, 115–16, 143.
11. *Ibid*, 121; E 101/391/15.
12. E 372/207, m. 50.
13. *Register of Edward the Black Prince, 1346–1365* (4 vols, London, 1930–33), IV, 247, 323.
14. For the following details, see Nicolas, *op. cit*, 115–18, 121–2.
15. *Expeditions to Prussia and the Holy Land made by Henry Earl of Derby*, ed. L. Toulmin-Smith (Camden Society, second series, LII, London, 1894), xv–xvi.
16. *CPR, 1350–4*, 172, 191; *Cartulaire de Louis de Male, comte de Flandre, 1348 à 1358* (2 vols, Bruges, 1898 & 1901), I, no. ccccxxx; *Knighton*, II, 68–9.
17. *Liber de rebus memorabilioribus sive chronicon Henrici de Hervordia*, ed. A. Potthast (Göttingen, 1895), 286.
18. *Knighton*, II, 69.

19. *Scriptores Rerum Prussicarum*, ed. T. Hirsch, M. Söppen and E. Strelkhe (5 vols, Leipzig, 1861–74), II, 516, n. 453.
20. *Baker*, 119–20; *Chronique des quatre premiers Valois*, 13–14.
21. *Knighton*, II, 69–70. He was at the palace of the Savoy on 10 July (DL 41/9/7, no. 1).
22. *Knighton*, II, 69–70. King John's letter has been published in *Scriptorum Brunswicensia Illustrantium*, ed. G. G. Leibnitz, II (Hanover, 1710), 47–50.
23. *Baker*, 121–2.
24. *Scriptorum Brunswicensia Illustrantium*, II, 47–50.
25. *Foedera*, III, i, 248; *CPR, 1350–4*, 317.
26. *Knighton*, II, 71.
27. *Chronographia*, II, 251.
28. *Ibid; Scriptorum Brunswicensia Illustrantium*, II, 47; *Knighton*, II, 71; *Chronique des regnes de Jean II et de Charles V*, 36; *Chronique des quatre premiers Valois*, 25.
29. Arch. nat, KK 8, fo. 102.
30. *Chronique des quatre premiers Valois*, 25.
31. *Knighton*, II, 71–3; *Baker*, 121–2.
32. *Scriptorum Brunswicensia Illustrantium*, II, 49–50.
33. *Knighton*, II, 73; Arch. nat, KK 8, fo. 122.
34. *Knighton*, II, 73; M. Galway, 'Froissart in England', *University of Birmingham Historical Journal*, VII, i (1959), 27, 29, 33–4.
35. *Les jurades de la ville de Bergerac*, ed. G. Charrier (4 vols, Bergerac, 1892–5), i; *Records of the Borough of Leicester*, ed. M. Bateson (4 vols, London, 1899–1923), II, 77; *Knighton*, II, 73.


Chapter IX

1. É. Perroy, 'Quatre lettres du cardinal Guy de Boulogne (1352–1354)', *Revue du Nord*, XXXVI (1954), 161; *CPL*, III, 51; O. Raynaldus, *Annales ecclesiastici ab anno MCXCVIII* (15 vols, Lucca, 1747–56), VI, 563–4.
2. C. Eubel, *Hierarchia catholica medii aevi* (Munich, 1898–1900), I, 19. The cardinal was not, however, at the conclave (*Ibid*, n. 3; Raynaldus, *op. cit*, VI, 564).
3. *Innocent VI: lettres closes, etc*, I, fasc. 1, nos. 45–6; *lettres secrètes, etc*, I, fasc. 1, nos. 83–4; G. Mollat, 'Innocent VI et les tentatives de paix entre la France et l'Angleterre (1353–1355)', *Revue d'histoire ecclésiastique*, X (1909), 730–1.
4. *Foedera*, III, i, 253–5. The English envoys returned on board the *Tromphorn* and arrived in London between 15 and 19 March (E 101/313/12, 17–19, 41; E 372/197, ms. 38r–d, 41r).
5. *Innocent VI: lettres secrètes, etc*, I, fasc. 1, nos. 253, 272, 275, 284; *CPL*, III, 482.
6. Perroy, *op. cit*, 162.
7. *Ibid*.
8. *Foedera*, III, i, 260–1. The duke was at Leicester on 22 July (*Records of the Borough of Leicester*, II, 89–90).

9. E 101/620/7.

10. *Foedera*, III, i, 261–2.

11. F. Bock, 'Some New Documents Illustrating the Early Years of the Hundred Years War (1353–1356)', *Bulletin of John Rylands Library*, XV (1931), 61–6, 79, 84–91.

12. *Rot. Parl*, II, 251–2, no. 32.

13. This is not dated (*Innocent VI: lettres closes, etc*, I, fasc. 1, no. 182; Mollat, *op. cit*, 732, n. 4), although elsewhere attributed to 13 July (*CPL*, III, 611–12). Clearly it was issued after the truce of 26 July, to which it refers, and presumably after 2 August, when the pope announced Pelegrini's departure to the cardinal (*Innocent VI: lettres closes, etc*, I, fasc. 1, no. 198; *CPL*, III, 612–13; Mollat, *op. cit*, 735–6). Mollat thought that the truce referred to was that of 10 March and not that of 26 July (*op. cit*, 732, n. 4).

14. E 101/620/7.

15. *Rot. Parl*, II, 252; *Innocent VI: lettres closes, etc*, I, fasc. 1, no. 198; *CPL*, III, 612–13; Mollat, *op. cit*, 735–6.

16. *Innocent VI: lettres closes, etc*, I, fasc. 1, nos. 197–9; *CPL*, III, 612–14; Mollat, *op. cit*, 735–6.

17. *Rot. Parl*, II, 252.

18. *Foedera*, III, i, 268.

19. *Ibid*, 269.

20. E 101/313/13–16; E 372/198, ms. 38d, 39d, 41d.

21. Arch. nat, J 637, no. 7.

22. J. Du Tillet, *Recueil des guerres et traictez d'entre les rois de France et d'Angleterre* (Paris, 1588), 66–7, 78.


## Chapter X

1. *Foedera*, III, i, 263; E 372/198, m. 39d.

2. R. Delachenal, 'Premières négociations de Charles le Mauvais avec les Anglais (1354–1355)', *Bibliothèque de l'École des Chartes*, LXI (1900), 272.

3. For the following remarks on the disputed succession and the ensuing conflicts, see Lucas, *op. cit*, 535–9, 542–3, 557–8; Pirenne, *op. cit*, II, 177–8, 180; P. J. Blok, *History of the People of the Netherlands*, trans. O. A. Bierstadt and R. Putnam (5 vols, New York and London, 1898–1912), I, 313–15; Abbé Hossart, *Histoire ecclésiastique et profane du Hainaut* (2 vols, Mons, 1792), II, 145–6.

4. *Foedera*, III, i, 206–7.

5. *Ibid*, 212.

6. E 101/313/3.

7. *Foedera*, III, i, 216.

8. *Ibid*, 215.

9. *Ibid*, 220.

10. *Ibid*, 227.

11. *Ibid*, 234. Burton drew wages from 6 December 1351 to 26 February 1352 'alaint en messaige le roi en Holande' (E 101/313/9).

12. *Foedera*, III, i, 235; *Knighton*, II, 69.

13. *Cartulaire des comtes de Hainaut*, ed. L. Devillers (6 vols, Brussels, 1881–96), I, 355.
14. Blok, *op. cit*, I, 315. A safe-conduct was issued for her to return on 16 March 1352 (*Foedera*, III, i, 241).
15. *Foedera*, III, i, 250; E 101/313/10 & E 372/197, m. 38 (their expenses accounts).
16. *Foedera*, III, i, 252–3.
17. He returned to London on the conclusion of the negotiations (E 101/313/19; E 372/197, m. 38d).
18. *Foedera*, III, i, 263.
19. Delachenal, *loc. cit; Cartulaire des comtes de Hainaut*, I, 772, no. 27; E 372/198, m. 39d.
20. It was returned to the chancellor of England by Lancaster's clerk Henry de Walton and cancelled on 5 April 1354 (*Foedera*, III, i, 252–3).
21. Blok, *op. cit*, I, 316; Hossart, *op. cit*, 146.
22. *Cartulaire des comtes de Hainaut*, I, 773, no. 7.
23. Blok, *op. cit*, I, 316.
24. *Ibid; Foedera*, III, i, 364.
25. *Knighton*, II, 116.

# Chapter XI

1. R. Delachenal, *Histoire de Charles V* (5 vols, Paris, 1909–31), I, 75–83; *Venette*, 194, 202–3. It was not, however, until the sixteenth century that he was given the sobriquet *el Malo* (S. Honoré-Duvergé, 'L'origine du surnom de Charles le Mauvais', *Mélanges d'histoire du moyen âge dédiés à la mémoire de Louis Halphen*, Paris, 1951, 345–50). Much of the correspondence upon which this chapter is based has been published in *Froissart*, ed. Lettenhove, XVIII, 350–60, and in Delachenal, 'Premières négociations', *cit. supra*, 253–82. Cf. Delachenal, *Charles V*, I, 83–4.
2. *Knighton*, II, 71, 73; *Chronique des quatre premiers Valois*, 25; *Scriptorum Brunswicensia Illustrantium*, II, 47.
3. E 101/171/3, fos. 22v, 23r.
4. *Foedera*, III, i, 271.
5. E 372/198, m. 39d.
6. *CCR, 1354–60*, 3; *Foedera*, III, i, 273.
7. He was at Vienne on 31 January and Lyons on 1 February (Perroy, 'Quatre lettres', *cit. supra*, 162–3).
8. Lancaster's forces were assembled at Southampton. On 5 March his wardrober, William de Horwich, received £1,000 advance on the wages of the duke and his retinue going to Normandy (E 404/504/9) and on 26 May following he was paid £1,592 13s 6d 'in recompense for diverse costs and expenses which he had stood in arraying and getting ready both himself and his men-at-arms to go to Normandy' (E 403/374, m. 7).
9. Published and analysed by Bock, 'Some New Documents', *cit. supra*, 70–73, 91–3.

10. *Foedera*, III, i, 275.

11. Bock, *op. cit*, 61–6, 84–91.

12. B. Mendl and F. Quicke, 'Les relations politiques entre l'empereur et le roi de France de 1355 à 1356', *Revue belge de philologie et d'histoire*, VIII (1929), 481–92. For the Dauphiné, see Delachenal, *Charles V*, I, 34–5.

13. For this and other letters from Guy de Boulogne, see Perroy, *op. cit*, 162–4.

14. E 372/198, m. 38d; E 101/313/24.

15. *Foedera*, III, i, 275–6.

16. Delachenal, 'Premières négociations', *cit. supra*, 279.

17. *Rot. Parl*, II, 262.

18. E 403/374, m. 10.

19. Edinburgh University Library, MS 183, fo. 53v.

20. Cf. *CCR, 1354–60*, 32–3, and BM Cotton MS Caligula D III, fo. 41.

21. Instructions for its observation in Brittany and Aquitaine had in fact been issued from Guines on 6 April and, subsequently, by Edward III on 18 May (*Foedera*, III, i, 277–8).

22. Mollat, *op. cit*, 739 ff.; Bock, *op. cit*, 74 ff.

23. De la Bere drew wages for the period 20 May to 12 August for his journey to Avignon 'in comitiva confessoris domini regis, videlicet Johannis de Woderone' (E 101/313/23). He received a prest on them on 24 May and a courier was sent to Dover with letters for him on 26 May (E 403/374, m. 7).

24. *Foedera*, III, i, 283–4.

25. The clergy and nobles appointed proctors on the same day. These were: Richard de Wimundewold, Richard de Drax, William de Loughborough and William de Lynn, dean of Chichester, doctors of civil law, and Edmund de Grimsby and John de Welwick, bachelors of civil law. They were empowered to confirm whatever might be concluded by the English ambassadors (*Ibid*, 284–5), and all of them appear to have gone to the curia or to have been there already (*CPL*, III, 518, 541–2, 547).

26. C 81/1334/7; *CCR, 1354–60*, 83.

27. E 403/374, m. 19.

28. *Ibid*; E 372/200, m. 37; E 101/171/3, fo. 33; E 101/313/22.

29. He was accompanied by 14 esquires and a sergeant-at-arms, 2 masters, 7 clerks, 7 officials and 24 boys in a retinue of 60 horse (E 101/313/21).

30. E 403/374, m. 19; *Foedera*, III, i, 289.

31. Lancaster drew a prest on his wages for the mission to Avignon as early as 4 October (E 403/375, m. 2).

32. Published and analysed by Bock, *op. cit*, 74–6, 94–6.

33. Lancaster began to receive the king's pay on 28 October (E 101/313/25) and Arundel on 29 October (E 403/377, m. 8).

34. E 101/171/3, fo. 33. The duke received £30 from a number of Dover burgesses for the shipment of his horses on 3 November (E 101/313/25). He may have been at Amiens on 4 December (BM, Cotton MS Caligula D III, fo. 41).

35. *Knighton*, II, 78–9.

36. Lancaster's expenses account, which has been published by Bock, *op. cit*, 96–7, is to be seen in conjunction with E 404/5/34. For that of Arundel, cf. E 403/375, m. 8, and E 403/377, ms. 8 & 11.

37. Perroy, *op. cit*, 163.

38. Delachenal, *Charles V*, I, 89; cf. *Baker*, 124, and *Knighton*, II, 78. For their departure for the curia, cf. *Froissart*, ed. Luce, IV, li, n. 2, and Mollat, *op. cit*, 741, n. 3.

39. Mollat, *op. cit*, 740.

40. *Ibid*, 740–1.

41. *Baker*, 123–5.

42. The *Anonimalle Chronicle*, 32, *Avesbury*, 421, *Reading*, 118, and *The Brut*, 304–5, all blame the French for their breakdown, but the latter three accounts are closely related (see Tait's note in *Reading*, 256). The *Anonymi Cantuariensis* gives no reason.

43. *Reading*, 118; *The Brut*, 305; Walsingham, *Historia Anglicana*, 277–8, and *Chronicon Angliae*, 31. *Baker*, 124–5, excludes Guy de Boulogne.

44. *Froissart*, ed. Lettenhove, XVIII, 364–5.

45. See two letters of Edward III published in *Foedera*, III, i, 303, and Delachenal, *Charles V*, I, 92, n. 3.

46. *Grandes Chroniques*, ed. Paulin, VI, 14; *Froissart*, ed. Luce, IV, 131; *Lescot*, 95.

47. *Knighton*, II, 78. However, this part of the chronicle may have been written many years later (see V. H. Galbraith, 'The Chronicle of Henry Knighton', *Fritz Saxl, 1890–1948. A Volume of Memorial Essays*, ed. D. J. Gordon, London, 1957, 136–48).

48. Delachenal, 'Premières négociations', *cit. supra*, 264–70, and 280–2 for the text of the 'projected treaty'; *Charles V*, I, 87–91.

49. Mollat, *op. cit*, 739–40. For Tennerie's role at Bruges and Avignon, see above p. 125 and *Catálogo del Archivo General de Navarra*, II, no. 672.

50. E. Petit, 'Séjours de Jean II (1350–1356)', *Bulletin historique et philologique* (1896), 605.

51. *Fragments d'une chronique inédite relatifs aux evénéments militaires arrivés en Basse-Normandie de 1353 à 1389*, ed. L. Delisle (Saint-Lô, 1895), 4.

52. See the expenses accounts of these messengers enrolled on E 403/375, ms. 12, 17, 27, and E 101/171/3, fo. 30v.

53. Mollat, *op. cit*, 741, n. 4; *CPL*, III, 615; Perroy, *op. cit*, 161, n. 1.

54. Delachenal, *Charles V*, I, 87; Mollat, *op. cit*, 741, n. 3.

55. Delachenal, 'Premières négociations', *cit. supra*, 269; *Charles V*, I, 89; Mollat, *op. cit*, 742. As early as 4 January 1355 Navarrese treasury officials were instructed to pay Arnaldo de Barbazan for a journey to Avignon to treat with the Cardinals of Boulogne and Arras on Charles' behalf (*Catálogo del Archivo General de Navarra*, II, no. 662).

56. *Foedera*, III, i, 268; E 403/374, m. 19.

57. *Rot. Parl*, II, 264.

58. *Baker*, 125, n. 2.

59. *Anonimalle Chronicle*, 32 & n. 2.

60. *Froissart*, ed. Lettenhove, XVIII, 364–5.

61. For these and the ensuing remarks on Charles IV and his policy, see Mendl and Quicke, *op. cit*, 477–93, 495–6; A Leroux, *Recherches critiques sur les relations politiques de la France avec l'Allemagne de 1292 à 1378* (Paris, 1882), 243–52, 257–9; P. Fournier, *Le royaume d'Arles et de Vienne, 1138–1378* (Paris, 1891), 452–3.

62. *Froissart*, ed. Lettenhove, XVIII, 362–4.

63. They arrived back in England on 28 March (E 101/313/25; E 403/377, m. 8; E 404/5/34).

## Chapter XII

1. *Knighton*, II, 79; *Anonimalle Chronicle*, 32.
2. The ships arrested for the embarkation of the troops under the duke's command were assembled at Rotherhithe flying his *stremers* (*Avesbury*, 425). The admirals of the northern and southern fleets were to have accompanied him (E 403/377, ms. 18 & 24), and the keeper of the king's wardrobe, assisted by the controller and the clerk of the king's navy, were responsible for the payment of sailors and troops (ibid, ms. 14–38).
3. *Grandes Chroniques*, ed. Paulin, VI, 16–17. For the details of the build-up of Navarrese forces in Normandy, see *Catálogo del Archivo General de Navarra*, II, nos. 706, 722–8, 730–2, 736, 739–41, etc.
4. C 81/1334/22; C 61/67, m. 5.
5. *Avesbury*, 425–6; *Rot. Parl*, II, 264.
6. Delachenal, *Charles V*, I, 107.
7. *Ibid*, 106.
8. *Avesbury*, 426.
9. *Grandes Chroniques*, ed. Paulin, VI, 16–17.
10. Between then and the following May they were being paid by Edward, first directly from the Exchequer, and then by way of Lancaster's treasurer-of-wars, William de Driffield (E 403/377, m. 37; E 403/380, ms. 6 & 7). Enríquez was ready to sail for Normandy from Fuenterrabia and other ports on 7 June 1355 (*Catálogo del Archivo General de Navarra*, II, no. 706). For his role and that of Ramirez in France, see *ibid*, pp. 471 & 482, and Delachenal, *Charles V*, II, 1, 2 n. 1, 421–2.
11. C 76/33, m. 6.
12. H. J. Hewitt, *The Black Prince's Expedition of 1355–1357* (Manchester, 1958), 40.
13. On 1 October orders were therefore given to arrest ships for the expedition, and on 1 and 10 October letters of protection were issued to several of those going to the duchy with the duke (C 75/33, m. 4).
14. *Rot. Parl*, II, 264; *Avesbury*, 427–31; *Knighton*, II, 83–6; *Baker*, 125–6; Walsingham, *Historia Anglicana*, I, 280.
15. After 26 November letters of protection, which had been issued to those 'going across the sea' with him on 20 October and 1 November, were again issued to those 'going to Brittany' with him; on 30 November a mandate was issued instructing him to take administrative action in the duchy and on 15 December orders were given for the arrest of ships to be assembled at Plymouth to transport the troops under his command to the duchy (C 76/33, ms. 2–4).
16. *Baker*, 126, 291; *Avesbury*, 431–2,:450; *Knighton*, 85; *Rot. Parl*, II, 264–5. He was paid wages for service 'cum rege in guerra sua in partibus Scocie' (E 361/4, m. 2), appears to have been with the king at Newcastle-upon-Tyne on 31 December (C 81/365/22966), and was among the witnesses to the instru-

ments by which Edward Balliol surrendered all his rights to the Scottish throne to Edward at Roxburgh on 20, 25 and 27 January, and to the royal confirmation of the Berwick charter at Westminster on 28 March (*Foedera*, III, i, 317–18. 320–2; *Rot. Scot*, I, 787–8, 792).

17. E 403/380, m. 12.

18. On 12 March William de Driffield was paid the first advance on the wages and regard for a quarter of a year of the duke and his retinue of 8 bannarets, 100 knights, 191 esquires and 300 mounted archers going to Brittany in the royal service (E 403/378, m. 34, and 380, m. 5). A second advance was paid to him on 11 April, a third on 12 May and a fourth on 23 May (E 403/378, m. 40, and 380, ms. 3 & 5). Letters of protection were issued to those going to the duchy with him on 13 and 20 March, and between 10 and 20 May their number greatly increased (C 76/34, ms. 14–18). Preparations for the transport of the troops took a similar turn. On 12 March commissions were issued for the arrest of ships for their passage (C 76/34, m. 17); three days later Thomas Dautre was paid for his costs in going to Southampton for that purpose (E 403/378, m. 35) and the sheriff of Southampton was instructed to provide the equipment necessary for the embarkation of the troops (C 76/34, m. 17) and delivered it to the marshal of the duke's household (E 372/201, m. 42v). Michael de Grendon, one of the king's sergeants-at-arms, was paid his wages for going to Southampton with a royal clerk, Richard de Derby, to arrest shipping for the duke's passage (E 403/380, m. 1). From March until early in June, Derby was engaged in paying the wages of the sailors at Southampton, and on 22 April masters of ships of other southern ports were also paid an advance on the wages of the sailors (E 403/378, ms. 36 & 41–2; E 403/380, ms. 1, 2, 8, 9, 12); Ralph de Kesteven was responsible for this at Sandwich, Winchelsea and Shoreham during April and May (E 403/380, m. 24). At the beginning of June carpenters and masons were conducted to Southampton for embarkation with the forces (E 403/380, ms. 9, 13).

19. Delachenal, *Charles V*, I, 140–174.

20. E 403/380, m. 1.

21. *Avesbury*, 461–2.

22. Delachenal, *Charles V*, I, 160–2.

23. *Ibid*, I, 161.

24. The ensuing account of the campaign is based on the dispatch, published in *Avesbury*, 462–5, and on Delachenal, *Charles V*, I, 171–2, 175–9, 186.

25. His letters were dated at Cachan on 2 June, Antony on 3 June, Saint-Clair-de-Gometz on 5 June, Saint-Arnoul-en-Yvelines on 7 June, Gué-de-Longroi on 7 and 8 June, and subsequently at Chartres (Arch. nat, J 188B; JJ 84, nos. 546, 561, 563, 569, 597–8, 686; *Froissart*, ed. Luce, IV, lxx, n. 2).

26. It was imperfectly obeyed and had to be reiterated on 7 or 8 June (Delachenal, *Charles V*, I, 186).

27. Arch. nat, J 188B, no. 1.

28. Arch. nat, JJ 84, nos. 554, 562, 567–8, 574, 592, 626, 630, 640.

29. *Foedera*, III, i, 332; L. Delisle, *Histoire du château et des sires de Saint-Sauveur-le-Vicomte* (Valognes, 1867), 88–9.

30. *Foedera*, III, i, 333.

31. He had arrived by 20 August, when he was given a royal licence to return to Normandy (*ibid*, 338).

32. *Ibid*, 340. He was still in England on 8 October, when a letter was written to him about the growing support for Godfrey d'Harcourt during his absence from Normandy (BM, Cotton MS Caligula D III, fo. 42r, no. 28).

33. J. Le Patourel, 'Edouard III, "roi de France et duc de Normandie", 1356–1360', *Revue historique de droit français et étranger*, 4e série, XXXI (1953), 317–18.

34. *Avesbury*, 468; *Baker*, 139; E. Déprez, 'La "Querelle de Bretagne", de la captivité de Charles de Blois à la majorité de Jean IV de Montfort (1347–1362), I: Pendant la captivité de Charles de Blois (1347–1356)', *Mémoires de la société d'histoire et d'archéologie de Bretagne*, VII (Rennes, 1926), 48–9.

35. *Foedera*, III, i, 335–6.

36. A. Le Moyne de la Borderie, *Histoire de Bretagne* (6 vols, Rennes, 1896–1914), III, 548–50. There is a letter of his dated at Vannes on 12 August (C 76/38, m. 3).

37. E 403/380, m. 23.

38. Delachenal, *Charles V*, I, 179–84.

39. Hewitt, *op. cit*, 102, 104, 107.

40. *Ibid*, 100–1, 104. The letter has been published by Delachenal, *Charles V*, II, 381–4.

41. Delachenal, *Charles V*, I, 190.

42. Bibl. nat, Pièces originales, vol. 1612, Labatut, no. 3.

43. Ibid. and vol. 106, Ars, no. 11; vol. 265, Beguin, nos. 2–4; vol. 1732, Locu, no. 2; Clairambault, vol. 213, p. 9481, no. 58.

44. Ibid.

45. He may have intended to accompany Lancaster to Normandy (*Rot. Parl*, II, 264; *Knighton*, II, 80) and he subsequently conducted the raid from Calais.

46. Delachenal, *Charles V*, II, 383.

47. *Chronicon Briocense*, *Chronicon Britannicum* and *Chronicon Britannicum alterum* in P. H. Morice, *Mémoires pour servir de preuves à l'histoire ecclésiastique et civile de Bretagne* (3 vols, Paris, 1742–46), I, cols. 8, 43, 113–14; *Anonimalle Chronicle*, 36; *Chronique des quatre premiers Valois*, 45, 58; *Baker*, 142.

48. E 36/278, m. 88d; cf. *Black Prince's Register*, IV, 145.

49. E 159/123, m. 254; E 101/68/4, no. 72.

50. *Foedera*, III, i, 421; *CPR, 1361–4*, 495; Arch. nat, JJ 89, no. 181; V. Ménard, *Histoire religeuse, civile et militaire de Saint-James de Beuvron* (Avranches, 1897), 61–2; further references in Fowler, *Henry of Grosmont*, Appendix C 8. He appointed Sir Thomas de Uvedale and Sir Thomas Fogg as his lieutenants at Domfront, Bois-du-Maine, Messei and Condé-sur-Noireau (Arch. nat, Xɪa 21, fos. 73v–5v, no. 3) and Richard Sholl and William de Tutbury as constable and receiver at Avranches (Arch. nat, JJ 89, no. 181). Uvedale was his lieutenant in Brittany (cf. below, pp. 183–4), and Sholl had letters of protection to go abroad in his retinue on 4 July 1355 and 23 August 1359 (C 76/33, m. 9; C 76/38, m. 16).

51. S. Luce, *Histoire de Bertrand du Guesclin* (1876), 188.

52. Bibl. nat, Pièces originales, vol. 1474, Hangest, nos. 8, 13, 14; Luilly, nos. 4–5; vol. 2103, Nully, nos. 2–4; vol. 2343, Portal, no. 8.

53. *Foedera*, III, i, 342. See above n. 32.

54. *Ibid*.

55. E 403/380, m. 24; 384, m. 1.

56. *Chronique du Mont-Saint-Michel*, I, 5; *Fragments d'une chronique inédite*

*relatifs aux evénéments militaires arrivés en Basse-Normandie*, 6; Ménard, *op. cit*, 61–2.
57. BM, Cotton MS Caligula D III, no. 59.
58. Bibl. nat, Moreau, vol. 700, fos. 73r–5r.
59. *Knighton*, II, 99; *Foedera*, III, i, 385.

## Chapter XIII

1. *Chronicon Britannicum alterum* in Morice, *Mémoires*, I, col. 113.
2. P. Jeulin, 'L'hommage de la Bretagne en droit et dans les faits', *Annales de Bretagne*, XLI (1934), 380–473; 'Un grand "Honneur" anglais. Aperçus sur le "comté" de Richmond en Angleterre, possession des ducs de Bretagne (1069/71–1398)'. *ibid*, XLII (1935), 265–302.
3. J. Le Patourel, 'L'administration ducale dans la Bretagne montfortiste, 1345–1362', *Revue historique de droit français et étranger*, 4e série, XXXII (1954), 144–7.
4. See map.
5. K. A. Fowler, 'Les finances et la discipline dans les armées anglaises en France au XIVe siècle', *Les Cahiers Vernonnais*, no. 4 (1964), 62–3.
6. Above, pp. 42–4.
7. E 101/175/5.
8. *Foedera*, III, i, 508; Morice, *op. cit*, I, cols. 1537–8; E 101/175/1, nos. 65, 66. On Coupegorge's career, see E. Déprez, 'Une lettre missive du prétendant Jean de Bretagne, comte de Montfort', 9–11. He was receiver of Duke John III's lands in England in 1339 (*CCR, 1339–41*, 334), treasurer of Brittany in 1343–5 (E 372/188, m. 55), and was granted a life annuity of 400 *écus* from the revenues of the duchy by Edward III (E 101/175/6, no. 21). Barbu had been retained as a councillor by one of Lancaster's predecessors as lieutenant, was granted an annuity by Henry 'for his good counsel and service', and had represented Montfort's interests during the drafting of the treaty of Guines in 1354 (ibid, no. 11; 175/7, no. 15). Callac was a native of the diocese of Vannes (B.-A. Pocquet du Haut-Jussé, *Les papes et les ducs de Bretagne*, 2 vols, Paris, 1928, I, 351) and had been retained in royal and ducal service in Brittany by a previous lieutenant, Sir Robert de Herle (E 101/175/1, no. 30; 175/6, nos. 23–4). Kaër had played an important role as admiral of the duke and keeper of the coast at Auray (*CPR, 1340–3*, 210). During the critical month of February 1342, he was joint captain of the castle and town of Brest (Arch. nat, J 241B, nos. 43 & 43 bis; De la Borderie, *Histoire de Bretagne*, III, 484; cf. Morice, *op. cit*, I, col. 1428).
9. C 76/33, m. 6; *Foedera*, III, i, 335–6, 361–2.
10. *Avesbury*, 462; Delachenal, *Charles V*, I, 175; Déprez, 'La Querelle de Bretagne', *cit. supra*, 47–9; E 403/380, m. 16.
11. Déprez, 'Une lettre missive', *cit. supra*, 2–9; *Froissart*, ed. Lettenhove, XII, 168.

12. Bock, 'Some New Documents', *cit. supra*, 4–11; Déprez, 'La Querelle de Bretagne', *cit. supra*, 50 ff; C 76/34, m. 10.

13. *Chronicon Britannicum* and *Chronicon Briocense* in Morice, *op. cit*, I, cols. 8, 43; *Chronique des quatre premiers Valois*, 58; Morice, *op. cit*, I, col. 1512.

14. He had arrived there by 24 November (Morice, *loc. cit.*); cf. *Froissart*, ed. Luce, V, 87, 305, for his dilemma.

15. Morice, *op. cit*, cols. 1513–14.

16. Bibl. nat, Clairambault, vol. 96, no. 5; 106, no. 166; 16, no. 168; 86, nos. 45 & 146; Luce, *Histoire de Bertrand du Guesclin*, 192–3.

17. Arch nat, JJ 87, no. 127.

18. *Chronicon Britannicum alterum* in Morice, *op. cit*, I, col. 113; *Froissart*, ed. Luce, V, xxii, n. 2.

19. S. Luce, 'Du Guesclin au siège de Rennes', *Bibliothèque de l'École des Chartes*, LII (1891), 615–18; *Histoire de Bertrand du Guesclin*, ch. vii; De la Borderie, *op. cit*, III, 551–9; Delachenal, *Charles V*, I, 266–7, 308.

20. *Cuvelier*, I, 41 ff.

21. Luce, 'Du Guesclin au siège de Rennes', *loc. cit;* J. Lemoine, 'Du Guesclin, armé chevalier', *Bibliothèque de l'École des Chartes*, LVI (1895), 84–9; A. Molinier, *Les sources de l'histoire de France* (6 vols, Paris, 1901–6), IV, 70–71.

22. *Knighton*, II, 93; Luce, *Histoire de Bertrand du Guesclin*, 218.

23. *Foedera*, III, i, 349.

24. *Black Prince's Register*, IV, 269.

25. *Foedera*, III, i, 353; Bibl. nat, Moreau, vol. 700, fos. 73r–5r. He left London for Rennes on 7 May and arrived back there on 30 July (E 101/313/27; E 403/387, m. 6).

26. *Foedera*, III, i, 359; E 101/313/32; E 372/202, m. 34d.

27. *Cuvelier*, I, p. 43, lines 1114–17.

28. *Chronique des quatre premiers Valois*, 58.

29. *Anonimalle Chronicle*, 40.

30. Morice, *op. cit*, I, col. 1512.

31. *Foedera*, III, i, 361–2.

32. *Lescot*, 112, n. 1.

33. E 403/382, m. 2.

34. BM, Cotton MS Caligula D III, fo. 42r, no. 28.

35. E 403/382, m. 13.

36. Bibl. nat, Moreau, vol. 700, fos. 73r–5r.

37. E 101/313/27; E 403/387, m. 6.

38. E 101/313/32; E 372/202, m. 34d; Bibl. nat, français 25701, no. 116.

39. *Chronique de Jean II et Charles V*, 111; *Knighton*, II, 95; *Chronicon Britannicum alterum*, cols. 113–14.

40. *Cuvelier*, I, 74, lines 1983–2007.

41. Bibl. nat, Moreau, vol. 700, fos. 73r–5r.

42. For what follows, see Fowler, 'Les finances', *cit. supra*, 62–4, 74–8.

43. *Foedera*, III, ii, 1189, 1205.

44. C 81/297/16125.

45. £4,173 of this was not received in 1359–60 because of the rebellion of many parishes (£2,287 11s 11d) and the poverty and inability to pay of others (£1,885 10s 4¼d). Nevertheless, the remaining £10,562 was raised (almost twice the annual revenue of Gascony in the years 1348–61), and amounted to

85% of total revenues received by the treasurer (£12,873). In the following two years the revenues of Bécherel were made over to William Lord Latimer, then lieutenant of the duchy, and those of Ploërmel to Richard Grenacres, then captain of the town; but at Vannes they continued to be collected by the treasurer and ransoms continued to form a high proportion of total receipts: 76% in 1360–61 and 72% in 1361–2.

46. In 1359–60 they brought in £746, but seem normally to have been farmed out for £1,200.

47. For £640.

48. £473 in 1359–60 and £1,083 in the entire period from September 1359 to June 1362.

49. £8,783 for the wages of the lieutenant and his retinue, £6,255 for those of the captains and garrisons of the three principal towns, together with divers other payments and allocations, and £426 for the wages of the treasurer.

50. See above, pp. 44–5.

51. Bibl. nat, Moreau, vol. 700, fos. 73r–5r.

52. See below, pp. 183–5.


## Chapter XIV

1. *CIPM*, XI, 92–116, no. 118; *CPR, 1358–61*, 580; *CFR, 1356–8*, 163–6; DL 41/4/12.

2. J. Nichols, *A Collection of the Wills of the Kings and Queens of England* (London, 1780), 83–7.

3. See Appendix II.

4. R. Somerville, *History of the Duchy of Lancaster*, I (1953), 35–40.

5. C 81/324/18888–9.

6. For the ensuing remarks on the palatinate, see Somerville, *op. cit*, 40–45.

7. M. McKisack, *The Fourteenth Century* (1959), 254–5.

8. DL 27/38; *CDRS*, IV, 3.

9. *GEC*, II, 59–60; VII, 409.

10. E. W. M. Balfour-Melville, *Edward III and David II* (1954), 6–7.

11. *Ibid*, 15–16; 'Papers Relating to the Captivity and Release of David II', *Miscellany of the Scottish History Society*, 3rd series, IX (1958), 6–7, 49–50, 55–6.

12. Walsingham, *Historia Anglicana*, I, 286.

13. Somerville, *op. cit*, 358.

14. For an outline of his career, see A. H. Thompson, *The History of the Hospital and New College of the Annunciation of Saint Mary in the Newarke, Leicester* (Leicester, 1937), 85–6, and Somerville, *op. cit*, 358, 363, 376.

15. E 101/15/12.

16. *CPP*, I, 46.

17. DL 27/155; *CPR, 1354–8*, 381; Thompson, *op. cit*, 30; *Records of the Borough of Leicester*, II, 113–14.

18. *CPR, 1348–50*, 350.

19. C 81/341/20581; *CPR, 1358–61*, 556; *1361–4*, 50; *CCR, 1354–8*, 601.

20. Somerville, *op. cit*, 86.

21. Peter de Wotton (1343–7): E 404/502/4; DL 25/984 & 27/323; E 372/191, m. 54d. William de Horwich (1353–4): *CPP*, I, 242; E 404/504/9; E 403/373, ms. 10, 31; E 372/198, m. 39d. Robert de Burton (1358–9): DL 29/288/4719.

22. Peter de Wotton (1347): Somerville, *op. cit*, 359. Richard de Melbourne (1351, 1353, 1359): *CPP*, I, 215, 238; DL 29/288/4719 & 367/6130. Richard de Walton (1353): *CPP*, I, 240. Nicholas de Colshull (1353–4, 1356, 1358–9): Somerville, *op. cit*, 359; DL 29/367/6130 & 725/11833.

23. Nicholas de Hume (1340–3): E 403/314, m. 4; 331, ms. 1, 4. John Gynewell (1344–6): E 403/332, m. 2; 336, ms. 8, 49; 337, m. 9. Henry de Walton (1348–53): Somerville, *op. cit*, 358–9; *CPP*, I, 193; E 403/341, m. 19; 359, m. 18; 362, m. 27; 365, m. 10; C 76/26, m. 4; C 61/62, m. 6; DL 29/212/3246, m. 1d; DL 42/11, fo. 24v. William de Driffield (1354–7): Somerville, *op. cit*, 359; E 403/375, ms. 2, 9; 377, ms. 12, 27, 36, 37; 378, ms. 34, 40; 380, ms. 3, 5; 384 m. 15. Nicholas de Colshull (1355, 1358): Somverville, *op. cit*, 359; E 403/375, m. 28; 388, ms. 35, 41; 392, m. 16.

24. *CPR, 1327–30*, 442.

25. E 403/294, m. 13; BM, Cotton MS Nero C VIII, fo. 263; E 404/493/8 & 501/303; C 76/12, m. 8.

26. C 76/15, m. 18; 19, m. 19; 20, m. 6; C 61/58, m. 2; DL 25/1235.

27. Somerville, *op. cit*, 359; *CPP*, I, 49; DL 27/36.

28. *CPP*, I, 56; DL 27/323; DL 42/11, fo. 52v.

29. E 101/25/9; E 372/191, m. 54d.

30. C 76/20, m. 15; 25, m. 5.

31. *CCR, 1346–9*, 521.

32. C 76/27, ms. 4, 24; 32, m. 4; 33, m. 9; Somerville, *op. cit*, 358.

33. Somerville, *op. cit*, 354, 357.

34. C 76/38, m. 16.

35. Somerville, *op. cit*, 359.

36. *Ibid*, DL 42/1, fo. 69, no. 42.

37. E 43/81; E 404/500/265 & 508/37; E 101/168/3, fos. 10v, 12v; 170/20, fo. 60v.

38. E 404/500/157; E 101/170/20, fo. 82v; *CPP*, I, 240 (treasurer *at* Bergerac).

39. DL 29/507/8226.

40. John Gynewell (1343–5), Sir Peter de la Mare (1347–8), Sir Hugh Berwick (1350, 1353), Walter atte Bergh (1351, 1353–4), Sir Robert de la Mare (1355), Robert de Syngleton (1356) and John Cockayn (1360): Somerville, *op. cit*, 359–60, and, for Gynewell: *CPR, 1343–5*, 366, 384; DL 27/36; *CPP*, I, 49; for Peter de la Mare: DL 42/11, fo. 52v; for Bergh: DL 29/725/11833.

41. Somerville, *op. cit*, 360; C 76/12, m. 3; 15, m. 18; 19, m. 19; 20, m. 6; 24, m. 16; 27, ms. 4, 24; 32, m. 4; 33, m. 9; 38, m. 16; C 61/58, m. 2.

42. *CCR, 1349–54*, 203, 219, 370; C 81/1730/9, 23, 25–6, 28–9, etc.

43. Thompson, *op. cit*, 30; C 81/1724/33 (Andrew Braunche); E 159/123, m. 327 (John Cockayn); C 81/1724/58 (Peyure); DL 37/2/104 (Radcliffe).

44. SC 1/40/109.

45. *CPR, 1327–30*, 442.

46. *CPR, 1350–4*, 464; *1361–4*, 50; DL 28/32/17, fo. 38r, & 18, nos. 1 & 2.

47. In 1336 (E 101/15/12), 1338–40 (C 76/12, m. 8), 1342–3 (C 76/17, m. 26), 1345–6 (E 101/25/9, m. 3) and 1347 (C 76/25, m. 25).

48. *CPR, 1350–4*, 464; *CIPM*, XI, 95, no. 118.

49. DL 25/3460.

50. C 76/38, m. 16. Cf. SC 1/40/109.

51. C 81/1724/33.

52. *CPR, 1338–40*, 101.

53. In 1338–40 (C 81/1724/33; C 76/12, m. 8), 1340 (C 81/1724/43; C 76/15, m. 6) and 1342–3 (C 76/17, m. 26).

54. *CPR, 1350–4*, 298; *1354–8*, 51.

55. E 403/373, m. 22.

56. E 403/368, m. 11.

57. *CPR, 1340–3*, 424.

58. In 1347 (G. Wrottesley, *Crécy and Calais*, London, 1898, p. 150) and 1359–60 (C 76/38, m. 16).

59. Minstrels and pipers: *Records of the Borough of Leicester*, II, 109 and *passim*; *Black Prince's Register*, IV, 90, 283. Tailors and armourers: C 76/12, m. 8; 34, m. 15; 35, m. 7. Carpenters and cooks: DL 42/11, fo. 52v; DL 28/32/18, nos. 12 & 13; *CPR, 1354–8*, 103; *JGR*, I, i, 748, & ii, 1468. Bakers and fish-mongers: C 76/12, m. 18; C 76/34, m. 14.

60. *Records of the Borough of Leicester*, II, 80.

61. W. A. Pantin, *The English Church in the Fourteenth Century* (Cambridge, 1955), 49.

62. Somerville, *op. cit*, 361; *CPP*, I, 166.

63. *CPP*, I, 56, 78, 108, 151, 166, 213, 271; *CPL*, III, 325, 332; *CPR, 1345–8*, 435; *1350–4*, 3, 47.

64. *CPP*, I, 226, 238, 244.

65. Somerville, *op. cit*, 361.

66. *Ibid*, 358; *CPP*, I, 111.

67. *CPP*, I, 242.

68. For an account of his career, see A. H. Thompson, 'The Registers of John Gynewell, Bishop of Lincoln, for the Years 1347–50', *Archaeological Journal*, LXVIII (1911), 302–6.

69. For his career, see Somerville, *op. cit*, 358–9; *CPP*, I, 132, 151–2, 225, 238–9, 282.

70. *Ibid*, 270, 298; *CPR, 1354–8*, 608.

71. *CPP*, I, 132, 282; *CPR, 1350–4*, 65; DL 28/32/17, fo. 12v.

72. *CPP*, I, 240.

73. DL 29/288/4719.

74. For the ensuing remarks, see *CPR, 1338–40*, 101; *1345–8*, 129; *1348–50*, 549; *1350–4*, 36, 182; *1354–8*, 132; *CCR, 1354–60*, 366; Tout, *Chapters in the Administrative History of Medieval England*, IV, 136–7.

75. DL 27/155 (Ufford); W. Dugdale, *The Baronage of England* (2 vols, London, 1675–6), I, 579 (Hastings); SC 1/42/64 (Swinford); DL 42/1, fo. 90r (Brace-bridge); DL 42/11, fo. 52v (Felstede).

76. For this and all subsequent references to military and diplomatic service in the duke's retinue, see 'A nominal roll of the men who served in Lancaster's retinue on military and diplomatic missions' in Fowler, *Henry of Grosmont* (Leeds University Ph.D. thesis), Appendix C 9.

77. *CPR, 1348–50*, 542; *1361–4*, 50; DL 25/3323.

78. *CPR, 1348–50*, 50.

79. DL 42/1, fo. 192r.

80. *Records of the Borough of Leicester*, II, 65.

81. See Appendix III, Table 1.

82. Fowler, *op. cit*, 683 ff.

83. See Appendix III, Table 2.

84. His steward Sir Hugh Berwick, his wardrober Robert de Burton and his doctor Richard of Ireland. For their careers, see Fowler, *op. cit*, 683–4.

85. For the numbers of those who served abroad with Lancaster which are given in this paragraph, see Appendix III, Table 1. Further details on their careers and other marks of connection with the duke are given in Fowler, *op. cit*, 703–6.

86. See Appendix III, Table 3.

87. Ibid.

88. He was in receipt of an annuity of £40 in the manor of Methwold in Norfolk in 1358–9 (DL 29/288/4719 & 4720). For his lieutenancy in Brittany, see E 101/175/1, nos. 78 & 80; 175/6, no. 1; C 76/36, m. 13.

89. He witnessed a charter of the duke at Reyte manor, near London, on 1 February 1359 (*JGR*, I, i, 739). For his property in Lincolnshire, see E 159/123, m. 126, and for his role in Brittany, *Foedera*, III, i, 403; C 76/35, m. 9; C 76/36, m. 11.

90. *CPR, 1358–61*, 225. For his property in Lincolnshire, see E 159/123, m. 126, and for his work in Aquitaine, *Froissart*, ed. Lettenhove, IV, 241, 246; XVII, 161.

91. E 403/380, ms. 6 & 7.

92. E 101/174/12. Florak had acquired a life annuity of 10 marks in the manor of Collingbourne Ducis in Wiltshire by 10 November 1350 (*CPR, 1350–4*, 8), and witnessed the foundation charter of Newarke College in 1356 (A. H. Thompson, *The History of the Hospital and New College of the Annunciation of Saint Mary in the Newarke*, Leicester, 1937, p. 30). He served, or was intended to serve, in the duke's *comitiva* on at least three occasions. His parents had been granted property in Amesbury, Wiltshire, by Earl Thomas (G. A. Holmes, *The Estates of the Higher Nobility in Fourteenth-Century England*, Cambridge, 1957, p. 136). For Walton, see above, n. 22.

93. E 404/508/51–79.

94. De la Mare acquired the manor of Berwick St James in Wiltshire from him sometime before 10 March 1349 (*CPR, 1348–50*, 268) and held it until his death in or about 1382 (*JGR*, II, ii, 766). He served on at least seven missions abroad with the duke, was steward of his lands in 1355 (*CPP*, I, 271) and subsequently acted as one of the executors of his will and as one of his feoffees (see below, pp. 217–18). He witnessed at least four of his charters (DL 25/248, 1860 & 2303; *CPR, 1348–50*, 469; Thompson, *op. cit*, 30). His elder brother Peter was also very active in the duke's service (Fowler, *op. cit*, 685–6). Cosington, possibly a native of Cosington in Leicestershire, acquired a grant for life of the manor of Hartley Mauditt in Hampshire (*CPR, 1361–4*, 50; *CIPM*, XI, 95) and held land of him at Clyve in Kent and Kingston Bagpuize in Berkshire (*CIPM*, XI, 108). He served on at least four missions in the duke's *comitiva*. Cok is described as 'nostre cher compaignon' in one of his letters close (DL 41/10/34, no. 66).

95. *Froissart*, ed. Lettenhove, IV, 303, calls him 'un bon chevalier engles'. He served on no less than seven missions in the duke's *comitiva*.

96. E 159/123, ms. 99d & 125.

97. *Froissart*, ed. Lettenhove, IV, 303, 306, 337, 338, 355, 505; XVII, 177.

98. *Foedera*, III, i, 73. Stafford crossed to England prior to November 1346 (E 404/490/180) and Cok had replaced him by 24 January 1347 (C 61/60, ms. 19 & 25), although he was not formally appointed until 3 March 1347 (C 61/59, m. 13).

99. See above pp. 107–8.

100. For his service in Aquitaine, see E 101/25/9, m. 3, and *Froissart*, ed. Luce, III, 61, 64, 70. He acquired the manors of Weston Patrick and Wynchfeld-by-Odyham, Hants, and an annuity of £20 in the manor of King's Somborne, Hants, by grant of the duke (*CPR, 1361–4*, 50; *CIPM*, XI, 95).

101. *Froissart*, ed. Luce, III, 46; *CPR, 1345–8*, 560.

102. For his captaincy of Aiguillon, see M. Bertrandy, *Étude sur les chroniques de Froissart* (1870), 151, 354.

103. See above, p. 156 and n. 50.

104. See above, pp. 167–71.

105. For his lands in Lincolnshire, see E 159/123, m. 139, and for his service in Aquitaine, *Froissart*, ed. Lettenhove, IV, 214, 216, 218, 253, 337, 338.

106. See above, p. 177

107. C 76/17, ms. 22 & 26; C 76/20, m. 15; E 372/191, m. 54d.

108. E 404/508/47; C 76/26, m. 9; C 76/27, m. 4.

109. E 404/508/61; E 403/355, m. 19; E 372/195, m. 46.

110. E 404/504/9.

111. E 372/198, m. 39d.

112. E 403/380, ms. 6 & 7.

113. PRO, *Lists and Indexes*, XXXV (Various Accounts), 129–31.

114. See above, p. 181.

115. Notably those of Roos, Holand, Melbourne, Neville, Longeford and the Greys of Codnor; others, like the Everinghams of Lastingham, Audeley, Asteley, Bures, Colvill, Hastang, Ferrers, Florak and Lestraunge, John de Dalton, Hugh Meignill and John de Twyford served both Thomas and Henry: Fowler, *op. cit*, ch. 14 and Appendices C 9 and J, for service with Henry; for service with Thomas and John of Gaunt, see Holmes, *op. cit*, 70–3 and Appendix 2; *JGR*, I, i, 103, 803; ii, 945 & index, 393, sub John Neville; S. Armitage-Smith, *John of Gaunt* (London, 1904; reprinted 1964), 441, 445; DL 29/262/4069 (Roos); DL 41/1/37 (Neville); C 81/1730/4, 5 & 7 (Holand, Ferrers and Lestraunge).

116. DL 41/9/5, no. 10; DL 28/32/17, fo. 38.

117. Somerville, *op. cit*, 356.

118. Fowler, *op. cit*, Appendices C 9 and J; Somerville, *op. cit*, 354–7; Holmes, *op. cit*, 67–8; *CPR, 1327–30*, 442.

119. Sir Peter de la Mare and Sir Hugh Berwick held the manors of East Garston and Market Lavington in 1349 and 1352 respectively, and Sir Robert de la Mare that of Berwick St James in 1349 (*CPR, 1348–50*, 261, 268; *1350–4*, 146). Sir John de Walkington and John de Aldewyncle held the manor of North Standen in 1349 and 1361 respectively (*CPR, 1348–50*, 366; *1361–4*, 50), and Sir Frank de Hale that of Weston Patrick in 1361 (*CPR, 1361–4*, 50). Sir Hugh de Camoys held the manor of Longstock in 1350 and Sir Stephen de Cosington that of Hartley Mauditt in 1361 (*CPR, 1348–50*, 573; *1361–4*, 50; *CIPM*, XI, 95, no. 118). Philip de Popham and Thomas de la Ryvere each held an annuity of £10 in the manor of King's Somborne in 1353 and 1361 respectively, and Sir Thomas Florak held one of 10 marks in the manor of Collingbourne Ducis in

1350 (*CPR, 1350–4*, 8, 464; *CIPM*, XI, 95, no. 118). See Somerville, *op. cit*, 18 and 38 for the inheritance of these manors by Lancaster and his wife.

120. Compare the nominal roll of men who served in Lancaster's retinue and the list of his donees (Fowler, *op. cit*, Appendices C 9 and J) with the list of Gaunt's retainers published by Armitage-Smith, *op. cit*, Appendix III, 440–6, and *JGR*, I, ii, index.


## Chapter XV

1. J. Elton, 'The Chapel of Saint Mary del Key, Liverpool', *Transactions of the Historic Society of Lancashire and Cheshire*, LIV, new series XVIII (1904), 78–85, 94–5; *A History of the Chantries Within the County Palatine of Lancaster*, ed. F. R. Raines (2 vols, Chetham Society, LIX & LX, Manchester, 1862–3), I, xxxiv, 86, and II, 208, n. 7.

2. *The Coucher Book or Chartulary of Whalley Abbey*, ed. W. A. Hulton (4 vols, Chetham Society, X, XI, XVI & XX, Manchester, 1847–9), IV, 1146–8, 1154–8, 1164–6, 1169–71; DL 42/1, fos. 74–5; *CPR, 1358–61*, 506–7; Somerville, *op. cit*, 46, 51; *VCH Lancashire*, II, 135–6. He also granted the rectory of Preston to the abbey, but this was not realized (H. W. Clemesha, *A History of Preston in Amounderness*, Manchester, 1912, pp. 29–30; *VCH Lancashire*, II, 136–7).

3. *Knighton*, II, 74; A. H. Thompson, *The Abbey of Saint Mary in the Meadows, Leicester* (Leicester, 1949), 30, 33; J. Nichols, *The History and Antiquities of Leicester* (4 vols. in 8, 1795–1815), I, ii, 262.

4. *CChR, 1341–1417*, 444–5; *The Coucher Book of Furness Abbey*, ed. J. C. Atkinson (3 vols, Chetham Society, new series, IX, XI & XIV, Manchester, 1886–8), II, i, 205, no. 22.

5. Nichols, *op. cit*, I, ii, 295–6; *CPR, 1348–50*, 19; *VCH Norfolk*, II, 433–4, no. 60, 451; F. Blomefield and C. Parkin, *An Essay Towards a Topographical History of the County of Norfolk* (5 vols, Fersfield, Norwich and Lynn, 1739–75), I, 424.

6. E 326/11958; LR 14/71; C 81/300/16406, 364/21022 & 376/24318; *CPR, 1343–5*, 354; *1348–50*, 560; *1354–8*, 134; *1358–61*, 295; *CCR, 1360–4*, 491.

7. *CPR, 1358–61*, 246.

8. *CPL*, III, 545.

9. *CPR, 1354–8*, 178, 488.

10. *CPR, 1348–50*, 372.

11. *CPR, 1338–40*, 467; *1340–3*, 257, 287, 397; *1343–5*, 197, 209, 547; *1345–8*, 283, 452; *1348–50*, 38, 367, 421; *1350–4*, 71, 146; *1358–61*, 271.

12. Somerville, *op. cit*, 46–7; *CPR, 1350–4*, 354, 378–9; *1358–61*, 275.

13. For the details in this paragraph, see *CPR, 1348–50*, 19; *1354–8*, 134; *1358–61*, 246, 295; Elton, *op. cit*, 94; DL 42/1, fos. 74–5; *The Coucher Book of Whalley Abbey*, IV, 1154–8.

14. For the following account, see Thompson, *The History of Newarke College*, chs. 1–3, and 'Notes on the Colleges of Secular Canons in England', *Archaeological Journal*, LXXIV (1917), 139–239.

15. DL 41/9/4, ms. 4, 6. Isabel and Edde of Leicester, a young girl from Dudford called Juliane Pollard, Roger de Mirfield (a poor man who had lost his hands) and Nicholas de Camme (a pantry boy of the earl) were among the first poor folk to be admitted (ibid, ms. 10, 12–14; DL 41/9/5, m. 30).

16. DL 41/9/4, m. 9; DL 41/9/5, m. 31.

17. *The Itinerary of John Leland In or About 1535–1543*, ed. L. Toulmin-Smith (5 vols, London, 1906–10), II, 15–16.

18. *Le Livre de Seyntz Medicines*, ed. E. J. F. Arnould (Anglo-Norman Texts, II, Oxford, 1940). This has been very fully analysed by the editor in his *Étude sur le Livre des Saintes Médecines du duc Henri de Lancastre* (Paris, 1948) and, more briefly, 'Henry of Lancaster and his "Livre des Seintes Medicines"', *Bulletin of John Rylands Library*, XXI (1937), 352–86. I am indebted to Professor M. D. Legge for the suggestion that the work was a task set by his confessor and for the help she has given me with the text.

19. *Froissart*, ed. Luce, III, 63; IV, 16.

20. '. . . par grant desir d'estre preisez, puis amez, puis perduz . . .' (*Livre*, 72).

21. L. Fox, *Leicester Castle* (Leicester, 1944), 19; *Records of the Borough of Leicester*, II, 109; *Black Prince's Register*, IV, 90, 283.

22. '. . . pur faire moi et les autres hors de sens—car bien y est celui q'est yvres . . .' (*Livre*, 20).

23. '. . . c'est a entendre q'ils ne sont mye si apparaillez ne si prestes de moi reporter ariere come ils sont d'aler la . . .' (*Ibid*, 75).

24. *Records of the Borough of Leicester*, II, xx, 67–8.

25. *Ibid*, xx, 65, 68, 77, 79.

26. For an early manifestation of this, see *CPR, 1334–8*, 434.

27. Thompson, *The Abbey of Saint Mary in the Meadows*, 32–3; L. Fox, *Leicester Abbey* (Leicester, 1949), 32–3.

28. *Livre*, 17.

29. *Ibid*, 244.

30. *Ibid*, 82.

31. *Ibid*, 93.

32. See above, pp. 127–8.

33. The translation is that of Arnold, *op. cit*, in *Bulletin of John Rylands Library*, XXI (1937), 375.

Chapter XVI

1. This account of the Reims campaign is largely based upon Delachenal's *Histoire de Charles V*, II, chs. iv & v, and the sources cited there. The principal evidence which has come to light since its publication consists of the wardrobe account of William de Farley (E 101/393/11), which records payments to the English expeditionary forces and helps to fill in some gaps in the king's itinerary (see A. E. Prince, 'The Strength of English Armies in the Reign of Edward III', *English Historical Review*, XLVI, 1931, 367–8; *The Anonimalle Chronicle*, 367–8; Tout, *Chapters in the Administrative History of Medieval England*, IV, 145), and a narrative of the expedition in *The Anonimalle Chronicle*, 49–50, which gives

a full and valuable itinerary of the English army after the treaty of Brétigny. This treaty and the abortive treaties of London which gave rise to the campaign have also been the subject of an important reinterpretation (J. Le Patourel, 'The Treaty of Brétigny, 1360', *Transactions of the Royal Historical Society*, 5th series, X, 1960, 19–39).

2. He was lodged there from his arrival in London on 24 May 1357 until 4 April 1359, when he was taken to Hertford castle. On 4 August following he was removed to Somerton castle in Lincolnshire (Delachenal, *op. cit*, II, 56–7, 77–8, 142–3, 179, 183).

3. In 1358 his letters were dated at Leicester on 3 April, Tutbury castle on 24 June, Liverpool castle on 20 July (*JGR*, I, i, 738, 740–1), and he was at Leicester on 8 October (E 403/394, m. 5; E 404/5/35). In 1359 his letters were dated at Reyte manor, near London, on 1 February (*JGR*, I, i, 739) and at Leicester castle on 20 June (*CPR, 1358–61*, 566).

4. *Reading*, 130–2, 273–5; *Eulogium Historiarum*, 227. *Knighton*, II, 99, however, by implication excludes him from the jousts at Windsor. He accompanied Blanche to Leicester shortly before the wedding (*Records of the Borough of Leicester*, II, 109).

5. For the following account of the negotiations of 1357–9, see Le Patourel, *op. cit*, 19–31. There are two letters which appear to relate to Lancaster's presence at Westminster for the conclusion of the second treaty of London in the spring of 1359 (BM, Harley 4971, fos. 13v–14r).

6. É. Perroy, 'France, England, and Navarre from 1359 to 1364', *Bulletin of the Institute of Historical Research*, XIII (1935–6), 153.

7. Delachenal, *op. cit*, II, 141, n. 1, 144; Prince, *op. cit*, 367, n. 4; E 404/495/40–41, 82, 88–91.

8. It included the Black Prince, Lancaster, 10 earls, 20 bannarets, 870 knights, 3,800 men-at-arms, 5,500 mounted archers, 300 household clerks and the like, 30 grooms and porters, 200 artificers and 1,100 Welsh foot (Prince, *op. cit*, 368).

9. Delachenal, *op. cit*, II, 150.

10. For a full account of these political events, see Delachenal, *op. cit*, I, chs. 8–10, II, ch. 1.

11. *Ibid*, II, 119–32; Perroy, *op. cit*, 152.

12. For these remarks and the next two paragraphs, see Delachenal, *op. cit*, II, 145–57.

13. *Ibid*, 146–7.

14. *Ibid*, 146; *Anonimalle Chronicle*, 44; *Scalacronica*, ed. Stevenson, 186–7, ed. Maxwell, 145–6.

15. *Scalacronica*, ed. Stevenson, 186, ed. Maxwell, 145.

16. It was made up of 6 bannarets, 90 knights, 486 esquires, 423 mounted archers, 91 Welsh foot, 5 vintenars, a constable, doctor, standard-bearer and crier (E 101/393/11, fo. 79v).

17. Delachenal, *op. cit*, II, 147–8. See map IV.

18. *Scalacronica*, ed. Stevenson, 187, ed. Maxwell, 146; *Froissart*, ed. Luce, V, lvi, n. 2, 193, 392–4. Guy de Châtillon was appointed lieutenant on 14 July 1359 (Arch. nat, JJ 89, no. 442).

19. Delachenal, *op. cit*, II, 150–1.

20. *Anonimalle Chronicle*, 44. For the strength of their respective retinues, see E 101/393/11, fos. 79r–80r.

21. *Scalacronica*, ed. Stevenson, 187, ed. Maxwell, 146.
22. *Anonimalle Chronicle*, 44. According to *Froissart*, ed. Luce, V, lviii, 194, 200 & 394, who appears to have been at Calais when the English troops disembarked there (M. Galway, 'Froissart in England', *University of Birmingham Historical Journal*, VII, i, 1959, p. 23), the junction took place between the town and the abbey of Licques (Pas-de-Calais, arr. Boulogne, cant. Guines), and Sir Thomas Gray, who took part in the campaign, implies that they met after Edward left Calais (*Scalacronica, loc. cit.*).
23. Delachenal, *op. cit*, II, 148, 151; *Anonimalle Chronicle*, 44–5.
24. Delachenal, *op. cit*, II, 151–2, and the sources cited there; *Anonimalle Chronicle*, 45.
25. This may be deduced from an incident there involving Bartholomew de Burghersh (Delachenal, *op. cit*, II, 152), who was a soldier in Lancaster's column (*Scalacronica*, ed. Stevenson, 188, ed. Maxwell, 148).
26. *Knighton*, II, 105. The junction could not have taken place near Beaurieux or Amifontaine, as conjectured by H. Moranvillé, 'Le siège de Reims, 1359–1360', *Bibliothèque de l'École des Chartes*, LVI (1895), 93 n. 3, since neither of these places was on the Black Prince's route (see map IV).
27. Delachenal, *op. cit*, II, 153 & n. 5.
28. *Chronique de Jean II et Charles V*, 251–2; Moranvillé, *op. cit*, 93; *Froissart*, ed. Luce, V, lx. Edward was at Verzy on 25 and 26 December, 1, 5 and 6 January (*Foedera*, III, i, 453; *Anonimalle Chronicle*, 167; *Lescot*, 208).
29. Delachenal, *op. cit*, II, 153–4, 154 n. 1, 160–1, 161 n. 1.
30. *Ibid*, 157, 159.
31. *Istorie*, ed. Muratori, XIV, cols. 587–8. See Delachenal, *op. cit*, II, 157 n. 3.
32. *Knighton*, II, 170.
33. For these operations, see Moranvillé, *op. cit*, 94–8, and Delachenal, *op. cit*, II, 159–60.
34. Delachenal, *op. cit*, II, 153, 160–1.
35. *Foedera*, III, i, 474; Delachenal, *op. cit*, II, 170 n. 4. See below, pp. 205–6.
36. Delachenal, *op. cit*, II, 161. Edward's letters were dated at Pogny on 18, 19 and 26 January (*Lescot*, 208), but at 'the town of Saint-George by the castle of Beaufort in France' on 25 January (*CPR, 1358–61*, 328). The castle of Beaufort, now Montmorency (Aube, arr. Arcis-sur-Aube, cant. Chavagnes) is situated south of the Marne. According to *The Anonimalle Chronicle*, 45, after crossing the Marne the army raided as far as Châtelraould-Saint-Louvent, and we know Edward to have been at Trouan on 2 February (*ibid*, 167). The halt at Pogny was not made to transact the ransom of the duchy of Bar, as suggested by Delachenal (*op. cit*, II, 161 n. 5), but to repair the bridge over the Marne (*Anonimalle Chronicle*, 45; *Scalacronica*, ed. Stevenson, 189, ed. Maxwell, 149). The ransom was negotiated at a later stage, probably at Méry (*Anonimalle Chronicle*, 45; *Froissart*, ed. Luce, V, 223).
37. Delachenal, *op. cit*, II, 161–3; *Scalacronica*, ed. Stevenson, 189, ed. Maxwell, 150.
38. *Anonimalle Chronicle*, 45. Delachenal, *op. cit*, II, 163, following E. Petit, *Histoire des ducs de Bourgogne*, IX, 183, conjectured that the junction took place at Tonnere.
39. *Anonimalle Chronicle*, 45–6, 167.
40. *Ibid*, 168.

41. Delachenal, *op. cit*, II, 163–4.

42. His letters were dated there on 28 February, 1, 8 and 16 March (*CPR, 1358–61*, 328–9; *Lescot*, 208), and the various instruments of the treaty concluded there are dated 10–20 March (Arch. dép. Côte d'Or, série B, nos. 11922–5).

43. *Froissart*, ed. Luce, V, 225.

44. Delachenal, *op. cit*, II, 165–6.

45. See above, p. 102.

46. Delachenal, *op. cit*, II, 166–9. The negotiations appear to have begun while Edward was before Reims (*Chronique des quatre premiers Valois*, 100) and the initiative seems to have been taken by the Burgundians (Arch. nat, X1a, 27, fos. 231r–2r, no. 39; *Chronicon Angliae*, 40; *Knighton*, II, 110). For further details concerning the negotiations, see Arch. nat, X1a 22, fos. 268v–9r, no. 95.

47. Arch. dép. Côte d'Or, B 11922; *Foedera*, III, i, 473–4. Cf. Delachenal, *op. cit*, II, 169–71.

48. Arch. nat, X1a 21, fos. 261v–2r, no. 32; Delachenal, *op. cit*, II, 173 n. 4.

49. Around 20 March, when the negotiations at Guillon were completed. Delachenal, *op. cit*, II, 173, did not think that Edward was heading for Paris at this juncture, but his route across the Cure and the Yonne was the obvious one to take (see map IV).

50. Delachenal, *op. cit*, II, 173–6.

51. *Ibid*, 172–3.

52. *Ibid*, 185 & n. 3; *Anonimalle Chronicle*, 46.

53. *Knighton*, II, 111. Cf. *Anonimalle Chronicle*, 46.

54. Delachenal, *op. cit*, II, 186.

55. *Ibid*, 186–8.

56. *Knighton*, II, 110–111.

57. *Lescot*, 144.

58. *Venette*, 98–101.

59. S. Luce, *Histoire de Bertrand du Guesclin* (Paris, 1876), 543–5, Pièces Justificatives, XX.

60. Delachenal, *op. cit*, II, 189–90.

61. *Reading*, 135–6. Cf. *Froissart*, ed. Luce, V, lxix, 230–1, 423; *Anonimalle Chronicle*, 46; *Lescot*, 144–5; *Knighton*, II, 111; *Scalacronica*, ed. Stevenson, 193, ed. Maxwell, 156–7; *Venette*, 102; *Chronique de Jean II et Charles V*, I, 259.

62. *Froissart*, ed. Luce, VI, 1.

63. *Scalacronica*, ed. Stevenson, 193, ed. Maxwell, 158.

64. *Chronicle(s) of London*, ed. Nicolas, 64, ed. Kingsford, 13. The *Anonimalle Chronicle*, 46, calls it 'mauveys lundy'.

65. *Eulogium historiarum*, III, 228; *Scalacronica*, ed. Stevenson, 193–4, ed. Maxwell, 158.

66. E 101/393/11, fos. 79r ff.

67. *Knighton*, II, 112. Cf. *Anonimalle Chronicle*, 46; *Lescot*, 145; *Venette*, 102, Other chronicles which mention the storm are: *Froissart*, ed. Luce, VI, iv, 4–5. 238; *Reading*, 137; *Chronique normande*, 152.

68. Delachenal, *op. cit*, II, 192, and the sources cited in n. 2; *Anonimalle Chronicle*, 46–7; *Chronique normande*, 152.

69. Delachenal, *op. cit*, II, 192; *Knighton*, II, 112; *Anonimalle Chronicle*, 47.

Edward's letters were dated at Tournoisis and Nids on 18, 27 and 28 April (*Lescot*, 209).

70. *Froissart*, ed. Luce, VI, 4.

71. See below, p. 219.

72. The comments of the *Chronique normande*, 149, on the failure of the campaign and the French refusal to risk a battle are apposite.

73. *Froissart*, ed. Luce, VI, 4.

74. *Ibid.*

75. Delachenal, *op. cit*, II, 192–6. Edward's letters were dated at Sours on 5, 6, 8 and 9 May (*Lescot*, I, 209).

76. Delachenal, *op. cit*, II, 196–201. For what ensues, see La Patourel, *op. cit*, 31–3.

77. Delachenal, *op. cit*, II, 200, 207–11.

78. *Anonimalle Chronicle*, 49.

79. *Ibid*, 168; *Lescot*, 209.

80. Delachenal, *op. cit*, II, 211–12.

81. *Ibid*, 212 n. 3; *Anonimalle Chronicle*, 49–50.

82. *Anonimalle Chronicle*, 49–50.

83. Lancaster and his retinue came off the king's pay on 23 May and the remainder of the army between then and 31 May (E 101/393/11, fos. 79r ff.).

84. He drew wages in that capacity from 25 May to 29 September (ibid, fo. 87r), and was succeeded by Sir Thomas Holand on the following day (*Foedera*, III, i, 509, 510).

85. Delachenal, *op. cit*, II, 212; *Scalacronica*, ed. Stevenson, 196, ed. Maxwell, 161; Luce, *op. cit*, 543–5, Pièces Justificatives, XX.

86. E 101/314/3; E 404/6/40. His letters were dated at Leicester on 15 August (*Records of the Borough of Leicester*, II, 111–13), but at Cowick, near Goole, Yorkshire, on 12 August (*JGR*, I, i, 745).

87. For what follows, see Le Patourel, *op. cit*, 33–9.

88. *Foedera*, III, i, 518, 531, 534; Arch. nat, JJ 96, no. 140 & K 166 (reconciliation of King John and Charles of Navarre).

89. *Chronique de Jean II et Charles V*, 326–7 & n. 1; *Lescot*, 147, no. 313.

90. *Froissart*, ed. Luce, VI, xv, 53; *Chronique de Jean II et Charles V*, 320–1.

91. E 101/314/3; E 404/6/40.


## Chapter XVII

1. *Knighton*, II, 32, 118.

2. DL 42/11, fo. 24r–v.

3. See above, p. 197.

4. His letters were dated there on 12 April 1348 (SC 1/40/7), 24 August 1349 (*CPR*, *1348–50*, 469), 3 June 1350 (SC 8/12667), 20, 23 and 24 February 1351 (*The Coucher Book of Whalley Abbey*, IV, 1146–8; *CPR*, *1358–61*, 242), 10 July 1352 (DL 41/9/7, no. 1), 18 and 28 April 1353 (SC 1/50/176; *JGR*, I, i, 736), 17 March and 5 July 1354 (*CPR*, *1358–61*, 242; DL 42/11, fo. 67v) and 1 December 1360 (SC 1/42/66). They were dated London on 10 October 1344

(DL 27/36), 20 January, 1 March and 2 December 1347 (DL 25/2185; DL 42/1, fo. 199, no. 26; DL 27/155; *CPR*, *1348–50*, 19), 13 and 17 March 1354 (Delachenal, 'Premières négociations', *cit. supra*, 277–80), at Reyte manor, London, on 1 February 1359 (*JGR*, I, i, 739); and he was at Westminster on 16 May 1342 (*CPR*, *1340–3*, 530; *Foedera*, II, ii, 1194), 24 October 1353 (SC 1/40/122), 31 October 1354 (Bock, 'Some New Documents', *cit. supra*, 94–6) and 28 March 1356 (*Rot. Scot*, I, 792).

5. His letters were dated there on 1 February, 6 July, 12 August and 12 October 1351 (DL 41/9/7, no. 4; *CPR*, *1354–8*, 381; *1358–61*, 242).

6. *Foedera*, III, i, 215, 217–18.

7. *Records of the Borough of Leicester*, II, xx, 60, 67–8, 76–7, etc.

8. He was at Leicester on 1 November 1341 (*CPR*, *1361–4*, 200), immediately after Michaelmas 1343 (*Records of the Borough of Leicester*, II, 60), after 15 August 1344 (*ibid.*), on 28 and 30 November 1344 (DL 25/2184; DL 42/1, fo. 198; *Knighton*, II, 30), 1 August 1349 (*CChR*, *1341–1407*, 444–5), 16 and 17 November 1352 (DL 41/9/7, no. 2; DL 41/10/34, nos. 60–61 & 77), 22 July 1353 (*Records of the Borough of Leicester*, II, 89–90), 28 February, 24 and 27 March, 20 April and 13 June 1356 (Nichols, *History of Leicester*, I, ii, 295–6; Thompson, *The History of Newarke College*, 29; DL 25/1860; DL 27/159; *CCR*, *1354–60*, 318–19), 5 July 1357 (E 40/11440), 3 April and 8 October 1358 (*JGR*, I, i, 738; E 403/394, m. 5; E 404/5/35), before 19 May 1359, on 20 June 1359 and on 15 August 1360 (*Records of the Borough of Leicester*, II, 109, 111–13; *CPR*, *1358–61*, 566) and 6, 11, 15, 20 and 23 March 1361 (*Records of the Borough of Leicester*, II, 113–24; *CFR*, *1356–9*, 159).

9. For the ensuing remarks, see Fox, *Leicester Castle*, 13–24.

10. *Records of the Borough of Leicester*, II, xix–xx.

11. L. Fox and P. Russell, *Leicester Forest* (Leicester, 1948), 28, 31–2, 34, 44, and DL 29/212/3246 for the hunting lodge in the Frith.

12. Maude was six in November 1347 (*CIPM*, IX, 54, 57).

13. Lancaster did not return from Gascony until 1 January 1347 (E 101/25/9; E 372/191, m. 54d) and Blanche was born between then and 3 May following (*GEC*, VII, 410 note g).

14. *GEC*, I, 243; II, 60–61.

15. *CPR*, *1343–5*, 224; *Foedera*, III, i, 10, 11. See above, p. 46.

16. Isabella died between 30 January 1348 and 4 February 1349 (*CCR*, *1346–9*, 428; *1349–54*, 5), and Joan on 7 July 1349 (*GEC*, IX, 383).

17. R. Atkyns, *The Ancient and Present State of Glosteshire* (London, 1712), 490.

18. DL 27/36; *GEC*, VII, 410 note g.

19. *GEC*, XII, i, 177; *CIPM*, IX, 16, 57; *CCR*, *1346–9*, 344, 347.

20. M. Galway, 'Froissart in England', *cit. supra*, 27 & n. 23.

21. *The Complete Works of Geoffrey Chaucer*, ed. W. W. Skeat (7 vols, Oxford, 1897), I, 277–322, especially 306–9, 311, 321.

22. *Froissart*, ed. Lettenhove, II, 8.

23. Lancaster's letters were dated at Whalley on 16 December 1360 and 2 January 1361 (DL 42/1, fos. 74–5, no. 58). He was summoned to parliament on 20 November 1360 (*CCR*, *1360–4*, 147) and this sat from 24 January to 18 February (W. Stubbs, *The Constitutional History of England*, 5th ed, 3 vols, Oxford 1896, II, 433 n. 1).

24. DL 37/2, m. 30d & *CPR*, *1361–4*, 251 (Richard of Ireland, who had a grant

for life of the site of the manor of Ulnes Walton in Lancashire from him);
Treaty Roll, sub 16 October 1360 (John Gouche, who appears to have accompanied him on the Reims campaign); *CPR, 1358–61*, 545 (Pascal of Bologna).
Richard of Ireland was subsequently surgeon to Edward III (*CPR, 1364–7*,
402) and died in 1372 (*JGR*, I, i, 270); Pascal of Bologna was one of the wardens
of the hospital of St Mary Magdalen, Preston, in 1355, canon of London in
1358 and prebend of St Paul's in 1361 (*CPL*, III, 597; *CPR, 1358–61*, 545).

25. It has been published several times, in full or in abstract, by J. Nichols,
*A Collection of the Wills of the Kings and Queens of England* (London, 1780),
83–7; N. H. Nicolas, *Testamenta Vetusta* (2 vols, London, 1826), I, 64; A. W.
Gibbons, *Early Lincoln Wills* (Lincoln, 1888), 24; E. Baines, *History of the
County Palatine and Duchy of Lancaster* (4 vols, London, 1836), I, 334–6; and
has been translated into English by A. H. Thompson, *The History of Newarke
College*, 37–9.

26. *CPR, 1358–61*, 580.

27. *Ibid*, 575. A later agreement between Gaunt and the trustees provided that
the latter should have sufficient timber for works on the college as ordered by
Henry (DL 42/2, fo. 234).

28. *Records of the Borough of Leicester*, II, 124; *Reading*, 150.

29. C 81/1334/53.

30. *Ibid, CFR, 1356–9*, 157–8.

31. *Black Prince's Register*, IV, 73.


# Appendix I

1. E 159/123, m. 254.
2. E 101/68/8, no. 60.
3. E 101/25/9; E 372/191, m. 54d.
4. E 372/191, m. 54d.
5. E 101/24/20; E 372/191, m. 35.
6. E 43/78; E 403/336, ms. 14, 22; 337, m. 14; E 404/490/174 & 503/139.
7. E 372/190, m. 41; E 404/501/335–9.
8. E 372/190, m. 41; E 404/501/372–3.
9. E 159/123, m. 254.
10. E 101/25/9; E 372/191, m. 54d.
11. E 101/68/8, no. 60.
12. E 372/191, m. 54d.
13. E 404/501/335–9.
14. E 403/339, m. 44.
15. E 101/25/9; E 372/191, m. 54d; E 403/336, ms. 8, 21, 49; 337, m. 9; 339, ms. 6, 13.
16. E 404/508/47. On him, see above, pp. 179, 185.
17. C 76/20, m. 15; E 372/191, m. 54d. On him, see above, pp. 179, 185.
18. *CPP*, I, 111.
19. E 372/191, m. 54d; E 403/336, m. 14; 337, m. 14; 339, ms. 6, 42.

20. *Foedera*, III, i, 64; E 403/336, ms. 21–2.

21. *Foedera*, III, i, 68; E 403/336, ms. 22–3, 26, 29.

22. E 101/24/20; E 372/202, m. 35.

23. *Foedera*, III, i, 77.

24. E 101/25/9; E 372/191, m. 54d; E 403/336, m. 49.

25. *Foedera*, III, i, 79.

## Appendix II

1. Somerville, *op. cit*, 78, 84–5, 90–3.

2. DL 41/4/11; *CIPM*, XI, 92–116, no. 118.

3. G. A. Holmes, *The English Nobility in the Reign of Edward III* (University of Cambridge, D.Phil. thesis, 1953), Appendix D, 267–74; C. D. Ross and T. B. Pugh, 'Materials for the Study of Baronial Incomes in Fifteenth-Century England', *Economic History Review*, second series, VI (1953), 185–94.

4. DL 28/32/17. This is incomplete and must therefore be used with caution. In the figures given in the accompanying table gross values relate to rents, farms and other fixed profits, casuals to sales of produce, etc. Feudal incidents and profits from franchises and courts are listed for assessment in the document, but no figures are given.

5. Viz, realized gross profits in 1347–8. They amounted to £3,559 11s 6½d if £53 3s 5½d rents not received is included, and £3,563 9s 0d if £3 17s 5½d fall in rents charged is included.

6. Viz: £4 8s 4d in Lancashire, £36 10s 1¼d in Tutbury Honor, £58 3s 9d in Bolingbroke Honor and £142 15s 4d in Leicester Honor.

7. DL 29/507/8226.

8. DL 29/212/3246.

9. Of the remainder, £62 15s 0d was paid out in fees and annuities to officers and others, £8 6s 1d in alms and £3 10s 0d in repairs.

10. *CFR*, *1356–68*, 163–6.

11. *CPR*, *1358–61*, 580; *1361–4*, 50. Bergerac reverted to the Crown on his death.

12. DL 28/32/17.

13. The principal Norfolk possessions (the manors of Gimingham, Thetford, Methwold and Tunstead) were put in charge at over £700 in the years to Michaelmas 1359 and 1360 (DL 29/288/4719–20), the manors of Rushden and Raunds and the manor and hundred of Higham Ferrers at over £230 in the years to Michaelmas 1348, 1356 and 1363 (DL 28/32/17; DL 29/324/5292–3), and Matlock at £27 10s 1½d in 1361–2 (DL 29/367/6135). The possessions in which he enfeoffed his executors which are not accounted for are: the manor of Waithe, Lincs, the hamlets of Challenge Wood and Newborough, Staffs, the hundreds of Gallow and Brothercross, Norfolk, and the knights' fees and advowsons in Norfolk.

14. Somerville, *op. cit*, 78, 84, 92.

# Index

Auray, keeper of the coast of, 281 n. 8
Autry, 204
Auxerre, 204
Avenel, John, 120
Avesbury, Robert of, 56, 60, 150
Avignon, 48–9, 77, 85, 97–8, 111, 113,
    115, 120, 125, 129, 131–43, 146–7,
    158, 178, 196, 219, 267 n. 37 & 41,
    276 n. 23 & 31, 277 n. 49 & 55
Avranches, 140, 156, 164; constable and
    receiver at, 280 n. 50

Baddeby, John de, 223
Baildon, Roger de, 92
Bajamont, 61; castle of, 54, 263 n. 31
Baker, Geoffrey, 85, 89, 106–7, 109, 138,
    142
Balliol, Edward, 29–31, 175
Bannockburn, battle of, 30
Bantelu, Gil de, 125
Bapaume, 201
Bar, duchy of, 130, 144, 206, 291 n. 36;
    duke of, 204
Barbazan, Arnaldo de, 277 n. 55
Barbu, Jean, 160, 281 n. 8
Bardi, banking house of, 35–6
Barley, Alan de, 140
Barlow, manor of, 182
Barraut, Bernard, 72
Barton, manor of, 188
Baume, Galois de la, 78
Bavaria, 118; William, duke of, count of
    Holland and Zeeland, 117–20, 123
Bayeux, 140, 153
Bayonne, 23, 39, 44, 53, 94, 147; bishop
    of, 47; canon of, 87, *La Dieu Garde* of,
    269 n. 40; *prévôté* of, 42
Bazadais, 40, 53, 67
Bazas, 53, 64–5, 67; captain of, 64
Béarn, Bernard of, 86; vicomté of, 53
Beauce, 208
Beauchamp, John de, 203; captain of
    Calais, 100; admiral of the fleet east of
    the Thames, 270 n. 42
Beaufort, 23, 26, 172, 226; castle of, 291
    n. 36
Beaumanoir, Jean de, 90
Beaumont, 57, 63
Beaumont, Henry de, titular earl of
    Buchan (1312–40), 25–6, 29–30, 175,
    256 n. 14; Isabella, daughter of, *see*
    Lancaster, Henry of Grosmont, first
    duke of
Beaumont, John de, 26, 216, 256 n. 15
Beaumont-de-Lomagne, 87–8
Beaune, 207
Beaurieux, 291 n. 26
Beauvais, Guillaume Bertran, bishop of,
    112, 209; Jean, bishop of, lieutenant in
    Gascony, Saintonge and Languedoc
    (1339, 1341–5), 39

Beauvaisis, lieutenant in, 201
Beauville, 61
Beauvoir-sur-Mer, 90–2, 238
Beche, Nicholas de la, seneschal of
    Aquitaine (1343–5), 47
Bec-Hellouin, 152
Bécherel, 159, 166–7, 169, 283 n. 45;
    receivers at, 184
Bedford, 28; John, duke of, 165
Beguer de la Russelle, Pierre, 69
Belleville, Jeanne de, widow of Olivier III
    de Clisson, 90–2
Belleville-Clisson, fief of, 78
Belper, 176
Benedict XII, pope (1334–42), 31, 33
Bentley, Sir Walter, lieutenant of Brittany
    (1350–3), 85, 89–92, 169–70
Bere, Sir Richard de la, 132–3, 276 n. 23
Berg, count of, 33
Bergerac, 54, 56–61, 67, 71, 154, 172, 226,
    232–3, 262 n. 9, 296 n. 11; captains of,
    57–8, 232–3; consuls of, 109; treasurer
    of, 177, 284 n. 38
Bergh, Walter atte, 178
Berkshire, 226
Berwick, Sir Hugh, 178, 186, 284 n. 40,
    286 n. 84, 287 n. 119
Berwick St James, manor of, 286 n. 94,
    287 n. 119
Berwick-on-Tweed, 30–2, 37, 103, 148,
    158, 257 n. 12, 279 n. 16
Bétheny, 203
Béthune, 80, 98–9, 101, 201
Beverley, Sir Robert de, 268 n. 26
Bièvre, river, 208
Blaby, William de, 225
Blackburn, bailiwick of, 187; chase, 187
Blanquefort, 42, 63
Blasimon, 53
Blaye, 39–40, 42, 54, 68, 259 n. 6, 262 n. 6
Blois, Charles of, 37, 113, 129, 159,
    161
Blount, John, 27, 178, 182; family of, 27
Blyth, 27
Boccanegra, Egidio, 45–6, 105
Boëse, 207
Bohun, Oliver de, 36, 258 n. 25
Bois-du-Maine, 156, 280 n. 50
Bolingbroke, castle 172; honor, 173, 218,
    225–6, 296 n. 6; steward of, 176
Bologna, Pascal of, 217, 295 n. 24
Bolton, 27
Bonnegarde, 42
Bonneval, 58, 209
Bordeaux, 39–40, 42, 44, 47–8, 52–4, 56,
    58–66, 68–70, 73–4, 86, 88, 92, 96, 148,
    194, 197, 224, 227, 259 n. 6, 261 n. 37,
    263 n. 24, 264 n. 50, 268 n. 15, 269 n. 38
    & 41; constable of, 40, 43–4, 50, 58,
    64–5, 71, 73–4, 88, 91, 177, 223, 231,
    233, 259 n. 11 & 12, 266 n. 93; con-

303

Kent, Edmund of Woodstock, earl of
(1321–30), 25; John of, 140
Kerman, William, 35
Kesteven, Ralph de, 279 n. 18
Kettering, 176
Kidwelly, castle of, 23, 172; lordship of,
189
Kilburn, 176
King's Somborne, manor of, 178, 189,
287 n. 100 & 119
Kingston Bagpuize, 286 n. 94
Kingston Lacy, manor of, 214, 294 n. 5
Knighton, Henry, 25, 56, 71, 102, 106,
108–9, 136, 139, 203, 207–8
Knowles, Sir Robert, 151, 157

La Barre-de-Monts, 90–1, 238
Labatut, Pierre de, 154
Lacépède, 64
La Cerda, Charles de, 93–4, 98; house of,
122
Lacy, Alice de, countess of Lincoln, 23, 173
Ladit, Tomás de, chancellor of Navarre,
124
Laforce, 57
Laigle, 122, 142–3, 153
Lalinde, 57
La Marche, Jacques de Bourbon, count of,
constable of France (1354–6), 87–8, 108
La Mongie, 57
Lampant, 90–2, 238
Lancashire, 23, 173–4, 178, 222, 225–6,
261 n. 46, 296 n. 6
Lancaster, 174, 187; castle of, 172; county
palatine of, 173–4, 177; *Gode Beyete* of,
269 n. 40; honor of, 24; St. Leonard's
Hospital at, 187
Lancaster, Blanche of, daughter of Henry,
3rd earl of, 23, 26–7, 217, 256 n. 16,
290 n. 14
Lancaster, Blanche of, daughter of Henry,
4th earl and 1st duke of, 174–5, 197, 216,
225, 294 n. 13
Lancaster, Edmund Crouchback, 1st earl of
(1267–96), 23
Lancaster, Eleanor of, daughter of Henry,
3rd earl of, 23, 26–8, 46, 48, 216, 256 n.
15
Lancaster, Henry, 3rd earl of (1326–43),
23–8, 72, 172, 176–8, 185–6, 188, 191,
194, 213, 218, 225–6, 256 n. 4, 8 & 16,
257 n. 22
Lancaster, Henry of Grosmont, earl of
Derby (1337–61), 4th earl (1345–61)
and 1st duke (1351–61) of, birth, early
life and marriage, 23–4, 26–8; campaigns
in Scotland, 29–33, 37, the Low
Countries, 34, 257 n. 14, 258 n. 17, and
Brittany, 37–8, 258 n. 33, 259 n. 34; imprisonment in the Low Countries, 35–7;
negotiates truces, 34–5, 38, 71, 78–80,

Lancaster—*continued*
87–8, 98–9, 112–13, 116–17, 120, 238–9;
peace negotiations, 39, 48–9, 97, 102,
111–14, 129–39, 143–4, 207, 209–13,
240, 261 n. 37 & 41; negotiations with
Castile, 39, 45–7, 261 n. 37; negotiations
with Flanders, 79–83, 98–100, 234–7;
appointed lieutenant in Aquitaine and
Languedoc (1344), 46–8 (1345–7), 51
(1349–50), 84; preparations for his
first expedition to Aquitaine, 49–52,
222–4, 230–2, 261 n. 45–6; his first
campaign there, 53–65, 232–3; his
second campaign there, 66–70; rewards
for service in, 71–2; consequences of,
72–4; at siege of Calais, 70–1; becomes
earl of Lancaster, 72; appointed
lieutenant in Flanders, Calais and elsewhere in France (1348), 79; second
expedition to Aquitaine, 85–9, 268 n.
14–15; lieutenant in Poitou (1349–50),
85, 89, 91, 237–8; at naval battle off
Winchelsea, 92–4; conducts raid through
Artois and Picardy, 100; expedition to
Prussia, 105–6; duel in Paris, 106–10;
mission in Holland, 117–20; negotiations with Charles of Navarre, 122–9,
139–44; negotiations with the emperor,
138, 144–6; campaign in Normandy,
147–8, 150–3; projected juncture with
the Black Prince, 154–6; fortresses
taken on return from Loire valley,
156–7; lieutenant in Brittany (1355–8),
148, 154, 156, 158, 160 ff, 239–40;
besieges Rennes, 161–5; his estates,
172 ff; his landed income, 225–6; made
duke of Lancaster and granted palatine
powers in Lancashire, 173–5; created
earl of Moray, 175; his officers, 176–81,
185; his retinue, 181–6, 227–9, 234;
his benefactions, 187–92; his *Livre de
Seyntz Medicines*, 26, 193–6, 219; his
last campaign, 201 ff; at jousts and
tournaments, 77, 103–5; his residences,
214–15, 294 n. 4–5 & 8; his family, 215–16;
relations with Edward III, 218–19; his
work as soldier, administrator and
diplomat, 19–20, 219–21; his will,
217–18; his death, 218
Lancaster, Isabella of, daughter of Henry,
3rd earl of, 23, 26, 187, 216, 256 n. 16,
294 n. 16
Lancaster, Isabella de Beaumont, wife of
Henry, 4th earl and 1st duke of, 26–8,
174, 186, 192, 215–17, 256 n. 14, 287 n.
119
Lancaster, Joan of, daughter of Henry, 3rd
earl of, 23, 26–7, 216, 256 n. 16, 294 n.
16
Lancaster, John of, son of Edmund
Crouchback, 1st earl of, 23

U

305

Moray, 32; Henry of Grosmont, earl of (1359–61), 175; John Randolph, earl of (1332–46), 31; Thomas Randolph, earl of (1312–32), 29–30, 175
Morbecque, Jean, lord of, 150
Moret, 207
Morgyng, lordship of, 189
Morlaix, battle of, 220
Morley, Sir Robert de, admiral of the northern fleet, 93
Mortain, 122, 140
Mortimer, Roger, see March, earl of
Mottisfont Priory, 26
Mowbray, John Lord, 26, 216, 256 n. 16
Mucidan, 58
Murimuth, Adam, 48, 56, 60

Namur, Louis de, 99; Robert de, 94
Nantes, 89, 159–60, 270 n. 46
Narbonne, 88
Nassington, prebend of, 181
Navarre, 46; Blanche of, 23; Philip of, 108, 150–1, 153, 156–7, 168, 220; chancellor of, see Ladit
Neath, 24
Needwood, 27
Nesle, 202; Guy de, 86, 268 n. 17
Neufchâtel, Jean de, 205
Nevers, county of, 81, 98, 101, 205–6; Louis de, count of Flanders, 76, 81
Neville, Hugh, 49; Sir John de, 185; family of, 287 n. 115
Newborough, 296 n. 13
Newcastle-under-Lyme, castle of, 172
Newcastle-upon-Tyne, 31, 37, 279 n. 16
Newmarch, John, 217
Newmarket, 28
Newstead, 176
Nids, 209–10, 293 n. 69
Nieulay Bridge, 71
Ninove, Henry of Flanders, lord of, 80
Niort, 68
Nogent-sur-Marne, 23, 172, 226
Noirmoutier, 90–1
Norfolk, 218, 226, 286 n. 88, 296 n. 13; earl of, 25
Normandy, 86, 104, 114, 123–6, 128–9, 136, 140–2, 146–53, 155–8, 160, 162, 168, 170, 185, 197–8, 210, 215, 220, 227, 275 n. 8, 278 n. 3 & 10, 280 n. 31, 32 & 45; lieutenants in, 156–7, 168, 211
Northampton, 27, 104; treaty of, 29; William de Bohun, earl of (1337–69), 20, 34–6, 38, 44, 49, 51, 66, 75, 97, 155, 166, 202–3, 207, 211, 258 n. 33, 261 n. 52
Northamptonshire, 23, 178, 218, 226
Northburgh, Michael de, archdeacon of Suffolk and keeper of the privy seal, 88, 102, 112, 132–4, 140, 142–3
North Standen, 178, 287 n. 119

Northumberland, 32, 37, 172, 226
Norwich, 33; William Bateman, bishop of (1344–55), 77–8, 85, 97, 100, 112, 133–4, 140
Nottingham, 31–2; castle, 25; parliament at, 33
Noyers, 205

Offémont, lord of, 78
Ogmore, castle, 23, 172; lordship, 189
Orchies, 80, 98–9, 101
Orléans, 209; duke of, 152
Orly, church of, 207
Orwell, 34, 258 n. 17
Oulton, 176
Oxford, 27; earl of, 202
Oye, 80, 129

Paderborn, bishop of, 106
Paris, 16, 102, 107–11, 113, 122–3, 126, 132–3, 140, 152, 161, 184, 197–8, 200, 206, 210–11, 219, 221, 266 n. 15, 292 n. 49; butcheries of Saint-Marceau and Saint Germain, 208; captain of, 200; Châtelet, 125; John of, 109; Louvre, 108–9, 160; monastery of Carmelite friars in, 208; Pré-aux-Clercs, 108; Sainte-Chapelle, 109; Saint-Germain-des-Prés, 108; suburbs of, 208; treaties of, 15, 39, 255 n. 5
Pas-de-Calais, 78
Passenham, manor of, 182
Pech Bardar, 64
Pelegrini, Hugo, 102; Raymond, canon of St Paul's, 97, 114–16, 274 n. 13
Pellegrue, 57
Pembrey, advowson of, 189
Pembroke, Laurence de Hastings, earl of (1340–8), 28, 56, 60–1, 66, 70, 222–4, 263 n. 23
Pendleton, 187
Penhoet, lord of, 162
Penthièvre, 154
Percy, Henry, 25–6, 37
Pérignac, abbey of, 64
Périgord, 40, 53, 58–9, 61, 63; seneschal of, see Montigny
Périgueux, process of, 16
Péronne, 201
Perot, Roger, 178
Perth, 30–2
Peruzzi, banking house of, 35–6
Peterborough, 27
Peyure, Nicholas, 179, 284 n. 43
Philip III, king of France (1270–85), 17
Philip IV, king of France (1285–1314), 17–18
Philip V, king of France (1316–22), 17
Philip VI (of Valois), king of France (1328–50), 17–19, 27–8, 30–1, 33–4, 39–40, 42, 64, 70–1, 75–82, 85–7, 89–92,

308

311

Waverley, William de, 223
Welbourne, John de, 179, 185, 224
Wells, canonries and prebends in, 179–81
Welwick, John de, 113–14, 134, 276 n. 25
Wesenham, John de, 223
Westminster, 44, 47–8, 76, 99, 129, 197, 211–12, 223–4, 279 n. 16, 290 n. 5, 294 n. 4; Collegiate Church at, 192; King's Chapel at, 119, 135
Weston, Walter, 45
Weston Patrick, manor of, 287 n. 100 & 119
Weymouth, 258 n. 33
Whalley, 216; abbey, 187–8, 288 n. 2
Whitecastle, 23, 172
Whitton, Phillip de, 222, 269 n. 42; William de, 222
Wiltshire, 23, 184, 186, 216, 226; warden of the sea coast of, 214
Wimundewold, Richard de, 276 n. 25
Winchelsea, 147, 279 n. 18; naval battle off, 93–5, 219
Winchester, 25, 223
Windsor, 77, 104, 290 n. 4; jousts at, 197; park, 218; St George's Chapel at, 188, 192

Witleseye, William de, archdeacon of Huntingdon, 114–15
Witney, 27
Woderone, John de, 113–15, 132–3, 276 n. 23
Wollaston, manor of, 189
Woodstock, 28, 140
Wotton, Peter de, 179, 185, 224, 284 n. 21–2
Wrightington, Geoffrey de, 222
Wymondham, advowson of, 189
Wymondwold, Richard de, 87–8
Wyther, Thomas, 25, 256 n. 8

Yonne valley, 206, 292 n. 49
York, 30; archbishop of, 93; minister, 27; St Mary's Abbey at, 163; canons and prebends of, 179–80
Yorkshire, 23, 160, 178, 226
Ypres, 34, 76, 80–2

Zeeland, 75, 96, 117–20, 130, 185; count of, see Bavaria
Zewele, Gorsorn de, 145
Zierickzee, 182

312